Hidden Dimensions

Pacific Rim Archaeology

This series is an initiative of UBC Laboratory of Archaeology and UBC Press. It provides a source of scholarly reporting on significant new archaeological research along the entire Pacific Rim – spanning the region from Southeast Asia to western North America and Pacific Latin America. The series will publish reports on archaeological fieldwork in longer monograph form as well as edited volumes of shorter works dealing with contemporary themes.

The general editors of the series are Michael Blake and R.G. Matson, both faculty members in the Department of Anthropology and Sociology at the University of British Columbia.

The first volume in the series is *Hidden Dimensions: The Cultural Significance of Wetland Archaeology*, edited by Kathryn Bernick. It presents the best papers from a conference on the topic held in Vancouver, British Columbia, in April 1995.

Edited by Kathryn Bernick

Hidden Dimensions:
The Cultural Significance of
Wetland Archaeology

UBCPress / Vancouver

Printed in Canada on acid-free paper ∞

ISBN 0-7748-0632-X

Pacific Rim Archaeology (ISSN 1483-2283)

Canadian Cataloguing in Publication Data

Main entry under title:

Hidden dimensions

(Pacific Rim archaeology, ISSN 1483-2283)
Papers presented at a conference in Vancouver, 1995.
Includes bibliographical references and index.
ISBN 0-7748-0632-X

1. Water-saturated sites (Archaeology) – Congresses. I. Bernick, Kathryn N.
II. Series: Pacific Rim archaeology series.

GN786.H52 1998   930.1   C97-910982-5

UBC Press gratefully acknowledges the ongoing support to its publishing program from the Canada Council for the Arts, the British Columbia Arts Council, and the Department of Canadian Heritage of the Government of Canada.

Cover illustrations: basket drawings by K. Bernick; basket fragment from Tsawwassen, BC, photo by M. Lay, courtesy UBC Laboratory of Archaeology; flint daggers, courtesy Aime Bocquet, Centre de Documentation de la Prehistoire Alpine; and wooden bowl from archaeological site in New Zealand

UBC Press
University of British Columbia
6344 Memorial Road
Vancouver, BC V6T 1Z2
(604) 822-5959
Fax: 1-800-668-0821
E-mail: orders@ubcpress.ubc.ca
http://www.ubcpress.ubc.ca

Contents

Preface and Acknowledgments / viii

Introduction / xi
Kathryn Bernick

Prologue: Wetland Worlds and the Past Preserved / 3
J.M. Coles

Part 1: Human Adaptations to Wetland Environments

Introduction / 27

Wetlands and Hunter-Gatherer Land Use in North America / 31
George P. Nicholas

Wetland Archaeological Sites in Aotearoa (New Zealand) Prehistory / 47
Cathryn Barr

Wetlands-Associated Sites in the Russian Far East:
A Review of Environment, Chronology, and Paleoeconomy / 56
Yaroslav V. Kuzmin

Prehistoric Wetland Sites in Sweden / 64
Lars Larsson

Part 2: Wet-Site Perspectives, Past and Present

Introduction / 85

The Importance of the Biskupin Wet Site for Twentieth-Century
Polish Archaeology / 89
Wojciech Piotrowski

Ancient Maya Use of Wetlands in Northern Quintana Roo, Mexico / 107
Scott L. Fedick

The Death of the Wildwood and the Birth of Woodmanship in Southeast England / 130
D.M. Goodburn

Stylistic Characteristics of Basketry from Coast Salish Area Wet Sites / 139
Kathryn Bernick

The Boston Back Bay Fish Weirs / 157
Elena B. Décima and Dena F. Dincauze

Part 3: Fishing Technologies on the Northwest Coast

Introduction / 175

A Comparative Chronology of Northwest Coast Fishing Features / 180
Madonna L. Moss and Jon M. Erlandson

Fishing Weirs in Oregon Coast Estuaries / 199
Scott Byram

Wet-Site Contributions to Developmental Models of Fraser River Fishing Technology / 220
Ann Stevenson

The Montana Creek Fish Trap I: Archaeological Investigations in Southeast Alaska / 239
Robert C. Betts

The Montana Creek Fish Trap II: Stratigraphic Interpretation in the Context of Southeastern Alaska Geomorphology / 252
Greg Chaney

Part 4: Preservation and Conservation in Practice

Introduction / 269

Essex Fish Traps and Fisheries: An Integrated Approach to Survey, Recording, and Management / 273
Paul J. Gilman

The Humber Wetlands Survey: An Integrated Approach to Wetland Research and Management / 290
Robert Van de Noort

The Role of Monitoring in the Assessment and Management of
Archaeological Sites / 302
Mike Corfield

Observations Resulting from the Treatment of Waterlogged Wood Bowls
in Aotearoa (New Zealand) / 317
Dilys A. Johns

Supercritical Drying of Waterlogged Archaeological Wood / 329
Barry Kaye and David J. Cole-Hamilton

Footing the Bill: Conservation Costs in the Private Sector / 340
Katherine Singley

Contributors / 357

Index / 359

Preface and Acknowledgments

The first waterlogged archaeological artifact I remember seeing came from the bottom of a two-metre-deep excavation pit at the Musqueam Northeast site in Vancouver. My sister Ruthie found it while screening a bucketful of sludge on a rainy day in June 1973. Further work at the site, under the direction of Charles E. Borden and David J.W. Archer, produced a large and varied assemblage of perishable artifacts and drew my attention to wet-site archaeology.

I have excavated several wet sites and analyzed a number of collections of basketry, cordage, and wooden artifacts. Until recently, I had assumed that such specimens are rarely preserved. This misconception was derived, in part, from the low profile wetland archaeology has within the profession and the tendency for a few spectacular finds, such as Ozette Village in Washington state, to eclipse ordinary water-saturated archaeological sites. In 1991 I conducted an overview study of wet sites in the lower Fraser River region of British Columbia, originally designed to generate leads for planning a field project. I was amazed at the large number of wet sites I "discovered" by looking at forgotten collections in local museums and reading field journals and unpublished reports. I concluded that, in addition to attention from researchers and resource managers, wet sites need and deserve public access – including the dissemination of information through publication. This volume represents one step in that direction.

As editor of a book mainly written by others, my greatest debt is to the authors who submitted their work to be published in it. I especially appreciate everyone's conscientious attention to details, indulgence of my editorial eccentricities, and patience with the publishing schedule.

The UBC Laboratory of Archaeology has played an instrumental role in the creation of this book. I sincerely thank R.G. Matson and Mike Blake for their time and advice and for trusting that a collection of conference papers could be transformed into a monograph. They took on the task of soliciting anonymous peer assessments, encouraged and facilitated completion of revisions recommended by the assessors, and directed the final manuscript to UBC Press. The UBC Laboratory of Archaeology, the Department of Anthropology and Sociology, and the Museum of Anthropology generously provided logistical support while I worked on the manuscript, for which I am grateful. Joyce Johnson of the UBC Laboratory of Archaeology deserves my very special thanks for myriad practical services.

I thank Ann Stevenson for facilitating the book project. As co-organizer of the conference that generated the contributions published here, Ann collaborated with me in the early stages of publication planning, performed miracles with budgets, shared crises, and gave constructive comments on introductory sections. I acknowledge Silvia Bergersen, Bryony and John Coles, Dale Croes, David Grattan, Warren Hill, Sharon Keen, Al Mackie, Madonna Moss, Phyllis and Jim Mason, Linda Vanden Berg, and many other friends and colleagues who have provided advice, practical assistance, and moral support over the past two years. Scott Byram and Phil Hobler generously provided illustrations for the introductions; Mike Blake, Joyce Johnson, and David Pokotylo facilitated my learning CorelDraw to computer-draft maps. I am grateful to Jean Wilson at UBC Press for supporting this publishing project and to Holly Keller-Brohman for overseeing conversion of the manuscript into a book. The copyediting was done by Judy Phillips.

This volume originated in a 1995 conference of the same name, *Hidden Dimensions: The Cultural Significance of Wetland Archaeology*. As a spin-off of the conference, the publication owes its existence to the success of that event and international participation that exceeded expectations. I take this opportunity to thank the UBC Museum of Anthropology for hosting the conference, the Archaeological Society of British Columbia and the Wetland Archaeology Research Project (WARP) for co-sponsoring it, and the Katzie, Musqueam, Tsawwassen, and Sto:lo nations for helping to develop the program. A modest financial subsidy of publication costs has been provided to UBC Press through the UBC Laboratory of Archaeology with residual funds from the 1995 *Hidden Dimensions* conference. I gratefully acknowledge financial support for the conference from the Government of Canada through the Department of Canadian Heritage's Access to Archaeology Program; the British Columbia Ministry of Small Business, Culture, and Tourism through the British Columbia Heritage Trust; and the British Columbia Ministry of Investment and Job Training through a Partners in Science Awareness grant. In-kind and/or financial support of the conference was also provided by the University of British Columbia First Nations House of Learning, the Museum of Anthropology, the Department of Anthropology and Sociology, the Laboratory of Archaeology, the Museum of Anthropology Volunteer Associates, and the Department of Botany; the Simon Fraser University Department of Archaeology; and the Archaeological Society of British Columbia.

The full list of everyone who contributed to the success of the conference and to this volume as its legacy is too long to include here. I single out for acknowledgment those who joined Ann Stevenson and me on the conference organizing committee – Helmi Braches, Greg Brass, Don Coolidge, Reet Kana, Dena Klashinsky, Joyce Johnson, John Maxwell, Anna Pappalardo, Susan Sirovyak, and Allison Young; and the session organizers whose initiative and vision shaped the conference program – Astrida Blukis Onat, Mary-Lou Florian, Doug Glaum, David Grattan, Kim Lawson, Dana Lepofsky, Judy Logan, Sonny McHalsie, Gordon Mohs, Madonna Moss, George Nicholas, and Allison Young. Thank you, everyone.

Kathryn Bernick
Vancouver, BC

Introduction

Kathryn Bernick

The discovery of fragile ancient objects always imparts a measure of excitement to an archaeological field project. When the finds – appearing suddenly in the slippery, oozing mud – consist of items made from plant material that should have decayed long ago, the feeling of exhilaration can be unforgettable, infectious, and addictive. The appeal of wet sites transcends emotional fascination, however, invoking intellectual appreciation for the unparalleled quality and variety of data they can provide.

Considering the potential wealth of information wetlands contain, it seems amazing that they have not attracted widespread attention from archaeologists. The explanation lies in a number of factors, among them reluctance to diverge from traditional research and to acquire new skills; the increased costs, labour, and time required for wet-site investigations; logistical and procedural conservation concerns; and the challenge of working in wetland environments. This volume aims to promote involvement in wetland archaeology by sharing practical experiences, as well as by providing glimpses of the tremendous promise of wet sites.

Raising awareness of wetland archaeology acquires a timely dimension when viewed from the perspective of current environmental concerns. Wetlands comprise a significant source of information about the past because they have been intrinsically connected with the history of humankind, and also because their water-saturated state preserves material evidence that would otherwise be absent from the archaeological record. Drainage and "reclamation" of wetlands directly threaten the continued existence of these invaluable and mainly still unknown, non-renewable cultural resources. Thus, the issues of site preservation and land management loom large on the agendas of those concerned with wetland archaeology.

Wet Sites

Wet landscapes have figured significantly in the development of human societies and in the lives of many people through the ages. Some contributors

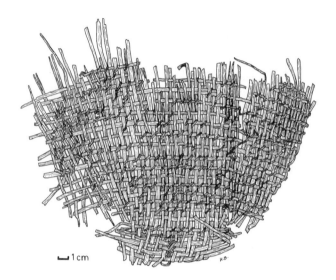

∟1 cm

Figure 1. Basket woven in plaited-wrapped-twining technique with cross-stitching to secure the "start" (centre of basket bottom), 3,000 years old, from the Musqueam Northeast site in Vancouver, British Columbia. *DhRt 4:10744. Drawing by K. Bernick.*

to this volume describe the variety of wetlands and of cultural adaptations to them. Others concentrate on particular locations that hold material remains of past human presence in wetland environments. These places, where archaeological evidence has been preserved in wet land, have become known as wet sites. Archaeologists use the term "wet site" for convenience – certainly it rolls off the tongue and word processor more smoothly than "archaeological site where waterlogged vegetal cultural materials are preserved in an oxygen-free environment in water-saturated soil below the water-table." In addition, "wet site" conveys the essential character of these unique places – they are utterly and thoroughly wet.

When water drives out the air that is normally present even in fine-grained tightly packed soil, the lack of oxygen inhibits the growth of bacteria and fungi that feed on organic matter. Although anaerobic (oxygen-free) environments support some decay organisms, wood and bark can survive, albeit in weakened condition, for thousands of years. To qualify as a "wet site," a water-saturated anaerobic location must contain wood that is not only old but also archaeological. A wet site contains perishable cultural artifacts – items composed of wood or other plant material, made or used by people or resulting from human activities.

Archaeological wood may also be preserved under conditions that do not involve waterlogging and therefore do not fall within the domain of wetland archaeology. These include preservation as charcoal (burnt wood), as well as by desiccation in arid environments, by freezing in permafrost or glaciers, and for comparatively short periods of time (a few centuries), in permanently damp conditions. Shipwrecks, even when thoroughly waterlogged and encased in mud at the bottom of the ocean, do not qualify as true wet sites because they are not at terrestrial locations. Other very wet archaeological sites that are not "wet sites" include locations that became submerged at some time after decomposition of any perishable cultural remains they may have contained. For example, earthquake-induced tectonic activity or a reservoir dam may permanently inundate archaeological sites where normal decay processes had already taken their toll.

Wet sites share certain characteristics regardless of the type of wetland in which they occur. In addition to the presence of artifacts and associated remains made from normally perishable materials, which introduces new categories of objects to the archaeological record, the wet context requires the development of specialized excavation techniques. Because waterlogged artifacts begin to shrivel up and disintegrate upon exposure to air, they require immediate conservation treatment as well as special storage conditions. Attending to the physical integrity of the artifacts imposes a major

Figure 2. The Kwatna River site of Axeti (FaSu 1) on the central coast of British Columbia was excavated by Simon Fraser University field schools, 1969-1971. This view shows excavation of intertidal waterlogged deposits with hand tools and also with water pressure. With time, water excavation using hoses supplied by pumps and by gravity from large oil drums (right foreground) became the preferred method. This is the first archaeological use of hydraulic excavation techniques on the northwest coast of North America. *Photo by P.M. Hobler.*

responsibility, especially since decisions about conservation may have long-lasting effects. Wet sites also preserve abundant biological remains, increasing the need for specialists who can identify, analyze, and interpret the data.

The preceding definitions and discussion of wet sites view them from the present – that is, the environment, preservation conditions, and cultural contents as they are today. Yet, the fact that we investigate these sites now and describe them in the present tense does not diminish the importance of their respective past histories. In addition to satisfying curiosity, understanding how a particular site came into being constitutes a crucial perspective for designing effective site protection measures, implementing a resource management program, and choosing appropriate methods of object conservation. It also bears directly on the accuracy of reconstructions of the cultural activities that took place at the site.

Not least, it should be emphasized that wet sites occur in wetlands. These sites are foci of activity on landscapes that have covered a significant portion of the earth and have been closely associated with human populations. Even though they do not always contain wet sites, wetlands comprise potential settings for preserved waterlogged materials. Understanding the nature of the relationship between people and wetlands provides a context for wet-site investigations. Moreover, exploring how people related to wetlands in the past constitutes an important direction for research, especially since many of these landscapes are threatened with extinction.

Figure 3. Kwatna River mouth on the central coast of British Columbia where archaeologists from Simon Fraser University excavated, 1969-1971. The Axeti waterlogged site (FaSu 1), imperilled by shifting stream channels, is near the end of the island (centre of photograph). In this view the tide is high and the wetland largely inundated. *Photo by P.M. Hobler.*

The *Hidden Dimensions* Conference

Our impetus for convening a conference on wetland archaeology began with the realization that the precarious state of wetlands and their cultural resources in southwestern British Columbia, Canada, required a public forum. The conference coincided with a UBC Museum of Anthropology exhibition *From Under the Delta: Wet-Site Archaeology in the Lower Fraser Region of British Columbia*. The exhibition features 130 objects made from wood and bark, most of which had never before been on public view. The artifacts in the display, which depict aspects of woodworking, basketry, cordage, and fishing technology, represent local collections dating from the past four millennia. The exhibit also addresses cultural resource management issues with an emphasis on the views of local First Nations communities. In the course of developing the exhibition, it became apparent that wetland management, site preservation, object conservation, and advancing the concerns of indigenous peoples are global issues. Thus, the original concept of a half-day symposium to enhance a museum display developed into a timely international event attended by some 200 people.

The conference *Hidden Dimensions: The Cultural Significance of Wetland Archaeology* was held by the UBC Museum of Anthropology and co-sponsored by the Archaeological Society of British Columbia and the Wetland Archaeology Research Project (WARP). It took place on the University of British Columbia campus in Vancouver, April 27-30, 1995. The program was developed in cooperation with the Katzie, Musqueam, Sto:lo, and Tsawwassen nations. These and numerous other organizations and individuals helped put together a stimulating and enjoyable gathering. The intention in publishing a selection of the proceedings is to build on the momentum of the conference in order to advance the issues of wetland archaeology.

In addition to three days of symposia and plenary sessions, the *Hidden Dimensions* conference featured public events and workshops that comprised an integral part of the proceedings. Sessions on the first day included a workshop on land management from the perspective of wet-site archaeology, organized by Doug Glaum of the British Columbia Archaeology Branch; a workshop on teaching children about wetland archaeology, organized by Kim Lawson of the British Columbia Archaeology Branch; and a public forum on First Nations' heritage and the Fraser River, organized by Gordon Mohs and Sonny McHalsie of the Sto:lo Nation and Greg Brass of the UBC Museum of Anthropology. These three sessions brought together archaeologists, conservators, and wetland experts from around the world, people from British Columbia First Nations, and from the local archaeology, land management, and education communities. The vibrancy of the discourse on that first day continued throughout the conference, reverberating in the oral scientific presentations and generating an ambience of intellectual excitement.

Despite its pivotal role, the public component of the conference is absent from the published proceedings – except for J.M. Coles' revised text of his excellent and well-received public talk. The decision to focus on publishing scholarly papers reflects the conceptual structure of the event as a combination of discussion for the benefit of participants and of formally delivered contributions to knowledge. In this, as in other aspects of planning the conference, Ann Stevenson and I (the co-organizers) took direction from the communities we consulted – local First Nations, professional and avocational archaeologists, conservators, and cultural resource managers.

The chapters in this volume explore academic research themes such as human adaptation to wetland environments and the contributions of wetland archaeology to reconstructions of culture history, as well as related practical issues of land management and object conservation. The selection represents the topical and geographical scope of the scientific conference sessions and includes about one-third of the presentations. Several conference papers that are absent from this collection comprise portions of research that will be available in other publications.

The scientific program of the conference was shaped in large part by the vision and enthusiasm of respondents to the call for contributions, particulary by those who organized symposia. For example, George P. Nicholas organized a session on human adaptations to wetland ecosystems, with presentations about research in Europe, North Africa, Asia, the North and South Pacific, and North America. Madonna L. Moss brought together researchers to discuss their experiences of fishing sites where wooden features and perishable artifacts have been preserved. Allison A. Young (PhD candidate at the University of British Columbia) can take credit for the good representation of participants from Alaska. Among other promotional efforts, she organized a symposium on the research potential of wet sites in Alaska aimed primarily at archaeologists tangentially involved in wetland research – but who ought to pay more attention to wet sites.

Well-seasoned wetland archaeologists also found the conference instructive and intellectually stimulating. European participants accustomed to professional gatherings about wetland archaeology found the *Hidden Dimensions* conference particularly rewarding for the insight provided by exposure to research, ideas, and concerns of people from other continents (see Van de Noort 1995). Conference participants were privileged to be able to hear about several research projects for which there is little published information in English. For those who work on the west coast of North America, excavations of waterlogged wooden villages in northern Europe presented stunning contrasts to collections of broken fishhooks and discarded baskets, or alignments of stakes on intertidal beaches. A special presentation related the excavation, preservation, and reconstruction of the Āraiši Lake Fortress site in the Baltic region, where Jānis and Zigrīda Apals of the Latvian Institute of History have investigated 75 percent of the site, including 145 dwellings and several thousand artifacts from the ninth to tenth centuries AD. The Āraiši wet site is now an open-air museum near Cēsis, Latvia.

The symposium organized by David Grattan and Judith A. Logan of the Canadian Conservation Institute drew high praise from participants. In this session, conservators from Canada, the United States, England, Scotland, and Japan presented papers describing their work concerning wet-site conservation and preservation. Notably, three new processes for the conservation of waterlogged organic materials were introduced. In addition to supercritical drying (Kaye and Cole-Hamilton, this volume), two treatments developed in Japan were reported and discussed. One, described by Setsuo Imazu, involves impregnation of waterlogged wood with lacitol (a sugar alcohol). A paper by Fumio Okada and several of his colleagues reported on experimental use of high molecular-weight alcohols, specifically cetyl alcohol and stearlyl alcohol. Conservation and preservation were also addressed within other symposia and in poster presentations (the article by Johns in this volume originated as a poster). Mary-Lou E. Florian (emerita, Royal British Columbia Museum) organized and presented a workshop on species identification and material analysis.

The Volume

The chapters in this volume, as well as the conference that generated them, share several underlying themes. These include the capacity of wetlands for remarkable preservation of archaeological evidence, the interconnectedness of people and wetlands, the dynamic nature of wetlands and the archaeological evidence they contain, and concern about the future of these cultural resources.

Wetlands, as reiterated explicitly or implicitly by nearly every author and conference presenter, are credited as archaeological archives par excellence. The potential presence of artifacts and other archaeological evidence that would in most other circumstances quickly decompose gives wetlands a special status. Their anaerobic deposits comprise a source of information that is not normally available and that can be considered a precious cultural resource. Because archaeologists normally base their interpretations on only a small portion of the material culture, the availability of additional types of data inevitably increases the validity of reconstructions.

The prologue by J.M. Coles is an eloquent contribution to the cause of promoting wetland archaeology. Coles relates the amazing attraction wetlands have held for people throughout the history of the world and still hold for archaeologists today. Though the examples are mainly drawn from Europe, his captivating account invokes the need for increased concern with wetlands internationally. Coles' essay originated as a public talk delivered at the *Hidden Dimensions* conference (rather than a scientific presentation); however, his message is addressed equally to professional archaeologists.

The chapters following the prologue are grouped by general topic into four sections proceeding from general to specific and from theoretical to practical. Each section is preceded by introductory comments that contextualize the presentations. Although the collection as a whole reflects the scope of the conference symposia, it does not retain the integrity of those sessions. This necessary change results from the availability of only a selection of the presentations and the essential requirement to organize the volume in a useful format.

Part 1 consists of four chapters that discuss environmental and historical contexts of wet sites, wetland archaeology, and past human adaptation to wetland environments. These overviews of wetland use are followed by case studies – in Part 2, five examples of wet-site research projects featuring specific sites, regions, or collections, and in Part 3, five that examine wet-site evidence for fishing technologies in the Northwest Coast culture area. Part 4 addresses applied aspects of wetland archaeology. The first three chapters in Part 4 discuss cultural resource management programs in England. The second facet of wetland conservation, that is, stabilization and preservation of waterlogged materials, is addressed by the last three contributions.

The immense geographic and topical scope of this volume highlights the global nature of wetland archaeology issues. It also presents an editorial challenge. Authors were encouraged to provide background information for readers from other parts of the world and other disciplines and to define technical terminology.

The style of citing radiocarbon ages follows that outlined in the journal *American Antiquity* (1992: 57:755-756). Accordingly, radiocarbon dates reported for the first time are given as uncalibrated ages BP with details provided by the respective laboratories including sample identification number, 1σ standard error, material, and whether the date was corrected for isotopic fractionation. Laboratory abbreviations conform to those used in the journal *Radiocarbon*. Citation of radiocarbon dates that have been calibrated (corrected by reference to tree-ring curves) are identified as such and include a reference to the particular calibration program. General references to archaeological time periods are given in years BP or as calendar years AD or BC, depending on the context of the discussion.

Readers unfamiliar with archaeological conventions should note that in most countries identification codes are assigned to sites when they are registered with an official government or other institutional authority. The site numbering systems vary among jurisdictions. The Smithsonian Trinomial System used in the United States includes alpha-numeric codes for state and county as well as the site number. In Canada, site codes are based on a map grid system.

If this volume helps to increase attention to wetland archaeological resources, it will have achieved its goal. Wetland archaeology provides unparalleled opportunities to rectify some of the biases in our current knowledge of past human behaviour. At the same time, wetland archaeology faces the enormous challenge of alleviating threats to the continued existence of the data. Environmentally sensitive archaeological resources are vanishing along with the shrinkage of wetlands, and rescued perishable artifacts too often suffer irreparable major damage due to lack of knowledge, inadequate conservation facilities, and insufficient money. This publication adds its voice to lobby for societal acknowledgment and acceptance of the immense responsibility to care for the fragile heritage of the world.

Reference Cited

Van de Noort, Robert
  1995 Hidden Dimensions, Vancouver: Conference Report. *NewsWARP* (Wetland Archaeology Research Project, UK) 17:4-5.

Hidden Dimensions

Prologue:
Wetland Worlds and the Past Preserved

J.M. Coles

The idea that beneath the waters of lakes and seas, and buried deep in muds and in peatbogs, there lie drowned villages and ancient civilizations is very common in many parts of the world. Under the deep waters and lakes, bogs and shallow seas, the tales and legends say, are the well-preserved remains of once-prosperous and thriving towns, where the people bustled about, building houses, raising children, working and playing, until disaster struck and their world was ended. The stories written down, or more often passed down by oral tradition, are often moralistic, that is, they make the point that the villages were drowned and lost forever because the people had done something wrong, had offended the powers, and had therefore been punished.

In the southeastern part of France, in the foothills of the Alps, there are many lakes, some large, some small. The area is very fertile and now is settled and worked for pasture, agriculture, and vineyards. One of the lakes, called Paladru, is a beautiful body of water and is now a popular tourist resort. The towns and villages around this lake were established only a few centuries ago, but there is good archaeological evidence that people lived along the shore in small farming communities and as fisher folk for many centuries before the recent towns were established.

Around the southern end of Lake Paladru there is a local legend, a story told long ago by a monk to a traveller:

Here by the lake was once a prosperous village, somewhat given to boasting of its wealth and hospitality. One day, the Lord God set out to find if the villagers were as hospitable in deed as they were in word. Disguising Himself as a pilgrim, He walked into the village and sought shelter. One and all, rich and poor, the

This chapter is a revised version of a public talk given by the author at the *Hidden Dimensions* conference.

*householders turned Him away. Angry and indignant, the Lord God smote
the village, which sank and was overwhelmed by the waters of the lake.*

Lake Paladru was used by fishermen over the centuries, and they occasionally brought up fragments of wood or other objects in their nets, and
thus kept alive the story of the drowned village. When the level of the lake
was low, in some winters, posts from an ancient settlement would sometimes be exposed, but most of the time they were under the water. The lake
recently became a popular holiday resort, and many tourists paddled about
and swam, and the site was often explored by divers and damaged by visitors. So a major archaeological campaign was mounted to excavate in and
around the wooden posts and timbers, mostly under water. The site was
soon identified as a small medieval fortified village, rather like a defended
manor house, and it was dated to the decades around AD 1000 – just about
the right age for the legend of the Lord God's curse to be delivered and for
the tradition of the drowned village to survive in the region.

Before the site was studied we knew very little about medieval settlement
in this part of eastern France, in Burgundy. It was a time just before the
great stone castles and abbeys were built, and written records are very sparse.
For archaeologists M. Colardelle and E. Verdel (1993), it was in a way prehistory, with little visible on the ground and not much in the historical
records, and there was no real idea about the character and extent of settlement in the region. Environmental studies showed that the area at this
time, AD 1000, was covered by dense forest with little trace in the pollen
record of clearances and cultivation. So the archaeologists, beginning to
excavate the posts at the lake's edge, had little to go on.

One of the reasons archaeologists dig wet sites is because they can expect,
most times, to recover evidence that is well preserved by waterlogging. This
is an obvious point that needs no emphasis here. So, at the Paladru site,
called Charavines Colletière, the expectation was that enough posts and
timbers would be recovered to create a reconstruction view of the settlement. By an extensive study of the tree-rings and by dendrochronology,
Colardelle and Verdel succeeded in the dating of the various structures,
both relatively and absolutely. They also managed to recover enough other
evidence to recreate the drowned world of Charavines Colletière and to
explain its existence. The whole archaeological process took about 20 years
to complete.

The story begins for us in AD 1003, probably in the springtime. A small
group of settlers arrived on the southern shore of the lake and began to
clear the forest and to build, in a very short time, a small fortified village –
three wooden buildings, set close together, and various workshops. The
archaeologists suggest that the main building may have been 14 m high,
perhaps with a tower as lookout post (Figure 1). The buildings were

Figure 1. Charavines Colletière. A reconstruction of the fortified village. *From Colardelle and Verdel 1993.*

enclosed by a strong palisade, and there was a landgate and a watergate. The village was set just beside the lake where the shoreland was clear enough for rapid building. The plan of the village, as well as the many thousands of artifacts recovered, suggest that the owner and family lived in the main (manor) house, and that a smaller building set at the water's edge was at first a stable, then was changed into a second dwelling house after only 10 to 15 years.

Around the village there was dense forest with chestnut, walnut, and box trees, but parts were soon cleared for grazing animals and for plough fields. The settlers grew rye and wheat (for bread), oats (for horses?), barley (for beer?), grapes (for wine), and other crops for cloth. The bones of animals were abundant on the site and suggest that the people butchered on average one pig every month, and that they also kept sheep, goats, cattle, and hens. The wildwood, lakeshore, and lake waters were exploited for deer, hare, various birds, and fish such as perch, dace, and roach. The wetland was also rich in plant foods – cherries and sloes, crab apples, hips and haws, strawberries, raspberries and blackberries, acorns, beechnuts, walnuts, chestnuts, and hazelnuts. All this detailed evidence of the foods was preserved in the wet silt and muds of the lake, and had to be sieved and sorted by an extensive program. The perch, for example, was identified only by its scales, as no bones of this species had survived.

So far, this evidence suggests a group of people, farmers and gatherers, exploiting their landscape, living and eating well. But they were also more than farmers. The excavators recovered many pieces of horse gear – spurs and bits and wooden saddle frames. These suggest that horses were kept for riding, not ploughing, and perhaps for riding out to battle because there were many iron weapons such as axes and lance heads. We might envisage a small band of armed and armoured men riding out when the occasion demanded action. To support the cavalry and the whole society, craftsmen worked in the village making leather clothing, including shoes, and working with wood for furniture and smaller items such as plates, bowls, cups, and spoons. Spinning and weaving of wool, flax, and hemp are attested by the fragments of textiles and small tools, and wooden combs were made for weaving or for wearing.

Because the conditions of preservation were so good, and probably because the settlement had been abandoned in a hurry, the archaeologists also found many things that we do not often see on ancient sites. For example, there were many musical instruments, such as flutes, parts of bagpipes, and pieces of stringed instruments. The people also amused themselves playing games, with discs for backgammon perhaps, and chess pieces and dice. This was no ordinary farmstead, we think, but who were these people and why were they living here on the shore of the lake? That they were wealthy is clear, not only from the clothing, iron weapons, gaming pieces, and musical instruments, but also from a few very valuable jewels, such as a piece of horse harness made of precious stones set in a golden mount. So we can envisage a small settlement of a wealthy family with its dependants and associated labourers, self-sufficient, well-fed and well-equipped for defense and attack. But what did it mean? Here the archaeologists could present an explanation based on wider fields of evidence.

The settlement was new in this region. It was a frontier post trying to establish an existence in a small but distinct region in Burgundy in the years just after AD 1000. Two other small settlements were established farther north along Lake Paladru at about the same time, according to field surveys. These three settlements may have been in competition with one another for the land, and for the whole territory of Burgundy; or perhaps they had combined forces against another power. This was a time when the great landowners of France began to expand their holdings, and there was one, called Gilbert, who was active in Burgundy. But it was also the time when the great religious orders – the Carthusians – were asserting themselves and acquiring new lands. By the twelfth and thirteenth centuries, the land of Burgundy was divided between these powers. So our small fortified settlement was probably a part of this competition, in an early phase. It was successful for a time after its establishment in AD 1003. The settlement grew, extended its clearances, probably took in more land, and gained in strength; its strong palisade and towered building asserted its power to all who approached. It could look forward to expansion and stability. Perhaps it was hostile to strangers, wary about visitors, and did not want to share its undoubted wealth.

And then matters began to go wrong. There is evidence that about 30 years after its foundation, there were two bad years of rainfall. Crops failed, the land became waterlogged, the animals suffered, and finally the lake waters rose and drowned the settlement. The people left, probably hurriedly, leaving behind their fine buildings, workshops, storerooms and stables, and some of their personal possessions, games, clothes, horse gear, weapons, and jewels. All were drowned beneath the waters of Lake Paladru. But the tradition of their presence, the defended manor house, the fortified wealthy village, and its hostile and unfriendly attitude must have lingered on in the memories of those poorer people who lived away from the lake and who perhaps had to serve the more powerful lakeshore village. In this way, the tale told by the monk to the traveller, of the inhospitable village drowned beneath the waters, persisted until this day, and the French archaeologists have now succeeded in illuminating the tale in a vivid way, confirming the doomed village, explaining its existence, and coming close to understanding the lives of those who once lived there. It will be illuminating in a different way if the reader considers how little of this story would have survived the passage of time had this site been dried out, and all its organic components allowed to decay.

The wetlands of the world now cover about six percent of the land surface, and that figure is shrinking every day as more and more wetlands are destroyed. They can be marshes, swamps, wet valley bottoms, river deltas, shallow lake shores, and peat bogs, and they can be beautiful, colourful, rich in plants and animals, or flat and desolate, uncomfortable places for most people. In the past, wetlands were more extensive than today, and maybe 90 percent of all wetlands are now damaged or destroyed (Coles 1991). In recent years, some wetlands have been looked on as wastelands, suitable only for quarrying of peat, dumping of urban waste, draining into pasture or arable land, or consolidating for urban and motorway expansion. In the past it was different, I think. Ancient people were attracted to wet areas not because they wanted to live in the wet, but because of the wealth in plants and animals (wildfowl, fish, eels, mammals, reeds, withes, and plant foods), the ease of travel and transport (in the absence of roads), and in some cases because of the isolation and defense offered by certain wetlands.

Even in the past, few people chose or dared to settle, to actually live, in the lake waters, in the marshlands, or in the swamps and bogs. Instead, they perched, like a row of swallows, on the edge of wetlands, harvesting the wild wealth and the tamed shorelands. They tried to avoid the marsh sickness – malaria – and doubtless they wondered at the will of the wisp – the flickering lights in the rising mist. In the vast treeless bogs, the harvest was poor and here the bog surfaces were avoided, except when peat was dug for fuel and building blocks, or when wooden roads had to be built to cross from one island to another, or when the bog provided burial places for treasure and bodies. In time, many roadways, bodies, boats, platforms, and settlements were overwhelmed by rising waters or by peat formation, and they were waterlogged and sealed until recent times.

The history of wetland archaeology is very long, and it may be worth noting two or three of the pioneers, both for the sites they uncovered and for the concerns of wetland archaeology that they experienced and developed. The first recorded discoveries in the wetlands of the Old World, in Europe, were made about 600 years ago, when peat digging revealed wooden roadways, wheels, barrels, weapons of iron, bronze tools, gold ornaments, and sometimes human bodies (Coles and Coles 1989). Almost all of these were abandoned, stolen, sold, destroyed, and almost all are lost. By the nineteenth century in Europe, huge canals were being dug, railways and roads built across boglands, towns constructed in river valleys, and peatlands dug by the peasantry. Discoveries came thick and fast, log boats from the rivers of Scotland, crannogs from the boglands of Ireland, and pile dwellings from the Alpine lakes. In the winter of 1853-1854 in Switzerland, the lake levels fell and the wooden piles of ancient settlements stood clear of the water (Figure 2). In the silt lay stone axes, bone tools, and pottery shards, as well as wooden artifacts, and the antiquarians began to trawl the silts, both underwater and newly exposed, using hoes, rakes, scoops, and other destructive tools. Dredging brought up hundreds of objects of the Stone and Bronze ages (Keller 1878), and, combined with the thousands of wooden piles, evoked images of ancient lake-dwellers, combing the shores and waters for their daily sustenance and living lives of tranquillity affected by

Figure 2. The posts or piles of a prehistoric lakeshore village, exposed during low water at Bevaix-Treytel, Switzerland. *From M. Egloff, in Coles and Coles 1989.*

Figure 3. An idealized view of a lakeshore pile-supported settlement about 5,000 years ago. Modern archaeology suggests that this view is substantially incorrect, both structurally and in the appearance of the clothing worn. *Drawn by Y. Reymond, after a painting by Hyppolythe Coutau 1896.*

nothing except the threat of rising waters (Figure 3). The proper excavation of these sites was beyond the capabilities of the antiquarians, as most of the sites lay submerged beneath the water or were buried by silt or peat. One ingenious explorer in Lake Geneva, Adolphe van Morlot, armed himself with a pick, a butterfly net, a bucket for his airflow, and lead boots, and conducted an underwater assessment, commenting, "It was strikingly poetical to stand amidst those ancient posts in the bluish twilight" (Coles and Coles 1989:20). He was the first underwater archaeologist whose determination surpassed his technique, and doubtless he was considered an eccentric by his fellow antiquarians.

In England, a medical student named Arthur Bulleid came to hear of the discoveries in Switzerland, and he searched for four years in the Somerset moors until he too discovered a lake village. The site, near Glastonbury, was excavated between 1892 and 1907, and its fine preservation of round houses, fences, and organic artifacts made it one of the best-known prehistoric sites in western Europe. The Lake Village has continued to create interest and is still the subject of research and interpretation (Coles and Minnitt 1995). Bulleid was a scientist, quiet and methodical in his work, and the Lake Village benefits from his careful excavations and records. But he was also determined, and managed to excavate the entire Lake Village.

Equally determined was a contemporary in America, a man named Frank Cushing. In the late nineteenth century, the west coast of Florida was being settled, and various areas of peaty soil were dug to prepare them for orchards and other crops. At a place called Key Marco, some wooden, bone, and shell objects were recovered from a peaty "muck," and through a combination of coincidences, Cushing heard of the site and was determined to seize the opportunity; he too had read about the Swiss Lake Dwellings. He was by all accounts an eccentric archaeologist, and his eccentricities served

him well at Key Marco (Gilliland 1989). The site was in effect a collapsed marina, and the infill of muck contained hundreds of organic objects, carved, engraved, and painted. Cushing and his small team laboured to recover masks, models, tools, and weapons. Almost all disintegrated before their eyes, and it is only the drawings and photographs of Cushing's draughtsman that allow us to contemplate the wealth of artistry of the prehistoric Calusa Indians whose site Cushing had stumbled upon (Figure 4). Today, the site of Key Marco is obliterated (Purdy 1991), unlike the Glastonbury Lake Village, where a farsighted local society has preserved its remnants.

Figure 4. A painted board from Key Marco, Florida. It may have formed part of a ceremonial display on the edge of a prehistoric marina about 1,000 years ago. The bird is probably a kingfisher. *From Gilliland 1989.*

Since the early discoveries in the Alpine lakes, work has continued decade by decade, and today a formidable array of technologies can be directed
on the material remains. Aerial photographs have exposed the lines of posts
beneath the cold, clear waters of some Alpine lakes, and underwater excavation has carefully retrieved material from individual floors of houses, identified through specialist examination of wooden posts, wall plates and
uprights, floorboards, doorways, pathways, and even remains of bedding.
In some cases, cofferdams have been erected around sites, the water pumped
out, and excavations carried out using land-based methods. By radiocarbon
dating and dendrochronology (tree-ring counting), we know that the
lakeshore settlements existed from about 4000 BC to sometime after
1000 BC. We can begin to understand how some ancient houses were built,
not just the shape and size but also the character of the walls, the roof
structure, and the materials used in all aspects (e.g., Arnold 1990, Coles
1992) (Figure 5). Pine, oak, and ash were preferred trees, providing good

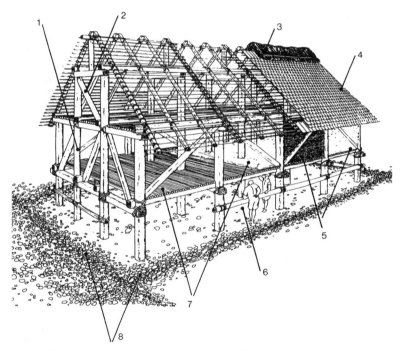

Figure 5. A Bronze Age house, recreated from the well-preserved evidence on
Alpine lakeshore and underwater sites. Note the following: (1) the height of the
building is based on fallen uprights; (2) the details of the superstructure are known
from fallen pieces; (3) pollen and macroscopic plant remains indicate reed ridge
thatch; (4) pine and oak shingles were recovered; (5) Wall panels of wattle survive;
(6) the height of the ground floor is deduced from the wood structure, floor
deposits, hearths, etc.; (7) the floor of poles was covered by clay; and (8) the
pathways lead to other houses. *From Arnold 1990 and Coles 1992.*

straight stems and planks. One site in Lake Neuchâtel in Switzerland provides an example of how much we have learned about the structure of houses, and comparison with the normal bare postholes on dry sites hardly bears thinking about – if you are a dryland archaeologist. And we know that most of the settlements were constructed on the lakeshores rather than in the lake waters. The piles upon which the house platforms and floors rest were not free-standing but were driven deep into the soft sediments to help stabilize and support the structures.

Another site, at Hornstaad-Hörnle in south Germany, provides yet more striking evidence of the value of wetland investigations (Schlichtherle 1990). Here a series of small hamlets existed. If dried out, the archaeologist would be presented with a bewildering palimpsest of postholes difficult to disentangle. Because the posts of all the houses have survived, they can be dated individually and linked to one another in a relative sequence, using the tree-ring signatures of each, then joined to a master dendrochronology that gives absolute calendar years BC (Figure 6). One of the settlements at Hornstaad began in 3586 BC, with one house; between 3571 and 3564 BC repairs were needed, new wood was put in place, and several new buildings were erected. From 3541 BC to 3531 BC there was much new building, and again between 3521 BC and 3517 BC. A final episode of activity took place between 3511 and 3507 BC. There are two things to say about this. First, the whole settlement, with at least four phases, existed for only 90 years or so; archaeologists of the past might have postulated several

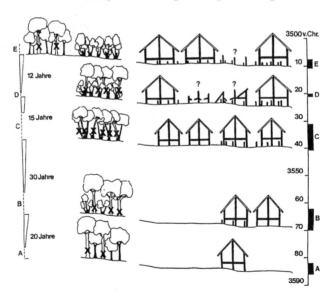

Figure 6. A reconstruction of the houses in the settlement at Hornstaad-Hörnle and the size of trees used at various building phases. *From Billamboz 1990.*

centuries for its existence. Second, the wood used in the structures can be identified and aged so that we can deduce the size of trees selected and how the mixed oak forest of Hornstaad was managed (Billamboz 1990). Several large trees that had clearly been protected or conserved by the earlier builders were used in the final episode of the building. This speaks of an "owned" woodland.

A third site, in France, provides us with a fine example of how the lakeside muds have preserved not only structures but also a wide range of objects and debris contemporary with the buildings (Bocquet 1990, 1994). From Charavines les Baigneurs in Lake Paladru, Neolithic evidence has been recovered of the small areas of forest cleared for cultivation, and of the wheat, barley, peas, poppies, flax, and garlic grown there. Animal bones, of cattle, sheep, and goats indicate a mixed economy, which included the collection of apples, acorns, hazelnuts, beechnuts, grapes, various berries, and Chinese lantern – all good to eat. A variety of wild seeds such as marjoram, thyme, and lime were perhaps used as a flavouring in the cookhouse. The wild woodland was harvested for different species of wood suitable for maple handles, boxwood combs and spoons, holly spindles, lime bowls, elder tubes, silver-fir whisks or beaters, and yew bows, and fine beechwood handles were attached to flint dagger blades with birchbark gum and tied with a fir twig (Figure 7). On a dry site we would have found only the flint. Oak was used for dugout canoes and beech for paddles, and stone net weights show that the lake was fished. Wild birds and eggs were probably taken from the reed beds. The whole structure of the site, which lasted in two phases, each of only 20-30 years, suggests a total reliance on the immediate environment of the settlement, with very little evidence of resources obtained from farther afield.

One of the features of many wetland settlements is that the immediate environment is often very rich in variety and quantity of resources so that, in theory, an extensive menu of foods could have been collected and prepared for home consumption. One settlement, the Glastonbury Lake Village, has had its Iron Age foods assessed by a wetland chef and her willing assistant, and they (Bryony and John Coles) prepared a menu based on what was found, what was there on the site, and, in some cases, what was potentially there but not identified in the early excavations. Even with allowances for enthusiasm, it was a formidable presentation (Coles and Minnitt 1995) (Figure 8).

What of the personal lives of the people who lived at Cortaillod, Hornstaad, and Charavines, and the many other contemporary sites? We know little about individual lives and personal habits, so when we find intimate details, they have an immediate attraction. In an early settlement at Hornstaad, for example, someone was chewing birchbark gum, and left a few gobs with his or her tooth marks imprinted. Perhaps they were stuck on a Neolithic bedpost. We have very little evidence of prehistoric clothing, perhaps due to its fragile nature, although at one site, Irgenhausen, conditions were so good for preservation that many pieces of textile were recovered, including some with elaborate decoration (Figure 9). They show what we have lost on wetland sites. The absence of textiles on other sites is likely because clothing, worn by owners, was removed when the settlements were abandoned, along with other precious materials. Why abandoned? It was probably due to one or more of the following: land exhaustion, human threat, rising damp, and rising or falling lake levels. Certainly, in some cases, it was the sudden rise of the waters, as we have seen at Charavines Colletière, and the good preservation of post tops and other wood on many sites suggests that submergence was rapid.

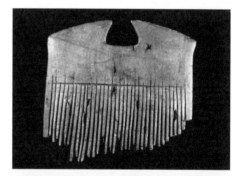
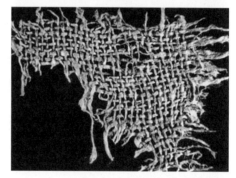

Figure 7. Some artifacts from Charavines: two flint daggers with beechwood and fir handles, a boxwood comb, plant-fibre cloth, and some wooden spoons and ladles. *From Bocquet 1990.*

All this evidence is important for archaeologists who try to re-create, in writing and by illustrations, the conditions of the past and the human responses to the opportunities presented by ancient wetlands. But there are serious problems for those of us who want to demonstrate the successes and

MENU

Water cress soup made with duck stock, served with comfrey fritter
Sweet oar weed fried in nut oil and wild celery soup
Reed mace spikes and common mallow soup
Bean and duck egg salad with brooklime
Hazelnut cutlets with herb and kelp salad

Fish etc.
Tench cooked in crab apple juice with steamed laver
Smoked eel and wild celery
Pike steak and boiled marsh samphire
Terrine of eel and frogs' legs with nettle tips
Crayfish with herbs and waterlily tubers

Meat.
Filet of heron and stewed nettle with brooklime salad
Wild boar cooked with bog myrtle berries
and served with crab apple sauce and sea kale
Grouse or duck (in season) and raised bog cranberry sauce
with sea beet and crab apple pickle
Beaver tail roast with hazelnuts, peas and comfrey sauce
Saltmarsh lamb and sea purselane, with wild cabbage and meadowsweet
Roast swan with reed mace shoots and sea holly sweetmeats
Teal served with watercress and samphire

Sweet trolley.
Goat cream cheese and honey
Reedmace pancakes with honey or apple jelly
Raspberries with cheeses
Bilberry crumble

Tea or coffee.
Coffee: acorn, dandelion root, goosegrass
Tea: mint, limeflower, heather flower
(served with angelica crystallised fruits)

Drinks.
Beer: nettle, heather, bog myrtle, sweet gale, crab apple cider
Wine: birch sap, oak leaf, elderflower, blackberry

Afters.
fennel seed chews, willow bark aspirin, marshmallow chews

Figure 8. A wetland menu drawn up from the archaeological and environmental evidence at the Glastonbury Lake Village. *From Coles and Minnitt 1995.*

Figure 9. A reconstruction of textile designs from Neolithic Irgenhausen, Switzerland. *Schweizerisches Landesmuseum, Zürich.*

potential rewards of wetland archaeology to the public at large, to the uncommitted and unpersuaded. It is important for us to show that the ancient heritage is interesting and worthy of efforts to preserve it. Underwater sites, and sites consisting mostly of wood, cannot be easily displayed in the open for all to see – they decay upon exposure and fail to retain any semblance of integrity if neglected. In some areas of the world today, real efforts are being made to use the rich evidence from wetlands to illuminate the past and to educate young people. In Japan, in Ireland, in western North America, and in Latvia and Poland, very significant and substantial reconstructions and displays have succeeded in attracting the public, but perhaps the best example of a specific and targeted approach is, again, Swiss in origin.

In the Alpine region there is a long tradition of wetland archaeology on the well-preserved lakeshore settlements of the Neolithic and Bronze Age. In 1990, an experiment was set up to build on these traditions and to demonstrate how archaeology could move away from strict legislation and laboratory analyses to meet the public face to face (Ruoff 1992). The essential question was: could serious scholarly archaeology be presented to the public in such a way as to attract, interest, and educate? Plenty of museums and open-air displays draw people regularly, but many people, and segments of society, never go to museums. Could they be drawn in, and could they become interested in the heritage, without the need to descend into fantasy worlds and exaggerations? The Swiss organized an exhibition, renting a small

Figure 10. The 1990 reconstruction of a Bronze Age village near Zürich, with visitors arriving by dugout. *Photo by J.M. Coles.*

island in the lake just outside Zürich. A replica of a Bronze Age settlement was built on the island, based upon the excavation plans of a prehistoric site nearby. The houses of the well-preserved settlement had wooden floors and roofing timbers as well as identifiable walls, hearths, and entrances, so the exhibition houses were probably very close in appearance to the originals. On the shore, the archaeologists erected large exhibition halls for special displays, experiments, and lectures. The public was invited to almost everything – to the workshops where children and adults could try their hands at making pottery, stone tools, bread, and baskets; to the open areas where children could try archery (shooting at straw animals) or drag wooden carts laden with aged parents (or the reverse); and to the lake where parents could paddle families in log boats out to the island village (Figure 10). Boats, often of a particularly unstable character, were offered to unsuspecting Zürich businessmen and their clients, or so it seemed to those of us who purport to know about such things. Neolithic and Bronze Age food was provided, and many a bottle of Lake Village beer drunk.

The exhibition was put on for only six months, and it clearly cost much money; various accidental and deliberate burnings of the prehistoric houses occurred, and replacements rapidly created. Almost 400,000 visitors came to the exhibition, including many thousands of school children and, on return visits, their parents. The enthusiasm shown by all created an atmosphere of excitement and stimulation that augured well for future endeavours. A number of lessons were learned there:

• Archaeologists learned a good deal about their subject because of the numerous direct and simple questions asked by the public.

- The public learned how archaeologists worked and why they think the past and its struggles and achievements are important.
- The public heard about the threats posed by industry and pollution to the Alpine lakes and to their storehouses of information.
- The children learned about technology, science, and heritage, and were introduced to the handling of tools, the care of livestock, and the excitement of real things, in contrast to the instant, yet wholly passive, "entertainment" offered by TV, videos, and the like.

One aspect deliberately excluded from the exhibition was the display of human remains, either skeletal or fleshed. This was in part due to the extreme rarity of "bog bodies" from Alpine Europe, and in part due to the desire to present a living/working display devoid of the distractions of ritual. Nonetheless, the preservation of human bodies from certain wetlands is yet another attraction for the public, and a continuing cause for research and concern on the part of archaeologists. No one can fail to be interested in the accounts of the discoveries of human remains: "The most shudderingly entrancing of all ... the Ancient Briton who suddenly emerged from the peat ... when the turf-diggers were at work ... The peat-dark skin was still stretched over the bones of his face. The eyes had gone but the eye-sockets were dark with mystery" (Turner and Scaife 1995:205). This is but one of many evocative descriptions of bodies from the bogs of northwestern Europe (Coles and Coles 1989; Glob 1969). The records of peat-digging over the past 200 years in this region are full of such encounters – a spade of peat comes up with a hand, or part of a head still with hair and skin, or a

Figure 11. A bog body from Rendswühren, Germany, preserved in waterlogged peat for about 2,000 years. *Photo by J.M. Coles.*

peat bank collapses to reveal a complete body lying at rest, or contorted in an unnatural position. The first photograph of a bog body was taken in 1892, just when Key Marco was being discovered, and the Glastonbury Lake Village too, and more of the Alpine settlements were being explored. All of the bog bodies were found by peasants and many of the bodies were abandoned through fear, destroyed, or taken to the churchyard for burial. Some of the bodies were incomplete, and often they consisted only of skin and hair without bones or flesh. Some were only heads, chopped through at the neck. Some were badly decayed and only fragments of feet or hands survived. Some had clothing, a coat or skirt, a headband, shoes of leather, or a cloak, occasionally laid near the naked body (Figure 11).

The most famous bog body is the Tollund man from Denmark – "the dead and the sleeping, how they resemble one another." He was naked except for a cap of leather, but was wrapped in a skin. He was 30-40 years old, with cropped hair and stubble on his chin. A leather noose around his neck had been used to strangle him. Before death he had a last meal of a soup with barley, linseed, and many other seeds. Other bodies tell the same story.

There are over 2,000 bog bodies now known from northern and western Europe, but many are not prehistoric bodies, but rather the outcome of more recent accidents, fights, or murders. A small number, perhaps as few as 200 or as many as 500, date back to the Iron Age of the region (ca. 800 BC to AD 300). The records of many of these bodies are old and sparse, and few bodies have survived discovery. It seems that a significant proportion of the humans were male, aged 20-35, who had been deliberately killed by their societies (Turner and Scaife 1995). They were hanged, strangled, stabbed, cut or beaten to death, and the bodies were then placed in pits or pools in the peatbogs. Others may have been placed elsewhere, and their bodies disappearing completely or reduced to less informative skeletons. Many of the bog bodies have evocative histories, some quite extraordinary.

In 1879 at a place called Huldremose in Jutland, the peat cutters discovered a woman's body clad in voluminous clothing. She was lying deep in the bog and there were sticks over her body, as if to hold her down. The local doctor was called to investigate, and he duly reported to the National Museum in Copenhagen along the lines of:

> *The body was dried, like a mummy, and stiff, but the clothes are very fine. I took the remains to my house, undressed the body, gathered all the clothes, washed them and hung them out to dry on the line. I put the body into a box and buried it in the churchyard. What should I do next?*

So much for conservation. The museum telegraphed back: *We want the clothes please, and also the body.* So off they went, by steamship, to Copenhagen. The body was later sent to the University Department of Anatomy where it

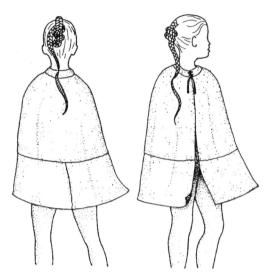

Figure 12. Reconstruction of a skin cape worn by a young woman with an elaborate hairstyle. She was strangled and put in a bog pool at Elling, Denmark, about 2,000 years ago. *From K. Ebbesen, in Coles and Coles 1989.*

promptly disappeared. The clothes survived and are the finest Iron Age set ever discovered. Among them are a short cape of sheepskin with an inner lambskin cape-lining, a woven scarf held by a bird bone pin, a very full plaid wove shirt in various browns, and a leather belt. The woman also had a horn comb in a pocket and a hair band and leather strap in a purse made of an animal bladder. Near the body the peat cutters also found a sack-like tubular dress made of wool.

But what of the body? It was lost in the university for 75 years, and rediscovered in the "museum archives"; perhaps it had been mistaken all this time for a rather slow-moving member of staff. The woman had long reddish hair (probably dyed by the peat) tied with a cord, but most of the hair had been detached during her tidy-up at the doctor's house. Other bog bodies occasionally have elaborate hair arrangements (Figure 12). The woman had been hacked by an axe, which almost severed her right arm, possibly the cause of her death.

Of the many bodies discovered in the peat of northern and western Europe, only a few have survived at all well, and there are very significant differences in their degree of preservation. Essentially, the bodies have been preserved because they were put into cold peat or water-filled holes, thus excluding maggots and rotting, and natural sphagnol encouraged the transformation of the skin into a kind of leather. The skin goes dark, and the hair often turns reddish brown. One of the most thought-provoking bodies is

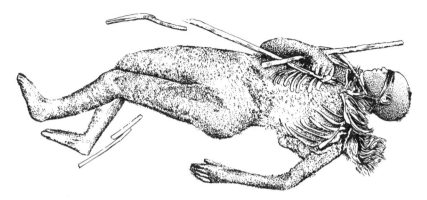

Figure 13. The young girl of Windeby, north Germany, blindfolded, head partly shaved, laid or pinned in a bog pool. *Illustration by M. Rouillard.*

that of the Windeby girl, 14 years old, who was put into a bog pool and perhaps pinned down by stones and poles. Her blonde hair had been shaved off on one side of her skull, yet she still wore a bright headband of brown, yellow, and red threads with tassels, pulled down over her eyes (Figure 13).

Why were people like her put into the pools and holes in the dark, frightening bogs? What had they done to deserve such a fate, or to be selected for such a fate? We do not know, but the Roman historian Tacitus wrote about the people of the north and provided some indication of the system of punishment in the northern societies. Whether Tacitus exaggerated or distorted his information is unknown, but he was not likely to look upon these people favourably, as they had not submitted to Roman rule. He wrote that there were special penalties for those who had been found guilty of particular misdemeanours, of adultery, cowardice, treachery, and other criminal activities. The punishments included shaving of hair, beatings, submergence in the bog, and strangling. Perhaps, therefore, all the bog bodies represent the undesirables of the societies of the north and west, in the centuries around the birth of Christ. For whatever reason, they provide us with our first real look at the faces of our European distant ancestors. Perhaps the Irish writer R.B. Sheridan summed it up for many: "Our ancestors are very good kind of folk, but they are the last people I should choose to have a visiting acquaintance with" (Coles and Coles 1989:197).

These discoveries of clothing and bodies are only a part of long-lived traditions in this area of burial or deposition of objects (Coles and Coles 1996). Some of these – stone and bronze tools and weapons, gold ornaments, pottery, textiles, and wooden artifacts – were put with care in the bog pools, rivers, and other wet places; perhaps they were offerings to the powers of the world, undamaged and thus still useful. Many other objects, including boats, weapons, and in some cases humans, were damaged and broken, and thus sacrificed. We still have to come to terms with this abundance of evidence – to say that they were offerings to the gods is too easy and explains nothing. To which powers? For what purposes? To placate, persuade, anticipate, donate? There is a panoply of explanations that have so far been advanced, but none capable of confirmation. One reason why we cannot seem to get closer to an understanding of the forces that drove and persuaded people to deposit their wealth and their possessions, and the lives of some, into the underworld of the northern wetlands is because we have always concentrated on the objects – the weapons, tools, ornaments, clothes, and bodies – instead of looking at the places of deposition where the actions took place. The pools, streams, peat bogs, and damp valley bottoms were probably significant elements in these events, just as much as the objects themselves; we know little about such places, and it is an ever-diminishing source of information as more and more wetlands disappear or are severely damaged (Coles 1995). The real test for archaeologists of this and the next decade is to conserve what we have, and to preserve what we suspect still remains in our threatened wetlands. The hidden dimension of the past is a fragile resource and deserves our best efforts to work for its survival.

References Cited
Arnold, B.
   1990 *Cortaillod-Est et les villages du lac de Neuchâtel au Bronze final: Structure de l'habitat et proto-urbanisme.* Archéologie neuchâteloise 6. Editions du Ruau, Saint-Blaise, Switzerland.
Billamboz, A.
   1990 Das Holz der Pfahlbausiedlungen Südwestdeutschlands. Jahrringanalyse aus archäodendrologischer Sicht. *Bericht der Römisch-Germanischen Kommission* 71:187-207.
Bocquet, A.
   1990 Le village néolithique des 'baigneurs' à Charavines, Lac de Paladru (Isère). In *Die Ersten Bauern 2. Pfahlbaufunde Europas,* pp. 205-209. Schweizerisches Landesmuseum, Zürich.
   1994 *Charavines il y a 5000 ans.* Faton, Dijon.
Colardelle, M., and E. Verdel
   1993 *Chevaliers-paysans de l'an mil au lac de Paladru.* Editions Errance, Musée Dauphinois, Paris.
Coles, B.
   1995 *Wetland Management: A Survey for English Heritage.* WARP Occasional Paper 9, Dept. of History and Archaeology, University of Exeter, UK.
Coles, B. (editor)
   1992 *The Wetland Revolution in Prehistory.* WARP Occasional Paper 6, Dept. of History and Archaeology, University of Exeter, UK.
Coles, B., and J. Coles
   1989 *People of the Wetlands: Bogs, Bodies and Lake-Dwellers.* Thames and Hudson, London.
Coles, J.M.
   1991 *From the Waters of Oblivion.* C.J.C. Reuvens Lezing 2. Stichting voor de Nederlandse Archeologie, Assen, Netherlands.

Coles, J., and B. Coles
1996 *Enlarging the Past: The Contribution of Wetland Archaeology.* Society of Antiquaries of Scotland Monograph Series No. 11 and WARP Occasional Paper 10, [Edinburgh].

Coles, J., and S. Minnitt
1995 *"Industrious and Fairly Civilized": The Glastonbury Lake Village.* Somerset Levels Project and Somerset County Council Museum, Taunton, UK.

Gilliland, M.
1989 *Key Marco's Buried Treasure: Archaeology and Adventure in the Nineteenth Century.* University of Florida Press, Gainesville.

Glob, P.V.
1969 *The Bog People: Iron-Age Man Preserved.* Faber, London.

Keller, F.
1878 *The Lake Dwellings of Switzerland and Other Parts of Europe.* 2nd ed. Longmans, London.

Purdy, B.
1991 *The Art and Archaeology of Florida's Wetlands.* CRC Press, Boca Raton, FL.

Ruoff, U.
1992 The *Pfahlbauland* Exhibition, Zürich 1990. In *The Wetland Revolution in Prehistory*, edited by B. Coles, pp. 135-146. WARP Occasional Paper 6, Dept. of History and Archaeology, University of Exeter, UK.

Schlichtherle, H.
1990 *Siedlungsarchäologie im Alpenvorland I.* Forschungen und Berichte zur Vor- und Frühgeschichte in Baden-Württemberg. Theiss, Stuttgart.

Turner, R.C., and R.G. Scaife (editors)
1995 *Bog Bodies: New Discoveries and New Perspectives.* British Museum, London.

Part 1:
Human Adaptations to Wetland Environments

Introduction

The archaeological story of wetlands has numerous plots and a seemingly endless selection of settings. Wetlands occur in many places and in many forms, and the ways in which people have interacted with wetlands have varied through time and over space. The approaches archaeologists take to investigating human adaptation to wetlands also vary, as amply demonstrated in this volume.

The chapters in Part 1 review archaeological evidence for wetland use over broad areas and long periods of time. (Studies of specific wetland uses and individual projects appear in other sections of the volume.) Each overview emphasizes, for a different part of the globe, the intrinsic connection between people and wetlands. The authors illustrate that patterns of human exploitation and occupation of wetlands vary according to place and culture, and temporally within regions. These examples lead to the synthetic conclusion that in one form or another wetland-human associations have been going on for a very long time, apparently whenever and wherever the opportunity arose.

Despite their centrality, the role of wetlands in the history of humankind is poorly documented. Wetlands and wet sites have received notably less consideration from archaeologists than have dryland settings, which has biased interpretations and reconstructions of the past. The oversight is particularly disturbing in light of present-day environmental threats to wetlands and the prospect that their archaeological evidence may soon disappear.

Wetlands are dynamic ecological habitats that do not remain stable through time. Human adaptations to wetland landscapes also continually evolve, sometimes in consort with the altered microenvironments. Shifts in sea levels and other natural phenomena may affect topographic and biological features of wetlands with potentially significant implications for human populations habituated to those environments. Moreover, because cultural events also cause people to modify their perception of and interaction with the natural environment (including wetlands), the

Figure 1. This view of the Pitt-Alouette wetlands near Vancouver, British Columbia, shows at least two waterlogged sites. The archaeology of the area remains virtually unknown despite a precarious future in the face of accelerating urban expansion. *Photo by K. Bernick.*

archaeological record can be complex. The continuously evolving nature of wetlands and their widespread association with people accentuates the importance of understanding the paleoenvironment as a context for archaeological interpretation.

The extensive inventory of human-wetland associations revealed by the chapters in the *Hidden Dimensions* volume reinforces the assertion that wetland archaeology warrants increased attention. People used wetlands in numerous ways. The most frequently cited include exploitation of resources (wetland foods and manufacturing materials), settlements (lake-side villages), and burials (bog bodies). These – and the many other uses – were not always manifested in the same way, and exploring the differences comprises an important direction for archaeological research. Lars Larsson's review of Swedish wetland sites includes, for example, reflections on cognitive explanations of changes in past human behaviour as intimated by wetland data. Discussions of variability in wet-site data from other perspectives appear elsewhere in this volume (e.g., Bernick, Byram).

Public awareness of environmental issues has made the term "wetland" a household word. However, the straightforward colloquial (and dictionary) meaning – wet land – does not satisfy the requirements of increasingly compartmentalized schemes for land management, and the distinctions recognized in local dialects are too diverse for broad systematic application. Consequently botanists, soil scientists, geographers, and other environmental scientists have constructed classification systems defining numerous types and subtypes of wetlands (e.g., Cowardin et al. 1985). Most archaeologists are content to think about wetlands (when they do, that is) in the generic sense and in their research describe specific habitats relying on the implicit connotations of vernacular terms – bogland, estuary, fens, marsh, mire, muskeg, peatbog, swamp, tideflat, etc. Distinctions between these, however, may have important implications for land management and locally for predictive modelling of settlement patterns.

Although not all wetlands and former wetlands contain archaeological wet sites (where normally perishable organic material has been preserved), wetlands as part of the natural environment hold considerable interest for archaeological inquiry. Yet, as J.M. Coles points out in the prologue, this aspect of the human past has been doubly neglected. The spectacular finds recovered from wet sites tend to attract the spotlight, too often leaving the wetlands themselves in the shadows.

Two chapters in this section of the volume specifically address the role of wetlands as environments available to people in the past. In the first, Yaroslav V. Kuzmin summarizes archaeological information for 13,000 years of human settlement in wetland landscapes of the Amur River valley and the nearby Primorye region and Sakhalin Island in eastern Asia. He observes that different types of wetlands were present and that they were used in different ways at different times.

George P. Nicholas surveys human adaptation to wetland environments on the continent of North America. He places his review in the context of the spatial and temporal dimensions of wetlands as human landscapes and discusses the reciprocal implications of evolving natural and cultural events. The concept of human landscapes permeates discussions of wetland archaeology (also see Van de Noort, this volume). Intensive use of an area clearly affects the natural environment, and evolving natural features elicit changes in behaviour. This holds true for all organisms with a connection to wetland habitats, not only humans.

In Scandinavia, archaeologists have investigated numerous wetland sites. Lars Larsson provides a chronologically ordered review of wet-site history and human adaptation to wetlands in southern Sweden. He does so in the context of the culture history of the region, emphasizing the connection between geographical and cultural changes, as well as the prevalence and diversity of wetland use in all eras.

The opposite situation prevails in New Zealand, where, as Cathryn Barr outlines, wetlands and wet sites have received little notice from archaeologists despite their abundance and apparent economic importance in the past. Unlike the other contributors to this section, Barr places her discussion of wet sites within a resource management perspective. Her conclusions, nonetheless, parallel those indicated for other parts of the world: in Aotearoa (New Zealand), people used wetlands continuously from early times, and inattention from archaeologists has led to biased reconstructions of the past.

The four chapters in this section discuss the environmental and historical contexts of wet sites, wetland archaeology, and past human adaptation to wetland environments. The authors give examples of many types of archaeological resources in wetland habitats. Surveys of a similar nature from other parts of the world would undoubtedly reveal parallel histories of wetland use and archaeological research, as well as additional examples and experiences.

Reference Cited

Cowardin, Lewis M., Virginia Carter, Francis C. Golet, and Edward T. LaRoe
  1985 *Classification of Wetlands and Deepwater Habitats of the United States.* Revised ed.; originally published 1979. Fish and Wildlife Service, US Department of the Interior, Washington, DC.

Wetlands and Hunter-Gatherer Land Use in North America

George P. Nicholas

Wetland environments have had an important role in human affairs around the globe and throughout antiquity. Across North America, swamps, marshes, bogs, estuaries, and other types of seasonally inundated lands are components of most regional landscapes (e.g., Finlayson and Moser 1991, Niering 1985). The importance of these settings as resource bases for past and present hunting and gathering peoples is demonstrated by widespread incorporation of wetland flora and fauna into economic and subsistence practices (e.g., Coles and Coles 1989, Nicholas 1995). Wetlands may also have satisfied land-use needs for economic buffer zones, defensive refugia, and even spiritual/sacred places – all of which contribute to what can be termed a prehistoric cultural geography. Without reference to the role of wetlands, our knowledge of hunter-gatherer social and economic diversity remains incomplete, and our recovery of representative sites incomplete (see Nicholas 1994).

Much of the conference on which this volume is based was devoted to the hidden dimensions of the past as revealed at individual sites. This chapter focuses on spatial and temporal dimensions of wetland use, and on the range of wetland adaptations represented in the archaeological and ethnographic record from across North America that relate to hunter-gatherers during the late Pleistocene (pre-10,000 BP) through Holocene (post-10,000 BP) periods. Here I refer to those small-scale societies commonly cited in the anthropological literature and characterized by generally egalitarian, non-sedentary bands frequently consisting of several extended families, with a low population density and a seasonally oriented economy based on non-domesticated food sources.

The type of research we initiate on the patterns and processes of land use depends on appropriate scales of inquiry. Figure 1 illustrates four aspects of research on wetland-related archaeology and human ecology that are defined, at least heuristically, by temporal and spatial parameters. Determining how individual wetlands were exploited, for example, provides an important avenue into (1) reconstructing life in the past, and (2) exploring human ecosystems. In the first case, wetlands may preserve the types of organic materials usually absent from archaeological sites, as attested to by many of the presentations in this volume. The recovery of basketry from sites on the northwest coast of North America (Bernick, this volume), wooden masks and statuary from Key Marco, Florida (Gilliland 1989), and fabric and human remains, including recoverable DNA, from the Windover site, Florida (Doran and Dickel 1988), all provide us with invaluable information about the richness of daily life in the past and about the health of human populations. Indeed, if there is to be a North American equivalent of "Ötze, the Ice Man," that 5,000-year-old corpse found frozen in the Italian Alps, it will be from a wetland setting. As for exploring human ecosystems, we can investigate the role of wetlands in terms of their contributions to the economy of individual societies. For example, the recovery of beaver remains from many Paleoindian- and Archaic-period sites in the northeastern United States, which date between 11,000 and 3,000 years ago, indicate a seasonal and recurring exploitation of wetlands. For more recent times, Fowler (1986, 1990) and others have documented significant use of wetland flora and fauna by Paiute groups in the Great Basin and at other North American locations.

Both approaches are vital, but there are additional dimensions and scales of investigation no less important. Shifting the scale of inquiry from individual sites to regional landscapes allows us to address questions concerning the dynamic nature of the landscape and associated human ecosystems, as well as the processes of human adaptation. We can investigate, for example, the contribution of individual wetlands to the heterogeneous character of a landscape, as in California, where extensive wetlands contributed to a resource base that supported an unusually large population and facilitated the development of semi-permanent villages (Moratto 1984). At even larger

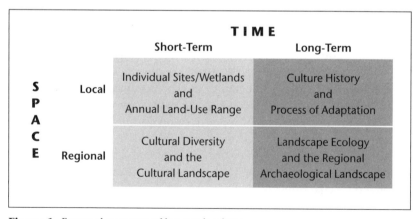

		TIME	
		Short-Term	Long-Term
S **P** **A** **C** **E**	Local	Individual Sites/Wetlands and Annual Land-Use Range	Culture History and Process of Adaptation
	Regional	Cultural Diversity and the Cultural Landscape	Landscape Ecology and the Regional Archaeological Landscape

Figure 1. Four scalar aspects of human land use.

and longer-term scales, we can evaluate the degree of ecological contrasts between wetlands and other environmental components to illuminate possible causes for changing settlement patterns (for examples from the northeastern United States, see Nicholas 1988, Robinson et al. 1992). Finally, a long-term perspective allows us to move beyond static models of human ecology and land use to reveal hunting and gathering peoples as populations that responded to constantly changing conditions through social, demographic, and technological change, while a large-area perspective enables us to look for indicators of cultural diversity in the past (Nicholas 1994:39).

The Importance of Wetlands

Perhaps the foremost attraction that wetlands have to people is the variety of seasonally available resources. Wetlands have relatively high values of biological productivity, diversity, and reliability (see Nicholas 1991, also Williams 1991), and can provide a dependable source of wetland-associated plants and animals for food, medicine, and other purposes. For example, cattail (*Typha* spp.) was particularly important to many peoples. Not only are different parts of the plant edible throughout the year, but the pollen can be processed into storable flour. In the Columbia River basin, cattail bags lined with fish skin were used for storing dried salmon meal (Hunn 1990:192). In addition to cattail, tule (*Scirpus* spp.), reed (*Phragmities* spp.), and other similar wetland plants provided material for baskets, mats, sandals, and buildings across North America and elsewhere (Figure 2).

Wetlands have been widespread across the North American continent since the end of the last ice age 15,000 years ago, not only in non-glaciated northerly locations such as Beringia, where they contributed to what may have been a relatively heterogeneous environment, but also in mid- and low-latitudinal areas. Pleistocene megafauna such as mastodon and giant beaver favoured swampy settings (Haynes 1991:90). Across most of the continent, however, wetlands achieved their greatest extent prior to about 9,000 years ago, before the impact of the warm/dry climatic episode that followed. By about 5,000 years ago, a wide variety of swamps, marshes, and bogs could be found, including the bottomland hardwood swamps of the Southeast and the Mississippi valley, the playa lakes region of the southern prairies, and the prairie pothole region of the northern plains. Wetlands were far more extensive on the past landscape then they are today. Moreover, in the last century, wetlands have decreased substantially in size and extent as the result of modern land use, and especially as a result of changes to drainage due to land clearing and farming. The wetland systems present today and those that existed in the past exhibit markedly different degrees of local and regional human habitat values (and some have no direct value to humans). As in the past, small wetlands today tend to support a small number of biotic communities but may have been important sources of particular

Figure 2. Use of tule (*Scirpus* spp.) for mat covering in the interior of British Columbia. *PN 5281. Courtesy of the Royal British Columbia Museum, Victoria, BC.*

flora of use to people. Large wetlands may support a wider range of biotic communities and may have been important hunting and collecting areas that could be utilized intensively. In addition, certain types of past wetlands may have no modern analogues. In some areas, what may be termed "wetland mosaics" – ecological "conglomerations" of terrestrial and wetland components that formed within former glacial lake basins – may have been particularly attractive places on the early postglacial landscape. A wide variety of features can be associated with such settings in northeastern North America, including shallow lakes and ponds, emergent riverine systems, adjacent uplands, and mixed deciduous-coniferous forests, each of which has an associated biotic community. The attraction of such a heterogeneous setting is demonstrated by the hundreds of archaeological sites identified at Robbins Swamp (see Figure 3 for this and other site locations), a large wetland system that formed within a former glacial lake basin (Nicholas 1988, 1990). Currently the largest freshwater wetland in Connecticut, Robbins Swamp was substantially larger during the early Holocene (based on topography and hydric soils).

Figure 3. Map of North America showing locations mentioned in the text.

Relatively large wetlands and wetland mosaics are found elsewhere in North America in areas that were not glaciated, including the Dismal Swamp in Virginia (Bottoms and Painter 1979), the Central Valley area of California (Moratto 1984), and the Lahontan Basin in Nevada (Elston 1986). Clusters of small upland wetlands are also important, such as those in the Vermilion Lakes area of Alberta (Langemann and Dempsey 1993). Cannon et al. (1990:177) consider the types of wetlands found at the Warner Valley of Oregon "lake-side grocery stores," as they provided marsh plants (e.g., tule, cattail), birds, bird eggs, fish, and clams, with rabbits and ground squirrels available nearby, and antelope and bighorn sheep in adjacent uplands. Clustered wetlands such as these and individual swamps, marshes, and estuaries were foci of frequent seasonal resource exploitation in the past. They may also have been used in a more restricted way, as, for example, economic buffer zones that were utilized specifically because of temporary food shortages elsewhere or during times of drought.

Despite their general attraction to humans as a resource base, wetlands may have been a limiting factor in hunter-gatherer land use. In northern latitudes today and in the past, wetlands have supported a variety of fauna important to humans, such as woodland caribou and waterfowl, but the nature of muskeg may restrict substantially the exploitation of those resources, as well as limit travel. In the extensive swamps of Florida, travel was similarly constrained, often possible only with watercraft. The trackways of Britain illustrate an alternative solution, but one that is absent so far in ancient North America. Access to certain parts of the landscape may also have been restricted by cultural values of which we have no direct knowledge. The Windover cemetery site (Doran and Dickel 1988), for example, might represent a location that not only held special spiritual values but also served to delineate political territory. As areas to be used intermittently or avoided altogether, wetlands may have additionally served as buffer zones in crowded locations.

Finally, the importance of wetlands to hunting and gathering peoples may also be reflected in stories about beaver, otter, ducks, and other wetland-associated fauna. Such stories may reveal a deep understanding of basic ecological principles through cautionary tales (e.g., Dean 1992) that exemplify Native American traditional knowledge.

Human-Wetland Associations, Past and Present
The basic association between people and wetlands reflects the short-term and local perspective, which we can view here as ranging from the territory used by an individual band during the course of a year to a single site occupied for an afternoon. Across much of the continent, archaeological sites can be found near wetlands. From the Saginaw Valley of Michigan (Keene 1981) to the Delmarva peninsula of the Atlantic coast (Custer 1989) to Nuevo Léon, Mexico (Turpin and Eling 1983), to the Midwest (Styles et al. 1983) to the northern Great Basin (Sampson 1985), interior and coastal marshes, swamp forests, and other types of wetlands are present within the catchment areas of numerous archaeological sites and represent only some of the many different biotic zones seasonally exploited from individual camps. By contrast, many valleys in the Sierra Nevada of California contained wet meadows and riverine marshes that may have supported year-round occupations (Elston 1986). In fact, the apparent abandonment of many sites following the drowning of the Nevada marshlands indicates an economic specialization focused on lake-marsh resources. At Robbins Swamp, repeated periodic use of the same general locations may indicate recurring land-use behaviour, as illustrated by clustering of some of the

many pre-7,000 year old Paleoindian and Early Archaic sites identified there (Nicholas 1988).

Beyond site location, we can identify local technological adaptations. The Northern Paiute of the Great Basin, for example, used tule to construct baskets, bags, and boats (Fowler and Liljeblad 1986). They were heavily dependent on the waterfowl of nearby wetlands and made realistic duck decoys of tule covered with bird skins to lure ducks into the range of their arrows and nets (Wheat 1967). A similar focus on waterfowl in ancient times is reflected by numerous bola stones at Dismal Swamp (Bottoms and Painter 1979).

Harvesting of wetland resources continues today among many indigenous peoples, albeit at a much reduced scale, as Fowler (1986, 1990) has documented for various Great Basin groups. The Shuswap of the Interior Plateau, and indeed many other groups in northwestern North America, still seasonally collect wetland plants such as cattail, tule, wapato, water parsnip, Canada mint, sphagnum moss, bog cranberry, creeping snowberry, and trapper's tea, as well as the narrow-leaved grass used for pit-cooking (Nancy Turner, personal communication 1995). Shuswap consultants report that these and other traditionally used plants are increasingly difficult to find due to the loss of wetlands and the widespread impact of cattle. In response, there is increasing involvement of aboriginal groups in wetland management, such as at T'kumlups Marshes in Kamloops, British Columbia, which

Figure 4. T'Kumlups Marshes Wetland Restoration Project, Kamloops, British Columbia.

is the focus of a joint restoration project (Figure 4) by the Kamloops Indian Band and the federal and provincial governments.

Recognizing the opportunities that wetlands may have provided hunter-gatherers in the past has implications for identifying cultural diversity in the past. Despite its popularity, the term "hunter-gatherer" subsumes those ethnographic groups that are more accurately described as gatherer-hunters or as fisher-gatherer-resource managers, as well as those groups that exhibit characteristics of "complex" social relations, such as the Calusa of Florida (Marquardt 1988). In fact, economic diversity among neighbouring hunter-gatherers in the Great Basin was reported by Wheat (1967) and Fowler (1982) for several wetland-oriented groups, such as the Cattail-Eaters and Grass-Nut Eaters, all situated within a relatively small area. This hints at the degree of diversity, now lost in the archaeological record, that may have been represented in those areas where wetlands and other features supported relatively sedentary settlement or diverse forms of social organization.

High population density often occurs in areas where wetlands are extensive, a pattern documented in parts of Australia, where extensive utilization of swamp resources may have allowed a group's minimum territory size to be reduced (e.g., Lourandos 1987). In North America, evidence of territoriality relating to reduced mobility may be reflected in the repeated use of cemeteries associated with wetlands, such as Windover in Florida (Doran and Dickel 1988), or the Black Earth site in Illinois, which has up to 400 burials (Jefferies 1987). Recurring use of these cemeteries may identify them as special places on the cultural landscape that were maintained or revisited as part of recognized territories.

Identifying Past Cultural Geographies
Moving beyond individual sites, site distribution patterns reflect the larger landscape occupied contemporaneously by numerous bands. At this level, a focus on settlement associated with large wetland systems is revealed in some locations.

Between about 11,000 and 8,000 years ago, some large interior wetland systems may have provided regional foci for settlement, as reflected in the concentration on sites around places such as Robbins Swamp (Nicholas 1988), and in central Maine (David Sanger, personal communication 1992) and on the Delmarva peninsula (Custer 1989). At that time, the resource productivity and diversity of such locations was significantly higher than that of the surrounding uplands and the still-unstable coastal zone. There may thus have been a substantial degree of ecological contrast between such wetland-dominated settings and other ecozones, making interior wetland mosaics relatively distinct on the regional landscape. The relatively high number of early archaeological sites identified at Robbins Swamp, for example, reflects a strong attraction to an area that may have served as a core area for

Figure 5. Circular features associated with archaeological site at Stillwater Marsh, Carson Sink wetlands, Nevada. *Photo by Robert Kelly.*

settlement and resource procurement, with the uplands and the coast as secondary or seasonal procurement areas associated with individual or small clusters of sites.

An example of human response to comparable ecological contrast in the Great Basin is provided by the Carson Sink wetlands of western Nevada (Figure 5). There, Kelly (1990:259) suggests that resource abundance "in the context of regional resource scarcity" may have encouraged some degree of sedentism. Marshes in this area apparently became more productive around 1,500 years ago, encouraging a shift to a less mobile foraging pattern. Clustering associated with the changing productivity of wetlands and other landscape components may also be present in the archaeological record in California (Moratto 1984) and elsewhere across the continent.

Dynamic Landscapes and Cultures

Adopting a local, long-term focus, we see that often the same wetlands were used in different ways over time – sometimes by the descendants of previous occupants, sometimes by others. This recognition allows us, in turn, to investigate both the processes of adaptation and the historical dimensions of land use and social organization. Neither hunter-gatherers nor the landscapes they have occupied are static entities.

As an example of long-term land use, the archaeological record at Robbins Swamp reflects a 10,000-year sequence of regional cultural traditions – from Paleoindian through Archaic through Woodland – including some, such as the Hardaway component, seldom seen so far north. The different land-use patterns reflected by the hundreds of sites associated with this extensive swamp-riverine-terrestrial environment are responses to changing local and regional social conditions and environmental parameters. One major shift postulated is from use of Robbins Swamp as a core area after the first three or four thousand years of occupation to a secondary use area associated with other core areas. This is supported by the absence of ceramics indicative of late-period settlement and by the presence of numerous ceramic-period projectile points, which indicate that the swamp was never abandoned, but was used for seasonal or resource-specific harvesting.

At places such as Dismal Swamp, which had been the focus of settlement throughout the Holocene (Bottoms and Painter 1979), there are changes not only in how the large wetland was used economically but also in the manner in which resources were obtained. During the last several thousand years, after the marsh decreased in size and the swamp forest increased in response to changing environmental conditions, bola stones apparently could no longer be used effectively to hunt waterbirds, and were replaced by arrows.

Land-use changes are also documented in the marsh-dominated setting of Nightfire Island, in the Lower Klamath area of northern California (Sampson 1985). Here, settlement and economic systems correspond to local environmental fluctuations. Beginning about 7,000 years ago, hunter-trapper-foragers used the marshes for waterbird hunting. By 5,000 years ago, Nightfire Island had become a regular part of the subsistence round associated with semi-permanent villages. A similar pattern of wetland use occurs at other Great Basin locations, such as the Abert-Chewaucan Marsh Basin (Oetting 1990). Occupation there began 5,000 to 6,000 years ago, with a subsequent increasing focus on wetland resources, and by 4,000 years ago, pit-house villages were associated with the marsh.

Other examples of changing land-use patterns associated with wetlands are seen in the central states. At the Black Earth site, which is located on a shallow lake-wetland margin in southern Illinois, there is continued use of the same location by the same population over time, beginning in the Middle Archaic period about 6,500 years ago, continuing through the Woodland period 3,000 to 1,000 years ago, and finally into the Mississippian period of this millennium (Jefferies 1987). At the Koster site, there is increasing use of wetland resources in the catchment areas (Brown and Vierra 1983), which facilitated relatively high degrees of sedentism. At this and other locations in the Ohio, Illinois, and Mississippi river valleys, the increasing use of sumpweed (*Iva annua*) reported by Asch and Asch (1978) and of other wetland-associated plants may be tied to a pattern of lowland forest efficiency and plant harvesting (e.g., Smith 1994; Struever and Vickery 1973; Usner 1983) that ultimately led to plant domestication.

Long-term, local research may also reveal evidence of the impact of prolonged or intensive hunting and gathering, especially in areas where substantial settlements were developing. Intensive harvesting of plants may have influenced the trajectory of wetland development in some cases. In a study of the stratigraphic sequences of 36 North American peatbogs, Tallis (1983) found considerable variation in the direction of their development. His data suggest that at least some types of wetlands, particularly small ones, may be relatively sensitive to hydrologic, climatic, or other factors, including human intervention. Similarly, the hunting of beavers, which are major contributors to swamp development, may have subsequently influenced the character of the local landscape. Changes in the preferred types of foods people collected may reflect environmental change, over-exploitation, or both. Faunal remains from the marsh-side Nightfire Island site in northwest California for example, indicate an apparent shift from coot hunting during the initial occupation about 7,000 years ago to grebe hunting 500 years later, and finally to scaup hunting around 5,000 years ago (Sampson 1985). Even in heavily populated areas, however, some hunter-gatherers took an active role in swamp management and manipulation, as illustrated by late prehistoric and historical wetland use in southwestern Victoria in Australia (Lourandos 1987), though we currently lack a comparable North American example.

People on a Changing Landscape
A long-term, large area approach in land-use studies provides us not only with a wide geographic perspective but also with enough time depth to reveal types of cultural and ecological processes normally visible only with a perspective of at least several thousand years. We are dealing, in other words, with Big Archaeology and Big Ecology as defined, for example, by tensions between different ecozones or biotic provinces. Two particularly relevant topics are the responses of wetlands to climatic events, and changes in ecological contrasts at the regional level.

   Human responses to large-scale climatic change, such as the continent-wide, early Holocene warm/dry episode that began about 9,000 years ago, are reflected by shifts in settlement pattern and by changes in the extent, the number, and the composition of wetlands, and the manner in which they were used. By the middle Holocene, the large playa lakes of the western United States had dried up, leaving small lakes and wetlands. Subsequent changes in precipitation enlarged lakes and reduced marshes, leading to the abandonment of some Great Basin sites. On the Prairie Peninsula of the central continent, Warren (1990) has documented a similar mid-Holocene drop and subsequent rebound of water levels. In the Eastern Woodlands, this same climatic episode may have led to increased summer drought, which would have resulted in intensified use of interior swamps and marshes, which would have, in turn, influenced their developmental history.

Changes in the degree of significant ecological contrast between different landscape elements at the regional level would also have occurred throughout the last 10,000 years. Kelly, for example, notes that "we cannot understand marsh resource use without understanding spatial and temporal change in other Great Basin resources" (Kelly 1990:272). Across the northeastern United States, a geographic land-use focus on the ecologically distinct, large wetland mosaics apparently lasted until about 8,000 years ago when the increasing attractiveness of river valleys, the coastal plain, upland areas, and other non-wetland areas encouraged significant changes in settlement patterns. A decrease in the number of 8,000- to 7,000-year-old sites at Robbins Swamp, and a coeval increase in sites in the coastal and riverine areas, suggest that the primary pattern of land use became economically peripheral to core areas located in other river valleys. That Robbins Swamp and similar wetlands continued to be heavily travelled and utilized, if only on a seasonal or resource-specific basis, is demonstrated by a large number of sites dating to the last four or five thousand years; the attraction of these wetlands didn't decrease, that of other areas simply increased.

Comparable changes in degree of contrast between ecological zones affecting wetland use occurred in other places also. In Florida, interior swamps and marshes did not become extensive until between 6,000 and 4,000 years ago, when the regional landscape underwent substantial transformation (Watts and Hansen 1988). Shifts in site location and population size, influenced by large-scale events, occurred also in California. Whereas significant lake-marsh adaptations had developed there by the late Pleistocene (Moratto 1984), wetlands may have served as an economic buffer during the mid-Holocene, when warm ocean temperatures may have reduced the extent of offshore kelp beds and, subsequently, the productivity of the entire maritime resource base (Glassow et al. 1987).

Other Dimensions of Wetland-Oriented Research

This chapter has briefly examined aspects of the spatial and temporal dimensions of the role that wetlands had on past human landscapes. Wetlands have significant implications for hunting and gathering peoples. The special ecological characteristics of wetlands provided people with a variety of opportunities that may or may not have been realized. As the archaeological record associated with North American wetlands is more thoroughly explored, the importance of wetlands to hunter-gatherers and others in the past should become evident. A systematic focus on wetlands research may also reveal evidence of decreased mobility, surplus production and storage, territoriality, social stratification, increased population density, and increased cultural and economic diversity – behaviours atypical of "classic" ethnographic hunter-gatherers, but not of their past counterparts, who presumably would have occupied the most attractive places around.

Finally, attention to cultural diversity is integrally tied to cultural resource management, the primary mandate of which is the recovery of representative sites. Some types of economic activities, social behaviour, and material culture may be represented only in wetland settings. Without recognizing the importance of wetlands, which were an integral part of the past cultural landscapes of North America, our knowledge of hunter-gatherers remains incomplete.

Acknowledgments
Several portions of this chapter are based on a work in progress, "Wetlands and Hunter-Gatherer Land Use: A Global Perspective."
I thank Drs. Nancy Turner, Robert Kelly, and Robert Warren for providing helpful information, and the Secwepemc Education Institute/Simon Fraser University Program for providing travel funds to the *Hidden Dimensions* conference. I also thank Kathryn Bernick and several anonymous reviewers for their comments.

References Cited
Asch, N., and D. Asch
   1978 The Economic Potential of *Iva annua* and Its Prehistoric Importance in the Lower Illinois Valley. In *The Nature and Status of Ethnobotany,* edited by R.I. Ford, pp. 300-341. Museum of Anthropology, University of Michigan, Ann Arbor.
Bottoms, E., and F. Painter
   1979 Evidence of Aboriginal Utilization of the Bola in the Dismal Swamp Area. In *The Great Dismal Swamp,* edited by P.W. Kirk, Jr., pp. 44-56. University Press of Virginia, Charlottesville.
Brown, J.A., and R.K. Vierra
   1983 What Happened in the Middle Archaic? Introduction to an Ecological Approach to Koster Site Archaeology. In *Archaic Hunters and Gatherers in the American Midwest,* edited by J.L. Phillips and J.A. Brown, pp. 165-195. Academic Press, New York.
Cannon, W.J., C.C. Creger, D.D. Fowler, E.M. Hattori, and M.F. Ricks
   1990 A Wetlands Settlement in the Lake Abert-Chewaucan Marsh Basin, Lake County, Oregon. In *Wetland Adaptations in the Great Basin,* edited by J.C. Janetski and D.B. Madsen, pp. 173-182. Museum of Peoples and Cultures Occasional Paper No. 1. Brigham Young University, Provo, UT.
Coles, B., and J. Coles
   1989 *People of the Wetlands: Bogs, Bodies and Lake-Dwellers.* Thames and Hudson, New York.
Custer, J.
   1989 *Prehistoric Cultures of the Delmarva Peninsula: An Archaeological Study.* University of Delaware Press, Newark.
Dean, J.
   1992 *Wetland Tales: A Collection of Stories for Wetland Education.* Publication 92-17. Washington State Department of Ecology, [Olympia, WA].
Doran, G.H., and D.N. Dickel
   1988 Multidisciplinary Investigations at the Windover Site. In *Wet Site Archaeology,* edited by B.A. Purdy, pp. 263-289. Telford Press, Caldwell, New Jersey.

Elston, R.G.

1986 Prehistory of the Western Area. In *Great Basin,* edited by W. D'Asevedo, pp. 135-148. Handbook of North American Indians, vol. 11, William C. Sturtevant, general editor. Smithsonian Institution, Washington, DC.

Finlayson, M., and M. Moser

1991 *Wetlands.* Facts on File, New York.

Fowler, C.S.

1982 Food-Named Groups among Northern Paiute in North America's Great Basin: An Ecological Interpretation. In *Resource Managers: North American and Australian Hunter-Gatherers,* edited by N.M. Williams and E.S. Hunn, pp. 113-129. Westview Press, Boulder, CO.

1986 Subsistence. In *Great Basin,* edited by W. D'Asevedo, pp. 64-97. Handbook of North American Indians, vol. 11, William C. Sturtevant, general editor. Smithsonian Institution, Washington, DC.

1990 Ethnographic Perspectives on Marsh-Based Cultures in Western Nevada. In *Wetland Adaptations in the Great Basin,* edited by J.C. Janetski and D.B. Madsen, pp. 17-32. Museum of Peoples and Cultures Occasional Paper No. 1. Brigham Young University, Provo, UT.

Fowler, C.S., and S. Liljeblad

1986 Northern Paiute. In *Great Basin,* edited by W. D'Asevedo, pp. 435-465. Handbook of North American Indians, vol. 11, William C. Sturtevant, general editor. Smithsonian Institution, Washington, DC.

Gilliland, M.S.

1989 *Key Marco's Buried Treasure: Archaeology and Adventure in the Nineteenth Century.* University of Florida Press, Gainseville.

Glassow, M.A., L. Wilcoxon, and J. Erichson

1987 Cultural and Environmental Change during the Early Period of Santa Barbara Prehistory. In *The Archaeology of Prehistoric Coastlines,* edited by G. Bailey and J. Parkington, pp. 64-77. Cambridge University Press, UK.

Haynes, G.

1991 *Mammoths, Mastodons, and Elephants: Biology, Behaviour, and the Fossil Record.* Cambridge University Press, UK.

Hunn, E.S.

1990 *Nch'i-Wána, "The Big River": Mid-Columbia Indians and Their Land.* University of Washington Press, Seattle.

Jefferies, R.W.

1987 *The Archaeology of Carrier Mills: 10,000 Years in the Saline Valley of Illinois.* Southern Illinois University Press, Carbondale.

Keene, A.S.

1981 *Prehistoric Foraging in a Temperate Forest: A Linear Programming Model.* Academic Press, New York.

Kelly, R.L.

1990 Marshes and Mobility in the Western Great Basin. In *Wetland Adaptations in the Great Basin,* edited by J. Janetski and D.B. Madsen, pp. 259-276. Museum of Peoples and Cultures Occasional Paper No. 1. Brigham Young University, Provo, UT.

Langemann, G., and H. Dempsey

1993 The Vermilion Lakes Wetlands: Interpreting 10,000 Years of Human Occupation in Banff National Park, Alberta. In *Culture and Environment: A Fragile Coexistence,* edited by R.W. Jamieson, S. Albonyi, and N.A. Mirau, pp. 237-245. Archaeological Association of the University of Calgary, AB.

Lourandos, H.

1987 Swamp Managers of Southwestern Victoria. In *Australians to 1788,* edited by D.J. Mulvaney and J.P. White, pp. 292-307. Fairfax, Syme and Weldon, Sydney, Australia.

Marquardt, W.H.

1988 Politics and Production among the Calusa of South Florida. In *Hunters and Gatherers*

Vol. 1: History, Evolution and Social Change, edited by R. Ingold, D. Riches, and J. Woodburn, pp. 161-188. Berg, New York.

Moratto, M.J.
1984 *California Archaeology.* Academic Press, New York.

Nicholas, G.P.
1988 Ecological Leveling: The Archaeology and Environmental Dynamics of Early Postglacial Land Use. In *Holocene Human Ecology in Northeastern North America,* edited by G.P. Nicholas, pp. 257-296. Plenum Press, New York.
1990 *The Archaeology of Early Place: Early Postglacial Land-Use and Ecology at Robbins Swamp, Northwestern Connecticut.* PhD dissertation, University of Massachusetts-Amherst. University Microfilms, Ann Arbor, MI.
1991 Putting Wetlands into Perspective. In *The Role of Wetlands in Northeastern Prehistory,* Part 1, edited by G.P. Nicholas, pp. 29-38. *Man in the Northeast* 42.
1994 Prehistoric Human Ecology as Cultural Resource Management. In *Cultural Resource Management: Archaeological Research, Preservation Planning, and Public Education in the Northeastern United States,* edited by J.E. Kerber, pp. 17-50. Bergin and Garvey, Greenwich, CT.
1995 Wetlands and Hunter-Gatherer Land Use: A Global Perspective. Ms. in author's possession.

Niering, W.A.
1985 *Wetlands.* Alfred A. Knopf, New York.

Oetting, A.C.
1990 Aboriginal Settlement in the Lake Abert-Checaucan Marsh Basin, Lake County, Oregon. In *Wetland Adaptations in the Great Basin,* edited by J.C. Janetski and D.B. Madsen, pp. 183-206. Museum of Peoples and Cultures Occasional Paper No. 1. Brigham Young University, Provo, UT.

Robinson, B.S., J.B. Petersen, and A.K. Robinson (editors)
1992 *Early Holocene Occupation in Northern New England.* Occasional Publications in Maine Archaeology 9. Augusta, ME.

Sampson, C.G.
1985 *Nightfire Island: Later Holocene Lakemarsh Adaptation on the Western Edge of the Great Basin.* University of Oregon Anthropological Papers 33. Eugene.

Smith, B.D.
1994 *The Emergence of Agriculture.* Scientific American Library, New York.

Struever, S., and K.D. Vickery
1973 The Beginnings of Cultivation in the Midwest-Riverine Area of the United States. *American Anthropologist* 75:1197-1220.

Styles, B.W., S.R. Ahler, and M.L. Fowler
1983 Modoc Rock Shelter Revisited. In *Archaic Huntres and Gatherers in the American Midwest,* edited by J.L. Phillips and J.A. Brown, pp. 261-297. Academic Press, New York.

Tallis, J.H.
1983 Changes in Wetland Communities. In *Mires – Swamp, Bog, Fen and Moor. Ecosystems of the World, Volume 4A: General Studies,* edited by A.J.P. Gore, pp. 1-46. Elsevier, Amsterdam.

Turpin, S.A., and H.H. Eling, Jr.
1983 From Marshland to Desert: The Late Prehistoric Environment of Boca De Potrerillos, Nuevo Léon, Mexico. *North American Archaeologist* 14(4):305-323.

Usner, D.H., Jr.
1983 A Cycle of Lowland Forest Efficiency: The Late Archaic-Woodland Economy of the Lower Mississippi Valley. *Journal of Anthropological Research* 39:433-444.

Warren, R.E.
1990 People as Paleoenvironmental Indicators: Holocene Settlement Patterns and Environmental Change in the Eastern Prairie Peninsula. Paper presented at the Midwest Archaeological Conference, Evanston, IL.

Watts, W.A., and B.C.S. Hansen
   1988 Environments of Florida in the Late Wisconsin and Holocene. In *Wet Site Archaeology,* edited by B. Purdy, pp. 307-323. Telford Press, Caldwell, NJ.
Wheat, M.M.
   1967 *Survival Arts of the Primitive Paiutes.* University of Nevada Press, Reno.
Williams, M.
   1991 The Human Use of Wetlands. *Progress in Human Geography* 15(1):1-22.

Wetland Archaeological Sites in Aotearoa (New Zealand) Prehistory

Cathryn Barr

Human occupation of Aotearoa (the Maori name for New Zealand) has been brief in comparison with that of most countries in the world. Consequently, the archaeological record is similarly brief. Although the precise date of arrival of the first inhabitants is a matter of some debate among archaeologists, current thinking places the arrival of the ancestors of the Maori at around 1,000 years before the country was visited by Captain James Cook in 1769. Despite this relatively recent date for the arrival of humans, the history of ethnographic and archaeological study in Aotearoa is long and well documented.

The prehistoric inhabitants of Aotearoa, and the modern Maori who are descended from them, voyaged from one or more groups of islands in central Polynesia – from French Polynesia and from the Cook Islands (Figure 1). Whether there was initially one major settlement or a series of smaller settlements is not certain, but present evidence suggests that the first immigrants came from the eastern Pacific and shared a very similar culture and economy with other East Polynesians (see Davidson 1984; Irwin 1992; Sutton 1994).

The Maori society first observed by Europeans in the eighteenth century was still firmly rooted in its Polynesian background, exhibiting many of the characteristics common to other Polynesian societies. In some respects, however, it was distinctly different. The climate and landscape of Aotearoa forced new arrivals to adapt to an environment very different from that of the islands of East Polynesia. Ecological zones in Aotearoa range from warm, subtropical, coastal regions of Northland, to temperate, inland river basins and floodplains, and to dense podocarp forests, coastal beech forests, and snow-clad mountains of the South Island.

Food resources in the new land were also different. The only mammals present were two small bats (*Chalinolobus tuberculatus* and *Mystacina tuberculata*), although there was an abundance of forest- and ground-dwelling birds, such as the kakapo (*Stigops habroptilus*), the kiwi (*Apteryx* spp.), and

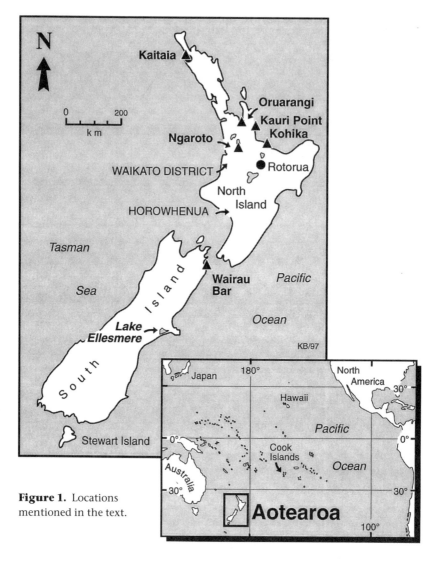

Figure 1. Locations mentioned in the text.

the now-extinct moa (*Dinornithiforms* spp.), which stood about 2 m high and could weigh up to 200 kg. The only domesticated animal brought from the islands was the kuri, or Polynesian dog (*Canis familiaris*). Chickens and pigs, important domesticates elsewhere in the Pacific, do not appear to have reached Aotearoa with the first human settlers. Immigrants also brought with them the kiore (Polynesian rat [*Rattus exulans*]) as a source of food, as well as a wide variety of cultigens, such as taro (*Colocasia antiquorum*) and kumara (*Ipomoea batatas*). Adaptation to both the natural environment and changing social conditions in the new land resulted in many human-induced alterations to landscape and the manipulation of environments.

Archaeological Studies in Aotearoa

For many years, archaeology and studies of pre-European use of and adaptation to the Aotearoa environment have concentrated on the extensive coastal middens and the form, function, and development of hilltop fortifications, or "pa." These highly visible sites are impressive, and early European settlers, as well as archaeologists, were understandably in awe of such major feats of engineering and construction built with wooden tools and human labour.

Studies of hilltop pa and midden sites have provided a good deal of information on changes that occurred in the economy and the material culture of the early inhabitants of Aotearoa. These studies have helped to chart cultural development from the early "moa hunter," or Archaic, period through to the period commonly referred to as Classic Maori culture, which dates from around AD 1500 and is characterized by hilltop fortifications (Schmidt 1995). It was this Classic Maori culture that existed at the time of, and ended with, the first contact with Europeans. Such studies have, however, resulted in what could be regarded as a biased view of archaeological information as it relates to land use and resource exploitation. Although ethnographic accounts such as those of Best (1976, 1977) and Taylor (1872) indicate that wetland areas were significant in pre-European land use, there have been limited excavations and little recent research of wetland sites.

Wetland Archaeological Sites

Aotearoa law defines as an archaeological site any area in which there is physical evidence of human activity pre-dating 1900. Using this definition, within the context of this chapter, any site located in an area of wet land – that is, in peat, in streams, on lake edges, and within lakes and streams themselves – is regarded as a wet archaeological site.

Wet archaeological sites in Aotearoa can be grouped into five categories determined on the basis of land use and evidence from physical remains (Barr 1989). These are:

(1) ditch features
(2) caches
(3) drowned dryland sites
(4) island pa/wetland habitation sites
(5) historic sites.

Of the five site types, the first four provide evidence of purposeful manipulation of the environment to aid in the procurement of resources or habitation during the pre-European era. Wet sites associated with land use by European settlers, such as flax milling, gum digging, and timber logging, are classified as historic sites. Although they illustrate the use of an area for the purpose of extracting a particular resource, historic sites are not discussed in this chapter, which aims to examine pre-European wetland use.

Ditch Features

There was considerable debate in the early 1900s as to whether archaeological ditch features in Aotearoa related to agricultural pursuits or the capture of eels (*Anguilla* spp.) and waterfowl (Skinner 1912, 1921; Wilson 1921, 1922). The accepted answer today is – both. In Northland, many of the inland valley and swamp plains are covered with a vast system of criss-crossing linear features. These are sometimes visible on the ground and show up clearly in aerial photographs.

In 1772, an officer travelling with Marion du Fresne noted in his journal the presence of vast, irrigated agricultural systems in the northern part of the North Island (Roux in McNab 1914:361). Initially it was suggested that these were for the cultivation of kumara, or sweet potato, but it is more likely that they were for growing taro, which prefers wet growing conditions. Regardless of the crop grown, the physical evidence suggests large-scale hydrological manipulation of the environment in these areas. Such use of the area must have altered the ecological diversity in the long term.

A different type of ditch system has been recorded in several locations elsewhere in Aotearoa, notably at Wairau Bar (Adams 1900) and across a land spit at Lake Ellesmere on the South Island. These ditches differ from those in the north of the North Island in that they do not appear to be systematic irrigation channels covering large areas, but rather, seem to be designed to control the outlets of the wetlands and lakes. Such control would have allowed the construction of *patuna* (eel weirs) and the capture of waterfowl from canoes (easy in the moulting season, when the birds cannot fly). Like the ditches in the North Island, these also display evidence of the manipulation of natural features and processes in order to obtain resources from an area.

Also included in the category of ditch features are natural streams and lake outlets that have undergone little physical alteration but that have been modified to the extent that a dam or weir has been constructed to aid in the capture of eels. These sites are often found today by farmers clearing drains or ditches that may once have been outlets for an area of wetland or a lake, but that are today part of drained farmland.

Today little remains of the ditch and drainage features of the past, and little research has been carried out to determine how such systems worked (Barber 1984; Johnson 1986). The formerly wet areas in which these features are located have been drained and are now prime farmland. In many cases, there is little physical evidence of such sites – often just modified stakes in a ditch. Artifacts associated with the past use of such areas still turn up in the course of drainage work, but not on the scale of drainage activities in the early part of the twentieth century.

Caches
These sites represent accidental or intentional deposition of cultural material in an area of wetland. In some instances, such deposits were made because of threat; in others, they were to aid in the preservation of wooden items such as agricultural implements. Cache sites may be represented by a single item or event, or, as is the case with a site at Kauri Point in the Bay of Plenty (Shawcross 1964), by deposition of one type of artifact at the same location over a long period. At this site, a large number of wooden head combs were recovered from a wetland area where they had been deposited to protect the mana of their owners. Archaeologists who excavated the cache in the 1960s noted that it was "not the normal assemblage of a settlement, but rather the result of some specific activities" (Shawcross 1968:4). Excavation of an assemblage such as this has allowed comment on stylistic changes in design of one type of artifact through time, and the development of certain carving styles.

Recent excavation of a site at Kaikohe in Northland provides a further example. This site was discovered by a farmer who was constructing a dam on his property. While digging out a small lake, the farmer noticed wooden artifacts in the spoil. Archaeologists from the New Zealand Department of Conservation excavated the undisturbed "island" remaining in the lake. During the excavation, more wooden agricultural implements were recovered. It is likely that these had been stored in the lake, or were hurriedly abandoned. In addition to wooden tools, gourd seeds (*Lagenaria siceraia*), hinau (*Elaeocarpus dentatus*) and miro (*Podocarpus ferrugineus*) berries, and a small amount of fish bone were also recovered (Slocombe 1996).

Drowned Dryland Sites
Drowned dryland sites provide a different type of archaeological information from that which is provided from sites that were wet during occupation or use. Drowned dryland sites allow insight as to how a "dry" site was constructed and organized. They also provide preserved organic cultural material that is missing from the ordinary dry archaeological record.

Drowned sites have become wet as a result of subsidence or flooding. Two examples of such sites in Aotearoa can be found in the Rotorua district, on central North Island: Ohinemutu village and a pa site in Lake Okataina. Comparison of photographs of Ohinemutu village from the late nineteenth century with the present-day site show that since the late 1800s, part of the small point of land on which the village site is located has been sinking into the lake. A visitor to the area in 1884 also reports how, with a "sound of hissing steam, the trembling earth opened, and the pa with all its people sank bodily into the lake" (Kerry-Nicholls 1974:57).

At Lake Okataina, the water level has risen between 10 m and 20 m as a result of the 1886 eruption of nearby Mount Tarawera. The higher water level created a small island where a headland containing a pa site once jutted into the lake. Palisade posts and cultural material associated with the use of this dryland pa are now preserved in the bed of the lake.

Island Pa/Wetland Habitation Sites

New Zealanders generally associate the term "pa" with hilltop fortifications, but island, or wetland, pa were also common in pre-European Aotearoa. This type of site, a habitation area that has been artificially constructed on the edge of, or even in, a lake or wetland, has been recorded in six locations throughout the country and is a common archaeological feature of the Waikato district. Ten of the 15 lakes in the district are known to have such sites located on them.

Island pa, or wetland habitation areas, were constructed using a variety of techniques. The missionary Richard Taylor observed the construction of one such pa in Lake Horowhenua in the early 1870s. He reports that

> first ... strong stakes [were driven] into the lake to enclose the required space; then ... large stones ... placed inside them, all kinds of rubbish being thrown in to fill up the centre; upon which alternate stratum of clay and gravel was laid until it was laid to the required height, on which the houses were then erected, and the pa surrounded with the usual fence. The only approach being by canoe they were then secure from any attack. (Taylor 1872:101-102)

Evidence from excavations in the Waikato district (Bellwood 1978; Cassels 1972; Pick 1968; Shawcross 1968), at Oruarangi on the Hauraki Plains (Best 1980), and Kohika in the Bay of Plenty (Irwin 1975), indicates that these sites were built up using successive layers of gravel, shell, and sand. In the case of Lake Ngaroto, the largest of the peat lakes in the inland Waikato basin, the stream outlet from the lake was blocked in order to raise the level of the water around several sites, which today are situated on the lake margin. Excavations at one of the sites at Ngaroto (Pick 1968; Shawcross 1968) suggest that this site (New Zealand Archaeological Association site number S15/9) was occupied continuously for several hundred years. Maori oral tradition suggests that the Ngati Apakura built the pa in the mid-1300s. Although excavations at the site failed to produce reliable material for radiocarbon dating, the depth of cultural deposit supports the oral traditions.

The site was finally abandoned in the early 1860s when the land surrounding the lake was confiscated by British troops following the New Zealand land wars.

The location of sites next to or in areas of wetland or lakes such as Ngaroto and nearby Mangakaware (Bellwood 1978) would have provided the inhabitants with good access to food resources – eel, freshwater mussels, waterfowl, and raupo (a lake reed, the pollen of which was used for bread; this plant was also used as material for house construction). In the Waikato district, the sites were close enough to dryland forest areas to allow the diet to be supplemented by game and cultivated crops. Cassels (1972) has suggested that, given the proximity of the sites at Ngaroto to a wide range of resources, it is likely that the sites were occupied year-round. Younger sites in the area appear to be smaller, with evidence of specialized collection of particular resources, and would have been used seasonally.

Lakeside locations would also have allowed good defensive capabilities; of the sites on the Waikato lakes, all had some form of defence structure. At Mangakaware and at two of the other lakes, palisade posts are still visible along the edges of the lakes. It was initially thought by archaeologists working at the sites located on Lake Ngaroto that the three sites had no defence system. It is now known, however, that there was a maze of stakes and posts just below the water surface, creating a hazard for those approaching the site who were unaware of their locations (they are still a hazard to yachts using the lake today).

Conclusion

Aotearoa presents the wetland archaeologist with a variety of site types and wetland environments in which to work. Sites of this nature are well documented in both ethnographic accounts and the files of the national Archaeological Association, but field-based research in recent years has been limited. Evidence available suggests that sites located in areas of wetland were occupied or in use early and continuously throughout Aotearoa prehistory.

The limited work that has been carried out on wet sites highlights the important role these sites play in understanding past land use in pre-European Aotearoa. Sites such as those with the drainage features in Northland, and with the canals and modified stream outlets for the capture of eels and waterfowl, and habitation sites such as Ngaroto all show purposeful selection and modification of wetland environments.

Acknowledgments
I would like to thank Hugh Barr, Matt Schmidt, Tony Roxburgh, and Neville Ritchie for reading and commenting on various versions of this paper.

References Cited

Adams, C.
1900 Ancient Canal, Marlborough, New Zealand. *Journal of the Polynesian Society* 9:169.

Barber, I.
1984 *Prehistoric Wetland Cultivation in Far Northern Aotearoa: An Archaeological Investigation.* Master's thesis, Anthropology Dept., University of Auckland, New Zealand.

Barr, C.E.
1989 *An Ecological Approach to the Management of Wet Archaeological Sites in New Zealand.* Master's thesis, Anthropology Dept., University of Auckland, New Zealand.

Bellwood, P.S.
1978 *Archaeological Research at Lake Mangakaware, Waikato 1968-1970.* New Zealand Archaeological Association Monograph 9. Dept. of Anthropology, University of Otago, Dunedin, New Zealand.

Best, E.
1976 *Maori Agriculture.* Government Printer, Wellington, New Zealand.
1977 *Fishing Methods and Devices of the Maori.* Government Printer, Wellington, New Zealand.

Best, S.
1980 Oruarangi Pa: Past and Present Investigations. *New Zealand Journal of Archaeology* 2:65-91.

Cassels, R.
1972 Human Ecology in the Prehistoric Waikato. *Journal of the Polynesian Society* 8(2): 196-248.

Davidson, J.
1984 *The Prehistory of New Zealand.* Longman Paul, Auckland, New Zealand.

Irwin, G.
1975 The Kohika Site, Bay of Plenty. *Whakatane and District Historical Society* 23(2): 101-104.
1992 *The Prehistoric Exploration and Colonisation of the Pacific.* Cambridge University Press, UK.

Johnson, L.
1986 *Aspects of the Prehistory of the Far Northern Valley Systems.* Master's thesis, Anthropology Dept., University of Auckland, New Zealand.

Kerry-Nicholls, J.
1974 *The King Country.* Capper Press, Christchurch.

McNab, R.
1914 *Historical Records of New Zealand.* Vol. 2. Government Printer, Wellington, New Zealand.

Pick, R.
1968 Waikato Island and Swamp Pa. *New Zealand Archaeological Association Newsletter* 11(1):30-34.

Schmidt, M.
1995 Pa Excavation and Radiocarbon Dating in New Zealand Archaeology: A Brief Presentation of Results. *Archaeology in New Zealand* 38(1):56-61.

Shawcross, F.
1964 An Archaeological Assemblage of Maori Combs. *Journal of the Polynesian Society* 73(4):382-398.
1968 The Ngaroto Site. *New Zealand Archaeological Association Newsletter* 11(1):2-29.

Skinner, H.
1912 Ancient Maori Canals, Marlborough. *Journal of the Polynesian Society* 21(3):105-108.
1921 The Awanui (Kaitaia) Lintel. *Journal of the Polynesian Society* 30(3):247-251.

Slocombe, A.
1996 Excavation of a Waterlogged Site near Kaikohe. *Archaeology in New Zealand* 39(1): 48-53.

Sutton, D.G. (editor)
1994 *The Origins of the First New Zealanders.* Auckland University Press, New Zealand.

Taylor, R.
  1872 On New Zealand Lake Pa. *Transactions and Proceedings of the New Zealand Institute*
    5:101-102.
Wilson, D.
  1921 Ancient Drains Kaitaia Swamp. *Journal of the Polynesian Society* 30(2):185-188.
  1922 Ancient Drains, Maori Drains, North Auckland. *Journal of the Polynesian Society*
    31(2):130-133.

Wetlands-Associated Sites in the Russian Far East: A Review of Environment, Chronology, and Paleoeconomy

Yaroslav V. Kuzmin

This chapter examines the history of wetland use in the Russian Far East in the area extending from the Bering Strait to 42° N latitude. The most extensively studied part includes Primorye, the middle and lower Amur River basin, and Sakhalin Island (Figure 1). Several hundred ancient sites, including Paleolithic, Neolithic, Bronze Age, Early Iron Age, and Middle Age sites, have been discovered by archaeologists during the last 130 years (Krushanov 1989).

Three principal types of wetlands are present in the area. These are: (1) coastal and river estuary lowlands of the Sea of Japan and Okhotsk Sea, (2) interior riverine lowlands (mainly the Amur River basin), and (3) interior lakeshore lowlands. About 200 ancient sites are associated with these kinds of landscapes. Until now there have been no published studies focusing on wetland use in prehistory for the southern Russian Far East. This chapter provides a short overview of archaeological and paleoecological data obtained as of 1994.

Data Sources

Several geoarchaeological methods, including geomorphology, palynology, chronometry, and zooarchaeology, were used to study the role of wetlands in human history. Data collected by me (Kuzmin 1994) and those resulting from previous archaeological and paleogeographical studies of the Russian Far East territory (Aleksandrova 1982; Andreeva 1977, 1991; Brodianski 1987; Djakov 1989, 1992; Korotky et al. 1980; Krushanov 1989; Markov 1978; Nikolskaya 1974; Okladnikov and Derevianko 1973) have been taken as a starting point for investigating human-environment interaction in wetland areas.

Paleoenvironment and Chronology

The earliest wetlands-associated sites in the southern Russian Far East are radiocarbon dated to ca. 13,000 BP. This time interval generally corresponds

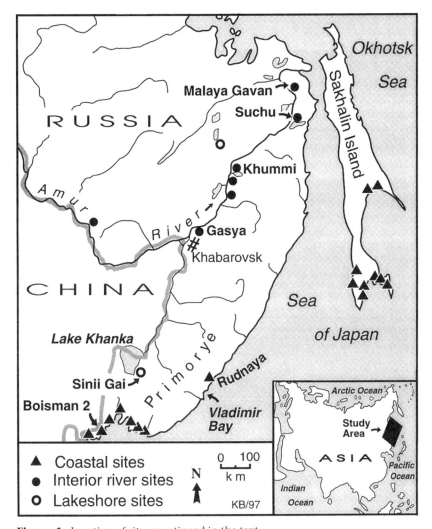

Figure 1. Location of sites mentioned in the text.

to the Late Paleolithic, which continued in Primorye and Sakhalin up to ca. 8000 BP (Kuzmin 1992a, 1992b). During the Late Glacial, 13,000-10,000 BP, the environmental conditions were colder and drier than now, whereas after 13,000 BP progressive warming began (Sakaguchi 1989; Verkhovskaya et al. 1992). In the early Holocene, 9000-8000 BP, thermophilous broad-leaved forests penetrated into southern Primorye (Korotky et al. 1980) and the southern part of the lower Amur River valley (Markov 1978).

The Paleolithic/Neolithic boundary corresponds in general to the Boreal/ Atlantic transition, ca. 8000 BP. After this time, the number of Neolithic sites increased rapidly in Primorye (Rudnaya and Boisman cultures), the lower Amur River basin (Malyshevo culture), and Sakhalin (Yuzhno-Sakhalinsk culture) (Kuzmin 1992c). These Early Neolithic cultures existed during the Atlantic period when environmental conditions reached their warmest and most humid levels of the last 10,000 years. During the phase of cooling and drying at the Atlantic/Subboreal transition, ca. 5000-4500 BP, Late Neolithic sites appeared in Primorye (Zaisanovskaya culture [Verkhovskaya and Esipenko 1993; Verkhovskaya and Kundyshev 1993]), the lower Amur River basin (Voznesenovskaya culture), and Sakhalin (Imchinskaya culture [Kuzmin 1992c]).

Bronze Age and Early Iron Age cultures existed in the continental Russian Far East during the late Subboreal and Subboreal/Subatlantic transition, ca. 3000-2000 BP. Climatic conditions 2,500 years ago were cooler and drier than the present (Korotky et al. 1980). The Early Iron Age cultures continued up to ca. 1200 BP, when the territories of southern Primorye and the middle Amur River basin were incorporated into medieval states (Krushanov 1989).

Paleoeconomy

Paleoeconomic data allow us to reconstruct human-environment interaction, especially human dependence on natural resources. In the continental Russian Far East throughout the Paleolithic and Neolithic periods, from 30,000 to 3,000 years ago, the most important economic activities were hunting, fishing, and gathering. During the Late Neolithic, ca. 4200-3700 BP, plant husbandry (and probably animal breeding) appeared in southern Primorye (Kuzmin 1995) and the middle Amur River valley (Nikolskaya 1974). They became economically important in the Bronze Age (ca. 3000-2500 BP) and in the Early Iron Age (ca. 3000-1200 BP). In the early Middle Ages, ca. 1200-1000 BP, arable agriculture was introduced to Primorye and the Amur River basin. On Sakhalin, an economy based on food production did not become established until the coming of Europeans and Japanese in the seventeenth and eighteenth centuries (Krushanov 1989).

Poor preservation of organic remains in archaeological sites limits paleoeconomic reconstructions of the Russian Far East. The most representative data are obtained from southern Primorye (Kuzmin 1994, 1995). In terms of hunting, the most important species in prehistoric and medieval times were hoofed animals such as Manchurian deer (*Cervus elaphus* L.), roe deer (*Capreolus capreolus* L.), red deer (*Cervus nippon* Temm.), elk (*Alces alces* L.), goral (*Nemorhaedus goral* Hard.), and wild boar (*Sus scrofa* L.). On some Bronze Age and Early Iron Age coastal sites located on the Sea of Japan and Lake Khanka, restricted marine hunting is indicated by rare bones of pinnipeds (*Phoca largha* Pall. and *Eumetopias jubatus* Schr.). The first reliable traces of fishing (i.e., fish bones) belong to the Early Neolithic, ca. 6800-5800 BP. Fishing was an important economic activity at coastal sites located near the Sea of Japan and Okhotsk Sea during the Early Iron Age, ca. 3000-2500 BP.

The main objects of terrestrial gathering in prehistory were Manchurian nuts (*Juglans mandshurica* Maxim.) and hazelnuts (*Corylus mandshurica* Maxim.). Gathering of marine molluscs began on the coast of Peter the Great Gulf in the Early Neolithic, ca. 6500 BP, and was widely practised on the southern coasts of Primorye (Brodianski and Rakov 1992) and Sakhalin in the Early Iron Age, ca. 3000-2500 BP (Figure 1).

Since the Late Neolithic, ca. 4200-3700 BP, millet (*Setaria italica* L.) cultivation occurred in southern Primorye in both the Bronze Age and Early Iron Age, ca. 3000-1500 BP (Janushevich et al. 1990; Kuzmin et al. 1994, Okladnikov 1964; Verkhovskaya and Esipenko 1993; Verkhovskaya and Kundyshev 1993). On Bronze Age sites dated ca. 3000-2500 BP (Kuzmin et al. 1994), the bones of domesticated animals such as pig and dog were identified (Krushanov 1989). These species were the most important resources throughout prehistoric and medieval times (Kuzmin 1995).

Types of Wetlands-Associated Sites in the Russian Far East

Coastal and Estuarine Sites

The earliest sites associated with coastal lowlands appeared in Primorye and Sakhalin during the Holocene climatic optimum, ca. 7000 BP, when the sea level was higher than at present. In southern Primorye on Boisman Bay, the Ryazanovka River mouth area was occupied, ca. 6500-5000 BP, by a shallow bight (or lagoon) with rich natural resources that included oyster (*Crassostrea gigas* Thung.) banks (Jull et al. 1994). The principal economic activities on the Boisman 2 site in the Early Neolithic, ca. 6500-5000 BP, were oriented to marine mollusc gathering, fishing, and hunting. People exploited the oyster banks for molluscs (Brodianski and Rakov 1992). The radiocarbon age of oyster shells from one of the natural beds in Boisman Bay is 6100 ± 55 BP (SOAN-3265) (Lyobov A. Orlova, personal communication 1994), which corresponds chronologically to human occupation of the area. The shallow bight disappeared at the Atlantic/Subboreal transition, ca. 5000-4500 BP, due to climatic deterioration and sea-level regression, and the Late Neolithic bearers shifted to terrestrial hunting and plant husbandry (Verkhovskaya and Kundyshev 1993).

Four hundred kilometres north from Boisman Bay, near the Rudnaya (Tetukhe) River mouth, a bight of transgressive type occurred ca. 6000-5000 BP. The Rudnaya site occupied the hill slope near the bight throughout the Neolithic and Bronze Age, ca. 7600-2500 BP (Djakov 1992; Kuzmin et al. 1994) (Figure 1). However, there is no evidence of marine mollusc gathering. Instead, the main economic activities were hunting, fishing, and gathering terrestrial plants and seeds. The difference between the Early

Neolithic economies of the Boisman 2 and the Rudnaya sites may be attributable to the absence of oyster banks in the Atlantic period near Rudnaya Bay. One of the northernmost findings of buried oyster banks on the Primorye coast occurs in the Vladimir Bay area, about 60 kilometres south from the Rudnaya site (Vladimir A. Rakov, personal communication 1994) (Figure 1). The radiocarbon age of oyster shells at this outcrop is 5570 ± 60 BP (SOAN-3365) (Lyobov A. Orlova, personal communication 1995).

During the climatic amelioration of the Subboreal period, ca. 3000-2500 BP, an abundance of Early Iron Age sites associated with coastal wetlands is known from the southern parts of Primorye and Sakhalin. The predominate economy was oriented to marine mollusc gathering, fishing, and hunting. During the Subboreal/Subatlantic transition, ca. 2500 BP, the coastal lagoons and wetlands disappeared or decreased due to cooling and sea-level regression. In southern Primorye, people moved to interior plains, and plant husbandry appears to have been the principal economic activity (Krushanov 1989).

Thus, coastal wetlands of the Russian Far East were used as an important subsistence base during the climatic ameliorations in the middle-late Holocene. Two phases of wetland occupation in the Atlantic period, ca. 7000-5000 BP, and in the Subboreal period, ca. 3000-2500 BP (Verkhovskaya and Kundyshev 1993), correspond to marine transgressions (Korotky et al. 1980) and the existence of shallow bights and estuaries with rich fish and mollusc resources.

Interior Riverine Sites

The majority of ancient sites associated with alluvial floodplains in the Russian Far East are located within the middle and lower Amur River basin. The paleoeconomic reconstructions for this region are limited mainly to the composition and typology of stone artifact assemblages due to an absence of organic remains (Krushanov 1989).

The initial exploitation of fish resources, which include both freshwater species and salmon, began in the interior riverine lowlands probably as early as ca. 13,000 BP, when the Incipient Neolithic sites Gasya and Khummi existed in the lower Amur River valley (Figure 1) (Okladnikov and Medvedev 1983; Z.S. Lapshina, personal communication 1994; A.J.T. Jull, personal communication 1995). Both sites are located at the top of the riverbank. In the Early and Late Neolithic, ca. 6000-3000 BP, the sites were located on riverbanks (Gasya, Khummi, and Suchu sites), as well as low floodplain terraces (Malaya Gavan site).

Riverine resources, together with wild animals and seeds, formed the subsistence base in this area throughout the entire Neolithic, ca. 13,000-3000 BP. There is no evidence of agriculture until the Early Iron Age, ca. 3000-2500 BP.

The distinctive feature of riverine-wetland use in prehistory is their long-term occupation during the Neolithic and Early Iron Age, ca. 13,000-1500 BP.

Interior Lakeshore Sites

There are few well-excavated sites associated with Lake Khanka and other interior lakes in the Russian Far East. The Sinii Gai site (Brodianski 1987), which is located on a hill slope near the swamps that surround Lake Khanka, was occupied during the Late Neolithic and Bronze Age, ca. 5000-2500 BP (Kuzmin et al. 1994). The principal economic activities represented were hunting, lake fishing, and terrestrial gathering. The finding of larga seal (*Phoca largha* Pall.) bones indicates sporadic pinniped hunting. Brodianski (1987) assumed that the Lake Khanka water-level fluctuations influenced human existence in the surrounding area. Unfortunately, the lack of archaeological and paleoenvironmental data prevents evaluation of the role of interior lake lowlands in prehistoric adaptations.

Conclusions

Based on data observed, two principal kinds of wetland use in prehistory may be inferred for the southern Russian Far East. First, the long-term occupation of wetland areas and the use of diverse natural resources such as fish, mammals, and seeds occurred in the vast riverine lowlands of the Amur River basin, beginning ca. 13,000 BP and continuing to the nineteenth century AD. The stability of this resource base encouraged the development of permanent human settlements in the Amur River valley during the Late Glacial and the Holocene. Second, the coastal lowlands were temporarily occupied during the climatic warmings of the Holocene. During this time, marine molluscs were an important natural resource used by people in the Early Neolithic, ca. 7000-5000 BP, and in the Early Iron Age, ca. 3000-2500 BP. During periods of climatic deterioration, people changed their living strategy either by introducing agriculture or by moving from the coast into the mainland in search of a stable subsistence base.

Acknowledgments

I am grateful to Dr. George P. Nicholas for the invitation to participate in the symposium "Wetlands and Past Human Ecosystems: Exploring the Long-Term and Large Scale Association" at the International Conference *Hidden Dimensions: The Cultural Significance of Wetland Archaeology* and to submit this paper. I am also grateful to colleagues who informed me about some unpublished data – Dr. A.J.T. Jull, Dr. Lyobov A. Orlova, Ms. Zoya S. Lapshina, and Dr. Vladimir A. Rakov. I greatly appreciate Dr. Kenneth B. Tankersley and Dr. George P. Nicholas for their help in correcting my English. I also appreciate the assistance of Ms. Kathryn Bernick and Ms. Ann Stevenson in obtaining travel funds.

My participation in the conference was supported in part by the International Science Foundation. Research for this publication was funded in part by grants from the Russian Foundation for Fundamental Investigations (RFFI), #94-05-16049 and #96-06-80688, and by grant #J9X100 (1995) from the International Science Foundation and RFFI.

References Cited

Aleksandrova, A.N.
  1982 *Pleistocene of Sakhalin.* Nauka Publ., Moscow. [In Russian]
Andreeva, Z.V.
  1977 *Primorye in Prehistory: The Iron Age.* Nauka Publ., Moscow. [In Russian]
Andreeva, Z.V. (editor)
  1991 *Neolithic of the Southern Far East: The Ancient Settlement in Chertovy Vorota Cave.* Nauka Publ., Moscow. [In Russian]
Brodianski, D.L.
  1987 *The Introduction into Far Eastern Archaeology.* Far Eastern State University Press, Vladivostok. [In Russian]
Brodianski, D.L., and V.A. Rakov
  1992 Prehistoric Aquaculture on the Western Coast of the Pacific. In *Pacific Northeast Asia in Prehistory: Hunter-Fisher-Gatherers, Farmers, and Sociopolitical Elites,* edited by C.M. Aikens and Song Nai Rhee, pp. 27-31. Washington State University Press, Pullman.
Djakov, V.I.
  1989 *Primorye in the Bronze Age.* Far Eastern State University Press, Vladivostok. [In Russian]
  1992 *The Multilayered Site Rudnaya Pristan and the Periodization of the Neolithic Cultures in Primorye.* Dalnauka Publ., Vladivostok. [In Russian]
Janushevich, Z.V., Y.E. Vostretsov, and S.A. Makarova
  1990 *Paleoethnobotanic Findings in Primorye.* Far Eastern Branch of the USSR Academy of Sciences, Vladivostok. [In Russian]
Jull, A.J.T., Y.V. Kuzmin, K.A. Lutaenko, L.A. Orlova, A.N. Popov, V.A. Rakov, and L.D. Sulerzhitsky
  1994 The Mid-Holocene Malacofauna of the Neolithic Site Boisman 2 (Primorye): Composition, Age, and Environment. *Reports of the Russian Academy of Sciences* 339(5):697-700. [In Russian]
Korotky, A.M., L.P. Karaulova, and T.S. Troitskaya
  1980 The Quaternary Deposits of Primorye: Stratigraphy and Paleogeography. *Proceedings of the Institute of Geology and Geophysics, Siberian Branch of the USSR Academy of Sciences* 429:1-234. Novosibirsk. [In Russian]
Krushanov, A.I. (editor)
  1989 *The History of the USSR Far East from Prehistory up to the Seventeenth Century.* Nauka Publ., Moscow. [In Russian]
Kuzmin, Y.V.
  1992a Geoarchaeological Study of the Late Paleolithic Sites in Primorye, the Far East Russia. *Quaternary Research* (Japan) 31(4):243-254.
  1992b Paleoecology of the Paleolithic of the Russian Far East. *Bulletin of Institute of Prehistory, Chungbuk National University* (Korea) 1:143-159.
  1992c Radiocarbon Chronology of the Stone Age Cultures of Southern Russian Far East. In *Abstracts of Papers Presented on the VIth Conference in Honor of V.K. Arseniev,* edited by A.M. Kuznetsov, pp. 189-192. State Teachers Training College, Ussuriisk. [In Russian]
  1994 Paleogeography of the Stone Age Cultures of Primorye (Far Eastern Russia). *Journal of Korean Ancient Historical Society* 15:379-424.
  1995 People and Environment in the Russian Far East from Paleolithic to Middle Ages: Chronology, Palaeogeography, Interaction. *GeoJournal* 35(1):79-83.
Kuzmin, Y.V., L.A. Orlova, L.D. Sulerzhitsky, and A.J.T. Jull
  1994 Radiocarbon Dating of the Stone and Bronze Age Sites in Primorye (Russian Far East). *Radiocarbon* 36(3):359-366.
Markov, K.K. (editor)
  1978 *The Sections of Quaternary Deposits in the Lower Amur River Basin.* Nauka Publ., Moscow. [In Russian]
Nikolskaya, V.V.
  1974 *About the Natural Tendencies of the Geographic Provinces Development in Southern Far East.* Nauka Publ., Novosibirsk. [In Russian]

Okladnikov, A.P.
1964 The Soviet Far East in the Light of Latest Achievements of Archaeology. *Voprosy Istorii* 39(1):44-57. [In Russian]
Okladnikov, A.P., and A.P. Derevianko
1973 *The Ancient Past of Primorye and Amur River Basin.* Far Eastern Publ., Vladivostok. [In Russian]
Okladnikov, A.P., and V.E. Medvedev
1983 The Study of Multilayered Site Gasya in Lower Amur River Basin. *Bulletin of Siberian Branch of the USSR Academy of Sciences* 23(1):93-97. [In Russian]
Sakaguchi, Y.
1989 Some Pollen Records from Hokkaido and Sakhalin. *Bulletin of the Department of Geography, University of Tokyo* 21:1-17.
Verkhovskaya, N.B., S.A. Gorbarenko, and M.V. Cherepanova
1992 The Changes of Natural Environment of Southern Japan Sea and Adjacent Mainland in the End of Pleistocene and in the Holocene. *Pacific Geology* 12(2):12-21. [In Russian]
Verkhovskaya, N.B., and L.P. Esipenko
1993 The Time of *Ambrosia artemisiifolia* (Asteraceae) Appearance in the Southern Russian Far East. *Botanical Journal* 78(2):94-101. [In Russian]
Verkhovskaya, N.B., and A.S. Kundyshev
1993 Environment of the Southern Primorye in the Neolithic and Early Iron Age. *Bulletin of Far Eastern Branch of the Russian Academy of Sciences* 4(1):18-26. [In Russian]

Prehistoric Wetland Sites in Sweden
Lars Larsson

A Country with Many Wetlands

The presence of wetlands and wetland archaeological sites in Sweden is directly related to the recent geological history of the region. During the last glaciation, Sweden was completely covered with an ice sheet, which began to recede from the southernmost parts of the country around 14,000 BP (uncalibrated). The geological structure of the bedrock, the deposition in various moraine formations, and the creation of kettle holes when blocks of buried ice melted meant that the young moraine landscape contained a large number of basins of varying sizes. The elongated shape of Sweden, with widely varying topography and climate, has contributed to radically different forms of human adaptation to the environment and use of lakes, shorelines, and watercourses. The degree of preservation of organic material in wetlands also varies. Preservation of settlement remains has been significantly affected by the dynamic relation between land and water. As a result of continuous melting of the ice in the northern parts of Scandinavia at the start of the Holocene, parts of southern Sweden were submerged, whereas the northern parts of the country, which had been pressed down by the ice sheet, were uplifted. In southernmost Sweden, the coastline is now more than 40 m higher than at the beginning of the Postglacial. In northern Sweden, the land has risen by more than 300 m – and is still rising.

The formation of bogs in Sweden has followed a process that is closely associated with the nutrient content of the soils. Oligotrophic lakes with the conditions required for quick filling with organic material existed only in southernmost Sweden and the islands in the Baltic Sea. Most Swedish lakes are eutrophic, which means they are very slow overgrowing. Some lakes were transformed into bogs in Preboreal times; a considerable number became overgrown (i.e., became bogs) during Atlantic times. In the Subboreal, which comprises the Neolithic and the Bronze Age (6000 BP to 2600 BP), many wetlands dried out and were covered with forests. At the start of the

Subatlantic period, which corresponds to the transition between the Bronze Age and the Iron Age, precipitation increased and raised bogs began to form, mainly in areas with low-nutrient soils.

A considerable part of the surface of Sweden is covered with raised bogs (von Post and Granlund 1926). The combination of a dense population and a long history of felling trees created shortages of fuel in the nineteenth century and led people in southern Sweden to cut peat on a large scale. Several archaeological sites were observed by peat cutters and a large number of artifacts were retrieved, thanks to a campaign in which posters depicting artifacts and describing their scientific importance were distributed to farmers. The relatively early development of pollen analysis in Sweden – already in the 1930s a significant number of bog sacrifices had been pollen-dated (Nilsson 1935) – further stimulated interest in the cultural significance of wetlands and drew attention to various remains of prehistoric settlement. In the central and northern parts of Sweden, because of the plentiful supply of firewood and the fact that peat cutting was restricted to the top layers of the raised bogs, few prehistoric finds have been discovered. This means unequal distribution of known locations of prehistoric remains in wetlands.

The preservation of prehistoric remains, particularly of organic material, has also been affected by the process of peat formation and the nutrient constituents of the soils. For example, different amounts of lime in gyttja and peat result in different preservation conditions – wood, but not bone, might be preserved in one layer, the opposite in another layer in the same stratigraphic sequence. Moreover, preservation conditions might vary considerably in different parts of the same bog.

Unfortunately, there are clear signs today that the number of well-preserved remains in wetlands is decreasing. Precipitation in the form of acid rain and accelerating drainage of wetlands mean that good preservation environments, not only for objects of an organic nature but also for metal objects, are quickly being destroyed (Borg et al. 1995).

Hunter-Gatherer Sites Under the Sea and in Bogs

Due to considerable rises in sea levels during the Late Boreal and Atlantic periods, there is very little evidence of coastal settlement during the preceding Late Glacial and early Postglacial periods in southern Sweden. What exists consists of individual finds that have been observed and noted in connection with sand-suction from the sea bottom. These include artifacts such as a worked flint and worked bones from the sea floor in the western part of the Öresund, the strait dividing Sweden from Denmark (Vang Petersen and Johansen 1993). Radiocarbon analysis of a worked reindeer bone gave an estimate of 12,140 BP (uncalibrated), indicating remains from the Hamburgian culture.

The Late Paleolithic remains found in the southern parts of the Öresund do not necessarily indicate the presence of settlements in the coastal zone. It is equally plausible that they represent short stays in conjunction with reindeer migrations over a land bridge that connected present-day Denmark and Sweden during certain periods, including from 11,300 BP to 10,900 BP and after 10,300 BP (uncalibrated dates) (Larsson 1994).

Settlement of the southern Scandinavian coastal area during the Preboreal and Boreal periods (11,200 BP to 8800 BP) is represented by several sites on the western coast of Sweden (Nordqvist 1995). One of the few Swedish shell middens, at Huseby Klev (Figure 1), is dated to the Boreal period (Hernek and Nordqvist 1995). For the late Boreal period, beginning about 9500 BP, we have more knowledge of settlements in southern Sweden.

In order to obtain information on coastal settlements, a marine archaeological investigation on the Swedish side of the Öresund was carried out in 1979 (Larsson 1983b). This was concentrated on what is now a submarine furrow corresponding to the prehistoric course of a river (Figure 2). Along this former river bed, investigations revealed a number of Late Mesolithic sites close to the present shoreline. From the study of sea charts, it was possible to trace the former course of the river, as well as the submarine elevations and depressions. Areas of particular interest in a submarine

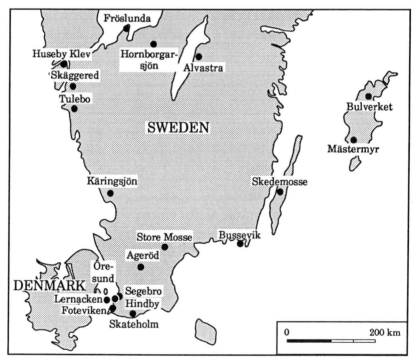

Figure 1. Southern Sweden with locations mentioned in the text.

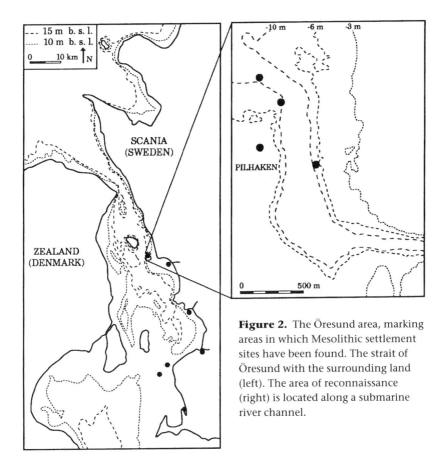

Figure 2. The Öresund area, marking areas in which Mesolithic settlement sites have been found. The strait of Öresund with the surrounding land (left). The area of reconnaissance (right) is located along a submarine river channel.

context were sampled, both from onboard ship and by divers. At least three Early Mesolithic sites were registered during this phase of investigation, at depths ranging from 6 m to 20 m below surface level (Figure 2). An additional site, located at the outermost part of the former river mouth, and discovered in 1992 at a depth of 7 m to 8 m, is partially layered in peat and has been dated to 8800 BP (Fischer 1993; Larsson et al. 1996). Finds of bone and worked wood make this a very important location for future investigations.

Coastal and Inland Settlements

The results of the investigations in the Öresund provide the basis for the argument that during the Boreal period, settlement in the coastal area was equally as intensive as in the hinterland (the latter of which is well proven). It indicates that choice of settlement location in the Early Mesolithic period was dictated by the same factors as those in the Late Mesolithic period. Whether these Early Mesolithic settlements were as extensive and of as permanent a character as their later variants is a question that we still cannot answer. Clearly, we must increase our knowledge of Early Mesolithic coastal settlement before we can draw conclusions as to the nature and form of settlement patterns during that period.

Surveys of the seabed in the southern part of the Öresund have been carried out since 1992 in connection with prospecting for bridge construction. The highest parts of the strait had been subjected to severe erosion by strong currents in the course of its transformation from a land bridge to a waterway. In spite of this, less-exposed areas have yielded cultural material dating from the late Boreal period, that is, a late part of the Maglemose culture (Fischer 1993). One of these sites is located at a depth of 7 m to 8 m and has been dated to approximately 9300 BP. Although some of the settlement remains are embedded in nodules of mud, as yet no organic material has been found to provide clues as to the ecological zones that were used by the inhabitants of the site. Tree roots discovered at Lernacken, off Limhamn, at a depth of 6.5 m have been dated to ca. 8700 BP (Fischer 1996), which indicates that significant quantities of saltwater did not find their way into the Baltic basin until after that time.

Bog Sites

Beginning in Preboreal times, a form of settlement appears that is particularly well known for the Early Mesolithic in southwestern Scandinavia, namely, the bog site – a small camp site featuring a hut structure located on gyttja and layers of peat at the edge of a lake that was in the process of becoming overgrown. To enable continued settlement, the area was often reinforced with small tree trunks, branches, and pieces of bark.

In some cases, structural details such as wall posts have been preserved, showing that the huts were light constructions intended for short-term use. Only a few examples of this type of settlement have been found in Sweden. These finds and their Danish counterparts show that the hut was rectangular, between 3 m x 3 m and 4 m x 6 m in size (Larsson 1990). Roofs and walls were probably made of bark or reeds. A site in Ageröds Mosse bog in the centre of the southern Swedish province of Scania has yielded a large collection of material remains, including tools of bone and antler dated to the late Maglemose culture, around 8800 BP (Larsson 1978a, 1978b).

The reason bog sites have had such a dominant role in the study of Early Mesolithic settlement is not that they are so numerous but that, due to good preservation conditions, they have unusually varied content, mostly of bone and antler but also of wooden artifacts. Bog sites are documented in southernmost Sweden. Similar examples of short-term seasonal settlement should also be represented in other parts of the country – which has been confirmed by the discovery of several camp sites in Lake Hornborgarsjön in Vastergötland (Kindgren 1983).

Figure 3. Perforated hazelnuts found in the Ageröd V bog site in southernmost Sweden, dated to 7500 BP.

The patterning of find locations and feature remains provides a basis for detailed analysis of the function of bog sites and the activities carried on there. For example, the spatial distribution of finds in relation to a postulated hearth has been interpreted as showing that the hut was divided into two activity areas, perhaps a men's side and a women's side (Grøn 1987).

Most bog sites are viewed as temporary camps of a seasonal character. This interpretation is supported, for example, by traces of extensive collecting in the form of hazelnut shells in the refuse layer outside the hut (Larsson 1983a).

Few bog sites have been found from the Late Mesolithic, mostly because the attractive lakes were by then completely overgrown, thereby losing their value for hunter-gatherers. In the Ageröds Mosse bog (Figure 1), there is a Late Mesolithic site – Ageröd V – corresponding in scale to those from the Early Mesolithic, with well-preserved material that includes wooden artifacts such as a bow, part of a leister, and fish traps. A necklace consisting of about 30 bored hazelnuts is a unique find (Figure 3). The site is dated to 7500 BP.

There is no Swedish equivalent to the Mesolithic submarine sites in southern Denmark, since sea level at that time was at least 4 m above its present level, along the entire Swedish coast. In some cases, one can follow refuse layers out into the bogs that 7,500 years ago were inlets of the sea. Layers rich in bone and antler are present in such settings in southern Sweden, and, in occasional cases, as at the Segebro site, wooden objects have been

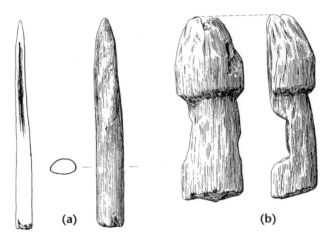

Figure 4. Wooden tools from the Segebro site in southernmost Scania, dated to 7800 BP: (a) tip of a spear with a slit into which a flint was set, (b) parts of a socket for shafting axes.

preserved – for example, part of a spear point and part of an axe shaft (Larsson 1982) (Figure 4).

In view of the considerable uplift of land in northern Sweden, one might expect finds of a marine character in bogs that were inlets of the sea in prehistoric times. Such finds, however, are extremely rare. Bog finds in northern Finland (e.g., a wooden elk head dated to 8500 BP and sleigh runners dated between 6100 BP and 5100 BP) show early human presence in the area (Edgren 1992). The earliest wooden skis from northern Swedish bogs are of similar age – 6000 BP (Baudou 1992). It should be borne in mind, however, that archaeological fieldwork in northern Sweden has concentrated on locations affected by the numerous construction projects to regulate rivers. No research has as yet been geared to the specific excavation of places where finds have been reported or where refuse layers from settlement sites can be expected to extend into wetlands.

The oldest Swedish human remains that have been recovered are those of a young woman found in Store Mosse (Figure 2), a bog in southern Sweden (Nilsson et al. 1979). She has been dated to the Boreal period. Judging by environmental circumstances (at the time of death, the lake at the location of the find was several metres deep), the woman drowned.

Land, Sea, and the Conceptual World

The great change in sea level during the Late Boreal and the Early Atlantic periods must not be regarded as ecologically critical for hunter-gatherer societies. New, abundant fishing environments were formed just as quickly as old ones disappeared. The social aspect should be far more interesting to study. The sea-level changes were so drastic that their effects must have been clearly identifiable in the landscape. Being forced to change one's physical orientation from one generation to the next probably also has consequences for one's conceptual orientation. Fishing on a shallow bank, knowing that their ancestors had lived there on firm land, must have significantly affected peoples' conceptual world. The stresses would have been of both a physical and a mental nature.

At Skateholm in southernmost Sweden (Figure 1), three cemeteries from the Late Mesolithic have been found (Larsson 1988a, 1988b). They were established directly on the shore, near settlement sites on islands. As the sea rose, people were forced to move to higher locations. The settlements and the cemeteries were gradually submerged. Why were the graves positioned on the shoreline? Is it possible that no one knew that the cemetery would become submerged within one or two generations?

One explanation is the view that the practice is a response to stress – stress created by natural processes that resulted in the submergence and reduction of the land area available for hunting and gathering. Hodder (1990) believes that dualism between the tame and the wild (or between *domus* and *agrios*) was of very great importance in the process of neolithization. In most examples of neolithization that he discusses, changes take place in inland settings and involve relatively small changes to the natural environment. The greatest changes that took place were thus the consequence of human activity. In southern Scandinavia, however, the greatest changes took place in the natural environment. Perhaps we are dealing with a form of territorial marking that is aimed not so much at other societies as against the changeability of nature, which threatened the social and intellectual situation of humankind. Could it be that the establishment of sea-side cemeteries quite simply represents an attempt to halt changing nature – an attempt to prolong the status quo? This idea may well be seen as an abstract somersault. Nonetheless, I believe that greater consideration must be given in future analyses to the conceptual relationship between people and the sea, in order to fully appreciate Late Mesolithic coastal societies.

Bogs and Bog Sacrifices in the Early Neolithic

No habitation bog sites have been documented in Sweden from the Early Neolithic, which began around 6000 BP. This does not mean, however, that interest in bogs had disappeared. What we see instead is a changed attitude to the use of bogs – wetlands became places of contact with the spirit world.

Peat cutting and drainage have uncovered a large number of Neolithic objects, the most common category being flint axes deposited in pairs (Figure 5). A recently conducted analysis of these wetland finds yields strong indications that the majority should be regarded as votive deposits (Karsten 1994). There are numerous instances of such bog finds. Their context has been clarified through excavations at a small bog near Hindby, in

Figure 5. Flint axes from the Neolithic, ca. 5500 BP, found in southernmost Sweden when a bog was being drained.

southwestern Scania (Figure 1), where several assemblages of objects were found – remains of a votive practice continuing through most of the Neolithic and into the Bronze Age. There were examples of axes deposited in pairs, but more commonly combinations of tools, sometimes broken before deposition, as well as bones of animals or humans (Karsten 1994). The simplicity of the sacrifices makes it difficult for the layperson to appreciate their value. There are probably similar depositions in other bogs, but they have not been observed, apart from easily recognized forms such as flint axes. It should be emphasized that the custom of using wetlands as votive sites was not introduced during the Neolithic. Similar deposits, albeit of a very limited scope, had occurred in the Mesolithic (Larsson 1978a). In some cases, Quaternary geological investigations have shown that the bogs in which votive deposits have been found were almost dried up at the time the sacrifices were made; they were only seasonally waterlogged.

The first depositions of human beings in wetlands occur in the Early Neolithic (Stjernquist 1981). There is no evidence of violence, and it is not clear whether the people had been sacrificed or were simply buried in this way. Human burials in wetlands also occurred in later periods of the Neolithic, but not to the same scale as in the Early Neolithic.

A find of quite a different character, in the Alvastra mire in south-central Sweden, dates to the middle of the Neolithic, about 5100 BP (Browall 1986). It features a wooden platform (investigated in several stages from 1903 to 1930, with resumed excavations in the 1970s) consisting of two almost square structures joined at an oblique angle. These two parts, with a total area of 450 m², are in turn divided into rectangular areas with hearths – 17 in number (Figure 6). The structure was linked to the nearby solid ground by two footbridges. The platform rests on oak piles driven deep into the mire. Dendrochronological studies tell us that the basic structure at the site was

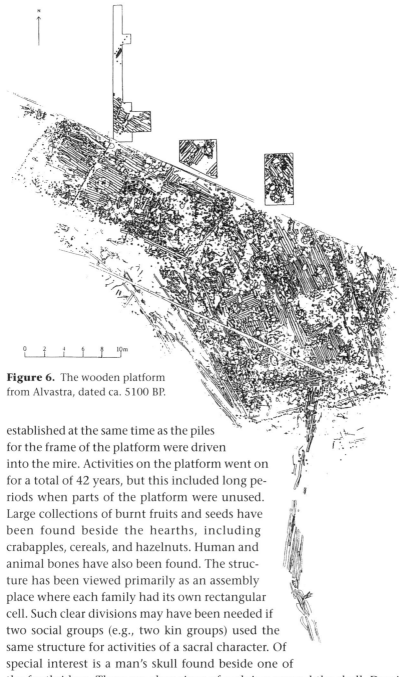

Figure 6. The wooden platform from Alvastra, dated ca. 5100 BP.

established at the same time as the piles for the frame of the platform were driven into the mire. Activities on the platform went on for a total of 42 years, but this included long periods when parts of the platform were unused. Large collections of burnt fruits and seeds have been found beside the hearths, including crabapples, cereals, and hazelnuts. Human and animal bones have also been found. The structure has been viewed primarily as an assembly place where each family had its own rectangular cell. Such clear divisions may have been needed if two social groups (e.g., two kin groups) used the same structure for activities of a sacral character. Of special interest is a man's skull found beside one of the footbridges. There are clear signs of scalping around the skull. Despite implications of this find, the local topography – close to a higher-lying shore – does not suggest that the structure had any defensive purpose. Data, albeit of a limited character, from peat cutting in Danish bogs among other sources, indicate that wooden structures in conjunction with finds of a votive character were not unusual (Rech 1979).

Bog Sacrifices in the Bronze Age and the Iron Age

The Bronze Age saw the continuation of the sacrificial custom that is well attested for the Neolithic. Bronze objects of both male and female character are encountered in bogs, as are less spectacular objects such as hair plaits and resin cakes, and in one case a mantle (cloak). The deposition practice is especially clear for the Late Bronze Age (3100 BP to 2600 BP), when large weapons and ornaments are absent from graves because of the prevailing custom of cremation and placement of the bones in small vessels. It is possible that the Bronze Age bog finds are associated with burial practices – that the depositions were seen as a way to transfer large objects to a buried person's life in another world. This interpretation, however, is based on written evidence from the Viking Age almost 2,000 years later, and it is doubtful whether it can be applied to the older material.

A significant bog find in recent decades is a collection of bronze shields found in a bog at Fröslunda (Figure 1) on a promontory on the southern shore of the large Lake Vattern (Hagberg 1988). Ploughing in 1985 turned up several thin fragments of bronze plate. The subsequent investigation found 16 shields of the Herzspung type, dated to the Late Bronze Age, about

Figure 7. Bronze shield from the Fröslunda votive find, dated to the Late Bronze Age, ca. 2800 BP. *86/572. Skaraborgs Länsmuseum Bildarkiv, Sweden.*

2800 BP (Figure 7). The significance of the find is related to the fact that only about 20 shields of this type were previously known in Europe. In some cases it has been possible to ascertain that sacrificed bronze objects were placed directly on relatively dry bog surfaces. Thus, they would have been exposed and visible for a long time.

In the Early Iron Age, 2500 BP to 1600 BP, the incidence of votive deposits increases. At this time, there were votive sites where different forms of sacrifice occurred over extended periods. The most prominent of such bog sacrifices is at Skedemosse (Figure 1), a limerich mire on the Baltic island of Öland (Hagberg 1967). Excavations were conducted in the 1950s and 1960s because gold arm rings had been ploughed up. Several depositions had been made in a former lake, beginning around 2000 BP. Most of the oldest votive deposits at Skedemosse consist of animal bones. Common assemblages include horses' heads, hooves, and tail bones, which have been interpreted to represent cult-related horse baiting or horse racing. In several cases, the bones show traces of marrow extraction, which indicates that the sacrifice was preceded by a meal. Among the bones there are also the remains of about 30 people who had been sacrificed. In the period 1800 BP to 1500 BP, a large number of weapons, parts of weapons, and horse equipment were deposited, in several cases after having been subjected to fire, chopped into pieces, or bent. These finds are viewed as gifts to higher powers for victory in battle. The most spectacular find from Skedemosse consists of seven gold arm rings, which weigh a total of 1.2 kg. The arm rings were found in one part of the investigated area. The finds in Skedemosse are interpreted as a tribal sacrifice, in other words, a matter that concerned much of the island's population.

Sacrificial acts from the same era but that concerned a smaller community, perhaps one or a few farms, also occurred. Best known are the finds from the small bog of Käringsjön (Arbman 1945). No weapons or objects of precious metal were found there; instead, the sacrifices consisted of objects such as wooden vessels and ards, as well as clay vessels containing food such as blood bread (Figure 8). These had been deposited beside a plank extending out into the shallow pond.

Not all the finds in water, however, are examples of sacrifices. In some cases they could have ended up in the water during transport, when a boat foundered or a sleigh went through the ice. One find interpreted in this way, from the mire of Mästermyr in Gotland (Figure 1), consists of three bronze cauldrons, three iron bells, a fire grid, and a wooden chest (Arwidsson and Berg 1983). The chest held a large number of very well-preserved iron objects, clearly showing that the owner was a smith. It contained all the equipment required for advanced work with wrought iron and even with fine metal. Some woodworking tools were also present. The find is dated to the Viking Age, ca. 1000 BP.

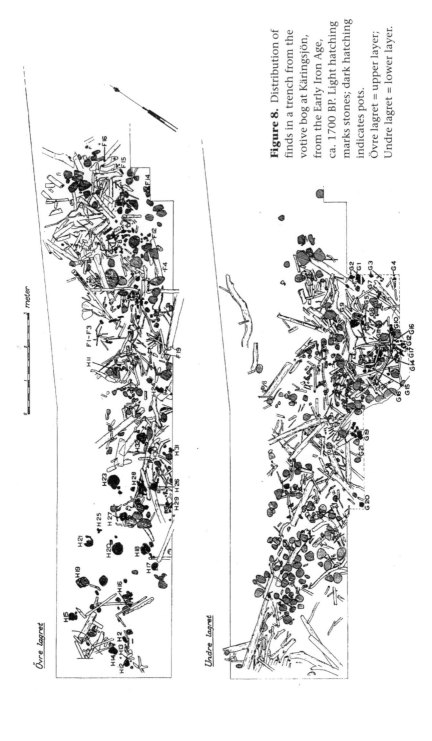

Övre lagret

Undre lagret

0   1   2   3 meter

Figure 8. Distribution of finds in a trench from the votive bog at Käringsjön, from the Early Iron Age, ca. 1700 BP. Light hatching marks stones; dark hatching indicates pots.
Övre lagret = upper layer;
Undre lagret = lower layer.

One category of antiquity that is seriously neglected in Swedish research is the remains of bridge structures and causeways built over wetlands. Several examples have been found during peat cutting, but only a few have been studied archaeologically and dated. The oldest are dated to the Roman Iron Age (Måhl 1988), but they probably existed much earlier (Schou Jørgensen 1988).

Ships and Stake Barriers

Although the extensive Swedish coasts functioned as important communication channels ever since the Stone Age, surprisingly few finds of prehistoric boats or parts of boats have been found. Evidence of lively shipping activities comes from hoards of axes made from southern Scandinavian flint and found along the coast of northern Sweden, and from the large number of ships depicted in Bronze Age rock carvings. Compared with the considerable number of Danish finds (Christensen 1990), it is remarkable that not a single dugout has been found at any of the excavated Swedish Mesolithic sites in bogs or on the coast. Moreover, none of the many wooden canoes found in bogs, of which only a small portion has been conserved, has been dated with certainty to the Neolithic. The oldest one, from Skaggered, near Gothenburg (Figure 1), is dated to the very latest phase of the Late Bronze Age, ca. 2600 BP (Rieck and Crumlin-Pedersen 1988).

It is only when we come to the Iron Age that archaeological finds give a picture of ancient vessels (Westerdahl 1989). There is considerable variation. Bog finds show that simple dugouts existed throughout the Iron Age. A find from the southernmost part of northern Sweden, from the fifth century AD, shows that dugouts were fitted with extra boards (Humbla 1950). A fragment fished off the coast of Gotland, in the Baltic, shows that this type was also used on the open sea (Rieck and Crumlin-Pedersen 1988). Also dated to the Iron Age are fragments of a bark boat from the western coast of Sweden (Westerdahl 1989).

In Sweden, the Late Iron Age boat is known mainly from graves where impressions in the soil show the positions of the rivets and other details (Nylen and Schönbäck 1994). In some cases, the damp soil preserved certain wooden details. Only in one place are large parts of several boats preserved. This is a barrier at Foteviken (Figure 1), consisting of at least five worn-out Viking ships that were filled with stones and submerged in the entrance to a natural harbour (Crumlin-Pedersen 1984). Only one of these ships has been raised. The barrier was probably built in connection with civil strife at the start of the twelfth century.

Other methods were also used to prevent enemy ships from penetrating important harbours, as is shown by barriers of stakes found at several places on the seabed. Barriers in a navigable channel at Bussevik, in the Blekinge archipelago (Figure 2), have been dated to the Viking Age (Westerdahl 1989).

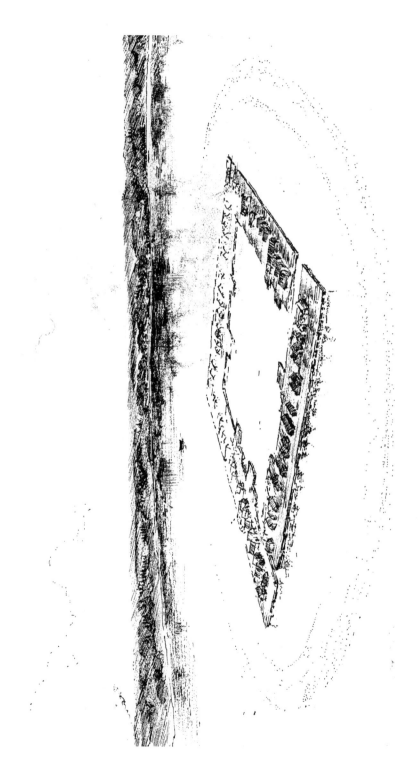

Figure 9. Reconstruction of the wooden structure known as Bulverket in Tingstäde Träsk, Gotland.

Outside Birka, Sweden's oldest trading town built at the start of the Viking Age, there are similar remains of extensive barriers.

A Viking-Age Wooden Fortress
Unlike the Baltic region (Apals 1993), there is very little evidence of wooden structures in lakes in Sweden. In one lake in southern Sweden, there are piles dated to the Bronze Age. The only remains of a substantial structure are in the shallow lake of Tingstäde Träsk in Gotland (Rönnby 1995; Zetterling and Boethius 1935), where a large assemblage of logs was found in the 1920s. These once formed wooden platforms comprising a square structure open in the centre. The sides of the structure, which is known as the Bulverket (Bulwark), were 170 m long, and much of the structure was surrounded by tree trunks forming a palisade. Houses were built by different techniques on the wooden platforms (Figure 9). Two small boats were found beside the structure. Few culturally distinctive objects have been recovered, however, ^{14}C dates give a relatively wide span – AD 1000 to AD 1200, or the Late Viking Age and Early Middle Ages.

The construction of the Bulwark shows certain similarities with structures on the eastern Baltic coast, in Estonia and Latvia. In most accounts of the Bulwark, the respective authors have tried to incorporate it in the cultural environment of Gotland (e.g., Rönnby 1995). It is more probable, however, that it represents influences from the southern and eastern coasts of the Baltic Sea, influences that are becoming increasingly clear from eleventh- and twelfth-century archaeological finds. The only possible Swedish counterpart occurs in a bog near Tulebo (Figure 2), on the western coast of Sweden (Wigforss 1993), where an area of 40 m x 100 m contains large quantities of wood shaped with axes. These are probably remains of a wooden defensive structure from about 1700 BP, which was burned and also destroyed in other ways.

Summary
Sweden is a country with an abundance of wetlands that provide the necessary conditions for preserving evidence of activities associated with human use of water and waterways in prehistoric times. The wetland archaeological resource is known mainly for the southern, densely populated part of the country where intensive use of natural resources, involving peat cutting and ditching, led to the discovery of a considerable number of artifacts, in some cases even the remains of boats and structures. These remains date to the whole of the prehistoric period and represent varying relationships with water.

During the Boreal and Atlantic periods, members of fisher-hunter-gatherer groups settled directly at the water's edge. As a result, rises in the seawater level and layers of vegetation deposited in lakes have preserved the remains of settlements. During the late Stone Age, Swedish wetlands assumed primarily ritual functions and became sites of sacrifices of – among other things – flint axes and human beings. The practice of offering sacrifices in wetlands continued during the succeeding Bronze Age and Iron Age, when valuable artifacts such as weapons and jewellery were deposited. Sacrifices of horses and humans occurred during the Early Iron Age.

Water has been used as communication routes in Sweden since early prehistoric times, although the earliest boat find dates only to the transition between the Bronze Age and the Iron Age, ca. 2600 BP. Even though boats were placed in graves, the number of well-preserved finds in wetlands is limited. Only one example of a fortification associated with wetlands has been found in Sweden. It is a large, four-sided structure from the Viking or Early Medieval period in a lake on the Baltic island of Gotland.

References Cited
Apals, J.
   1993 *Die Wohninsel Āraiši.* Cesis, Latvia. [In German]
Arbman, H.
   1945 *Käringsjön.* Studier i halländsk järnålder. (Käringsjön: Scientific pursuits of the Iron Age in Halland; summary in English.) Wahlstrom & Widstrand, Stockholm. [In Swedish]
Arwidsson, G., and G. Berg
   1983 *The Mästermyr Find: A Viking Age Tool Chest from Gotland.* Kungl. Vitterhets Historie och Antikvitets Akademien, Almqvist & Wiksell, Stockholm.
Baudou, E.
   1992 *Norrlands forntid – ett historiskt perspektiv.* Förlags A.B. Viken [Sweden]. [In Swedish]
Borg, G.C., L. Jonsson, A. Lagerlöf, E. Mattsson, I. Ullén, and G. Werner
   1995 *Nedbrytning av arkeologiskt material i jord. Målsättning och bakgrund.* Riksantikvarieämbetets och Statens Historiska Museer Rapport RIK 9. Riksantikvarieämbetet, Stockholm. [In Swedish]
Browall, H.
   1986 *Alvastra pålbyggnad: social och ekonomisk bas.* (The Alvastra pile dwelling: Its social and economic basis; summary in English.) Theses and Papers in North-European Archaeology 8. Institute of Archaeology, Stockholm. [In Swedish]
Christensen, C.
   1990 Stone Age Dug-Out Boats in Denmark: Occurrence, Age, Form and Reconstruction. In *Experimentation and Reconstruction in Environmental Archaeology*, edited by D.E. Robinson, pp. 119-141. Oxbow, Oxford.
Crumlin-Pedersen, O.
   1984 Fotevik. De marinarkæologiske undersøgelser 1981 og 1982. *Pugna Forensis?* Arkeologiska undersökningar kring Foteviken, Skåne 1981-83, pp. 7-68. Länsstyrelsen, Malmöhus Län. [In Swedish]
Edgren, T.
   1992 Den förhistoriska tiden. *Finlands historia I.* Helsinki. [In Swedish]
Fischer, A.
   1993 *Stenalderbopladser på bunden af Øresund.* Marinarkaeologiske førundersøgelser forud for etablering af en fast Øresundforbindelse. Skov- og Naturstyrelsen, Hørsholm, Denmark. [In Danish]
   1996 Rødder og stubbe af havsopslugte traeer. In *Marinarkaeologiske rekognosceringer efter fredede vrag og fortidsminder i højbrotraceet*, pp. 41-43. Marinarkaeologiske førundersøgelser forud for etablering af en fast Øresundforbindelse. Skov- og Naturstyrelsen. København. [In Danish]

Grøn, O.
1987 Seasonal Variation in Maglemosian Group Size and Structure: A New Model. *Current Anthropology* 28:303-327.

Hagberg, U.E.
1967 *The Archaeology of Skedemosse I-II*. Almqvist & Wiksell, Stockholm.
1988 The Bronze Shields from Fröslunda near Lake Vänern, West Sweden. In *Trade and Exchange in Prehistory: Studies in Honour of Berta Stjernquist*, edited by B. Hårdh, L. Larsson, D. Olausson, and R. Petré, pp. 119-126. Acta Archaeologica Lundensia Ser. 8, No. 16. Lunds Universitets Historiska Museum, Lund, Sweden.

Hernek, R., and B. Nordqvist
1995 *Världens äldsta tuggummi? Ett urval spännande arkeologiska fynd och upptäckter som gjordes vid Huseby Klev, och andra platser, inför väg 178 över Orust*. Riksantikvarieämbetet, Stockholm. [In Swedish]

Hodder, I.
1990 *The Domestication of Europe: Structure and Contingency in Neolithic Societies*. Basil Blackwell, Oxford.

Humbla, P.
1950 Björke-båten från Hille. *Från Gästrikland 1949*. Gävle, Sweden. [In Swedish]

Karsten, P.
1994 *Att kasta yxan i sjön. En studie över rituell tradition och förändring utifrån skånska neolitiska offerfynd*. (Throwing the axe in the lake: A study of ritual tradition and change from Scanian Neolithic votive offerings; summary in English.) Acta Archaeologica Lundensia Ser. 8, No. 23. Almqvist & Wiksell, Stockholm. [In Swedish]

Kindgren, H.
1983 Grävningar i Hornborgasjön. *Västergötlands Fornminnesförenings Tidskrift 1983-84*. [In Swedish]

Larsson, L.
1978a *Ageröd I:B – Ageröd I:D: A Study of Early Atlantic Settlement in Scania*. Acta Archaeologica Lundensia Ser. 4, No. 12. C.W.K. Gleerup, Lund, Sweden.
1978b Mesolithic Antler and Bone Artifacts from Central Scania. *Papers of the Archaeological Institute University of Lund 1977-1978*:28-67.
1982 *Segebro. En tidig atlantisk boplats vid Sege ås mynning*. (Segebro: An early Atlantic site at the estuary of the river Sege; summary in English.) Malmöfynd 4. Malmö Museum, Malmö, Sweden. [In Swedish]
1983a *Ageröd V: An Atlantic Bog Site in Central Scania*. Acta Archaeologica Lundensia Ser. 8, No. 12. Institute of Archaeology, Lund, Sweden.
1983b Mesolithic Settlement on the Sea Floor in the Strait of Öresund. In *Quaternary Coastlines and Marine Archaeology: Towards the Prehistory of Land Bridges and Continental Shelves*, edited by P.M. Masters and N.C. Flemming, pp. 283-301. Academic Press, New York.
1988a The Skateholm Project: Late Mesolithic Settlement at a South Swedish Lagoon. In *The Skateholm Project, I. Man and Environment*, edited by L. Larsson, pp. 9-19. Acta Regiae Societatis Humaniorum Litterarum Lundensis 79. Almqvist & Wiksell, Lund, Sweden.
1988b The Use of the Landscape during the Mesolithic and Neolithic in Southern Sweden. *Archeology en Landschap. Bijdragen aan het gelijknamige symposium gehouden op 19 en 20 oktober 1987, ter gelegenheid van het afscheid van H. T. Waterbolk*, pp. 31-48. Biologisch-Archaeologisch Instituut, Groningen, Netherlands.
1990 The Mesolithic of Southern Scandinavia. *Journal of World Prehistory* 4:257-309.
1994 The Earliest Settlement in Southern Sweden: Late Palaeolithic Remains at Finjasjön, in the North of Scania. *Current Swedish Archaeology* (Swedish Archaeological Society) 2:159-177.

Larsson, L., J. Ljungkvist, and C. Theander
1996 Submarine Settlement on the Bottom of the Öresund Strait, Southern Scandinavia. *NewsWARP* (Wetland Archaeology Research Project, UK) 19:8-10.

Måhl, K.
1988 Farvägar på Gotland. *Populär arkeologi* 2:42-44. [In Swedish]

Nilsson, T.
1935 Die Pollenanalytische Zonengliederung der spät-und postglazialen Bildungen Schonens. *Geologiska Föreningens i Stockholm Förhandlingar* 57(3):385-562.
Nilsson, T., T. Sjøvold, and S. Welinder
1979 The Mesolithic Skeleton from Store Mosse, Scania. *Acta Archaeologica* (København) 49:220-238.
Nordqvist, B.
1995 The Mesolithic Settlements of the West Coast of Sweden – with Special Emphasis on Chronology and Topography of Coastal Settlements. In *Man and Sea in the Mesolithic: Coastal Settlement above and below Present Sea Level*, edited by A. Fischer, pp. 185-196. Oxbow Monograph 53. Oxbow Books, Oxford, UK.
Nylen, E., and B. Schönbäck
1994 *Tuna i Badelunda. Guld Kvinnor Båtar* 1-2. (Tuna in Badelunda: Gold Women Boats; summary in English.) Västerås, Sweden. [In Swedish]
Rech, M.
1979 *Studien zu Depotfunden der Trichterbecher- und Einzelgrabkultur des Nordens*. Offa-Bücher 39. Karl Wachholtz, Neumünster, Germany. [In German]
Rieck, F., and O. Crumlin-Pedersen
1988 *Både fra Danmarks Oldtid*. Vikingeskibshallen, Roskilde, Denmark. [In Danish]
Rönnby, J.
1995 *Bålverket. Om samhällsförändringar och motstånd med utgångspunkt fron det tidigmedeltida Bulverket i Tingsträde träsk på Gotland*. (The Bulwark; summary in English.) Studier från UV Stockholm, No. 10. Riksantikvarieämbetet, Stockholm. [In Swedish]
Schou Jørgensen, M.
1988 Vej, vejstrøg og vejspaerring. Jernalderens landfaersel. In *Jernalderens Stammesamfund. Fra Stamme til Stat i Danmark* 1, edited by P. Mortensen and B. Rasmussen, pp. 101-116. Jysk Arkaeologisk Selskab Skrifter 22. Aarhus universitetsforlag, Århus, Denmark. [In Danish]
Stjernquist, B.
1981 Näbbe Mosse: A Mysterious Stone Age Lake. *Florilegium Florinis Dedicatum, Striae* 14:35-40.
Vang Petersen, and L. Johansen
1993 Sølbjerg I – An Ahrensburgian Site on a Reindeer Migration Route through Eastern Denmark. *Journal of Danish Archaeology* 10:20-37.
von Post, L., and E. Granlund
1926 *Södra Sveriges torvtillgångar* I. Sveriges Geologiska Undersökning Ser. C, No. 2. Norstedt & Söner, Stockholm. [In Swedish]
Westerdahl, C.
1989 *Norrlandsleden I: Källor till det maritima kulturlandskapet*. (Norrland Sailing Route: Sources of the maritime cultural landscape; summary in English.) Arkiv för norrländsk hembygdsforskning 24. Länsmuseet-Murberget, Härnösand, Sweden. [In Swedish]
Wigforss, J.
1993 Den vendeltida träanläggningen i Tulebo mosse. *Fynd* 2:65-74. [In Swedish]
Zetterling, A., and G. Boethius
1935 *Bulverket: En förhistorisk sjöbefästning i Tingstäde träsk på Gotland*. Svenska fornminnesplatser 10. Wahlström & Widstrand, Stockholm. [In Swedish]

Part 2:
Wet-Site Perspectives,
Past and Present

Introduction

This section of the *Hidden Dimensions* volume features case studies, that is, reports of specific sites, regions, or collections. They comprise examples of wet-site archaeological research from Poland, England, Mexico, and the east and west coasts of North America. Each author describes a different type of research, involving different types of evidence, from a different type of wetland setting. They demonstrate how wet-site data contribute to archaeology and how wet-site investigations have influenced the ways in which archaeologists address research questions.

As emphasized by J.M. Coles in the prologue and by the authors in the preceding section of this volume, wet sites contribute unique data for research on numerous questions about the past, including settlement patterns, subsistence economy, social organization, spiritual beliefs, ethnicity, technology, architecture, land use, and cultural ecology. Moreover, waterlogged deposits often contain abundant plant remains that provide invaluable information about ancient landscapes and climates.

The case studies in this section (as well as those on Northwest Coast fishing technologies, in Part 3) illustrate how wet sites can contribute to knowledge of local culture history. Where wetland settings make available material and features that would otherwise be absent from the archaeological record, the sum total of archaeological data is amplified. This observation supports a holistic approach to wetland preservation and the need to understand how the depositional context can be protected as well as the data (see Corfield, this volume).

Wet sites, though easy to define collectively in reference to environmental conditions, present an eclectic face when it comes to discerning common substantive concerns. From the perspective of site-specific archaeological research, the wetland setting becomes a depositional context for data used to investigate questions of regional, topical, and theoretical interest. One might argue, for example, that Kathryn Bernick's chapter on basketry technology has little to do with wetlands. Yet it is recognized as an aspect of

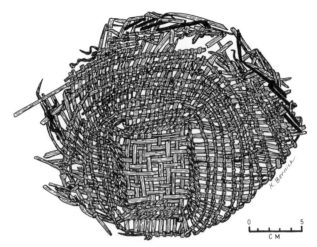

Figure 1. Three-thousand-year-old basket from the Musqueam Northeast
site in southwestern British Columbia. Woven from split withes of western red
cedar (*Thuja plicata*) in open-wrapped-twining technique with a twill-plaited
base. *DhRt 4:10737. Drawing by K. Bernick.*

wet-site archaeology by her colleagues who work with collections devoid of
perishable materials and by conservators who develop and apply treatments
to preserve waterlogged objects.

Lest one jump to the conclusion that wet-site archaeology can be defined
as involvement with perishables, it is important to remember that anthropological (and historical) archaeology does not restrict itself to artifacts.
Scott L. Fedick's investigations into the manipulation of wetlands to enhance resource yields clearly relate to wet sites even though conservators
may have difficulty seeing the relevance of his research since no perishable
artifacts have been found (yet). Perhaps the best way to view wet sites is to
see them as an integral part of archaeology, rather than to risk compounding the bias by isolating wet-site data.

The special importance of the wet-site resource lies in the presence of
materials that do not normally survive in archaeological contexts. "Perishable" artifacts give direct testimony of occupations such as woodworking
and basket making. Nets, canoes, and looms document methods of fishing,
watercraft styles, and weaving equipment that conventional archaeology
can only infer. The remains of wooden dwellings provide information on
architecture, and carvings in wood record artistic traditions that may enhance or alter interpretations based solely on artwork in stone and bone.

One advantage of wooden artifacts is that their organic composition
renders them easy to date by radiocarbon assay. Moreover, the preservation
of logs and specimens of trunk wood has spurred the refinement
of dendrochronology, which in turn has provided precise calendar years

(sometimes also seasons) for timbers used in ancient constructions. Two contributions demonstrate the scientific value of perishable materials when their ages can be confirmed. D.M. Goodburn reviews the insight gained from wet sites for reconstructing the ways in which people exploited ancient treeland in southeast England. In addition to learning about past human behaviour, Goodburn's research bears directly on paleoenvironmental reconstructions. Kathryn Bernick shows how basketry, preserved in wet sites on the northwest coast of North America, provides stylistic evidence for reconstructions of culture history. In this case, the wet-site evidence supports the established scheme at a time when the local archaeological community is leaning toward new interpretations.

In their respective chapters, Bernick and Goodburn draw conclusions from studying objects that were recovered from wet-site deposits. This highlights the observation that successful conservation of waterlogged artifacts has significant implications for the continued survival of archaeological evidence. Although objects can be analyzed and described before treatment, it is not always possible to do so. Moreover, treatments can alter the appearance, dimensions, and surface texture of artifacts in ways that may affect the very traits of interest for a particular research question. (See comments by Johns, this volume, on qualitative and quantitative effects of conservation treatment.)

Since wet-site archaeology is still relatively neglected, the full impact of perishables on the science of archaeology remains unknown. The example of the extensive excavations at the wooden village of Biskupin suggests that it could be considerable. Wojciech Piotrowski's account of 60 years of archaeological work at Biskupin, in Poland, illustrates the potential achievements, as well as problems and solutions to problems, that can be realized from a truly long-term project. Piotrowski credits the overall success of the Biskupin project to a prominent public profile that helped to secure research funds as well as sustained public, political, and professional commitments for preservation.

In contrast, Scott L. Fedick reports on the initial stages of a brand-new project in Mexico. Fedick describes agriculture-related features he observed in wetlands and suggests innovative explanations that credit the ancient Maya with the ingenuity to devise effective schemes to manipulate particular environmental systems.

In the last chapter in this section, Elena B. Décima and Dena F. Dincauze re-interpret Boston's "Boylston Street Fishweir" as a series of small, short-lived, simple tidal traps. Their presentation parallels those in the succeeding section on Northwest Coast fishing technologies, with a stress on the necessity for accurate paleoenvironmental reconstruction.

The projects described in these case studies represent approaches to research involving different types of wetland evidence. In part, this reflects the diversity of wetlands and the kinds of materials preserved in them, but it also reflects the scope of wetland-related archaeological research. The authors illustrate through specific examples the kinds of questions and answers wetland archaeology is uniquely suited to address.

The Importance of the Biskupin Wet Site for Twentieth-Century Polish Archaeology

Wojciech Piotrowski

"Biskupin" is the name of an archaeological site, a modern village, a lake, a peninsula, and a museum (Figure 1). The name has been traced to a church document written in 1325, in which the archbishop of Gniezno mentioned the village of Biskupin as being located in the place where it has existed ever since – 800 m to the west of the archaeological site (Żurek 1935:14). Within Poland, Biskupin has become a legend and a symbol of the great timber-building achievements of the tribes inhabiting this region in the

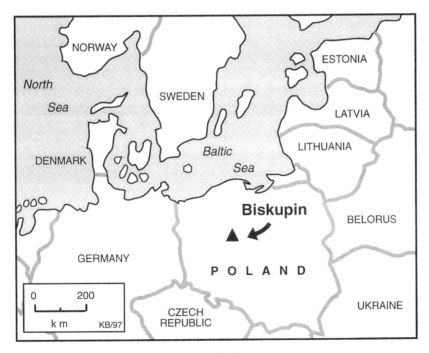

Figure 1. The location of Biskupin in Poland.

Figure 2. Professor J. Kostrzewski (right) and Dr. Z. Rajewski (left) in the Biskupin expedition's pottery magazine, 1936. *Photo Archives, Biskupin Museum.*

eighth to sixth centuries BC (the time of transition from the Bronze Age to the Iron Age). The image of Biskupin's reconstructed wooden tower has become one of the most popular national emblems. In September 1994, President Lech Waàe(sa designated the Biskupin archaeological reservation as a national historic monument.

For a description of the ancient settlement, its layout, its internal chronology, and the details of the structures and the artifacts, see Kostrzewski (1936, 1938), Piotrowski (1995), Rajewski (1950, 1959b), and Zajączkowski (1984). The discussion in this chapter addresses the impact of the excavations at Biskupin and its environs on Polish archaeology.

History of the Excavations

The discovery on the Lake Biskupin peninsula of a fortified settlement dating to the first millennium BC was the result of both chance and good judgement. At the beginning of the 1930s, flood control of the Gąsawka Rivulet lowered the water level of nearby lakes and turned some waterlogged areas into meadows. In the spring of 1933, Walenty Szwajcer, a teacher from Biskupin who often organized trips for his pupils, noticed a row of piles sticking out of the water of the lake near the flat, miry Biskupin peninsula. The discovery was made by chance, but Szwajcer's further actions (alerting

Figure 3. Biskupin excavations in 1938. *Photo Archives, Biskupin Museum.*

Figure 4. Northeastern area of 1938 excavations at Biskupin. *Photo Archives, Biskupin Museum.*

the local police, then county officials, and finally the Archaeological Museum and the Chair of Archaeology at Poznań University) followed from his absolute conviction that he had found a unique and ancient structure.

The conviction and determination of a village teacher led to the start of excavations by Professor J. Kostrzewski (1885-1968) and Kostrzewski's assistant Z. Rajewski (1907-1974) in 1934 (Figure 2). From that moment, events moved quickly. The first trenches revealed fragments of wooden floors and walls that had been preserved in excellent condition in the water-saturated ground. On the basis of pottery shards, and antler and bronze tools, Kostrzewski dated the settlement to 700-400 BC. During the years 1934-1939, about half (10,500 m^2) of the fortified settlement was uncovered (Figures 3 and 4). The settlement occupies the entire 2-ha peninsula (Figure 5). Because the excavations at Biskupin aroused great interest in the country, many sponsors were found to finance the work. Just before World War II – Germany invaded Poland on September 1, 1939 – work at Biskupin reached its apogee. In 1939, the Biskupin expedition included 50 professionals, 12 of who were archaeologists, the rest technical staff (in 1934, there were 30 professionals, 10 of them archaeologists). They supervised 200 local workers and the documentation process. During the last days of August 1939, as war became imminent, the excavated material

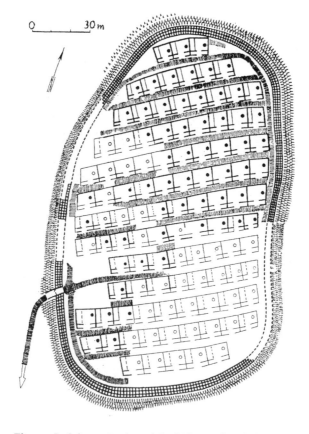

Figure 5. Schematic plan of the Biskupin fortified settlement.

Figure 6. The first reconstructions at Biskupin, 1938. *Photo Archives, Biskupin Museum.*

was transported in great haste to Poznań, a town 85 km southwest of Biskupin. Everyone was sorry to be leaving the site, as the wooden two-winged gate to the settlement had just been found.

The Germans carried out excavations at Biskupin from 1940 to 1942. They worked methodically, completely revealing, among other things, the settlement gate (Schleif 1944). In 1945, after the war ended, Biskupin was in lamentable condition. The dam, which had been erected around the Biskupin peninsula in 1935-1936, was broken in several places, and the excavation trenches were flooded by lake waters. The portion of the settlement that had been reconstructed (Figure 6) was destroyed, as were the expedition barracks, storerooms, and workshops. When Dr. Rajewski resumed excavations in 1946, he had to devote considerable energy to repair work, restoring the ancient structures to a state that would enable their further preservation and study. A second reconstruction was begun and interdisciplinary studies resumed.

Large-scale excavations were halted in 1974, because the wooden remains were decaying in the open air; this could not be stopped in spite of conservation efforts. During the 1970s and 1980s, most of the archaeological and conservational work at Biskupin was devoted to preserving the remains of the settlement, 75 percent of which had been excavated. Reconstruction continued, and the museum area and the conservation workshops were enlarged. For the past 10 years, the Biskupin Museum has been emphasizing the need to link interdisciplinary studies with active protection of the Biskupin settlement and its vicinity (Niewiarowski 1995; Rajewski 1959a, 1968b).

Biskupin's Contribution to Polish Archaeology

The popularity of Biskupin had, and still has, a positive influence on Polish archaeology. Researchers often mention Biskupin, comparing it with other scientific projects. It is a good point of reference for analyses and syntheses, especially for explaining so-called Biskupin-type settlements and Lusatian culture components (e.g., Niesiołowska-Wędzka 1991; Ostoja-Zagórski 1991). The importance of Biskupin is illustrated in the following summaries of its numerous contributions – to methodology (large-scale excavations, wet-site techniques, interdisciplinary studies, microregional focus, photographic documentation and cataloguing), to conservation, to knowledge, and to education (professional training, experimental archaeology, interpretation centre).

New Methodologies

It was at Biskupin that, for the first time in Polish archaeology, excavations were carried out on a truly large scale. This undertaking required changes to some standard methods that were characterized by the use of extreme caution and which were therefore prohibitively slow. The Biskupin peninsula was explored using a 10 m x 10 m grid layout, and the locations of all remains were recorded in three dimensions. During the 1934 excavation season, a 500 m² area was uncovered; in 1935, 2,000 m²; in 1936, 1,000 m² (Kostrzewski 1936, 1950).

This was also the first Polish excavation of a site protected by a wet environment. Archaeologists were confronted by methodological and technical problems, since not all exploration methods traditionally used at dry sites could be applied. The results of excavations at Swiss lake settlements were already known, but, in the 1930s, archaeologists had not yet developed efficient methods for excavating wet terrestrial sites. Therefore, many of the techniques initially applied to the waterlogged Biskupin peninsula were based on intuition. The practical experience gained at Biskupin helped to develop field techniques that have been applied in other wetland situations.

Here also interdisciplinary studies and archaeology were, for the first time in Poland, well coordinated. Kostrzewski's reputation enabled him to assemble a large team of researchers that included botanists, geologists, dendrochronologists, archaeozoologists, hydrologists, palynologists, anthropologists, architects, and engineers. The results of their collective effort are published as three volumes of Biskupin reports (Kostrzewski 1936, 1938, 1950). Most of the conclusions and hypotheses presented in these reports are still useful today, for example, Żurowski's (1950) considerations concerning the Biskupin reconstructions. Toward the end of the 1930s and in the post-World War II period, a successful venture of cooperation between representatives of different sciences was undertaken at Biskupin. Although not completely flawless, this venture achieved its purpose in the sense of integrating the expertise of various disciplines. The results of recent inter-disciplinary studies in the Biskupin microregion are also valuable for Polish archaeology because specialized analyses (palynological, hydrological, botanical, and pedological) have added considerably to our knowledge of the past, especially to our knowledge about the Neolithic, the period from the second century BC to the fourth century AD, and about the Early Middle Ages (Niewiarowski et al. 1992; Niewiarowski 1995).

Excavating the remains of the Lusatian settlement accounts for only part of the work of Biskupin archaeologists. Kostrzewski and Rajewski surveyed the surrounding area, rightly assuming that the fortified settlement must have been supported by satellite settlements situated around Lake Biskupin. Surface investigations covered an area of approximately 40 km² in the Biskupin microregion (Rajewski 1957:303) and found about 70 archaeologi-cal sites. Microregional studies continued in the 1950s and 1960s in refer-ence to other periods, such as the Paleolithic, Neolithic, and Early Middle Ages (Rajewski 1955, 1959b). The microregional research model was also applied in other regions of Poland (e.g., Opole in southern Poland, Gdańsk on the Baltic coast, and Gniezno, the first capital of Poland, 35 km south-west of Biskupin), especially in the late 1950s and early 1960s when excava-tion work was greatly intensified throughout the country in connection with the Polish State Millennium celebrations. In 1982, archaeologists from the Biskupin Museum carried out further surface investigations in the Biskupin microregion, increasing the number of known prehistoric and medieval archaeological sites to 126.

The methodology of archaeological documentation reached a new phase at Biskupin. Photography, beginning in the early years of excavation in the 1930s, became a major addition to the traditional methods of documenting finds. Wonderful black-and-white photographs were taken from small bal-loons, each with a camera suspended underneath and linked by a string to someone (usually archaeologist Wojciech Kočka) standing on the ground (Figure 7), as well as from large observation balloons, zeppelins (Figure 8), and planes (Rajewski 1975). A new system of cataloguing and classifying finds was developed. The magnitude of the excavations also required new forms of logistical organization – storehouses, carpentry workshops, and living quarters were built. For underwater work, divers from the navy were employed (Figure 9). A dam was constructed around the peninsula so that water could be pumped out of the trenches while exploration was in progress.

Conservation

The need to conserve the wooden structures of the settlement has been a continuing problem at Biskupin. At first, no one realized how quickly wet wood rots when removed from its natural environment. In the winters during the 1930s, some of the waterlogged finds and structures were covered with rush mats and moss. After World War II, various methods of preservation were used, such as permeating with ordinary salt, soaking in paraffin, and spraying with phenolon resins. These methods were only partly successful in halting the decay. Today, visitors to Biskupin can see in situ only the remains of the entrance to the settlement, and portions of the breakwater and foundation of the ramparts. The rest of the ancient structure is covered by a protective layer of earth and water. Both the old structures and the reconstructions are cared for by staff of the Biskupin Wood Conservation Laboratory (with L. Babiński as chief conservator), which since 1990 has been working in cooperation with the Canadian Conservation Institute (Bilz et al. 1994). Biskupin, where various conservation problems

Figure 7. Balloon photography at Biskupin in 1936.
Photo Archives, Biskupin Museum.

remain unsolved, serves as a warning to Polish archaeologists not to excavate rashly in wetland terrain (Mikłaszewska-Balcer 1981; Piotrowski 1991b). Since 1989, archaeologists and conservators at Biskupin have been receiving useful advice from John and Bryony Coles of the Wetland Archaeology Research Project (WARP).

Figure 8. Polish Air Force zeppelin above the Biskupin reconstructions in 1938. *Photo Archives, Biskupin Museum.*

Figure 9. Polish Navy divers at Biskupin, 1937. *Photo Archives, Biskupin Museum.*

Efforts to preserve the site itself have centred on environmental protection. At Biskupin, it was possible to include the entire 116.6-ha lake and its surroundings (all together more than 250 ha) in an environmental scheme that had been developed in 1992 by Biskupin Museum archaeologists and naturalists from Bydgoszcz (50 km northeast of Biskupin), and that had then been accepted by county officials. Also in 1992, an artificial barrier (designed by drainage experts from nearby Inowrocław) was constructed on the Gąsawka Rivulet flowing out of Lake Biskupin. The barrier successfully blocks the outflow from the lake, raising the water level. This has created favourable conditions for the waterlogged structures of the settlement, and, equally important, the barrier has not changed the hydrological conditions of the microregion (Piotrowski and Zajączkowski 1993). However, it will probably not be easy to continuously monitor this area, educate the local populace, and check any future industrial polluters.

Knowledge

Biskupin has provided some very valuable information about the people of the Lusatian culture who inhabited a large part of central Europe from 1300 BC to 400 BC. Biskupin is the only fortified settlement of this culture studied in detail. Researchers are particularly interested in the "urban phenomenon" of Biskupin (Niesiołowska-Wędzka 1991). Nonetheless, after 60 years of studies, certain questions remain unanswered, a situation that, in a way, increases the attraction of the place. Recent dendrochronological data have pushed back the beginnings of the Biskupin settlement to the middle of the eighth century BC. (The first set of absolute dates ranges from 747 BC to 722 BC; most of the samples were from trees that had been cut down in the late autumn or winter of 738-737 BC [Ważny 1993].) This means that current ideas about the origin of this type of fortified settlement must change. Until recently, Balkan, or even Greek and Anatolian, influences were suggested (Niesiołowska-Wędzka 1989). Now, Ważny et al. (1994) argue for an eastern Alpine source of influence or, alternatively, that Biskupin-type fortified settlements in central Europe originated in local tradition.

Another unanswered question concerns the ethnic status of the people of ancient Biskupin. Polish archaeology, until the 1970s, accepted Kostrzewski's assumptions that the settlement was built and inhabited by proto-Slavs. German archaeology before the end of World War II preferred an interpretation put forth by Professor G. Kossinna (1858-1931) that central Europe had been inhabited in the Bronze and Iron ages by Indo-Germanic folk (Kossinna 1902, 1926-1927). Kostrzewski (who, incidentally, had studied under Kossinna's professorship) maintained his opinion in this matter until his death in 1968. The issue is embedded in popular belief – most Poles are convinced that Biskupin was a Slavic or proto-Slavic settlement. However, it now seems that the truth is different – that Biskupin was neither proto-Slavic nor proto-Germanic. Science does not yet know the ethnic identity of the inhabitants of ancient Biskupin, though undoubtedly the Biskupin excavations have extended our knowledge of the era of transition between the Bronze and Iron ages. Most Polish archaeologists today agree with the opinion that Slavic tribes first appeared in southeastern Poland, although no earlier than the fifth century AD.

The Biskupin region has been an attractive place to live for thousands of years (Rajewski 1959b). However, finds from the Lusatian period have obscured those from earlier and later eras. In the Neolithic, there were already settlements of breeders and farmers on the Biskupin peninsula and near the lake. In the Early Bronze Age, people of the Iwno culture built a structure near the peninsula. It was first defined as a cattle enclosure but now is thought to have had a religious and trade-centre function. After Lusatian Biskupin fell, settlers came to the peninsula in the second and third centuries AD (during the Roman Influences period, which in this part of central Europe lasted from the first to the beginning of the fifth centuries AD). From the sixth to the mid-eleventh centuries, there was a small Slavic fortified settlement at Biskupin. From the second half of the eleventh century until 1325, a village existed on the southern shore of Lake Biskupin, about 300 m in a straight line from the Biskupin peninsula. The modern village was erected in 1325, 800 m in a straight line from the peninsula.

Education

Popularization and propaganda have played an important role in the story of Biskupin (Piotrowski 1991a). Before Biskupin, no archaeological remains or excavations in Poland were well known. Though the popularity results primarily from the conviction that the village by the lake was a creation of Slavic civilization, the circumstances are exploited to provide the public with information about prehistory in general (Piotrowska 1994). These efforts of public education have been so successful that, now, when the theory that the Lusatian settlement was proto-Slavic has to be retracted, Biskupin's image will not be changed. A knowledgeable public is receptive to new, even if less agreeable, hypotheses.

Professional Training

Even before World War II, many students helped the expedition at Biskupin as volunteers. Toward the end of the 1940s, Rajewski introduced an excellent scheme: he organized archaeological training camps (Archeologiczne Obozy Szkoleniowe, or AOS) (Rajewski 1952). Every student of archaeology in Poland had to spend at least one month at Biskupin. Students had to help with excavation work, listen to lectures, and participate in archaeological experiments. Such camps took place in the years 1951 to 1963. Their effects can still be seen in the network of contacts and cooperation among former participants. Today's young prehistorians, who often work in isolation from other centres, would certainly profit from attending such a camp. Archaeologists from the Biskupin Museum wish to return to the concept, though in slightly different form.

Experimental Archaeology

At Biskupin, experimental archaeology serves as a public education tool as well as a means for archaeologists to test ideas about ancient technology. The first experiments were carried out in 1935. Clay vessels were modelled and fired, and attempts were made to soften deer antlers using natural milk and oxalic acid. (Antler softened in this way is easier to work.) After World War II, experimental archaeology was undertaken at Biskupin on a large scale. Prof. W. Hołubowicz experimented with pottery, Dr. T. Dziekoński specialized in bronze casting, and others smoked fish and tried using ancient building techniques. Dr. W. Szafrański first carried out, in 1949, an experiment according to early medieval recipes, using the dry distillation of wood tar and pitch. Today, archaeologists at Biskupin grow small plots of plants that had been used in prehistoric times and keep herds of heath sheep and tarpan-like horses. Every year in May and June, a demonstration of ancient and medieval crafts takes place within the reconstructed area or in the experimental archaeology quarters (Figure 10) (Piotrowski and Zajączkowski 1991). Also, since 1995, the third week of September is devoted to an international event called the Biskupin Archaeological Festival.

Figure 10. Archaeology by experiment: building a bakery oven. *Photo by A. Ring.*

Figure 11. Biskupin peninsula, 1993. *Photo by A. Ring.*

Interpretation Centre
The idea of creating an archaeological reservation in Poland also first arose
at Biskupin. As early as 1935, Kostrzewski talked of establishing such a centre while the excavation work was still in progress. In the years 1936 to
1939, two huts and a fragment of the rampart, covered on the outside and
the inside with clay, were reconstructed (Figure 6). The reservation really
began to grow toward the end of the 1940s, and construction is still going
on. The Biskupin reservation covers an area of 26 ha and includes the remains and replica of the Lusatian culture fortified settlement on the peninsula (Figure 11), a dozen or so archaeological sites from various ages, quarters for experimental archaeology, a museum pavilion with a conference
room, a peasant cottage from the end of the eighteenth century, meadows,
forests, and ponds (Figure 12). The reconstructed structures have deterio-
rated and need to be rebuilt, giving archaeologists today a good excuse for
trying out new ideas and investigating hypotheses (Piotrowski and
Zajączkowski 1994; Rajewski 1968a; Zajączkowski 1991).

Conclusion
Biskupin has made a positive mark on twentieth-century Polish archaeology. More than 60 years of excavations at Biskupin and the surrounding
region is a sufficiently long period to determine both good and bad. Biskupin
was undoubtedly the inspiration and pride of Polish archaeology before
World War II. Throughout the 1940s and 1950s, it remained a symbol of all
that was new and undertaken on a large scale. Although the world of Polish

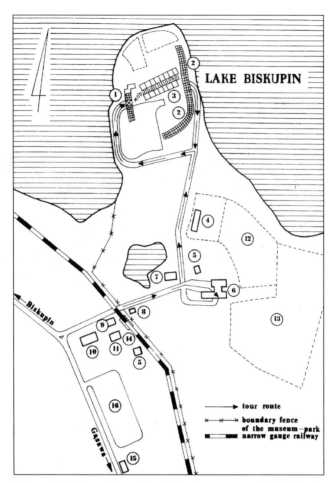

Figure 12. Plan of the archaeological museum-park in Biskupin, showing reconstructions of (1) the ancient gateway, (2) the ramparts, and (3) houses; (4) conservation laboratories, (5) toilets, (6) museum, (7) peasant cottage, (8) porter's lodge, (9) ticket office, (10) snack bar pavilion, (11) kiosk, (12) enclosure for sheep, (13) enclosure for horses, (14) narrow-gauge railway stops, (15) bus-stop, and (16) car park.

archaeology heard less about Biskupin in the 1970s and 1980s, Biskupin's time is not yet over. In recent years, Biskupin has enlarged its storage, tourist, and conservation facilities and organized its records. Its greatest problem is the conservation of remains at the wet site and, in this regard, Biskupin serves as a warning to Polish archaeologists. For scholars involved in questions of ethnicity, Biskupin is a reminder that changes in interpretation might be required when a theory is based on wishful thinking. For museum workers, it is a good example of how to organize an archaeological

Figure 13. Reconstructions on the Biskupin peninsula, 1994.
Photo by A. Ring.

reservation, and of the care that must be taken when reconstructing a site
(Figure 13).

How can Biskupin uphold its renown? The answer is simple if we look at
the current and potential contributions of research undertaken there today.
Dendrochronology, which provided the first absolute dates for Biskupin
(additional samples will be analyzed gradually), evoked a discussion among
Polish archaeologists about the transition between the Bronze and Iron ages,
and whether the Biskupin fortified settlement existed in the Late Bronze
Age or the in Early Iron Age, as well as the origin of Biskupin-type settlements. Interdisciplinary studies in the Biskupin microregion continue to
increase our knowledge of settlement processes and changes in the natural
environment during the last 10,000 years. There is talk of creating something called the Biskupin International Project. The idea is to use the experience gained at Biskupin to excavate a similar site at Izdebno (7 km northwest of Biskupin), which may turn out to be as much of a revelation as
Biskupin, and also to continue excavations at Biskupin itself. The Biskupin
International Project would include scholars from various countries who
are experienced in wetland archaeology. After all, Biskupin is part of the
cultural heritage of Europe and of the world.

Acknowledgments
I would like to thank Mrs. Alicja Petrus-Zagroba for translating the text, and I am very obliged to Ms. Kathryn Bernick for her accurate comments and good advice.

References Cited
Bilz, M., D. Grattan, and M. Horvath
   1994 The Test Treatment of Waterlogged Wood from the Biskupin Archaeological Site, Poland. In *Proceedings of the 5th ICOM Group on Wet Organic Archaeological Materials Conference (Portland, Maine 1993)*, edited by P. Hoffmann, pp. 23-40. ICOM Committee for Conservation Working Group on Wet Organic Archaeological Materials, Bremerhaven, Germany.
Kossinna, G.
   1902 Die indogermanische Frage archäologisch beantwortet. *Zeitschrift für Ethnologie.*
   1926-1927 *Ursprung und Verbreitung der Germanen in Vor und frühgeschichtlicher Zeit.* Germanenverlag, Berlin.
Kostrzewski, J. (editor)
   1936 *Osada bagienna w Biskupinie w pow. żnińskim.* (Bog settlement at Biskupin near Żnin; summary in French.) Nakładem Instytutu Prehistorycznego Uniwersytetu Poznańskiego, Poznań, Poland.
   1938 *Gród prasłowiański w Biskupinie w powiecie żnińskim. Sprawozdanie z prac wykopaliskowych w latach 1936 i 1937 z uwzględnieniem wyników z lat 1934-1935.* (Pre-slavonic settlement at Biskupin: Excavation report for 1936-1937 with additional results from 1934-1935; in Polish.) Nakładem Instytutu Prehistorycznego Uniwersytetu Poznańskiego, Poznań, Poland.
   1950 *Sprawozdanie z prac wykopaliskowych w grodzie kultury łużyckiej w Biskupinie w powiecie żnińskim za lata 1938-1939 i 1946-1948*, vol. 3. (Report of excavations at the Lusatian-culture town of Biskupin in 1938-1939 and 1946-1948; summary in French.) Polskie Towarzystwo Prehistoryczne, Poznań, Poland.
Mikłaszewska-Balcer, R.
   1981 Najważniejszy problem Biskupina – konserwacja drewna. (The most important problem of the Biskupin settlement – waterlogged wood conservation; in Polish.) *Z Otchłani Wieków* 47(3):155-161.
Niesiołowska-Wędzka, A.
   1989 *Procesy urbanizacyjne w kulturze łużyckiej w świetle oddziaływań kultur południowych.* (Urbanization processes in the Lusatian culture in the light of cultural action from the south; summary in German.) Polskie Badania Archeologiczne 29. Zakład Narodowy im. Ossolińskich, Wrocław, Poland.
   1991 Procesy urbanizacyjne w kulturze łużyckiej (Urbanization processes in the Lusatian culture; summary in English.) In *Prahistoryczny gród w Biskupinie*, edited by J. Jaskanis, pp. 57-80. Wydawnictwo Naukowe PWN, Warszawa.
Niewiarowski, W. (editor)
   1995 *Zarys zmian środowiska geograficznego okolic Biskupina pod wpływem czynników naturalnych i antropogenicznych w późnym glacjale i holocenie.* (An outline of geographic changes in the Biskupin region under the influence of natural and anthropogenic factors during the Late Glacial and Holocene; summary in English.) Turpress, Toruń, Poland.
Niewiarowski, W., B. Noryśkiewicz, W. Piotrowski, and W. Zajączkowski
   1992 Biskupin Fortified Settlement and Its Environment in the Light of New Environmental and Archaeological Studies. In *The Wetland Revolution in Prehistory*, edited by B. Coles, pp. 81-92. WARP Occasional Paper 6. Dept. of History and Archaeology, University of Exeter, UK.
Ostoja-Zagórski, J.
   1991 Problemy organizacji halsztackich wspólnot terytorialno - gospodarczych typu biskupińskiego. (The organization of Biskupin-type territorial economic communities in the Hallstatt period; summary in English.) In *Prahistoryczny gród w Biskupinie*, edited by J. Jaskanis, pp. 37-56. Wydawnictwo Naukowe PWN, Warszawa.

Piotrowska, D.
1994 Wykopaliska biskupińskie w świetle nauki i kultury. (Biskupin excavations in the world of Polish science and culture; in Polish.) *Żnińskie Zeszyty Historyczne* 11:30-43.
Piotrowski, W.
1991a 50 lat badań w Biskupinie (Fifty years of research at Biskupin; summary in English.) In *Prahistoryczny gród w Biskupinie,* edited by J. Jaskanis, pp. 81-105. Wydawnictwo Naukowe PWN, Warszawa.
1991b Biskupin bezpieczny – jak konserwować drewno sprzed 2500 lat? (Is Biskupin safe? How to conserve 2,500-year-old waterlogged wood; in Polish.) *Wiadomości Konserwatorskie* (Heritage Documentation Centre, Warszawa) vol. 3-4 (July 18-19): 27-30.
1995 Biskupin – The Fortified Settlement from the First Millennium BC. *Quaternary Studies in Poland* 13:89-99.
Piotrowski, W., and W. Zajączkowski
1991 Biskupin Archaeology by Experiment. *Experimentelle Archäologie Bilanz 1991: Archäologische Mitteilungen aus Nordwestdeutschland* (Staatliches Museum für Naturkunde und Vorgeschichte Oldenburg) 6:131-138.
1993 Protecting Biskupin by an Artificial Barrier. *NewsWARP* (Wetland Archaeology Research Project, UK) 14:7-11.
1994 Biskupin Reconstructions Problems. In *Les sites de reconstitutions archéologiques. Actes du colloque (Aubechies, 2,3,4,5 septembre 1993),* pp. 73-77. Ministére de la Région Wallone, Direction Générale de l'Aménagement du Territoire, du Logement et du Patrimoine, Division du Patrimoine, Aubechies, Belgium.
Rajewski, Z.
1950 Sprawozdanie z organizacji prac w Biskupinie w pow. żnińskim w latach 1938-1939 i 1946-1948 (Report of excavations at Biskupin in 1938-1939 to 1946-1948; summary in French.) In *Sprawozdanie z prac wykopaliskowych w grodzie kultury łużyckiej w Biskupinie w powiecie żnińskim za lata 1938-1939 i 1946-1948,* vol. 3, edited by J. Kostrzewski, pp. 1-11. Polskie Towarzystwo Prehistoryczne, Poznań, Poland.
1952 Archeologiczny obóz szkoleniowy w Biskupinie. (Archaeological training camp at Biskupin; in Polish.) *Z Otchłani Wieków* 21(4):141-146.
1955 O metodzie badań wczesno redniowiecznych zespołów osadniczych. (On the method of investigations of early medieval settlements; summary in English.) *Wiadomości Archeologiczne* (Bulletin archéologique polonais) 22(2):117-145.
1957 Wczesnośredniowieczne ośrodki wiejskie w świetle dotychczasowego stanu badań. (Early medieval rural settlements in the light of former and recent studies; in Polish.) In *Pierwsza sesja archeologiczna Instytutu Historii Kultury Materialnej Polskiej Akademii Nauk,* pp. 299-318. Zakład Imienia Ossolińskich, Wydawnictwo Polskiej Akademii Nauk, Warszawa-Wrocław.
1959a W 25 rocznicę rozpoczęcia badań wykopaliskowych w Biskupinie. (On the 25th anniversary of the first excavation season at Biskupin; in Polish.) *Z Otchłani Wieków* 25(2):130-132.
1959b Settlements of a Primitive and Early Feudal Epoch in Biskupin and Its Surroundings. *Archaeologia Polona* 2(1):85-124.
1968a Rezerwaty archeologiczne i muzea na wolnym powietrzu. (Archaeological reservations and open-air museums; summary in English.) *Archeologia Polski* (Instytut Historii Kultury Materialnej, Warszawa) 13(2):429-442.
1968b 35-lecie odkrycia Biskupina. (35th anniversary of the discovery of Biskupin; in Polish.) *Z Otchłani Wieków,* 34(4):238-239.
1975 Aerofotografia w badaniach terenowych w Polsce. (Aerial photography and archaeological field investigations in Poland; in Polish.) *Wiadomości Archeologiczne* (Bulletin archéologique polonais) 39(4):560-566.
Schleif, H.
1944 *SS-Ausgrabung Urstätt im Warthegau.* Posener Jahrbuch für Urgeschichte (erster Jahrgang):11-17.
Ważny, T.
1993 Dendrochronological Dating of the Lusatian Culture Settlement at Biskupin, Poland – First Results. *NewsWARP* (Wetland Archaeology Research Project, UK) 14:3-5.

Ważny, T., W. Piotrowski, and W. Zajączkowski
1994 Biskupin i dendrochronologia. *Żnińskie Zeszyty Historyczne* 12:4-14.
Zajączkowski, W.
1984 Biskupin, the Wooden Township of the Early Iron Age. *Popular Archaeology* (Bath, UK), May 1984, pp. 21-24.
1991 Stan i perspektywy rozwoju Oddziału PMA w Biskupinie. (The present state and perspectives of the Biskupin department of the State Archaeological Museum; summary in English.) In *Prahistoryczny gród w Biskupinie,* edited by J. Jaskanis, pp. 235-246. Wydawnictwo Naukowe PWN, Warszawa.
Żurek, J.
1935 *Wenecja i Biskupin.* Ekspedycja Wykopaliskowa Uniwersytetu Poznańskiego, Poznań, Poland.
Żurowski, T.
1950 Budowle kultury łużyckiej w Biskupinie – próba rekonstrukcji. (Lusatian-culture buildings at Biskupin – attempts at reconstruction; summary in French.) In *Sprawozdanie z prac wykopaliskowych w grodzie kultury łużyckiej w Biskupinie w powiecie żnińskim za lata 1938-1939 i 1946-1948,* vol. 3, edited by J. Kostrzewski, pp. 286-370. Polskie Towarzystwo Prehistoryczne, Poznań, Poland.

Ancient Maya Use of Wetlands in Northern Quintana Roo, Mexico

Scott L. Fedick

The ancient Maya of southern Mexico and Central America are perceived as perhaps the most advanced civilization to arise in the Americas during pre-Columbian times (Figure 1) (see Sharer 1994). Archaeologists have found evidence of the emergence of Maya culture about 1200 BC, with complex social organization developing during the Late Preclassic period, from about 400 BC to AD 250. The Classic period, approximately AD 250 to AD 900, witnessed the height of Maya achievements, curtailed by the disruption of the so-called Classic Maya collapse in the southern lowlands. The Postclassic period, from about the beginning of the tenth century to the time of Spanish contact in the early sixteenth century, witnessed a shift of political power and cultural achievement from the southern to the northern lowlands.

The Maya are renowned for their art, architecture, and intellectual achievements in mathematics, calendrics, and astronomy. Scholars have made many advances in recent years, revealing details of ancient Maya political organization, warfare, population levels, and religion, yet we still know relatively little about how the Maya satisfied their basic subsistence needs in the tropical lowland environment in which they flourished. Until the 1970s, it was generally believed that the environment of the Maya Lowlands could not support dense population levels and that the only viable form of agriculture for the region was the slash-and-burn system of *milpa* (maize field) cultivation that was described in modern ethnographies. Since the 1970s, as an increasing body of data on ancient Maya settlement patterns became available, it has been clear that the new picture of Maya population – high regional densities and urban centres – does not fit the model of extensive slash-and-burn cultivation. A variety of alternative or supplementary crops and cultivation systems have been suggested for the ancient Maya, and a growing appreciation for the diversity of both the natural landscape and Maya agricultural practices is emerging (see Fedick 1996). Along with advances in our knowledge of ancient Maya agriculture has come much debate, particularly over the use and management of wetlands for agricultural production.

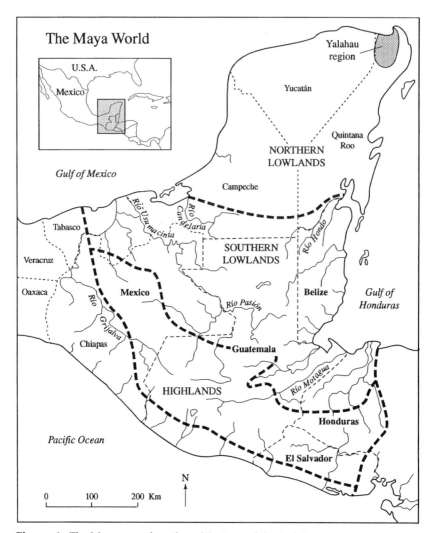

Figure 1. The Maya area of southern Mexico and Central America.

It was not until geographer Alfred Siemens' recognition of patterned ground in the wetlands of Campeche, Mexico, in 1968, and the joint investigations conducted in the early 1970s by Siemens and archaeologist Dennis Puleston, that evidence for ancient Maya use of wetlands was first brought to the attention of the world (Siemens and Puleston 1972; Pohl 1990). Researchers in the 1970s examined evidence for wetland cultivation along the Candelaria River of Campeche, along the Río Hondo of northern Belize, and in Pulltrouser Swamp, also located in northern Belize (Pohl, ed. 1990; Puleston 1977, 1978; Siemens 1978; Siemens and Puleston 1972; Turner and Harrison 1983). By the early 1980s, some archaeologists were assuming the perspective that virtually all wetlands of the Maya Lowlands were of similar agricultural development potential, representing the breadbaskets of ancient Maya subsistence (e.g., Adams 1980). Under these assumptions, vast areas of wetlands were drained by canals and transformed into intensive agricultural plots through the laborious construction of raised planting platforms similar to the Aztec *chinampas* of the Basin of Mexico (but more extensive in scale by a factor of 10 or 20).

Recently, researchers have begun to recognize the heterogeneity of wetland ecosystems in the Maya Lowlands and the diversity of local strategies employed by the Maya to exploit these varied resources. Wetlands of the region vary tremendously in hydrologic regimes and soils, and there is no single technology that the Maya could have used to bring all the wetlands under cultivation. Some types of wetlands may not have been cultivated at all. In other cases, cultivation may have been limited to exploitation of seasonal flooding cycles, without any human modification of the landscape. Channelizing the margins of wetlands may have been a more commonly used technique than previously recognized, whereas the construction of raised fields may actually have been very restricted (see Dunning 1996; Fedick and Ford 1990; Pope and Dahlin 1989; Siemens 1996). There is also growing evidence that the suitability of wetlands for agricultural development has changed through time in response to natural changes in climate and groundwater levels, as well as to human impact on the environment (e.g., Curtis et al. 1996; Hodell et al. 1995; Leyden et al. 1996; Pohl, ed. 1990; Pohl and Bloom 1996; Pope et al. 1996). As archaeologist T. Patrick Culbert has pointed out (Culbert et al. 1990), there were probably as many strategies of wetland cultivation as there were varieties of wetlands. It is with the explicit recognition of wetland heterogeneity that I present the findings of initial investigations into ancient use of wetlands in the Yalahau region of northern Quintana Roo, Mexico.

The Yalahau Region

Environmental Setting

Wetlands of the Maya region are concentrated in the southern lowlands (Figure 1), where up to 40 percent of the landscape is represented by various forms of wetlands. In contrast, the northern lowlands are generally characterized as arid and rocky, with water restricted to natural wells, or *cenotes,* that dot the landscape. The Yalahau region (Figure 1) stands in sharp contrast to these generalizations of northern lowland environment. This northeast corner of the Yucatán Peninsula receives more rainfall than the rest of the northern lowlands due to a pronounced climatic anomaly apparently associated with a "sea breeze convergence effect" that results in average annual rainfall of nearly 2,000 mm, comparable with rainfall of the southern lowlands (Isphording 1975).

The high rainfall of the northeastern peninsula has contributed to the development of a series of elongated karst depressions, or solution features,

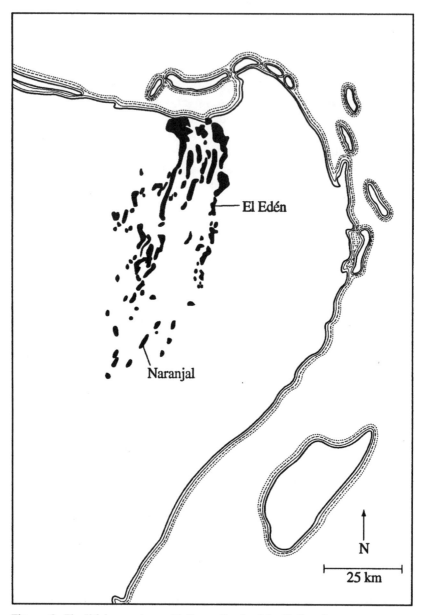

Figure 2. The Yalahau region, with the wetlands of the Holbox fracture zone indicated in solid black.

that apparently follow an underlying fault system, although the underlying structural geology is unknown (see Tulaczyk 1993). This lineament system of north-northeast-trending elongated depressions and aligned swales is referred to geologically as the Holbox fracture zone, as first characterized by geologist A.E. Weidie (1982, 1985). The Holbox fracture zone extends in well-developed form from the north coast to approximately 50 km south, with a maximum width of about 50 km east-west. Analysis of remote-sensing data by Scott Southworth (1985) proposed that the Holbox fracture zone extends, in less dramatic form, for another 50 km to the south, terminating at approximately N20°30' latitude in a concentration of karst terrain and *cenotes* just north of the ancient Maya centre of Cobá. The elongated depressions of the Holbox fracture zone contain a series of wetlands, referred to locally as *sabanas,* that remain saturated or inundated throughout the year (Figure 2). Recent investigations by geologist Slavomir Tulaczyk (1993) suggest that the wetlands were formed when the descending karst solution-corridors met the water table. Thus, the seasonal hydrological regime of the wetlands, as well as long-term fluctuations in the water table, are linked directly to groundwater levels.

The northern area of the Holbox fracture zone, where the wetlands are most prevalent, is referred to as the Yalahau region (Figure 3). Initial investigations by ecologists and biologists suggest that this wetland zone is characterized by perhaps the greatest biodiversity, and contains the highest number of endemic plant and animal species, in the Yucatán Peninsula (Lazcano-Barrero 1995; Snedaker et al. 1991). The core of the Yalahau region is for the most part uninhabited, although there are growing communities along the western and southern margins of the wetland zone, and the huge resort community of Cancún, only a short distance to the east, is currently spurring tremendous population growth in northern Quintana Roo. Two new "protected areas" have recently been established in the Yalahau region (Figure 4) to preserve the diverse ecosystems found in this unique area of the Yucatán Peninsula (Gómez-Pompa and Dirzo 1995). The Yum Balam Protected Area, established in 1994, covers 154,052 ha of land and encompasses much of the northern wetland area. The El Edén Ecological Reserve, on a privately owned tract of 1,492 ha, was established in 1990 just outside the southeast corner of the larger Yum Balam Protected Area. There has been little information available on the wetland ecosystems or the archaeology of the Yalahau region, but archaeological investigations undertaken since 1993 have produced some tantalizing results (Fedick and Taube 1995; Fedick and Taube, eds. 1995).

Archaeological Setting
The Yalahau region has been the subject of sporadic archaeological studies and visits over the years (see Andrews 1985). In 1937, Alberto Escalona Ramos

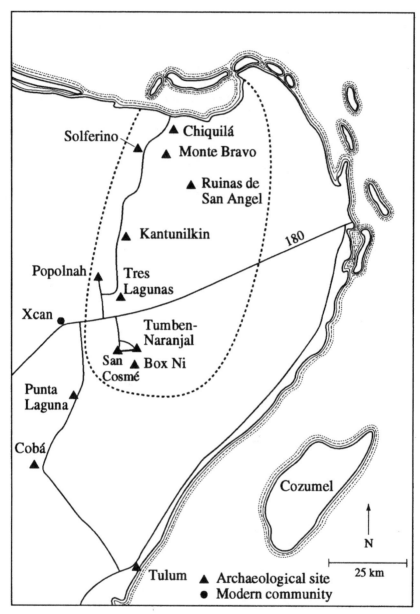

Figure 3. The Yalahau region (defined by dotted line), with locations of ancient centres indicated.

(1946) visited Kantunilkin and other sites in the vicinity (Figure 3). In 1954, William Sanders (1955, 1960) engaged in exploration and limited excavation near the communities of Kantunilkin, Solferino, Monte Bravo, and Chiquilá, all situated along the northwestern margin of the Yalahau region.

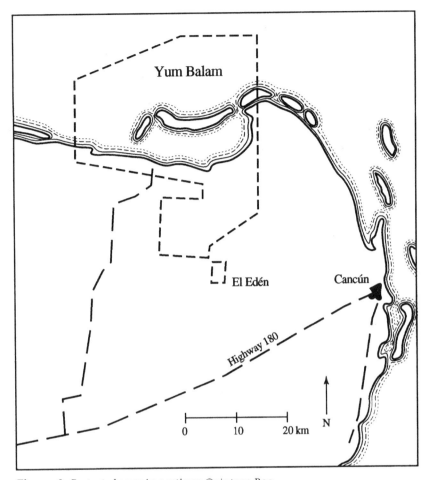

Figure 4. Protected areas in northern Quintana Roo.

In the 1980s, the sites of San Angel and Tumben-Naranjal were first re-corded and investigated by archaeologists Karl Taube, Edward Kurjack, Ruben Maldonado, and Sonia Lombardo (Lombardo 1987:116-117, 150-151, 156-159; Taube and Gallareta 1989).

In 1993, the Yalahau Regional Human Ecology Project was initiated by Scott Fedick and Karl Taube, with the first season of field investigations focusing on the site located at the modern village of Naranjal. The site has been known by the village name of Naranjal and, more recently, as Tumben-Naranjal (Figure 3) (Fedick and Taube 1995; Fedick and Taube, eds. 1995). The Yalahau Project documented architectural relationships between the Late Preclassic/Early Classic site of Tumben-Naranjal and those of the north-western peninsula such as Izamal and Aké (Taube 1995), developed data on the Postclassic reuse of earlier monumental structures (Lorenzen 1995), recorded settlement patterns associated with the site of Tumben-Naranjal and the adjacent Naranjal wetland (Fedick and Hovey 1995), investigated ancient use of wells in the area (Winzler and Fedick 1995), and mapped numerous ancient sites and roadways (Fedick and Taube 1995; Fedick and Taube, eds. 1995; Fedick et al. 1995; Mathews 1995; Reid 1995). Subsequent visits to the El Edén Ecological Reserve have resulted in the identification of numerous ancient settlements in the vicinity (1994-1996 field observations by Scott Fedick, Arturo Gómez-Pompa, and Marco Lazcano-Barrero). Archaeological evidence suggests that the Yalahau region was densely occupied during Late Preclassic/Early Classic times (ca. 100 BC to AD 400), and again during the Late Postclassic period (ca. AD 1250 to AD 1520). The high population density of the Yalahau region during ancient times makes the possibility of agricultural use of wetlands in the region particularly pertinent to our understanding of human use of the area in antiquity.

Investigations at the Naranjal Wetland

The site of Tumben-Naranjal and the village of Naranjal are at the southern end of a wetland within the southern area of the Yalahau region (Figures 2 and 3). The Naranjal wetland extends approximately 2.5 km north-south by 250 m east-west. It contains water throughout the year, with some seasonal variation in water level resulting in annual inundation along the narrow wetland floodplain (Figure 5). The terrain surrounding this wetland is relatively steep, and there are deep deposits of clays and dark, organic hydrosols within the wetland.

A systematic archaeological settlement survey was undertaken at Tumben-Naranjal in 1993 (Fedick and Hovey 1995), with one survey area located to the north of the site centre, along the southwest margin of the wetland, and a second survey area situated to the south of the site centre. Surveyors mapped a total of 70 ancient structures, as well as a variety of other features, including rock alignments, retaining walls, small stone enclosures, wells, and *sascabera* (quarry) pits. Information on terrain, forest cover, and soils was also recorded. Soils were identified according to local Maya classification with the assistance of residents from the modern village of Naranjal. The results of the systematic settlement survey reveal that large residential structures cluster on high ground around the margins of the wetland, whereas those structures situated at greater distances from the wetland tend to be much smaller and less elaborate. In addition to the systematic survey, a reconnaissance-level survey was conducted during 1993 and 1996 along the southeast side of the wetland, recording numerous large residential structures similar to those on the western side of the wetland. Reconnaissance was also conducted within the Naranjal wetland to potentially identify raised planting platforms or other features that might be currently submerged beneath the surface of the water. No constructed features were identified

Figure 5. The wetland at Naranjal (from western margin looking east).

within the main body of the wetland, although our preliminary examination cannot rule out their existence.

Of particular interest here are rock alignments and other features recorded along the margins of the wetland. The alignments consist of a nearly continuous line of single boulders stretching for approximately 50 m north-south, with two shorter segments running east-west for approximately 20 m and 12 m. The alignments are situated within the narrow floodplain on the southwest margin of the wetland: they were fully exposed on dry land during the dry season, but were submerged beneath about 10 cm of water with the onset of the rains in June. A retaining wall or embankment constructed of cobbles and boulders stretches for approximately 200 m along the southeast margin of the wetland, forming a band of relatively level terrain between the wetland and the settlement area.

Surface collection of ceramics in 1993 and test excavations undertaken in 1996 indicate a major occupation at Tumben-Naranjal during the later part of the Late Preclassic period and the early part of the Early Classic period, between approximately 100 BC and AD 400. There is scant indication of Late Classic occupation (ca. AD 600 to AD 900) and ample evidence of a Late Postclassic reoccupation (ca. AD 1250 to AD 1520).

Further reconnaissance was undertaken to the north of Naranjal, where 19 cleared and burned agricultural fields were checked along approximately 18 km of road running from the village of San Angel to the east and then

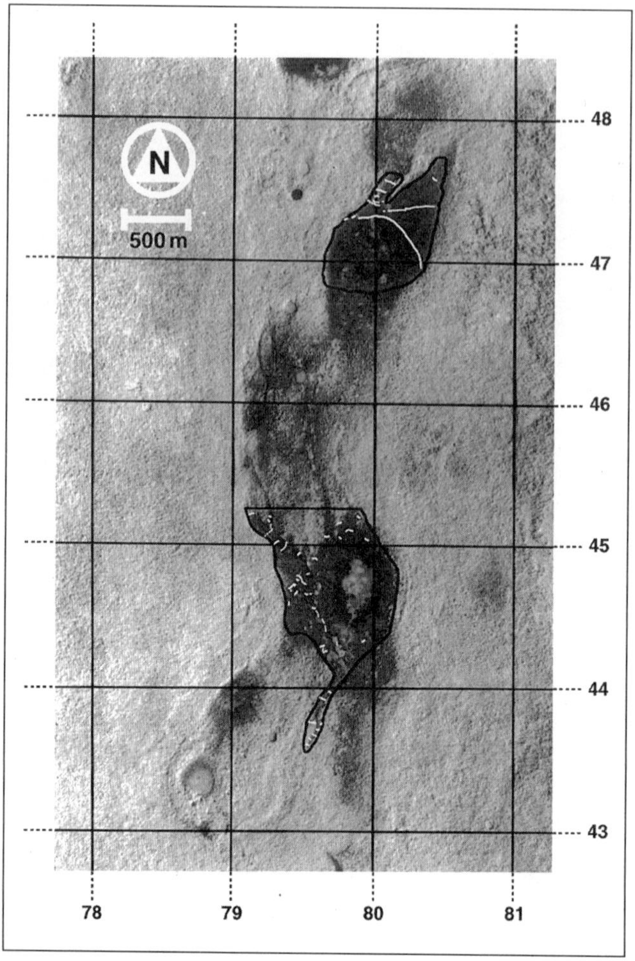

Figure 6. Aerial photograph (1980) of the El Edén wetland.
The 1-km grid represents the Universal Transverse Mercator
divisions as indicated on the 1:50,000 topographic map
(F16C49). Areas enclosed by black lines indicate areas surveyed
in 1996. White lines indicate locations of recorded rock-
alignment features.

the northeast. Five of the 19 checked fields contained the remains of ancient residential settlements, and all the fields with structures were within
500 m of a wetland.

Investigations at the El Edén Wetland

The El Edén Ecological Reserve is dominated by a wetland situated within a
large shallow karstic depression measuring approximately 5.5 km north-

Figure 7. Rock-alignment feature within the west-central area of the El Edén wetland (now designated as feature 96 A-22).

south by 0.8 km east-west (Figures 2, 4, and 6). Only a small area of the El Edén wetland contains standing water throughout the year, with most of the depression being subject to varying degrees of seasonal inundation. The terrain surrounding the wetland is relatively flat, apparently rising no more than 2 m above the margin of the depression within a radius of several kilometres.

In the spring of 1994, botanist Arturo Gómez-Pompa described to me a rock alignment he had discovered well within the wetland at the El Edén reserve. I visited the reserve in August 1994 and was shown this feature by Dr. Gómez-Pompa (Figure 7). During my inspection, I noted that there is actually a series of these rock alignments oriented perpendicular to the length of the wetland and running from one side to the other side of a channel that can be distinguished within the larger wetland. Four alignments were noted, approximately 80 m apart; two are distinct and two are partially exposed. Each alignment consists of one or two rows of unshaped, upstanding limestone slabs measuring up to 70 cm in length. The alignments are very sinuous, stretching for about 70 m between bedrock outcrops on opposite sides of the wetland channel. These bedrock exposures mark a slight transition in terrain between the lower portion of the wetland, with vegetation associations dominated by various mixes of cattail (*Typha latifolia*), sawgrass (*Cladium jamaisense*), and water lily (*Nyphaea* spp.), and the slightly elevated transition zone dominated by the logwood, or *palo tinto,* tree (*Haematoxylon campechianum*). The moist soils spanned by the alignments are only about 10 cm to 20 cm thick over limestone bedrock. The southernmost alignment was approximately 10 m north of standing water. The entire lower area of the wetland depression floods during the rainy season and would normally have been inundated by early August, except for the unusually dry conditions of 1994.

I participated in an environmental reconnaissance at El Edén during the summer of 1995 and noted many more rock alignments within the wetland (Fedick 1995). In 1996, I began a project to systematically record and study

Figure 8. Segment of an approximately 700-m-long rock alignment (feature 96 A-41) at the north end of the El Edén wetland.

the wetland features of El Edén and the associated ancient settlement. During the 1996 season we surveyed approximately half of the wetland and recorded 52 rock-alignment features within its main body (Figure 6). We plan to complete the survey and conduct excavations at a sample of these features in 1997. A study of ancient settlements associated with the El Edén wetland is being conducted by graduate student Bethany Morrison. Limited test excavations conducted in 1996 by Morrison at residential sites associated with the wetland indicate occupation during part of the Late Preclassic period (ca. 100 BC to AD 400), and no evidence of a Late Postclassic occupation, as is the case at Tumben-Naranjal. The dating of these residential sites is based on ceramics analyzed by Sylviane Boucher of the Instituto Nacional de Antropología e Historia, with the assistance of Sara Dzul G.

The rock alignments within the El Edén wetland vary in form in accordance with the local topographic setting and hydrology. The most prominent feature noted consists of an alignment of limestone slabs and boulders at the north end of the wetland, stretching for a distance of nearly 700 m between the west and east margins (Figure 8). The alignment traverses seasonally inundated land dominated by sawgrass and tasiste palm (*Paurotis wrightii*), crossing some areas containing calabash trees (*Crescentia cujete*). Boulders range from approximately 40 cm to 70 cm in diameter, and slabs average about 15 cm in thickness, with maximum diameters up to 115 cm. The rocks are arranged in single to double rows, with several segments of slabs remaining in upright positions, supported on one or both sides by smaller boulders (Figure 9). The rocks apparently rest on the limestone

Figure 9. Detail of an intact section of rock alignment 96 A-41.

bedrock, with immediately surrounding soils varying from 5 cm to 25 cm in depth. It is estimated that the alignment consists of over 2,000 large boulders and slabs, representing a substantial investment of labour.

North of the long alignment, as well as at the south end of the wetland, is a series of smaller alignments associated with the margins of natural depressions (10 m to 20 m in diameter) that are within the courses of shallow channels. The depressions and channels are dominated by various mixes of cattail, sawgrass, and water lily. The alignments are generally situated so as to block the lowest terrain along the depression margin (Figure 10). These alignments are constructed of limestone boulders averaging about 30 cm to 40 cm in diameter, in single to double rows, occasionally reaching two or three courses in height. Alignments also run perpendicular across the shallow channels in areas lacking depressions. These cross-channel alignments vary in width from 10 m to 66 m and are constructed of limestone boulders or slabs, ranging from about 40 cm to 70 cm in diameter.

A few alignments were recorded within swamp-forest vegetation dominated by logwood, with other trees, including black chechem (*Metopium brownei*), ya'axnik (*Vitex gaumeri*), and a wild relative of the coca tree (*Erythroxylon campechianum*). These alignments run between slightly higher bedrock outcrops and tend to be constructed of smaller rocks, averaging about 20 cm to 30 cm in diameter.

Variability of Wetlands in the Yalahau Region

Naranjal and El Edén represent two distinctly different varieties of wetlands. The Naranjal wetland rests within a relatively deep depression and is surrounded by hilly terrain, whereas the El Edén wetland is in a shallow depression that is surrounded by relatively flat terrain. As a result of the terrain, the El Edén wetland is subject to extreme fluctuations in the extent of surface area that is seasonally inundated. The narrow margin of the Naranjal wetland is seasonally inundated, but the majority of the depression remains flooded throughout the year. Correspondingly, the soils and vegetation are also strikingly different in these two wetlands. The Naranjal and El Edén wetlands represent examples along a continuum of wetland varieties present within the Yalahau region. In addition to the wetlands' inherent interest to wetland ecologists, their variety would have offered an intriguing range of possibilities, as well as challenges, to ancient Maya farmers.

Initial Suggestions for Possible Ancient Use of Wetlands in the Yalahau Region

How might the wetlands of the Yalahau region have been used by the ancient Maya? The two examples discussed here, the wetlands at Naranjal and at El Edén, indicate management strategies different from those that have been suggested for other lowland Maya wetland sites. Investigations of

Figure 10. Rock alignment (feature 96 A-42) situated so as to block the lowest terrain along the margin of a natural depression.

wetlands in the southern lowlands suggest that the most common form of wetland manipulation was channelization of the seasonally inundated margins of wetlands, with perhaps some construction of raised planting beds within permanently flooded zones. So far, neither of these management strategies is evident in the study area. In the Yalahau region, channelization of the wetland margins to facilitate cultivation would not have been practical, as the margins were for the most part either exposed bedrock or very thin soil. No raised platforms have been identified in the Yalahau wetlands, although their existence cannot yet be ruled out. The only possible agricultural features identified in the region so far are the rock alignments along the margin of the Naranjal wetland and those found throughout much of the El Edén wetland.

I suggest two possibilities for the agricultural use of wetlands in the Yalahau region. These suggestions are not mutually exclusive, and they are directed only at the conditions evident at the Naranjal and El Edén wetlands.

The first hypothetical use can be characterized as an intensive form of water-recessional cultivation. Various forms of water-recessional cultivation are known ethnographically for the Maya Lowlands (Carter 1969; Culbert 1978; Gliessman 1991; Wilk 1985). Under these cultivation systems, farmers plant in the moist soils that are exposed as waters recede along the margins of rivers or wetlands during the dry season. None of the ethnographic examples mentions intensification through the construction of rock alignments. As an intensified variation of water-recessional cultivation, the construction of rock alignments could have functioned to help retain soils and moisture, thereby increasing the productivity of the naturally thin soils and lengthening the growing season. At the El Edén wetland, crops could have been planted in sequence behind the alignments as the waters receded. According to this hypothesis, the use of wetlands at El Edén would represent an intensified form of an ethnographically known cultivation system. It should be noted, however, that unlike the extensive area of seasonally flooded land at El Edén, the relatively narrow flood-margin at Naranjal is not particularly conductive to water-recessional cultivation.

The second hypothetical use of wetlands in the Yalahau region can be termed the "fertilizer factory" method of cultivation. In 1993, several local farmers in the Naranjal area mentioned to me how people sometimes haul truckloads of muck and soil from the wetlands and deposit them in their home gardens. The wetland soils were said to be very fertile. Although I saw this as a technique that could have been used by the ancient Maya (minus the pick-up trucks), it was not until I talked with Dr. Ana Luisa Anaya, professor of chemical ecology at the National Autonomous University of Mexico, that I realized the potential significance of wetlands as sources of fertilizer. Dr. Anaya had collected and analyzed samples of periphyton from the El Edén wetland. Periphyton are complex communities of microbiota that are attached to substratums of either organic or inorganic materials. Periphyton communities consist of algae, bacteria, fungi, and animals, along with organic and inorganic detritus (see Wetzel 1983). Periphyton represent a vital component of freshwater wetland ecosystems, providing the main source of food for many grazing herbivores, and contribute significantly to the cycling of nutrients, particularly nitrogen and phosphorus (see Batzer and Resh 1991; Doyle and Fisher 1994; Grimshaw et al. 1993; Lamberti et al. 1989; Lane 1991; Marks and Lowe 1989; Mulholland et al. 1994). Dr. Anaya's (1995) analyses indicate very high levels of phosphorus, nitrogen, and organic matter, as well as a high cation exchange capacity – all indicators of high fertility from the perspective of plant growth. Moreover, phosphorus is the primary limiting nutrient for agriculture in the Yucatán Peninsula. Thus, the periphyton may represent a formerly unrecognized (by modern researchers) source of natural agricultural fertilizer that may have been exploited by the ancient Maya. The extensive, thick, and fast-growing periphyton could have been harvested as the waters receded and transported to nearby intensively cultivated gardens. The rock alignments at El Edén could have functioned to retain water longer into the dry season, thereby increasing periphyton growth and facilitating its collection from behind the rock-alignment dikes. The alignments around the margin of the Naranjal wetland could have functioned in a similar manner, and the thick organic deposits within that wetland may prove to be comparably high in nutrients. If periphyton and associated soils were transported to upland gardens, I would anticipate that these gardens would be nearby.

Suggestions for Testing the Hypotheses

How can these two hypotheses be tested archaeologically? Pollen and phytolith samples from the wetlands may provide some support for intensified water-recessional cultivation, but there is always the possibility that such plant materials were washed down into the wetlands from fields and gardens in the surrounding uplands. Cultivation experiments may at least test the plausibility of the water-recessional cultivation hypothesis. There is, however, a direct way to test the fertilizer-factory hypothesis. Wetlands contain assemblages of small freshwater organisms that would not live in well-drained upland environments and are unlikely to be transported from the wetlands into upland settings except if humans were to move wetland soils for fertilizer. These wetland organisms include ostracodes (minute crustaceans), small molluscs (snails and clams), and charaphytes (green algae that produce calcium carbonate shells). Remains of these organisms preserve in the archaeological record (e.g., Miksicek 1989; Palacios-Fest 1989), and, if recovered from upland home-garden contexts, may indicate ancient transport of periphyton or wetland soils.

Other Possible Uses of the Wetlands

In addition to the potential agricultural uses of the wetlands, the recorded features may be related to the management of a number of edible wetland resources. The most abundant of these resources are cattails, blue-green algae, and apple snails (*Pomacea flagellata*). The cattails that grow abundantly within the deeper areas of the wetlands represent a potentially significant food source. Cattails are referred to as "probably the most famous of all the edible plants of the Northern Hemisphere" (Harrington 1967:220); virtually all parts of the common cattail are edible and are used as food in many parts of the world (Morton 1975). The cattail rootstock or rhizome in particular is highly nutritious, containing as much protein as maize and more carbohydrates than the potato (Morton 1975:23). Blue-green algae, a major component of the periphyton of the Yalahau wetlands, is another potential food source worth considering. A number of blue-green algae species are known to have been used as a food by the Aztec and Inca peoples of the Americas (Coe 1994:100-101, 186). The apple snail, a large, edible, freshwater snail, is abundant in the Yalahau wetlands and is known to have been a significant food source to the ancient Maya (e.g., Andrews 1969; Moholy-Nagy 1978). All these resources – cattail, blue-green algae, and apple snails – are responsive to varying hydrologic regimes. Manipulation of hydro-period and water depth may have been accomplished through construction of features such as those found in the Yalahau wetlands.

Conclusion

The extensive wetlands of the Yalahau region represent a unique and potentially significant resource zone that may have been significant to ancient Maya subsistence. So far, only two of the dozens of wetlands of the region have been investigated, and both of these have evidence of ancient Maya manipulation. Field research currently underway will help clarify the use and dating of the rock alignment features that have been recorded in the Naranjal and El Edén wetlands. Field investigations so far suggest that occupation of the Yalahau region, and use of the wetlands, dates primarily from the Late Preclassic to Early Classic periods, about 100 BC to AD 400. At Tumben-Naranjal, occupation and possible use of the wetland is also evident for the Late Postclassic period, about AD 1250 to AD 1520. Several potential uses of the wetland have been suggested, including cultivation of domestic crops, harvesting of periphyton for fertilizer, and manipulation of wetland microenvironments to increase production of naturally occurring edible resources.

In conclusion, I reiterate that we will understand ancient Maya wetland cultivation systems only when we strive also to understand the complex and varied ecosystems of the region's wetlands. The wetlands of the Yalahau region are not like the riverine-associated swamps of northern Belize or the *bajos* of the Petén in Guatemala. Nor are wetlands within the Yalahau region alike; a great deal of ecosystem heterogeneity is evident. The true accomplishment of ancient Maya agriculture lies not in a uniform, monolithic system of cultivation but in the local agricultural variations within a complex and varied landscape.

Acknowledgments
Funding for the 1993 season of the Yalahau Regional Human Ecology Project was provided by the H. J. Heinz III Charitable Fund Grant Program for Latin American Archaeology, the UC-MEXUS Development Grant Program, the UCR-Mexico Collaborative Research and Training Group, the UC Riverside Academic Senate Field Research Travel Fund, and by Lic. Gaston Alegre of Cancún. My 1994 visit to the El Edén Ecological Reserve was funded by the UC Riverside Academic Senate Field Research Travel Fund. The 1995 ecological reconnaissance was supported by grants from the University Research Expeditions Program (UREP) of the University of California, and the Dean's Humanities and Social Sciences Research Committee of the University of California, Riverside. The 1996 season of archaeological investigations was funded by UC-MEXUS and by the Foundation for the Advancement of Mesoamerican Studies. Our archaeological research was conducted under permits issued by the federal office of the Instituto Nacional de Antropología e Historia (INAH), and with the assistance of archaeologists María José Con, Luis Leira G., and Enrique Terrones of the Cancún INAH office. Sylviane Boucher of CRY-INAH kindly identified ceramics for the project, with the assistance of Sara Dzul G. I am particularly grateful to Arturo Gómez-Pompa for inviting me to visit El Edén and for sharing with me his discoveries; his enthusiasm for ecological research in the Maya area is a great inspiration. Biologist Marco Lazcano-Barrero, director of the El Edén Ecological Reserve, has greatly facilitated our work at the reserve, and I thank him for all his help as both a friend and a colleague. Finally, many thanks to the numerous students and UREP volunteers who have participated in the archaeological and ecological research at Naranjal and El Edén.

References Cited

Adams, R.E.W.
1980 Swamps, Canals, and the Locations of Ancient Maya Cities. *Antiquity* 54:206-214.

Anaya, A.L.
1995 Richness of Bioactive Compounds in the Tropics. Paper presented at the Conference on Biochemical and Disease Diversity in the Mexican Tropical Forests, University of California, Irvine, March 31, 1995.

Andrews, A.P.
1985 The Archaeology and History of Northern Quintana Roo. In *Geology and Hydrogeology of the Yucatan and Quaternary Geology of the Northeastern Yucatan Peninsula,* edited by W.C. Ward, A.E. Weidie, and W. Black, pp. 127-143. New Orleans Geological Society, New Orleans.

Andrews, E.W., IV
1969 *The Archaeological Use and Distributions of Mollusca in the Maya Lowlands.* Middle American Research Institute, Publication 34. Tulane University, New Orleans.

Batzer, D.P., and Resh, V.H.
1991 Trophic Interactions among a Beetle Predator, a Chironomid Grazer, and Periphyton in a Seasonal Wetland. *Oikos* 60:251-257.

Carter, W.E.
1969 *New Lands and Old Traditions: Kekchi Cultivators in the Guatemalan Lowlands.* University of Florida Press, Gainesville.

Coe, S.D.
1994 *America's First Cuisines.* University of Texas Press, Austin.

Culbert, T.P., P.C. Magers, and M.L. Spencer
1978 Regional Variability in Maya Lowland Agriculture. In *Pre-Hispanic Maya Agriculture,* edited by Peter D. Harrison and B.L. Turner II, pp. 157-161. University of New Mexico Press, Albuquerque.

Culbert, T. Patrick, Laura J. Levi, and Luis Cruz
1990 Lowland Maya Wetland Agriculture: The Rio Azul Agronomy Program. In *Vision and Revision in Maya Studies,* edited by Flora S. Clancy and Peter D. Harrison, pp. 115-124. University of New Mexico Press, Albuquerque.

Curtis, Jason H., David A. Hodell, and Mark Brenner
1996 Climate Variability on the Yucatan Peninsula (Mexico) During the Past 3500 Years, and Implications for Maya Cultural Evolution. *Quaternary Research* 46:37-47.

Doyle, R.D., and T.R. Fisher
1994 Nitrogen Fixation by Periphyton and Plankton on the Amazon Floodplain at Lake Calado. *Biogeochemistry* 26:41-66.

Dunning, Nicholas P.
1996 A Reexamination of Regional Variability in the Prehistoric Agricultural Landscape. In *The Managed Mosaic: Ancient Maya Agriculture and Resource Use,* edited by Scott L. Fedick, pp. 53-68. University of Utah Press, Salt Lake City.

Escalona Ramos, Alberto
1946 Algunas Ruinas Prehispánicas en Quintana Roo. *Boletín de la Sociedad Mexicana de Geografía y Estadística* 61:513-628.

Fedick, Scott L.
1995 *Observations on Archaeological Features within a Wetland of the El Edén Ecological Reserve, Northern Quintana Roo, Mexico.* Report on file with the Instituto Nacional de Antropología e Historia, Cancún and México, DF, offices.

Fedick, Scott L. (editor)
1996 *The Managed Mosaic: Ancient Maya Agriculture and Resource Use.* University of Utah Press, Salt Lake City.

Fedick, Scott L., and Anabel Ford
1990 The Prehistoric Agricultural Landscape of the Central Maya Lowlands: An Examination of Local Variability in a Regional Context. *World Archaeology* 22:18-33.

Fedick, Scott L., and Kevin Hovey

1995 Ancient Maya Settlement and Use of Wetlands at Naranjal and the Surrounding Yalahau Region. In *The View from Yalahau: 1993 Archaeological Investigations in Northern Quintana Roo, Mexico,* edited by Scott L. Fedick and Karl A. Taube, pp. 89-100. Latin American Studies Program, Field Report Series No. 2. University of California, Riverside.

Fedick, Scott L., Dawn M. Reid, and Jennifer Mathews

1995 Preliminary Evidence for the Existence of a Regional Sacbe Across the Northern Maya Lowlands. In *The View from Yalahau: 1993 Archaeological Investigations in Northern Quintana Roo, Mexico,* edited by Scott L. Fedick and Karl A. Taube, pp. 129-137. Latin American Studies Program, Field Report Series No. 2. University of California, Riverside.

Fedick, Scott L., and Karl A. Taube

1995 The Yalahau Regional Human Ecology Project: Research Orientation and Overview of 1993 Investigations. In *The View from Yalahau: 1993 Archaeological Investigations in Northern Quintana Roo, Mexico,* edited by Scott L. Fedick and Karl A. Taube, pp. 1-21. Latin American Studies Program, Field Report Series No. 2. University of California, Riverside.

Fedick, Scott L., and Karl A. Taube (editors)

1995 *The View from Yalahau: 1993 Archaeological Investigations in Northern Quintana Roo, Mexico.* Latin American Studies Program, Field Report Series No. 2. University of California, Riverside.

Gliessman, Stephen R.

1991 Ecological Basis of Traditional Management of Wetlands in Tropical Mexico: Learning from Agroecosystems. In *Biodiversity: Culture, Conservation, and Ecodevelopment,* edited by Margery L. Oldfield and Janis B. Alcorn, pp. 211-229. Westview Press, Boulder, CO.

Gómez-Pompa, Arturo, and Rodolfo Dirzo

1995 *Reservas de la Biosfera y Otras Areas Naturales Protegidas de México.* Instituto Nacional de Ecología, México, DF.

Grimshaw, H.J., M. Rosen, D.R. Swift, K. Rodberg, et al.

1993 Marsh Phosphorus Concentrations, Phosphorus Content and Species Composition of Everglades Periphyton Communities. *Archiv fur Hydrobiologie* 128:257-276.

Harrington, H.D.

1967 *Edible Native Plants of the Rocky Mountains.* University of New Mexico Press, Albuquerque.

Hodell, David A., Jason H. Curtis, and Mark Brenner

1995 Possible Role of Climate in the Collapse of Classic Maya Civilization. *Nature* 375:391-394.

Isphording, W.C.

1975 The Physical Geology of Yucatán. *Transactions, Gulf Coast Association of Geological Societies* 25:231-262.

Lamberti, G.A., S.V. Gregory, L.R. Ashkenas, A.D. Steinman, et al.

1989 Productive Capacity of Periphyton as a Determinant of Plant Herbivore Interactions in Streams. *Ecology* 70:1840-1856.

Lane, J.M.

1991 The Effect of Variation in Quality and Quantity of Periphyton on Feeding Rate and Absorption Efficiencies of the Snail *Neritina reclivata* (Say). *Journal of Experimental Marine Biology and Ecology* 150:117-129.

Lazcano-Barrero, Marco Antonio

1995 Ecological Diversity in El Edén Reserve, Northern Quintana Roo. Paper presented at the Conference on Biochemical and Disease Diversity in the Mexican Tropical Forests, University of California, Irvine, March 31, 1995.

Leyden, Barbara W., Mark Brenner, Tom Whitmore, Jason H. Curtis, Dolores R. Piperno, and Bruce Dahlin

1996 A Record of Long- and Short-Term Climatic Variation from Northeast Yucatán: Cenote San José Chulchacá. In *The Managed Mosaic: Ancient Maya Agriculture and Resource Use,* edited by Scott L. Fedick, pp. 30-50. University of Utah Press, Salt Lake City.

Lombardo de Ruiz, S. (coordinator)
1987 *La Pintura Mural Maya en Quintana Roo*. Instituto Nacional de Antropologia e Historia, Chetumal.

Lorenzen, Karl J.
1995 Late Postclassic Reuse of Early Classic Monumental Architecture at Naranjal. In *The View from Yalahau: 1993 Archaeological Investigations in Northern Quintana Roo, Mexico*, edited by Scott L. Fedick and Karl A. Taube, pp. 59-77. Latin American Studies Program, Field Report Series No. 2. University of California, Riverside.

Marks, J.C., and R.L. Lowe
1989 The Independent and Interactive Effects of Snail Grazing and Nutrient Enrichment on Structuring Periphyton Communities. *Hydrobiologia* 185:9-17.

Mathews, Jennifer P.
1995 The Box Ni Group of Naranjal, and Early Architecture of the Central Maya Lowlands. In *The View from Yalahau: 1993 Archaeological Investigations in Northern Quintana Roo, Mexico*, edited by Scott L. Fedick and Karl A. Taube, pp. 79-87. Latin American Studies Program, Field Report Series No. 2. University of California, Riverside.

Miksicek, Charles H.
1989 Snails, Seeds, and Charcoal: Macrofossils from the Las Acequias Canal System. In *Prehistoric Agricultural Activities on the Lehi-Mesa Terrace: Perspectives on Hohokam Irrigation Cycles*, edited by Neal W. Ackerly and T. Kathleen Henderson, pp. 235-262. Northland Research, Flagstaff, AZ.

Moholy-Nagy, Hattula
1978 The Utilization of *Pomacea* Snails at Tikal, Guatemala. *American Antiquity* 43:65-73.

Morton, Julia F.
1975 Cattails (*Typha* spp.) – Weed Problems or Potential Crop? *Economic Botany* 29:7-30.

Mulholland, P.J., A.D. Steinman, E.R. Marzolf, D.R. Hart, et al.
1994 Effects of Periphyton Biomass on Hydraulic Characteristics and Nutrient Cycling in Streams. *Oecologia* 98:40-47.

Palacios-Fest, Manuel
1989 Late-Holocene Ostracodes as Hydrochemical Indicators in the Phoenix Basin. In *Prehistoric Agricultural Activities on the Lehi-Mesa Terrace: Perspectives on Hohokam Irrigation Cycles*, edited by Neal W. Ackerly and T. Kathleen Henderson, pp. 263-278. Northland Research, Flagstaff, AZ.

Pohl, Mary D.
1990 The Río Hondo Project in Northern Belize. In *Ancient Maya Wetland Agriculture: Excavations on Albion Island, Northern Belize*, edited by Mary D. Pohl, pp. 1-19. Westview Press, Boulder, CO.

Pohl, Mary D. (editor)
1990 *Ancient Maya Wetland Agriculture: Excavations on Albion Island, Northern Belize*. Westview Press, Boulder, CO.

Pohl, Mary D., and Paul Bloom
1996 Prehistoric Maya Farming in the Wetlands of Northern Belize: More Data from Albion Island. In *The Managed Mosaic: Ancient Maya Agriculture and Resource Use*, edited by Scott L. Fedick, pp. 145-164. University of Utah Press, Salt Lake City.

Pope, Kevin O., and Bruce Dahlin
1989 Ancient Maya Wetland Agriculture: New Insights from Ecological and Remote Sensing Research. *Journal of Field Archaeology* 16:87-106.

Pope, Kevin O., Mary D. Pohl, and John S. Jacob
1996 Formation of Ancient Maya Wetland Fields: Natural and Anthropogenic Processes. In *The Managed Mosaic: Ancient Maya Agriculture and Resource Use*, edited by Scott L. Fedick, pp. 165-176. University of Utah Press, Salt Lake City.

Puleston, Dennis E.
1977 The Art and Archaeology of Hydraulic Agriculture in the Maya Lowlands. In *Social Process in Maya Prehistory: Studies in Honour of Sir Eric Thompson*, edited by Norman Hammond, pp. 449-467. Academic Press, London.

1978 Terracing, Raised Fields, and Tree Cropping in the Maya Lowlands: A New Perspective on the Geography of Power. In *Pre-Hispanic Maya Agriculture*, edited by Peter D. Harrison and B. L. Turner II, pp. 225-245. University of New Mexico Press, Albuquerque.

Reid, Dawn M.
1995 Inter- and Intra-Site *Sacbeob* of the Naranjal Area. In *The View from Yalahau: 1993 Archaeological Investigations in Northern Quintana Roo, Mexico*, edited by Scott L. Fedick and Karl A. Taube, pp. 121-128. Latin American Studies Program, Field Report Series No. 2. University of California, Riverside.

Sanders, William T.
1955 *An Archaeological Reconnaissance of Northern Quintana Roo*. Current Reports No. 24. Carnegie Institution of Washington, Department of Archaeology, Cambridge, MA.

1960 *Prehistoric Ceramics and Settlement Patterns in Quintana Roo, Mexico*. Contributions to American Anthropology and History Vol. 12, No. 60, pp. 154-264. Carnegie Institution of Washington, Washington, DC.

Sharer, Robert J.
1994 *The Ancient Maya*. 5th ed. Stanford University Press, Stanford, CA.

Siemens, Alfred H.
1978 Karst and the Pre-Hispanic Maya in the Southern Lowlands. In *Pre-Hispanic Maya Agriculture*, edited by Peter D. Harrison and B.L. Turner II, pp. 117-143. University of New Mexico Press, Albuquerque.

1996 Benign Flooding on Tropical Lowland Floodplains. In *The Managed Mosaic: Ancient Maya Agriculture and Resource Use*, edited by Scott L. Fedick, pp. 132-144. University of Utah Press, Salt Lake City.

Siemens, Alfred H., and Dennis E. Puleston
1972 Ridged Fields and Associated Features in Southern Campeche: New Perspectives on the Lowland Maya. *American Antiquity* 37:228-239.

Snedaker, Samuel, John C. Clark, and Ingrid Olmstead
1991 *The Status of Biodiversity in Quintana Roo, Yucatan*. Division of Marine Biology and Fisheries, The Rosenthal School of Marine and Atmospheric Science, University of Miami, Miami.

Southworth, C. Scott
1985 Applications of Remote-Sensing Data, Eastern Yucatán. In *Geology and Hydrogeology of the Yucatán and Quaternary Geology of Northeastern Yucatán Peninsula*, by W. C. Ward, A. E. Weidie, and W. Back, pp. 12-18. New Orleans Geological Society Publications, New Orleans.

Taube, Karl A.
1995 The Monumental Architecture of the Yalahau Region and the Megalithic Style of the Northern Maya Lowlands. In *The View from Yalahau: 1993 Archaeological Investigations in Northern Quintana Roo, Mexico*, edited by Scott L. Fedick and Karl A. Taube, pp. 23-58. Latin American Studies Program, Field Report Series No. 2. University of California, Riverside.

Taube, Karl A., and Tomás Gallareta Negrón
1989 *Survey and Reconnaissance in the Ruinas de San Angel Region, Quintana Roo, Mexico*. Preliminary report of the 1988 San Angel Survey Project submitted to the National Geographic Society.

Tulaczyk, Slawomir M.
1993 *Karst Geomorphology and Hydrogeology of the Northeastern Yucatán Peninsula, Mexico*. Master's Thesis, Department of Geology, Northern Illinois University, De Kalb.

Turner, B.L. II, and Peter D. Harrison (editors)
1983 *Pulltrouser Swamp: Ancient Maya Habitat, Agriculture, and Settlement in Northern Belize*. University of Texas Press, Austin.

Weidie, A.E.
1982 Lineaments of the Yucatán Peninsula and Fractures of the Central Quintana Roo Coast: Road Log and Supplement to 1978 Guidebook. 1982 Geological Society of America Annual Meeting Field Trip No. 10, pp. 21-25.

1985 Geology of Yucatán Platform. In *Geology and Hydrogeology of the Yucatán and Quaternary Geology of Northeastern Yucatán Peninsula,* by W.C. Ward, A.E. Weidie, and W. Back, pp. 1-19. New Orleans Geological Society Publications, New Orleans.

Wetzel, Robert G. (editor)

1983 *Periphyton of Freshwater Ecosystems.* Dr W. Junk Publishers, The Hague.

Wilk, Richard R.

1985 Dry Season Agriculture Among the Kekchi Maya and its Implications for Prehistory. In *Prehistoric Lowland Maya Environment and Subsistence,* edited by Mary Pohl, pp. 47-57. Papers of the Peabody Museum of Archaeology and Ethnology, Vol. 77. Harvard University Press, Cambridge, MA.

Winzler, Susan, and Scott L. Fedick

1995 Ancient Wells and Water Resources of Naranjal and the Yalahau Region. In *The View from Yalahau: 1993 Archaeological Investigations in Northern Quintana Roo, Mexico,* edited by Scott L. Fedick and Karl A. Taube, pp. 101-113. Latin American Studies Program, Field Report Series No. 2. University of California, Riverside.

The Death of the Wildwood and the Birth of Woodmanship in Southeast England

D.M. Goodburn

Waterlogged archaeological sites are well known to contain preserved woody materials such as timber, roundwood, bast, and bark. Objects made of these materials, which are not preserved in the vast majority of archaeological sites, are often of great interest. They are commonly studied from many different perspectives, such as the technical, social, economic, and ceremonial. A hidden dimension of this artifactual material is its ability to tell us much about the complex interactions between people and trees in pre-industrial times. Of course, waterlogged woody materials are clearly ecofacts as much as artifacts.

It is a well-established practice to identify the species of wood used to make artifacts such as fish weir stakes or boat paddles. However, it is less common for archaeologists to consider the more subtle ecological information intrinsic to this type of material. It is already clear that, at least as early as the Neolithic, efforts were made to semi-domesticate wild native trees in England. The various techniques used in the past (and occasionally still today) to manage individual trees and groups of trees have been termed "woodmanship" practices by Oliver Rackham (1976). These practices are quite distinct from those of modern forestry that developed in Britain, beginning in the seventeenth century AD. Woodmanship practices are primarily concerned with the production of fuel and small structural materials on a sustainable basis, whereas forestry was primarily developed in Britain to produce larger timber for naval and other constructional purposes. Current work is showing that the details of woodmanship practices varied greatly through time and over space, reflecting different social and economic needs. This varied development to some extent mirrors that of early agriculture.

Museum of London Investigations

What follows is a brief summary of the approach used by the Museum of London Archaeology Service (MOLAS) to investigate the nature of ancient trees and treeland in southeast England. This approach was developed by me and other colleagues in MOLAS and has been employed since 1988 on most wet-site excavations. The term "treeland" refers to any land on which trees grow, including wildwood ("old-growth forest" in North American terms), coppice with standards, woodland, orchards, and hedges. Our approach to reconstructing past treeland has been inspired by the pioneering work of Oliver Rackham (1972, 1976) on standing timber buildings from later medieval times. For periods earlier than ca. AD 1200, we must look to the wet-site evidence. London is fortunate to have many waterlogged zones in which large amounts of well-preserved timber and roundwood have been found. The remains span the period from the Bronze Age to post-medieval times. Structural remains of many types have survived, including buildings, wharfs, bridges, boats, wells, wattle fences, trackways, and groups of reused timbers.

Wherever possible, we try to carry out the following procedure when excavating waterlogged timber and roundwood (Goodburn 1991a; Spence 1990):

(1) Timber and roundwood structures are first exposed, then recorded in plan view. The best-preserved sections are then drawn in elevation and photographed.

(2) These best-preserved areas are dismantled, and individual components drawn, described on standardized forms, and selectively photographed. We pay particular attention to the following features: size, shape, type of conversion (section of tree used), method of conversion (e.g., by sawing, by cleaving), and the major features of tree anatomy, knots, grain, presence of sapwood or bark. Evidence of reuse is also noted.

(3) Each timber is then sampled for tree-ring study, unless it is required for conservation and display. Structures of roundwood are also systematically sampled.

(4) Given sufficiently well-preserved material, attempts at graphic reconstruction of the following will be made, drawing on the results of the tree-ring and species identification work and the drawn field record: the parent log, the parent tree, and, where the evidence is particularly strong, the parent treescape (e.g., Figures 1, 2, and 3).

To improve our understanding of the archaeological finds, we have been carrying out experimental work in ancient woodland on the edge of London for the past eight years. Reconstructions of ancient structural woodwork have been made using the types of tools and trees that have the closest characteristics to those used originally (see Goodburn 1992; Goodburn and Redknap 1988).

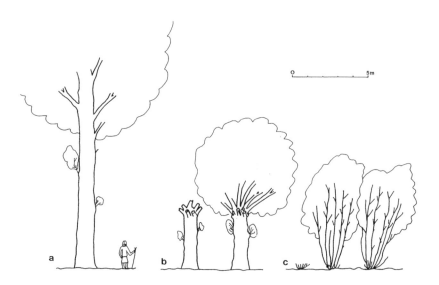

Figure 1. Typical sources of timber and roundwood in southeast England ca. AD 1000: (a) a wildwood oak ca. 300 years old, now extinct in England; (b) a pollarded oak ca. 100 years old (old pollards can still be seen in the London region); and (c) young oak and hazel coppice less than seven years old, such as can still be seen in the London region.

Reconstructing Past Treelands

The following summaries describe aspects of the collaborative work of this author and tree-ring specialists I. Tyers, N. Nayling, and the late H. Hibberd. "Tree-ring work" is used here as an umbrella term for species identification; annual growth ring counting; and, for samples with 50 or more rings, ring measuring and matching leading to dating (dendrochronology).

The archaeological woodwork from London is dominated by the two species of native oak (*Quercus robur* L. and *Q. petraea* Liebl.). However, the form, the age, and the type of oak used varied greatly, principally as a response to the application of varying woodmanship practices (Goodburn 1994) (Figure 1). Unfortunately, the two species are very closely related, and the timber of the two can not be distinguished by archaeobotanists. Other species found on London sites in smaller quantities include alder (*Alnus* sp.), beech (*Fagus* sp.), willow (*Salix* sp.), and elm (*Ulmus* sp.).

Cleft Boards from Wildwood or High-Forest Oaks

Timbers cleft and hewn from very large, straight-grained oaks are particularly common on London sites dating from the tenth to twelfth centuries AD, becoming much less common later. The trees were often worked into thin, wide, radially faced boards for buildings, boats, and cooper ed vessels (stave-built containers). Recently, small amounts of beech (*Fagus sylvatica*)

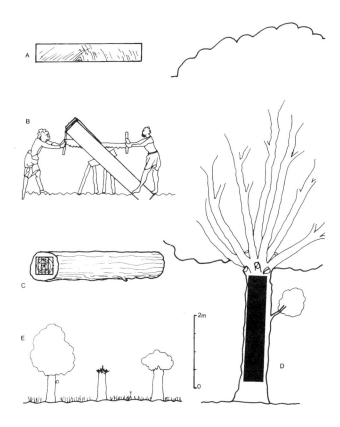

Figure 2. Reconstructed method of processing some pollarded oak stems in late medieval times: (a) a typical plank; (b) the method and type of conversion, see-sawing from a hewn square baulk; (c) the hypothetical parent log; (d) the hypothetical parent tree; and (e) the hypothetical treescape, a wood pasture.

have been found worked in similar ways. Typically, these great parent oaks were 200 to 300 years old, between about 0.7 m and 1.2 m in diameter, and grew very slowly in girth (i.e., they had narrow annual growth rings; Figure 3). Such oaks will grow only in conditions of tall, dense woodland, which must, at the time, have been either wildwood or perhaps very over-grown Roman-managed woodland. Oak trees with these characteristics are extinct in Britain today, and were apparently rare by about AD 1300, when it may be fair to say that the last large tracts of native English wildwood had been felled. Boards cleft from large wildwood oaks are found alongside different types of timber and small roundwood deriving from managed woodland, which shows that the contemporary treeland was a complex mosaic of types.

Figure 3. Reconstructed method of processing some large, straight, wildwood oaks in Anglo-Saxon and Norman times: (a) a typical radially cleft oak board; (b) the type and method of conversion and hypothetical parent log; (c) the hypothetical parent wildwood oak; and (d) the hypothetical treescape.

Sawn Planks from Pollarded Oaks

The woodmanship practice of "pollarding," where a tree is cut between about 1 m and 4 m above the ground and the rapid regrowth repeatedly harvested, is well known from later medieval times (Rackham 1976:22). Recent work in London can now take the dating of the practice back to the ninth century AD, which supports theories of early oak pollarding based on charter evidence (Rackham 1976:54).

A high proportion of excavated medieval sawn oak planks are of very short lengths, 1.6 m to 3.5 m long, but are often wide, about 0.5 m to 0.8 m. Typically, the logs these planks were cut from had mainly wide growth rings and rather curved, knotty grain. The method of conversion was by see-sawing (Figure 2b), which was reintroduced about AD 1180 after being lost with the departure of the Romans (Goodburn 1992:113). Experimental work has shown that this sawing method is particularly well adapted to the use of the short thick trunks of pollards (Figures 2b and 1b). Detailed analysis of the growth-ring sequences in several recently excavated thirteenth-century oak planks has found cessations of summer growth every 13 to 16 years, for a period of 60 years or so, in a sequence of otherwise rather wide growth rings. This patterning is similar to that in recent pollards and, together with the morphology of the planks, it is taken as evidence of some form of pollarding. The planks were in a structure with other timbers that were felled in AD 1241 (Figure 4). Since none of the timbers showed signs of reuse, it is likely that the parent pollard was felled about the same time. Therefore, this particular pollarding began in the 1180s. Interestingly, it is now clear why the matter of the ownership of pollard tree stems, or "bollings," was considered important in medieval times, even though they would generally have little value to a modern English forester.

Wattle Work from Coppice

Coppicing is the woodmanship practice in which trees are repeatedly cut down to ground level and the vigorous regrowth harvested (Figure 1c).

Figure 4. The landward face of a mid-thirteenth-century timber river wall containing see-sawn oak planking cut from a pollarded oak stem; exposed in a MOLAS basement excavation at Vintners Place, City of London. Scale: 1 m long. The crossing sloping saw marks indicative of see-sawing are just visible on planking of the bottom right. *Photo by M. Cox of MOLAS.*

However, many of the details of this practice in early periods are little known. Roundwood structures of early medieval date, such as wattle pit linings, hurdles (portable woven panels), and fences are relatively common finds in London. The weaves and types of rods used for the structures varied considerably. Some structures have a home-made appearance, with irregular rods of varied species and age; others are very neatly woven, with long regular rods such as can be produced only by pollarding or coppicing.

Pilot analysis of this varied material has shown some interesting patterns. Some structures were clearly being made from casually collected local hedgerow or orchard thinnings, and others were produced from systematically coppiced woodland. For fine wattle work, such as hurdles, the rods used were small and whole rather than cleft, as in recent English practice. This suggests that they were made from coppice cut on a short rotation. Detailed tree growth ring analysis indeed shows this to have been the case for some finely made structures. For example, in a wattle hurdle dating to ca. AD 1200, the uprights were six-year-old oak and the rods a mix of six-year-old hazel (*Corylus avellana* L.) and three-year-old oak.

Research into Roman Woodmanship Practices

Considerable work has been undertaken recently by MOLAS into the evidence for aspects of Roman-period woodmanship surviving in the remains of worked timbers. Unfortunately, very little Roman-period roundwood has been found and studied in London, so the insights achieved concern only medium- and large-sized trees. Some of the recent work has been published or is just about to be published, so it will not be described further here (Brigham et al. 1995; Goodburn 1991a, 1991b). However, a few words summarizing our state of knowledge can be included.

We have clear evidence for the Roman harvesting of huge wildwood oaks, alongside clear evidence for the use of oak from different forms of treeland, such as old oak coppice, and trees growing in open pasture or arable land. Additionally, there appears to have been a marked trend toward the use of younger, smaller oaks growing in more open, managed landscapes toward the end of the period ca. AD 200 to AD 400 (Figure 5). This seems to indicate a considerable taming of the wildwood during the Roman occupation.

Conclusions

It appears that the modern forestry practice of re-planting trees after harvesting was not a common feature in Britain before the seventeenth century. The exceptions include the establishment of some hedges and orchards and, during the Roman occupation of Britain, the introduction of chestnut (*Castenea sativa* L.), which is now naturalized and subject to woodmanship practices.

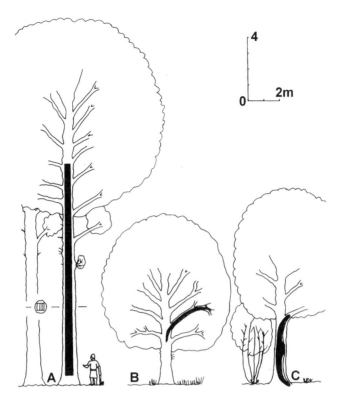

Figure 5. A reconstruction of some of the types of oak tree used for Romano-Celtic Blackfriars' ships dating to the mid-second century AD: (A) huge wildwood oaks for the sawn hull planks; (B) large, open grown oaks, probably from farmland, for the curved floor timbers and knees; and (C) standard trees from managed woodland or hedges for floor timbers and smaller hold-lining planking; such trees were part of the complex mosaic of treeland types in the hinterland of Londinium.

Most native British trees grow back with vigour from their established roots or regenerate from seed after felling. A tough living root-mat is left behind, requiring enormous effort to break up and remove. Only if repeated heavy grazing is maintained would dense wildwood be prevented from rapid regrowth. Thus, in many cases, it appears that the wildwood must have been rather gradually converted into various forms of managed woodland, such as wood pasture, with increasingly scattered old trees. Only much later could large areas of open arable farmland be established.

In the southeast of England in particular, there are considerable areas where woodmanship practices are still in use or have lapsed only relatively recently. Thus, the visitor is able to view treeland forms that, in many senses, are as much a product of human intervention as any field of wheat or concrete road. Such treeland comprises living monuments to the very distant past, which can be understood only by the dedicated and intelligent use of the wetland archaeological resource. Since this resource is precious, the archaeologist clearly has a duty to maximize the amount of information obtainable from it, by, in the first instance, systematic recording, sampling, and multi-disciplinary research.

I hope that this short summary has demonstrated the potential of waterlogged archaeological woodwork to increase our understanding of aspects of early woodmanship in a very concrete way. It is also to be hoped that charcoal identification, woodland pollen analysis, and historical, ecological, and archaeological studies of ancient treeland in the London area will refine and advance new understanding outlined here.

Acknowledgments

The line of research summarized here would have been impossible without the hard work of MOLAS excavation and specialist staff, particularly I. Tyers, the late H. Hibberd, N. Nayling, R. Bartkowiak, and G. Milne. However, I remain responsible for any errors in the text and figures used here.

References Cited

Brigham, T., D. Goodburn, I. Tyers, and J. Dillon
  1995 A Roman Timber Building on the Southwark Waterfront, London. *Archaeological Journal* 152:1-72.
Goodburn, D.
  1991a Waterlogged Wood and Timber as Archives of Ancient Landscapes. In *Wet Site Excavation and Survey,* edited by J. Coles and D. Goodburn, pp. 51-53. Museum of London and WARP, London.
  1991b A Roman Timber Framed Building Tradition. *Archaeological Journal* 148:182-204.
  1992 Woods and Woodland; Carpenters and Carpentry. In *Timber Building Techniques in London c.900-1400,* edited by G. Milne, pp. 106-130. London and Middlesex Archaeology Society Special Paper 15.
  1994 Trees Underground: New Insights into Trees and Woodmanship in South East England, AD 800-1300. In *Botanical Journal of Scotland* 46(4):658, 662.
Goodburn, D., and Redknap, M.
  1988 Replicas and Wrecks from the Thames Area. *London Archaeologist* 6(1):7-10, 19-22.
Rackham, O.
  1972 Grundle House: The Question of Timber in Certain East Anglian Buildings in Relation to Local Supplies. *Vernacular Architecture* 3:3-8.
  1976 *Trees and Woodland in the British Landscape.* Dent, London.
Spence, C. (editor)
  1990 *Museum of London Excavation Manual.* 2nd ed. Museum of London, London.

Stylistic Characteristics of Basketry from Coast Salish Area Wet Sites

Kathryn Bernick

Objects made from normally perishable materials that have been preserved in anaerobic deposits constitute a significant archaeological resource. In addition to being cultural specimens that might otherwise be known only by inference, perishable artifacts inform about the past through detailed analysis of their morphological and technological attributes. Basketry, which can reveal elusive sociological traits, is an apt example of the analytical capacity of wet-site finds.

Basketry comprises an aspect of material culture that is technologically complex, stylistically sensitive, and relatively abundant when present. Like ceramics, basketry artifacts have the potential to be cultural indicators and to provide insight about ethnicity (Adovasio 1986). On the northwest coast of North America, where ceramics are absent from the indigenous techno-logical repertoire, basketry is probably the most useful artifact type for understanding past cultural diversity (Bernick 1987; Croes 1992:104; Matson and Coupland 1995:312).

In the Coast Salish area of southwestern British Columbia and north-western Washington, basketry has survived in numerous water-saturated archaeological deposits (Figure 1). To date (1995), the oldest known speci-men yielded an AMS radiocarbon assay of 4400 ± 80 BP (Eldridge 1991:20). Other dated collections span the past three millennia (Bernick 1991; Croes 1977, 1992, 1995).

Waterlogged assemblages from the Coast Salish area typically contain large proportions of basketry – for example, basketry accounts for 40 percent of the perishable vegetal artifacts from the Musqueam Northeast site (Archer and Bernick 1990) and 29 percent from the Water Hazard site (Bernick 1989b). Although most of the objects are fragmentary, many are sufficiently intact to be readily recognized as remains of baskets (Figure 2). These finds pro-vide direct evidence for the antiquity of basket-making and present an opportunity to investigate stylistic variation through time.

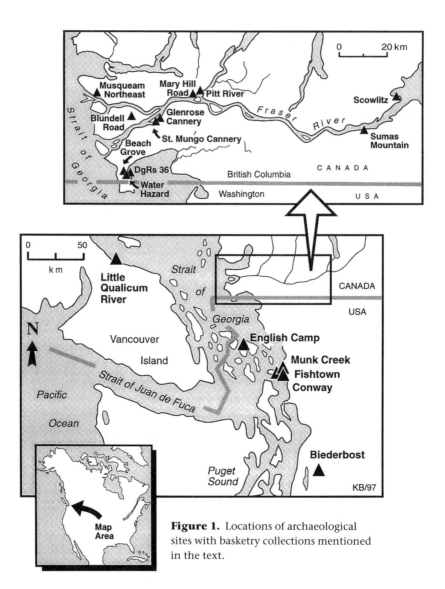

Figure 1. Locations of archaeological sites with basketry collections mentioned in the text.

Aims and Methods of Analysis

Basketry found in archaeological waterlogged contexts is nearly always flattened and broken, and colours seldom endure (the original presence of more than one colour might be detectable, but hues are not). However, many other features persist, including aspects of construction and structural decoration that I have found enlightening for stylistic comparisons (Bernick 1989a, 1991, 1994a). Even small fragments provide information about materials and weaving techniques, and they might also show trend-sensitive attributes such as rims and ornamentation. In addition, the organic

Figure 2. Basket fragment (DgRs 30:44) from the 1,700-year-old Water Hazard site in Tsawwassen, British Columbia. Open plain-twined weave with narrow bands of decoration and false-braid selvage. *Photo by Michael Lay, courtesy of the UBC Laboratory of Archaeology, Vancouver, BC, Canada.*

composition of basketry means that specimens can be directly dated (if samples for dating are obtained before conservation treatment), and this enhances the usefulness of isolated finds and collections that were recovered out of context.

The present discussion of stylistic variation in archaeological basketry centres on assemblages from the Fraser delta, though it also draws on data from other parts of the Coast Salish area. The rationale for including collections beyond the delta relates to the established recognition of the Coast Salish area as a cultural entity, from ethnographic, linguistic, and archaeological perspectives (Mitchell 1971; Suttles 1990).

This synthesis reflects my continuing research on Northwest Coast basketry. It is based on information gathered over the past 22 years from personal observation as well as from published and unpublished material. In terms of coverage, I have analyzed or assisted in the analysis of 16 Coast Salish area collections from British Columbia and have observed five from Washington. Available descriptions for the latter are preliminary and cursory (Blukis Onat 1976; Munsell 1976; Nordquist 1960a, 1960b, 1976; Sprague 1976; also see summary information in Croes 1977, 1995). Detailed descriptions of Coast Salish area basketry from British Columbia sites can be found in Arcas (1991), Archer and Bernick (1990), Bernick (1981, 1983, 1989b, 1994b), Eldridge (1991), and Laforêt (1971). The following summaries draw on these sources as well as personal observations. Table 1 gives sample sizes and ages. For site locations see Figure 1. Although additional assemblages, especially with large samples, would be advantageous, I believe that sufficient data are available now to identify characteristics that might be chronological or cultural markers.

Depending on the features displayed by particular artifacts and their completeness, systematically recorded data generally include observations about methods of construction (wall weave, reinforcements, selvage, corners, base weave, start, stitch orientation); basket size and shape, element widths, weaving gauge; material (species, plant part, preparation); handles (construction, method of attachment, placement); and decoration (placement, construction, design, evidence of colour contrast). The foregoing include most of the attributes recommended by Adovasio (1977) for basic analysis of basketry.

The baskets are classified by the predominant weaving techniques of the walls. In order to accommodate the range of weaving techniques found on

Table 1

Dated basketry collections from the Coast Salish area

Site name	Sample size[1]	Age[2]	Reference
Beach Grove (DgRs 1)	1	1600	Smith 1964
Biederbost (45SN100)	53	2000	Nordquist 1976
Blundell Road (DgRs 15)	1	2200	Bernick 1991
Conway (45SK59b)	52+	700	Munsell 1976
DgRs 36	2	2150	Arcas 1991
English Camp (45SJ24)	2	2000	Sprague 1976
Fishtown (45SK99)	15	1200	Blukis Onat 1976
Glenrose (DgRr 6)	5	4300	Eldridge 1991
Little Qualicum (DiSc 1)	22	1000	Bernick 1983
Mary Hill Road (DhRq 19)	3	900	BC Archaeolgy Branch, pers. comm. 1994
Munk Creek (45SK156)	1	1000	Dale Croes, pers. comm. 1995
Musqueam NE (DhRt 4)	184	3000	Archer and Bernick 1990
Pitt River (DhRq 21)	1	3000	Bernick 1981
Scowlitz (DhRl 16W)	5	1000	Bernick 1994b
St. Mungo (DgRr 2)	1-4	[4000]	Bernick, pers. observation 1993
Sumas Mt. (DgRm 1)	1+?[3]	[2000]	Bernick 1991
Water Hazard (DgRs 30)	102	1700	Bernick 1989b

[1] Number of basketry artifacts.
[2] Age of the basketry or the component containing the basketry, in approximate years BP; [ ] denotes age estimated for isolated finds based on presumed context.
[3] Confusion in site registry records suggests that not all finds designated DgRm 1 are actually from that site (see Bernick 1991).

the Northwest Coast, I have modified Adovasio's (1977) classification scheme. The terminology for wrapped weaves includes long-established terms such as "wrapped twining" (Mason 1988:72-74), as well as newly coined terms such as "dual-warp wrapping" (Eldridge 1991). See Figure 3 for definitions. "Selvage" refers to the finished edge of a piece of weaving, which on a basket comprises the rim.

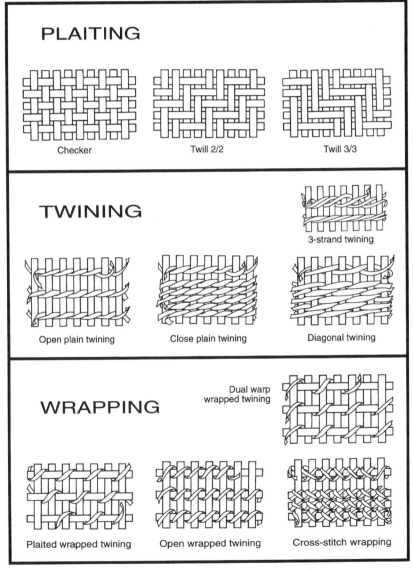

Figure 3. Weaving techniques recorded for baskets from the Coast Salish area.

For the purpose of stylistic comparison, I focus on characteristics that are both stylistic in nature and likely to have been observed if present. Thus, weaving gauge is excluded because it is not stylistically sensitive (Archer and Bernick 1990:152; Croes 1977:160), whereas starts, mends, splices, and methods of increasing the warp were not considered due to inconsistency of information. Although some attributes of basket handles, such as placement, likely have stylistic significance, I do not feel confident separating these from functional criteria and have therefore elected to exclude such data.

Methodologically, the comparisons rely on the presence/absence of particular characteristics. Detailed statistical analysis is precluded by the mainly small sample sizes, which would have severely limited interpretation. On the other hand, the study is enhanced by personal familiarity with the collections. My experience with basketry from other places (Bernick 1989a, 1994a) provides an additional perspective.

Basket Characteristics

Overall, archaeological baskets from the Coast Salish area display a recognizable Northwest Coast style. That is, in the context of North American aboriginal basketry, these specimens clearly fall within a Northwest Coast tradition. The set of weaving techniques (Figure 3) in combination with types of structural decoration and raw material distinguishes the collections from those originating in other culture areas. For example, none of the specimens is likely to be mistaken for an Arctic, Subarctic, Plateau, or Great Basin manufacture (see Mason 1988; Turnbaugh and Turnbaugh 1986).

However, most known archaeological baskets from the Coast Salish area differ from ethnographic Coast Salish baskets and also from those found in other parts of the Northwest Coast. Notably, the absence of coiling in ancient archaeological assemblages contrasts with its prevalence in ethnographic Coast Salish collections (Bernick 1987; Jones 1976). Detailed comparison within the Northwest Coast is constrained by the small number of archaeological basketry collections from other areas, though available data indicate that basketry in the Coast Salish area has been stylistically distinct for at least the past 3,000 years (Croes 1992:105-106).

Croes (1992:106) further argues for stylistic continuity through time within the Coast Salish area, based on statistical analysis of selected characteristics. Certainly some basketry features persist through time. However, the same data show differences when one looks at details of trend-sensitive attributes, such as selvage types and decoration, in combination with weaving techniques and materials. Moreover, this variation correlates with the ages of the respective collections.

Material

The material that is used to make a basket influences the choice of weaving technique and directly affects the appearance of the finished product. Most basketry from Coast Salish area wet sites is made from wood splints, mainly western red cedar (*Thuja plicata* Donn), though other species have also been identified, including yew (*Taxus brevifolia* [Raf.] Sarg.), fir (*Abies* sp.), and spruce (*Picea sitchensis* [Bong.] Carr.). Where plant part was determined, only spruce materials have been identified as root – the others are withes. Although exceptionally thin withes (and roots) are sometimes used whole, in most cases the wood materials were split longitudinally, resulting in "inner-splints" with two flat, light-coloured faces, and "outer-splints" with a curved surface that is dark coloured if the bark has been left on or shiny and light if the bark was removed. This colour contrast was exploited for decorative effect.

Bark materials include western red cedar secondary phloem (commonly called "cedar bark") and a hardwood bark that is either bitter cherry (*Prunus emarginata* [Dougl.] Walpers) or maple (*Acer* sp.). Both were used in the form of thin strips.

Wood splints as well as bark occur as basketry materials in all represented time periods. The oldest collection (Glenrose Cannery, 4300 BP) stands out from later assemblages by having relatively little cedar. Instead, fir-wood splints and cherry/maple bark strips predominate as weaving elements. Moreover, the fir-wood splints are thin in comparison with the occasional fir elements in younger assemblages. Hardwood bark has not been noted on younger archaeological basketry from the Coast Salish area. The Glenrose Cannery site collection includes open-work basketry with cherry/maple bark wrapping elements, as well as one checker-plaited specimen made entirely from cherry/maple bark.

Cedar bark is relatively sparse in archaeological basketry collections from the Coast Salish area, though it was sometimes used for close-twined basketry, and also occasionally as wrapping elements and for decorative weft rows on wood-splint ware. Checker-plaited basketry made from strips of cedar bark occurs in the Coast Salish area only in collections dating from the past 1,300 years.

Weave Types

Checker plaiting appears to have been a common way to make baskets throughout the time represented by the available collections. Twill plaiting, which in regular 2/2 or 3/3 interval is the usual weave technique for wood-splint basket bases, occurs only occasionally as a wall weave. Twill-plaited baskets from the Water Hazard (1700 BP) and Blundell Road (2200 BP) sites feature a conspicuous patterned twill weave enhanced by colour contrast (Figure 4).

Wrapped weaves are reported (in the Coast Salish area) only from sites in British Columbia, but not for collections aged 2400 BP to 1500 BP. In the

Figure 4. Fragmentary basket (DgRs 15:5) from the
Blundell Road site on Lulu Island, Richmond, British
Columbia. Patterned twill plaiting. Age: 2180 ± 170 BP
(SFU RIDDL 663).

early assemblages from Glenrose Cannery (4300 BP) and Musqueam Northeast (3000 BP), wrapped weaves predominate. Each of these assemblages
features different variants, including apparently unique wrapping techniques
unreported for other collections, ethnographic or archaeological. Wrapped
weaves from recent collections appear to have ethnographic parallels. For
example, open-wrapped-twined baskets from the Little Qualicum River site
(1000 BP) are like those made by Coast Salish and other Northwest Coast
groups (Jones 1976). A seemingly unique basket woven in its entirety in
close cross-stitch wrapping (Figure 5) – from the Mary Hill Road site (900 BP)
on the Fraser River – has technological analogues in present-day Puget Sound

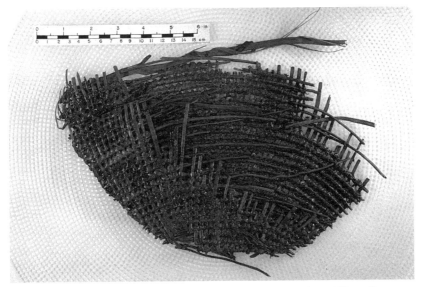

Figure 5. Basket woven in close cross-stitch wrapping, found in 1993 eroding from the Fraser River beach at the Mary Hill Road site (DhRq 19) in Port Coquitlam, British Columbia. Age: 900 ± 100 BP (Beta-73593/CAMS-14134; wood; δ^{13}C = -29.2 0/00).

basketry (personal observation, 1994). Nonetheless, no wrapped basketry is reported for archaeological collections in the Coast Salish area of Washington state.

Twined weaves appear as a major basketry technique only for the 2400 BP to 600 BP period. These are mainly made from wood splints in open plain twining. A few similar baskets occur in the Musqueam Northeast (3000 BP) collection. Baskets woven in close plain twining are present, but not common, in various-aged assemblages. Close plain twining, diagonal twining, and three-strand twining appear in ornamental contexts.

Selvages

To my knowledge, with the exception of close-twined baskets and some plaited cedar-bark specimens, all other archaeological examples from the Coast Salish area have wrapped rims. In other words, the top edge of the basket was finished by bending the standing ends of the warps approximately 90° and wrapping the resulting bundle with one or more flexible strands. The specific way in which this was accomplished varies somewhat within collections and notably through time.

The oldest examples of selvages, from the Musqueam Northeast site (3000 BP), feature two (or three) non-intersecting spiralling elements that wrap the warps two at a time (Figure 6a). On the outside face these rims

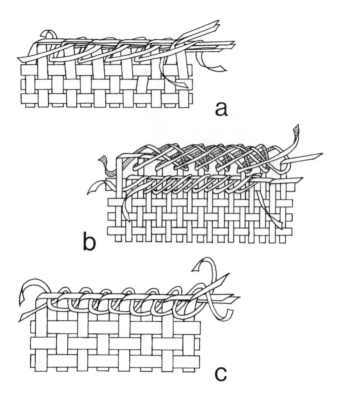

Figure 6. Diagnostic selvage types: (a) paired-warp two-strand wrapped, (b) false-braid (figure-eight wrapped), (c) hitched.

display diagonal stitches and appear "finished," whereas on the inside the wrapping stitches are vertically aligned and present an image of being the back, or wrong side, of the construction.

The 2400 BP to 1500 BP collections include some examples of nearly similar rim types; however, the predominant (74 percent) selvage type involves the addition of an elaborate figure-eight wrapped coil bundle (Figure 6b). The resulting "false braid" displays a diagonal design on both the outside and inside of the rim and a chevron motif on the top, or lip, edge. This elaborate false-braid selvage does not occur in younger or older collections from the Coast Salish area. Within the area, it has been recorded on baskets from the Fraser delta, lower Fraser River, San Juan Island, and Puget Sound, on specimens in checker plaiting, twill plaiting, and open plain twining.

Baskets from 600- to 1,300-year-old collections from the Fraser delta, Vancouver Island, and Puget Sound feature variants of what Croes (1977) calls "hitched" selvages. These involve narrow, inconspicuous wrapping strands (Figure 6c) and are reported for both wood-splint and cedar-bark specimens.

Some baskets from the Conway site (700 BP) have wrapped rims that superficially resemble the false-braid type, but they are more simply constructed and do not have added coil bundles.

Decoration

In regard to structural decoration on archaeological basketry from the Coast Salish area, the recent assemblages stand out for their plainness. In contrast, collections older than 1,500 years contain significant proportions of baskets that display evidence of decoration. Three methods of decoration have been documented: (1) horizontal bands effected by using a different weaving technique from that of the basket wall, (2) coloured horizontal or vertical stripes (perhaps also checks) produced by employing elements of contrasting colours, and (3) geometric-patterned twill plaiting. These methods all require deliberate, planned manipulation throughout the basket-making process. In some cases they are used in combination.

Basketry assemblages dating from 2400 BP to 1500 BP display all three types of decoration. The most common, which occurs on checker-plaited as well as open-twined baskets, features a narrow horizontal band immediately below the rim and often another narrow band several centimetres below the rim (Figure 2). These decorative bands are composed of one to three twined or wrapped rows and may incorporate reinforcements. Visually they display rows of diagonal stitches, generally all slanting up to the right (/). Occasionally, the stitches alternate direction in each row, producing a chevron motif. Some specimens feature colour enhancement of the horizontal bands. Even though each example is unique, the decorative style is remarkably consistent. Band width, placement, and general appearance are extremely similar in assemblages from the Fraser delta, Fraser valley, San Juan Island, and Puget Sound.

Wide vertical stripes are common in the Water Hazard collection (1700 BP), especially on open-twined baskets. These stripes have been produced by orienting some warp elements so that the bark-covered (dark) sides face out and placing other elements so that they display split-wood (light) faces. None of the examples is sufficiently complete to determine whether the stripes formed a pattern. This method of decoration is probably more prevalent than available documentation suggests, since most assemblages from the area were analyzed after conservation treatment had obscured evidence of colour contrast.

The third method of decoration, geometric-patterned twill, occurs on baskets from the Water Hazard (1700 BP) and Blundell Road (2200 BP) sites (Figure 4). Apparently, the geometric design covered the entire wall of the respective baskets, though the absence of a complete specimen precludes certainty. All-over patterned weave does not occur in older or younger archaeological collections from the Coast Salish area.

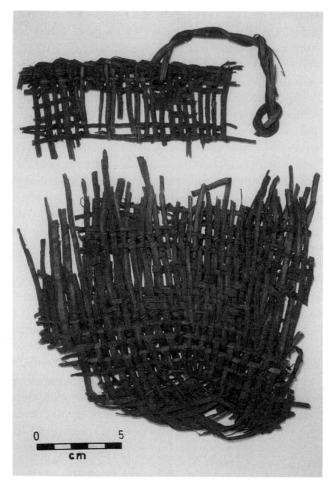

Figure 7. Basket (DhRt 4:10667/8) excavated in 1974 from the 3,000-year-old water-saturated component of the Musqueam Northeast site on Musqueam Indian Reserve 2 (on Point Grey near the mouth of the Fraser River). Woven in plaited-wrapped-twining with wide bands of twill plaiting.

Baskets from the Musqueam Northeast site (3000 BP) also often feature structural decoration. Generally, this consists of one, two, or three wide horizontal bands in a different weaving technique from that of the basket wall. The bands tend to be in the upper two-thirds of the wall and may be as much as 10 cm wide. In some cases, these bands may have been colour-enhanced by contrasting cedar-bark strips with split-wood elements. Although some baskets from the Musqueam Northeast site have decorative wrapped reinforcements that resemble the decoration on ca. 2,000-year-old specimens in appearance and placement, the overall impression of the Musqueam Northeast assemblage is of multiple wide bands, each basket in its own design. The mix of weaves varies considerably and combines different classes. For example, one checker-plaited specimen features three wide bands of diagonal twining; the plaited-wrapped-twined basket illustrated in Figure 7 is decorated with bands of twill plaiting. Croes (1977) characterizes the Musqueam Northeast baskets as "combination weaves" since the alternate decorative weaves occupy appreciable areas. A basket fragment from the Pitt River site (3000 BP) displays similar decoration.

The collection from the Glenrose Cannery site (4300 BP) is too small to define a general style; however, structural decoration is definitely present. For example, the specimen in dual-warp wrapping features a horizontal band, apparently just below the rim. Moreover, undated fragments from the St. Mungo Cannery site that are probably also about 4,000 years old display a series of horizontal bands, some in contrasting colour.

Stylistic Types

Considering material, weaving technique, selvage type, and decoration, archaeological baskets from the Coast Salish area clearly cluster into chronological groups that correspond to the ages of established archaeological cultures or phases. The following summaries of diagnostic characteristics for early, middle, and late time periods are accompanied by lists of the collections that display the respective stylistic types. Except where age can be extrapolated from archaeological context, undated collections are not integrated into the scheme.

- Early Period Basketry
  Age: older than 2900 BP.
  Cultural affiliation: Locarno Beach; tentatively also St. Mungo.
  Collections: Musqueam Northeast, Pitt River; tentatively Glenrose Cannery and St. Mungo Cannery.
  Diagnostic characteristics: relative techno-stylistic diversity; predominance of wrapped weaves including variants not known from other time periods; twill plaiting infrequent and plain, twining infrequent; sparse use of cedar bark; paired-warp wrapped selvages featuring multiple non-intersecting wrapping strands; structural decoration as multiple wide horizontal bands in alternate weaves; non-standardized decorative scheme. (Example: Figure 7.)

- Middle Period Basketry
  Age: 2400 BP to 1500 BP.
  Cultural affiliation: Marpole.

Collections: Water Hazard, DgRs 36, Blundell Road, English Camp, Biederbost; probably also Beach Grove and Sumas Mountain.

Diagnostic characteristics: relative techno-stylistic standardization; predominance of open plain twining and checker plaiting, no wrapped weaves; twill plaiting scarce but strikingly decorative when present; sparse use of cedar bark; elaborate false-braid selvage; structural decoration standardized, occurring as one narrow horizontal band at the rim and a second several centimetres lower, or as all-over patterned twill plaiting; chevron motif. (Example: Figures 2 and 4.)

- Late Period Basketry
  Age: 1300 BP to 600 BP.
  Cultural affiliation: Gulf of Georgia/Stselax.
  Collections: Little Qualicum River, Mary Hill Road, Munk Creek, Fishtown, Conway; tentatively Scowlitz.
  Diagnostic characteristics: relative techno-stylistic simplicity; predominance of open plain twining and checker plaiting; wrapped weaves present, but perhaps not in Puget Sound sub-area; cedar bark used for plaiting (except at Scowlitz); wrapped selvages in variants of "hitched" type; no structural decoration. (Example: Figure 5.)

The Glenrose Cannery site collection (five artifacts), which is 1,000 years older than any other dated specimens, is too small a sample for generalization – even with the addition of the St. Mungo Cannery site finds (four fragments, probably all from the same basket). Although the 4,000-year-old specimens differ in material from younger assemblages, I tentatively grouped them with the Musqueam Northeast collection based on the predominance of wrapped weaves and the presence of structural decoration. More examples are needed to evaluate whether they comprise a distinct stylistic group.

The Scowlitz basketry does not quite fit the stylistic type for its age, nor does it fit well into any of the other basket period types. This could be a factor of the small sample size (five items). Notably, however, the evidence of the basketry parallels conclusions about the lack of fit (into the regional sequence) of other artifact types from the Scowlitz site (Matson 1994). In other words, the stylistic characteristics of the basketry provide independent evidence for conclusions derived from stone artifacts. It is this type of agreement between basketry and stone (and bone, antler, and shell) artifacts that provides a new dimension of Northwest Coast culture history.

Discussion

The following comments address two issues highlighted by the stylistic summaries: the temporal associations of certain basket styles or types and the apparent techno-stylistic elaboration of Marpole-age (2400 BP to 1500 BP) collections. Both of these conclusions are somewhat controversial within the local archaeological community.

Archaeological research in the Coast Salish area has outlined a sequence of culture types that extends back to the seventh millennium BC. These were defined without the benefit of perishable assemblages and with a dearth of stylistically sensitive materials (though Mitchell [1990] and Matson and Coupland [1995] integrate perishables in recently published syntheses). Since not all the regional phases or culture types are well documented and the relationships among them are not well understood, potentially basketry can be highly instructive.

Close correlation between the grouping of the basketry and the independently defined phases/culture types was not expected. Like many other archaeologists who work in the Coast Salish area, I had predicted that when discovered and analyzed, perishable artifacts (such as baskets) would demonstrate cultural continuity throughout the past several thousand years (Bernick 1983:150). Instead, they can be seen to support out-of-favour theories of cultural dislocation (see discussion in Burley 1980:31-39). The basketry evidence sharpens, rather than diffuses, the differences among the archaeological cultures.

At the risk of compounding my "political incorrectness," I further observe that characteristics of the basketry support theories of a cultural "florescence" during Marpole times. The middle period basketry, which coincides in age with the Marpole phase (400 BC to AD 500), exhibits a degree of sophistication that is lacking in both older and younger assemblages. This observation parallels conclusions about other aspects of material culture, such as the incidence and elaboration of art objects, especially stone sculptures (Burley 1980; Matson and Coupland 1995:203-208; Mitchell 1990; cf. Holm 1990). Moreover, the notable standardization of techno-stylistic basketry attributes and the complexity of the preferred selvage construction during Marpole times hint at craft specialization, which also repeats suggestions that have been advanced on the basis of other artifact types (Holm 1990:191).

The congruence between basketry and other artifact types is also manifested in apparent similarities between late-period archaeological assemblages and the ethnographic record. The previously mentioned examples of open wrapped twining and cross-stitch wrapping illustrate techno-stylistic continuity during the past 1,000 years, and the same is probably true for plaited cedar-bark baskets. The late period basketry may also reflect geographic differences that have been noted for other aspects of Coast Salish culture, specifically in respect to a breach approximately at the entrance to Puget Sound (see Mitchell 1971). These lines of inquiry, though undoubtedly pertinent, fall outside the scope of the present discussion (and are made difficult by the paucity of documentation and examples of modern Coast Salish woven basketry).

The preceding discussion emphasizes stylistic differences even though considerable similarities also exist. All the assemblages from the Coast Salish area are recognizably Northwest Coast, which signifies a cultural tradition that is thousands of years old. Nonetheless, people in the Coast Salish area did not always make baskets in the same way. Details of basketry construction and style changed, and they did so at the same times as other changes appear in the archaeological record.

Conclusions

Although I am convinced that stylistic variation in basketry assemblages from the Coast Salish area reflects cultural diversity through time, available data do not suffice to interpret the nature of that diversity. Explanations may be forthcoming when we have more and larger samples, from all time periods and representing the full geographic range of the region and beyond. Analyzing and describing unreported existing collections (especially from Washington state) would be a logical starting point.

Culturally determined basketry attributes such as weave types, decoration, and selvage construction cross-cut functional and morphological categories and provide a means to trace ethnicity. Basketry assemblages from the Coast Salish area of British Columbia and Washington display that kind of stylistic variation. The observed variation clusters chronologically into periods that coincide with independently established phases/culture types, and mirror observations about artistic expression in other media. Thus, basketry, and wet sites that contain basketry, promise to be invaluable data sources for archaeological research in the Coast Salish area and the entire Northwest Coast.

Acknowledgments

I sincerely thank the British Columbia archaeological community for supporting my research into wet-site basketry over the years. I am grateful to Astrida Blukis Onat and Julie Stein for showing me specimens from Washington state and to Dale Croes for unpublished information on the Munk Creek find. Radiocarbon dates for DhRq 19 are courtesy of the British Columbia Archaeology Branch. Not least, thanks to Joyce Johnson for helping with photography.

References Cited

Adovasio, James M.
   1977 *Basketry Technology: A Guide to Identification and Analysis.* Aldine, Chicago.
   1986 Artifacts and Ethnicity: Basketry as an Indicator of Territoriality and Population Movements in the Prehistoric Great Basin. In *Anthropology of the Desert West,* edited by Carol J. Condie and Don D. Fowler, pp. 43-88. University of Utah Anthropological Papers No. 110. University of Utah Press, Salt Lake City.

Arcas Consulting Archeologists, Ltd.
   1991 *Archaeological Impact Assessment, South Delta Watermain and Storm Sewer Upgrading, South Delta, B.C.* Permit 1991-89. Report on file, British Columbia Archaeology Branch, Victoria.
Archer, David J.W., and Kathryn Bernick
   1990 Perishable Artifacts from the Musqueam Northeast Site. Ms. on file, British Columbia Archaeology Branch, Victoria.
Bernick, Kathryn
   1981 Perishable Artifacts from the Pitt River Site, DhRq 21. Ms. on file, British Columbia Archaeology Branch, Victoria.
   1983 *A Site Catchment Analysis of the Little Qualicum River Site, DiSc 1: A Wet Site on the East Coast of Vancouver Island, B.C.* National Museum of Man Mercury Series, Archaeological Survey of Canada Paper 118. National Museums of Canada, Ottawa.
   1987 The Potential of Basketry for Reconstructing Cultural Diversity on the Northwest Coast. In *Ethnicity and Culture,* edited by Réginald Auger, Margaret F. Glass, Scott MacEachern, and Peter H. McCartney, pp. 251-257. Proceedings of the 18th Annual Chacmool Conference. Archaeological Association, University of Calgary, AB.
   1989a *Basketry and Cordage from Hesquiat Harbour, British Columbia.* Royal BC Museum, Victoria, in press. Ms. 1989.
   1989b *Water Hazard (DgRs 30) Artifact Recovery Project Report.* Permit 1988-55. Report on file, British Columbia Archaeology Branch, Victoria.
   1991 *Wet Site Archaeology in the Lower Mainland Region of British Columbia.* Report on file, British Columbia Archaeology Branch, Victoria.
   1994a Basketry, Cordage and Related Artifacts. In *Masada IV: The Yigael Yadin Excavations 1963-1965, Final Reports,* pp. 283-317. Israel Exploration Society and the Hebrew University, Jerusalem.
   1994b *Waterlogged Deposits at the Scowlitz Site: Final Report of 1992-1993 Archaeological Investigations.* Permit 1992-117. Report on file, British Columbia Archaeology Branch, Victoria.
Blukis Onat, Astrida R.
   1976 A Fishtown Site, 45SK99. In *The Excavation of Water-Saturated Archaeological Sites (Wet Sites) on the Northwest Coast of North America,* edited by Dale R. Croes, pp. 122-145. National Museum of Man Mercury Series, Archaeological Survey of Canada Paper 50. National Museums of Canada, Ottawa.
Burley, David V.
   1980 *Marpole: Anthropological Reconstructions of a Prehistoric Northwest Coast Culture Type.* Department of Archaeology, Simon Fraser University, Burnaby, BC.
Croes, Dale R.
   1977 *Basketry from the Ozette Village Archaeological Site: A Technological, Functional, and Comparative Study.* PhD dissertation, Washington State University. University Microfilms, Ann Arbor, MI.
   1992 An Evolving Revolution in Wet Site Research on the Northwest Coast of North America. In *The Wetland Revolution in Prehistory,* edited by Bryony Coles, pp. 99-111. WARP Occasional Paper 6. Department of History and Archaeology, University of Exeter, UK.
   1995 *The Hoko River Archaeological Site Complex.* Washington State University Press, Pullman.
Eldridge, Morley
   1991 *The Glenrose Cannery Wet Component: A Significance Assessment.* Permit 1990-24. Report on file, British Columbia Archaeology Branch, Victoria.
Holm, Margaret Ann
   1990 *Prehistoric Northwest Coast Art: A Stylistic Analysis of the Archaeological Record.* Master's thesis, Department of Anthropology and Sociology, University of British Columbia, Vancouver.

Jones, Joan Megan
  1976 *Northwest Coast Indian Basketry, a Stylistic Analysis.* PhD dissertation, University of Washington. University Microfilms, Ann Arbor, MI.
Laforêt, Andrea
  1971 Two Basketry Fragments from Lulu Island. Ms. on file, Laboratory of Archaeology, University of British Columbia, Vancouver.
Mason, Otis Tufton
  1988 *American Indian Basketry.* Reprinted. Dover, New York. Originally published 1904, *Indian Basketry: Studies in a Textile Art without Machinery* (2 vols.), Doubleday, Page, New York.
Matson, R.G.
  1994 *Excavations at Scowlitz, Stage II: Report on the 1993 Excavations at Scowlitz.* Permit 1993-45. Report on file, British Columbia Archaeology Branch, Victoria.
Matson, R.G., and Gary Coupland
  1995 *The Prehistory of the Northwest Coast.* Academic Press, Toronto.
Mitchell, Donald H.
  1971 *Archaeology of the Gulf of Georgia Area, a Natural Region and Its Culture Types.* Syesis, Vol. 4, Suppl.1. British Columbia Provincial Museum, Victoria.
  1990 Prehistory of the Coasts of Southern British Columbia and Northern Washington. In *Northwest Coast,* edited by Wayne Suttles, pp. 340-358. Handbook of North American Indians, vol. 7, William C. Sturtevant, general editor. Smithsonian Institution, Washington, DC.
Munsell, David A.
  1976 Excavation of the Conway Wetsite 45SK59b, Conway, Washington. In *The Excavation of Water-Saturated Archaeological Sites (Wet Sites) on the Northwest Coast of North America,* edited by Dale R. Croes, pp. 86-121. National Museum of Man Mercury Series, Archaeological Survey of Canada Paper 50. National Museums of Canada, Ottawa.
Nordquist, Delmar
  1960a Basketry from Site 45SN100, General Comments. *Washington Archaeologist* 4(9): 2-6.
  1960b Open Plaited Basketry from 45SN100. *Washington Archaeologist* 4(11):2-5.
  1976 45SN100 – the Biederbost Site, Kidd's Duval Site. In *The Excavation of Water-Saturated Archaeological Sites (Wet Sites) on the Northwest Coast of North America,* edited by Dale R. Croes, pp. 186-200. National Museum of Man Mercury Series, Archaeological Survey of Canada Paper 50. National Museums of Canada, Ottawa.
Smith, Derek G.
  1964 *Archaeological Excavations at the Beach Grove Site, DgRs 1, During the Summer of 1962.* Bachelor's thesis, Department of Anthropology and Sociology, University of British Columbia, Vancouver.
Sprague, Roderick
  1976 The Submerged Finds from the Prehistoric Component, English Camp, San Juan Island, Washington. In *The Excavation of Water-Saturated Archaeological Sites (Wet Sites) on the Northwest Coast of North America,* edited by Dale R. Croes, pp. 78-85. National Museum of Man Mercury Series, Archaeological Survey of Canada Paper 50. National Museums of Canada, Ottawa.
Suttles, Wayne (editor)
  1990 *Northwest Coast.* Handbook of North American Indians, vol. 7, William C. Sturtevant, general editor. Smithsonian Institution, Washington, DC.
Turnbaugh, Sarah Peabody, and William A. Turnbaugh
  1986 *Indian Baskets.* Schiffer Publishing, West Chester, PA.

The Boston Back Bay Fish Weirs

Elena B. Décima and Dena F. Dincauze

The discovery of prehistoric aquatic features has been mostly an oddity in the archaeological record of New England. The discovery of fish weirs, understood as wooden or stone fences, enclosures, or barriers set in water for taking fish, is no exception.

The Boylston Street fish weirs of Boston, Massachusetts, have been well known among New England archaeologists since the publication of Frederick Johnson's excavation results in 1942 (Johnson 1942; see also Johnson 1949). The area where the weirs were once located is nowadays Back Bay (Figure 1), one of Boston's neighbourhoods; this area, filled during the nineteenth century, was once a large estuarine bay at the mouth of the Charles River.

The first exposure of the weirs' wooden stakes goes back to 1903, when excavators of a subway line under Boylston Street happened upon sharpened stakes. The stakes, clearly not the usual wooden pilings that support most of the old buildings of the area, were recognized as part of "what appears to be a prehistoric fish weir" (Boston Transit Commission 1913:44). Building construction on Boylston Street in 1939, 1957, and 1986, and in the immediate vicinity in 1946 (Figure 2), exposed additional segments of many weirs that once spread over more than 2 ha of the ancient bay.

The fish weirs have been described as a structure "composed of about 65,000 stakes ... distributed over more than two acres ... of mud flats and marsh land" (Johnson 1942:1), as large facilities for the exploitation of estuarine resources, and as large environment-modifying facilities (Dincauze 1985). The archaeological investigations of Johnson's team in the 1940s represent the first scientific examination of the structures, a remarkable study in interdisciplinary research (Johnson 1942). However, their interpretation relied on analogies with twentieth-century coastal weirs, which are built to trap large numbers of fish running in longshore currents of impressive speed and tidal amplitude.

The recent archaeological work of the 1980s supports a simpler picture. This interpretation proposes that the majority of the Back Bay weir

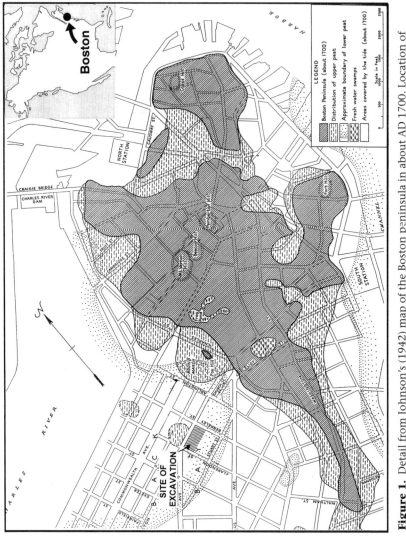

Figure 1. Detail from Johnson's (1942) map of the Boston peninsula in about AD 1700. Location of excavation is at left.

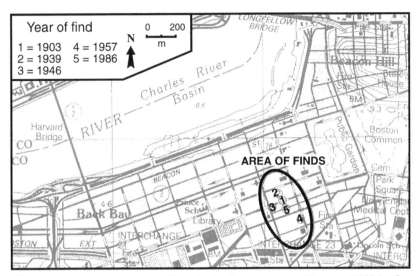

Figure 2. Location of fish weir finds in the Back Bay area of Boston. *USGS South Boston 1987.*

structures were built over a long period of time, as small, short-lived, uncomplicated tidal operations. The stakes and brushwork (horizontal wood) were designed to permit fish to swim over them during high tide; they then acted as barriers when the tide went out, preventing the fish from escaping the resulting enclosure. Baskets, bowls, scoops, and dip nets could have been used easily by women, men, and children to gather the fish almost effortlessly.

The 1986 Project

The construction of two 25-story buildings (covering 100 m x 78 m) in the Back Bay area, across from the old New England Life (NEL) building where Johnson's excavation had taken place (Johnson 1942), gave impetus to the 1986 archaeological project. The project was carried out by Timelines, Inc., with Dincauze as senior archaeologist and Décima as project archaeologist. The goals focused on obtaining a better understanding of the form, size, and function of the features, as well as obtaining possible evidence of human influence on the vegetation and estuarine fauna as an indirect result of the weirs' presence and function. It was expected that the results would augment and clarify the information gathered from the earlier exposures of the weirs.

The fieldwork, unfortunately, was far from ideal. It took place amid huge construction machines during the harsh New England winter. The team of archaeologists managed, nevertheless, to excavate two areas of the site, approximately 70 m apart (a total of approximately 7 m²), and to register

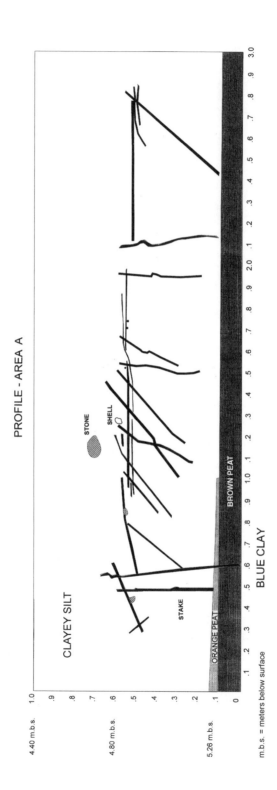

Figure 3. Profile view of Area A, showing stratigraphy and vertical distribution of stakes.

exposures of fish weir fragments in another 12 locations. Additionally, isolated stake finds were monitored and registered.

A master sediment core, obtained from the immediate vicinity of one of the excavation areas, provided samples for specialized studies of pollen, sediment, shell, and diatoms. Additional sediment samples were collected to process by flotation. Microscope examination of all the wood specimens and a tree-ring study completed the studies.

The fieldwork took place in two stages. The first stage, or "slurry wall phase," consisted of monitoring the machine excavation of sediments on three sides of the construction site where a slurry wall was being built; the object was to check for the presence of stakes and brushwork in order to potentially predict the locations of the weir structures. The second stage, or "foundation phase," included systematic and exploratory excavation.

Descriptive Results

Though the fieldwork was conducted in a piecemeal fashion, following the schedule and whims of construction, it was possible to observe segments of fish weirs that on analysis and radiocarbon dating proved to be part of a series of structures spanning more than 1,000 years.

Area A Structures

The results from the first excavation area (Area A), together with observations of nearby exploratory vertical units, clearly reveal the presence of stakes aligned in a roughly east-west direction. (In contrast, the majority of Johnson's concentrations or alignments across the street were oriented on a predominantly north-south direction.) The fieldwork unveiled a wooden structure that has no analogues with the lake and river weirs that prevail in the literature (e.g., Johnston and Cassavoy 1978; Petersen et al. 1994) or with the twentieth-century coastal weirs against which the Boylston Street "Fishweirs" were compared in the studies of the 1930s and 1940s. The bulk of the stakes and brushwork recovered from this first excavation appeared at an elevation of 4.76 m below Boston City Base (i.e., 1.72 m below USCGS Mean Sea Level) (Figure 3). With the exception of one stake, the bottom of which was embedded in a glacial blue clay substratum, all the wood was found within a clayey silt layer. Fourteen stakes and more than 90 brushwork fragments were recovered from this area. All but one of the recovered stakes (broken and unbroken) measure between 30 cm and 84 cm in length; the majority fall between 1 cm and 2.5 cm in diameter. All but three have broken tops. At the bottom, or deeper ends, 12 stakes are split, seven have been snapped, and three are now broken; two show signs of having been crushed against the sediments. None has been cut or shaped with tools. The irregularities of the scar surfaces (with jagged edges in some cases) suggest that the branches were probably torn by hand from trees, ripping the wood

Table 1

Radiocarbon dates from the Boston Back Bay fish weirs

Lab no.	Uncorrected ^{14}C date at 1σ	Sample locus[1]	Material	Depth below BCB[2] in cm	^{13}C corrected date at 1σ
Beta 24955	1790 ± 60	C8, s#54	sediment	-115, -123	1890 ± 60
Beta 24954	2090 ± 60	C8, s#46	sediment	-190	2170 ± 60
Beta 24953	3010 ± 80	C8, s#42	sediment	-225	3090 ± 80
Beta 24952	3470 ± 70	C8, s#36	sediment	-280	3540 ± 70
Beta 24951	3480 ± 110	C8, s#32	sediment	-305, -313	3570 ± 110
Beta 25163	3760 ± 70	SU11	wood, brush	-420	3700 ± 70
Beta 27611	3770 ± 80	SU10	wood, stake	vertical	3710 ± 80
Chicago 418	3851 ± 390	JH	wood	above stakes	—
Beta 27609	3950 ± 100	Area B, EU6	wood, stake	stake in blue clay	3910 ± 100
Wisconsin 1957	3990 ± 70	MU1	wood, stake	-482	3890 ± 70
Beta 27610	4200 ± 140	MU4	wood, stake	-550 (estimated)	4150 ± 140
Wisconsin 1958	4217 ± 70	MU1	wood, stake	-482	4120 ± 70
Geochron 14019W	4260 ± 60	MU1	wood, stake	-482	4175 ± 60
Beta 25161	4270 ± 70	MU9	wood, brush	-528	4260 ± 70
Geochron 14019B	4935 ± 130	MU1	wood, stake	-482	4315 ± 160
Beta 20107	4440 ± 90	MU1	wood, stake	-482	4340 ± 90
Humble Oil 1475	4450 ± 130	IBM	wood, brush	-510	—
Humble Oil 1474	4500 ± 130	IBM	wood, brush	-510	—
Beta 27606	4530 ± 80	Area A, EU5	wood, stake	vertical	4470 ± 80
Beta 25162	4550 ± 70	SU5	wood	-517	4540 ± 70
Beta 24950	4580 ± 80	C8, s#21	sediment	-405, -415	4630 ± 80
Beta 20106	4720 ± 70	MU1	wood, stake	-482	4690 ± 70

Beta 27607	4840 ± 170	Area A, EU5	wood, brush	horizontal	4750 ± 170
Humble Oil 1902	4860 ± 130	IBM	wood, brush	-510	—
Beta 24987/ETH		C8	sedge achenes	-489	5125 ± 115
Wisconsin 1959	5330 ± 70	SU6	wood	-550	5300 ± 70
Humble Oil 1118	5600 ± 140	IBM	lower peat	-568, -570	—
Beta 24949	5620 ± 90	C8, s#8-11	sediment	-505, -510	5630 ± 90
Chicago 417	5717 ± 500	JH	lower peat	-624	—

[1] Key to loci: C8 = master core, EU = excavation unit, IBM = old IBM site located within the 1986 project area, JH = John Hancock building, MU = monitoring unit, SU = sample unit.

[2] Boston City Base = 3.04 m above United States Coast Guard Service (USCGS) Mean Sea Level.

in the process. Whichever the cutting method, the result was a thinned end, and driving it into the soft clayey silt was likely effortless.

Sassafras (*Sassafras albidum*), hickory (*Carya* sp.), and dogwood (*Cornus florida*) are the three leading species amounting to 62.5 percent of the identified wood. Looking at the order of vertical and oblique stakes, from east to west, we see a tentative pattern to the species distribution, reflecting, perhaps, the stockpiling arrangement: the first four are hickory, the fifth and sixth are white ash (*Fraxinus* sp.), the seventh is sassafras, the next four are dogwood, the twelfth is sassafras, the thirteenth is maple (*Acer* sp.), and the last is birch (*Betula* sp.). Only six stakes are greater than 2.5 cm in diameter, three of these also being the longest. It is possible that these bigger stakes, driven deeper into the mud, supported and anchored the shorter and thinner stakes. The preserved weir remains include two of the bigger vertical stakes anchored in blue clay, approximately 11 m apart, and 18 thinner stakes. However, these represent a small segment of fish weir (the longest continuous segment for which we have information being less than 3 m).

Only one layer of brushwork was detected, within 25 cm of the tops of the stakes (whereas Johnson [1942] reports two layers of brushwork). Most of the brushwork, or horizontal wood, was lying on a plane perpendicular to the stakes, alongside or between stake alignments; it was not woven among them, as the term "wattles" implies. Thirty percent of the brushwork is sassafras. The pieces vary in length from 2 cm to 70 cm, but this is not representative of their original dimensions since many were found broken or broke while being excavated. With diameters of less than 2 cm (with a single exception), the horizontal wood is slightly thinner than the stakes.

Thus, the original structure would have consisted of sparse walls of oblique and vertical stakes with brushwork placed horizontally between them, against the top section of the stakes. Noticeable characteristics, shared by all the weirs we observed, include the small size of constituent branches, an absence of artifacts, and an absence of basketry, netting, cordage, or wattles that could have been part of a trap used in conjunction with weir leads. Radiocarbon analysis for two pieces of wood from this area gives dates of 4470 ± 80 BP and 4750 ± 170 BP (Table 1).

Area B Structures

The second excavation area (Area B) revealed a different picture: more brushwork (330 vs. 90) and fewer stakes (10 vs. 14) than in Area A (Figure 4). The stake distribution suggests a northwest-southeast alignment, with possibly two lines of stakes. The brushwork resembles an intersecting perpendicular lattice oriented northwest-southeast and northeast-southwest. Most of the brushwork is located 15 cm to 27 cm above the blue clay substratum (vs. 60 cm to 70 cm in Area A). The majority of the stakes are very short, ranging in length from 18 cm to 40 cm (whereas the average length throughout the site is around 50 cm), and all are driven through the underlying blue clay. All but two of the stake tops are broken. Three bottoms are snapped, four are torn and split, and one is slightly crushed. One of the unbroken top ends has been shaped to a point. Beech (*Fagus grandifolia*) and oak (*Quercus* sp.) seem to have been favoured in this area, accounting for 72 percent of the identified wood. One piece of wood from Area B was dated, yielding a date of 3910 ± 100 BP (^{13}C corrected).

This Area B structure has a large proportion of wood fragments that had been cut in the growing season, a characteristic present in "many" of the wood samples of Johnson's excavation (1942:84), about 100 m away, but quite rare in our total sample. These similarities and the proximity of the locations led us to entertain the hypothesis that the feature in Area B may be an end section of one of the weirs previously found in the NEL site.

Chronology

The research undertaken in the 1930s by Johnson's team suggested an age of between 3,700 and 3,400 years for the NEL weirs, based on desiccation of European bogs of the Subboreal period (Johnson 1942:122-123). The depth of the IBM stakes, recovered in 1946 during construction of the IBM building, suggested greater antiquity (Table 1); radiocarbon dating subsequently placed these weir fragments between 4,900 and 4,500 years of age.

Twenty-three ^{14}C dates obtained for the 1986 project definitely show that the archaeological features represent a series of constructions that range over approximately 1,500 years. The oldest dated weir element is about 5,300 years old, the youngest about 3,700 years old. This age range subsumes the IBM stakes, which are from the same area. The NEL features seem to belong to the late weir-building period. The few stakes to the southeast, undated, are estimated by the authors to be older than 5,000 years. The long time span demonstrates without doubt the existence of several fish weirs (rather than a single large one) that were constructed in Back Bay.

Specialized Analyses

Sediment

Analysis of the master sediment core shows that the fish-weir elements (at least those in the vicinity of the core location) are in a zone dominated by clay deposits. The clay source is probably glacial, redeposited on brackish waters quiet enough to support deposition of fine sediments. Tidal amplitude at this time in the inundation of the Gulf of Maine is estimated around 1 m at maximum. The sediment qualities in the weir zone are characteristic of subtidal muds. Three stratigraphic units (lower, middle, and upper) were recognized; at the base of the lower unit, which contains the fish weir structures, the geologists see a change in sediments, which they interpret as a

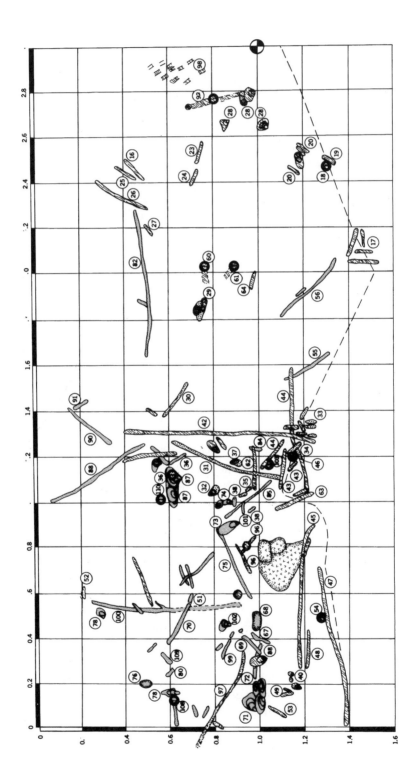

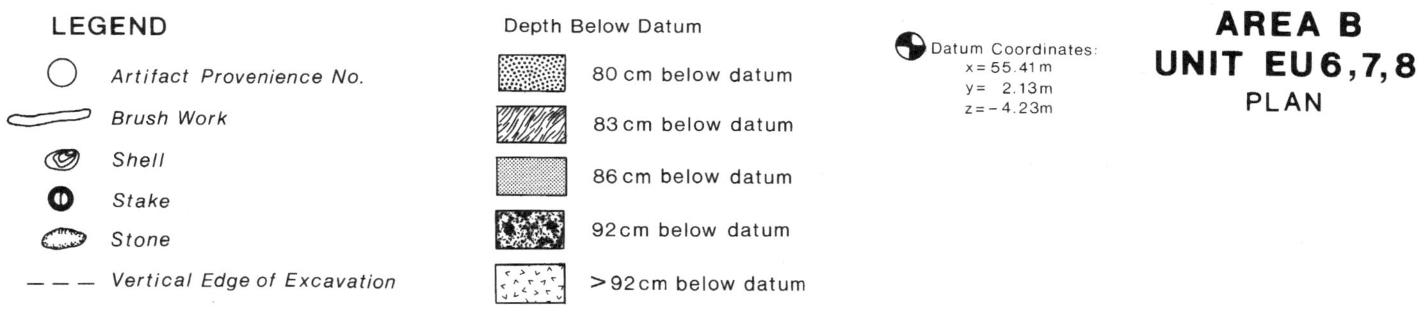

AREA B
UNIT EU 6,7,8
PLAN

Datum Coordinates:
x = 55.41 m
y = 2.13 m
z = -4.23 m

Depth Below Datum

80 cm below datum

83 cm below datum

86 cm below datum

92 cm below datum

> 92 cm below datum

LEGEND

◯ *Artifact Provenience No.*

⬭ *Brush Work*

🐚 *Shell*

● *Stake*

🥚 *Stone*

– – – *Vertical Edge of Excavation*

Figure 4. Plan view of Excavation Units 6, 7, and 8 in Area B showing distribution of finds.

transition from intertidal to subtidal environment (Rosen and Maybury 1988). Based on this analysis, they postulate that the fish weirs would have been set just below low-tide level in shallow and relatively quiet waters.

The grain-size chart registers an increase in particle size of sediments from layers dating just before 3500 BP, suggesting dramatic changes in local conditions. The changes, represented by increases in tidal amplitude and energy (reflecting rising sea level and a higher energy tidal system in the entire Gulf of Maine), affected the quiet, shallow water environment.

The younger weir structures of the 1986 excavations (SU10-12) and Johnson's trench across the street may reflect these changes. Both show an increase in the number and proportion of stout stakes and in the density of the wood (Johnson 1942:20-38, and personal observations) – an adaptation, perhaps, to stronger wave action and deeper water.

Pollen

The pollen diagram, which shows a predominance of hardwoods, agrees with other studies of the regional pollen rain at the time (Newby and Webb 1988). The ancient bay was rimmed with salt marshes, freshwater ponds, and swamps supporting alder (*Alnus* sp.) and red maples. Most of the species identified by pollen analysis are represented in the weir wood, white pine (*Pinus strobus*) being the conspicuous exception. The data do not indicate anthropogenic stress on the local vegetation, as might be expected if young wood were harvested in the quantities that have been calculated in earlier estimates (Johnson 1942:1). The pollen analysis (and the wood analysis) indicate a warm temperate climate during weir times, nearly like the present.

Wood

Two hundred and ten samples of wood were analyzed for species, number of growth rings, diameter, season of death (or time of harvest), and growth characteristics (compression and symmetry) at the University of Massachusetts, Boston (Kaplan et al. 1988). The species represented match those identified from pollen analysis, except for the noticeable absence of white pine in the weir structures (white pine was an important part of the forest of the time). In 92 percent of the cases, it was determined that the weir wood was harvested during the dormant season, before the middle of April and after the end of October. These results contrast with Johnson's (1942) findings at the NEL location, where most of the wood was harvested during the growing season.

The species analysis reveals some differences among the stake clusters. In Area A, the weir segment represented in units SU10, SU11, and SU12 has a predominance of beech, whereas the cluster in units SU6 and SU7 has mainly oak and no beech. In Area B, which is contemporary with the SU10-SU12 cluster, beech is the main species. Area A has the only stake cluster with a dominance of sassafras.

When the wood species data are compared to the radiocarbon sequence for the site, changes through time can be discerned. Specifically, sassafras, present in the older Area A structures, seems to have been replaced by beech and alder (*Alnus* sp.) in the younger SU10-SU12 cluster in our site. On the other hand, sassafras is the main species represented at the younger NEL site area.

Fauna

The number of fish bones recovered (113 fragments) constitutes a very small sample. Species include tomcod (*Microgadus tomcod*), flounder (Pleuronectidae), eel (*Anguilla rostrata*), herring (Clupeidae), and possibly sturgeon (*Acipenser* sp.). Most of the fragments (71) were unidentifiable. The predominant species is tomcod.

Today warm, brackish, shallow, estuarine waters in southern New England are home to several species of small fish, among them tomcod and mummichogs (*Fundulus heteroclitus*), or killifish. Tomcod are bottom feeders living in shallow brackish, or even fresh, water, ranging from Nova Scotia to New Jersey. They spawn during the winter in estuaries, where they may be numerous year-round. They can be taken in weirs or by hook and line. In habitat and size, tomcod are compatible with the function of small, inshore tidal weirs. Mummichogs, on the other hand, move inshore with the tide and may be easily caught in tidal pools until freed by the incoming tide. Weirs such as the Back Bay structure could have easily trapped mummichogs and other small inshore feeders. No mummichog bones were identified in our samples, but this could be because of their small size and fragility.

Discussion

Reinvestigation of the Boylston Street fish weir has demonstrated that there were many small weirs, rather than one large one, near the shore of the ancient Back Bay. The weirs spanned approximately one thousand years, during which time sea level was rising against the sloping shores. The ambiguity in functional interpretation following the initial investigations in the 1930s and 1940s appears to be the result of the application of an inappropriate analogue, specifically, large commercial weirs built to trap schools of fish by taking advantage of the energy of marine longshore currents.

The small weirs that we examined were built sequentially along the shores of the former bay, probably not very far from the coast of the time, in the intertidal zone. Our analysis shows changes through time in the characteristics of the saplings and the branches used to build the structures. The thin stakes were driven into the muddy deposits of the bay, sometimes extending into the top of the underlying blue clay. Lines of stakes and brushwork fences paralleled the shoreline along natural contours on the sloping fore-shore. As the sea level rose and the coastal environment changed, the builders used more robust stakes and apparently had to repair or reinforce weir structures, even in the summer. Increased higher tidal energy moved larger quantities of coarser sediments onto the foreshore, which likely buried the structures more frequently than did the fine sediments mobilized previously. Increased sedimentation rendered the weirs less efficient and required more frequent maintenance. The changing environmental conditions eventually rendered the facilities unusable. By 3500 BP, people had abandoned this stretch of coast.

The series of radiocarbon dates now available (Table 1) confirms that the Back Bay weirs existed during the Late Archaic period, when small groups of hunters-gatherers-fishers lived in New England. The absence of culturally diagnostic artifacts, in both the Johnson investigations and our own, precludes associating the builders, maintainers, and users of the many fish weirs with any particular tradition of the Late Archaic period. Chronologically, the weir features begin with the time of the Laurentian tradition and continue through the Small Point and the Susquehanna traditions (Dincauze 1975; Snow 1980). The time span indicated for the Back Bay weirs coincides with the time of construction and use of large freshwater river-current weirs in northeastern North America – at Atherley Narrows, Ontario, and at Sebasticook, Maine (Johnston and Cassavoy 1978; Petersen et al. 1994).

Late Archaic subsistence activities were oriented toward harvesting seasonally abundant resources. Exploitation of a wide range of terrestrial, riverine, estuarine, and maritime resources was characteristic of prehistoric economies in northeastern North America from initial settlement (about 12,000 BP to 10,000 BP). By the beginning of the Late Archaic period, ca. 6000 BP, land-use patterns include the partitioning of resource-collecting and residence areas. Foraging territories were approximately delimited by watersheds, and each group exploited its own particular area (Dincauze 1975). The technology and the workforce available in the Late Archaic period were entirely adequate to the task of constructing simple facilities to trap small fish swimming with the tide, like those indicated by the Back Bay finds.

Reconstruction of the spatial arrangement of the weir structures within Back Bay and understanding in detail how they would have been used await a more precise description of the environment of the area during the fourth and fifth millennia BP. We expect to learn such information from intensive spatial analysis of data within the investigated areas. Basically, we believe that the weirs were built as low fences following the curves of the paleoshores.

The full length of any one structure has not yet been reconstructed. We do, however, know that the coastal tidal weirs from the Late Archaic period are not comparable in size, construction, or method of operation to weirs that use strong currents in rivers or along ocean shores. Their only

Figure 5. Artist's rendering of Boston fish weir. *Drawing by Elaine Chamberlain.*

similarity is that all types are facilities for catching fish. Understanding the differences is critical to understanding the Back Bay weirs.

At the time the Back Bay weirs were built and used, environmental conditions differed considerably from those of the region today. Sea level was 1 m to 2 m lower, tidal characteristics differed, and the climate was warmer. Low tidal amplitude, low tidal energy, a sloping shore, and warm, brackish water of weir times are probably essential requirements for the fish-catching technology displayed by the Back Bay weirs. The low brush fences constructed with small, widely spaced stakes would not have withstood coastal currents. They would not have been designed to sieve fish out of strongly flowing water. Rather, they would have held fish near the shoreline during ebb tides, retaining them in reach of wading fisherfolk. They may have been inspired by the behaviour of small fish, such as mummichogs, that are trapped naturally in tidal pools at low tide (Bigelow and Schroeder 1953:163).

Conclusion

The Back Bay structures appear to have been small, uncomplicated operations, protruding little if at all above mean sea level, apparently built as spring weather warmed the waters of the bay. Constructed on a sloping foreshore in ways that required a very small workforce, the small weirs had relatively short use lives. They represent a simple, low-cost, dependable system that produced a reliable but undramatic supply of marine proteins (Figure 5).

Shallow, brackish waters of the Back Bay area 4,000 to 5,000 years ago provided a perfect setting for small tidal weirs. As a result of a changing microtopography and increasing sedimentation, the environment disappeared and the weirs were abandoned. This reconstruction, though based on analysis of the structures, is nonetheless speculative. Using modern analogies would potentially lead us further astray. The initial interpretation of the Boylston Street "Fishweir" errs for this reason. It is time to devote attention and innovative critical analyses to prehistoric freshwater weirs, lest we overestimate them in the image of our own technology.

Acknowledgments

The authors would like to thank Gerald D. Hines Interests, who funded the archaeological work, and all the construction workers at the site who, for two long years, helped and encouraged the field crew.

References Cited

Bigelow, Henry B., and William C. Schroeder
   1953 *Fishes of the Gulf of Maine.* Fishery Bulletin 74, vol. 53. [United States] Fish and Wildlife Service, Washington, DC.
Boston Transit Commission
   1913 *Report of the Chief Engineer Edmund S. Davis. Nineteenth Annual Report for the year ending June 13, 1913.* E.W. Doyle, Boston, MA.
Dincauze, Dena F.
   1975 The Late Archaic Period in Southern New England. *Arctic Anthropology* 12(2):23-34.
   1985 Research Design. In *Reconnaissance Archaeological Study for the 500 Boylston Street Project,* compiled by Michael Roberts, pp. 6-9. Prepared by Timelines, Inc., on file at the Massachusetts Historical Commission, Boston.
Johnson, Frederick
   1942 *The Boylston Street Fishweir.* Phillips Academy Foundation, Andover, MA.
Johnson, Frederick (editor)
   1949 *The Boylston Street Fishweir II.* Phillips Academy Foundation, Andover, MA.
Johnston, Richard B., and Kenneth A. Cassavoy
   1978 The Fishweirs at Atherley Narrows, Ontario. *American Antiquity* 43:697-709.
Kaplan, Lawrence, Mary B. Smith, and Lesley Sneddon
   1988 Wood Materials from 500 Boylston Street. Ms. prepared for Timelines, Inc., Littleton, MA.
Newby, Paige E., and Thomson Webb, III
   1988 Pollen and Sediments Records from 500 Boylston Street, Boston, MA. Ms. prepared for Timelines, Inc., Littleton, MA.
Newby, Paige E., P. Tzedakis, and Thomson Webb, III
   1987 Pollen and Sediment Records in Mendon, Massachusetts. Ms. on file, Public Archaeology Lab Inc., Pawtucket, RI.
Petersen, James B., B.S. Robinson, D.F. Belknap, J.Stark, and L.K. Kaplan
   1994 An Archaic and Woodland Period Fish Weir Complex in Central Maine. *Archaeology of Eastern North America* 22:197-222.
Rosen, Peter S., and Lynn Maybury
   1988 Geologic Evolution of the Inner Boston Harbor Estuary. Ms. prepared for Timelines, Inc., Littleton, MA.
Snow, Dean R.
   1980 *The Archaeology of New England.* Academic Press, New York.

Part 3:
Fishing Technologies on the Northwest Coast

Introduction

The Northwest Coast enjoys legendary status in the discipline of anthropology, comprising a unique culture area that according to European-based models of social evolution should not exist. Contrary to "textbook theories," the aboriginal societies of the northwest coast of North America achieved relatively high levels of social complexity based on a food-collecting subsistence economy centred on fishing. Scholars seeking to explain this seeming anomaly have amassed impressive amounts of ethnographic information over the years. Archaeological research, though obviously pertinent for understanding the development of the "Northwest Coast cultural pattern," has not received comparable attention. This, in part, is due to the large proportion of organic material, especially wood and bark, in the inventory of the indigenous material culture. Large items such as houses and watercraft, as well as furniture, coffins, and numerous small articles, were made entirely from perishable materials that do not normally survive in the archaeological record. Such materials are, however, preserved in water-saturated anaerobic deposits, and recent attention to wet sites has been expanding the horizons of anthropological archaeologists.

The authors of the chapters in Part 3 address aspects of fishing technology revealed by examining wet-site archaeological data. They discuss recent discoveries and current research with the intention of sharing information and ideas. It is important to remember, however, even while marvelling at the remarkably ancient and well-preserved vegetal remains, that these types of sites do not tell the whole story and that wetland archaeology is integrally connected to "dryland" archaeology. Moreover, wet-site archaeological research of fishing technologies is not unique to the Northwest Coast. (Two accounts of similar sites in other places appear in this volume – Décima and Dincauze's reinterpretation of a fish weir on the Atlantic coast of North America, and Gilman's account of management planning of intertidal fish weir features in England.)

A recurring theme in all five chapters about the archaeology of Northwest Coast fishing concerns the little attention accorded to wet sites. Whether they discuss artifacts, radiocarbon dates, or environmental context – all of which potentially can provide information about fishing activities that is not available from conventional archaeological sources – the authors comment on the scarcity of data and the difficulties this poses for interpretation.

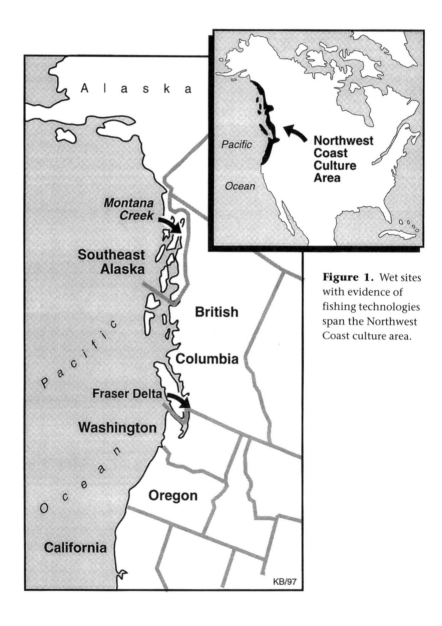

Figure 1. Wet sites with evidence of fishing technologies span the Northwest Coast culture area.

Ann Stevenson observes that archaeologists who regard fishing as a critical component of Northwest Coast cultures have based their interpretations largely on models (ideas) with little evidence of the fishing operations or of the variability in technologies that might signify economic differences through time. This potential for bias lies at the heart of wetland archaeological research the world over, and many other contributions to this volume address or allude to the issue.

The need for paleoenvironmental reconstruction comprises another subject emphasized in the chapters on Northwest Coast fishing. This need seems obvious; it is an established and recognized aspect of archaeological research (see Larsson, this volume) – and on the Northwest Coast has received increasing attention from scientists. The combination of a dynamic, geologically young coastline and archaeological sites situated in areas of land-sea interfaces intensifies the relevance of understanding relationships between fishing devices and topography at the time the devices were built and used. In other words, the authors promote the need to recognize that one does not simply "go fishing": one goes to a particular type of setting to fish in a particular way.

Greg Chaney's geoarchaeological study illustrates that understanding the depositional context provides essential information for interpreting cultural artifacts and the activities they represent. Chaney concludes that a basketry fish trap, described in a companion contribution by Robert C. Betts and originally believed to be an isolated find that had drifted downstream, had been used at the find-site, and the adjacent terrain would have been suitable for habitation at the time.

One reason for the dearth of information about Northwest Coast fishing sites involves the logistical problems of observing features in intertidal and submerged settings (the locations of fish traps) and of recovering artifacts from such settings. Robert C. Betts describes innovative (and complicated) techniques used to recover one relatively large, but unique, artifact. His experience illustrates the difficulties faced by archaeologists in remote areas working with highly fragile material that is environmentally sensitive and structurally weak. And that is only the excavation portion of the job – conservation treatment poses additional challenges.

Reviews of existing literature and newly recorded observations reveal considerable variation in fishing technologies and associated features on the Northwest Coast. Scott Byram, as well as Madonna L. Moss and Jon M. Erlandson, document and explore this variability by using survey data. This approach provides comparative data from numerous sites while avoiding the time-consuming aspects of wet-site excavation (though fewer types of data are forthcoming from survey). Moss and Erlandson look at the temporal distribution of weir features along the entire Northwest Coast, documenting weir fishing in the region over the past five millennia. They find an age difference between features in the north (Alaska) and in the south (Oregon), and suggest that geomorphological processes may in part be responsible.

Scott Byram looks in detail at data for weir sites on the Oregon coast (Moss and Erlandson's "southern" sub-area). He synthesizes archaeological, environmental, and documentary (ethnographic and historical) evidence and proposes a typology of weir features. The innovative aspect of his classification originates from an attempt to devise a scheme based on readily observable characteristics that could be used to predict the locations of archaeological features and to indicate the types of fishing technologies represented.

Before closing these introductory remarks, it may be useful to say a few words about the vocabulary of archaeological fishing sites. Despite (or perhaps because of) the widespread geographic popularity and great antiquity of fishing, there is no commonly recognized terminology for describing the various technological devices in detail. For example, the contributors to this section do not all use the words "weir" and "trap" in exactly the same sense – though where confusion might arise they discuss and define their respective usages. Moreover, the historical and ethnographic literature is plagued with inconsistent, undefined usage, and differentiating the archaeological remains of fish-dams, fences, and enclosures (all are types of weirs)

Figure 2. Mesh size, method of construction, and robustness of fish-weir components may indicate the species that were targeted. Lattice from the Osprey site (35CS130) in Oregon measures ca. 12 cm between horizontal weft rows. *Illustration by Scott Byram.*

from traps (which may be large enclosures) is not always possible. The need to describe fence-like features and their component parts introduces additional linguistic challenges (hurdle, wattle, brushwork, lattice, etc.). Clearly, an opportunity exists for someone to compose a glossary of archaeological fishing terminology.

Collectively, the authors in this section demonstrate that on the Northwest Coast, people have been fishing for a very long time, and that they have been catching various types of fish (not only salmon) using various devices (not only weirs). They argue that if fish and fishing are key elements in the development of Northwest Coast culture, accurate reconstruction requires attention to wet-site data and paleoenvironmental characteristics in relation to fishing activities. Since a considerable portion of fishing gear and devices consists of perishable material, foregoing such evidence risks biased interpretations of the past.

A Comparative Chronology of Northwest Coast Fishing Features

Madonna L. Moss and Jon M. Erlandson

The two most common Northwest Coast fishing features described in the anthropological literature are weirs and traps (e.g., Stewart 1977). A weir is typically understood to be a fence-like structure set in an estuarine tidal channel or stream for catching fish or guiding them into a trap. Archaeological remnants of these features usually consist of a series of upright wood stakes truncated through years of exposure. Some weirs functioned as small dams, extending across the entire width of a stream or tidal channel. More frequently, these linear arrangements of wood stakes did not completely cross stream or tidal channels and functioned in conjunction with a variety of different types of traps. Weirs were built in shallow waters to block the upstream movement of fish or to strand fish with the outgoing tide. A trap might consist of an arrangement of wood stakes, stones, or other elements left in place as an enclosure. Some traps involved portable and removable elements such as well-made basketry traps or lattice-work, or minimally altered brush or boughs woven into a framework. Because weirs and traps often co-occur, we sometimes use the terms interchangeably in this discussion.

Archaeological Studies of Northwest Coast Fishing Features

Northwest Coast fishing traps and weirs have been described in a wide range of ethnographic studies for over a century (Boas 1909; de Laguna 1960, 1972; Drucker 1937, 1951; Hewes 1947; Krause 1956 [1885]; Langdon 1977). In most cases, these works treat fishing weirs and traps as though they are exclusively of recent age. Pomeroy (1976) was the first archaeologist to examine Northwest Coast fishing sites explicitly as a special class of sites within a broad regional context. He reported 109 stone fish traps in the Bella Bella region of British Columbia (Figure 1), and although he was unable to directly date these exclusively stone structures, Pomeroy (1976:173) suggested they might be as much as 3,000 years old, based on their likely association with nearby shell middens of that age. Pomeroy (1976:173) indicated that

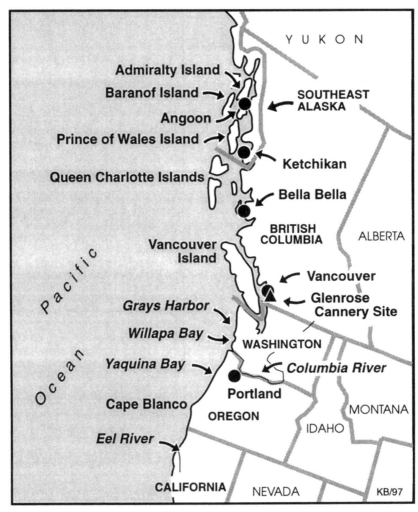

Figure 1. Locations mentioned in the text.

the northern Kwakiutl (Heiltsuk) had used these traps into the twentieth century. In 1981, Ackerman and Shaw reported stone weirs they described as "beach-front boulder alignments" located in two inlets on Revillagigedo Island, near Ketchikan, Alaska. Based on the testimony of local Tlingit, they suggested that these stone weirs fell out of use ca. 1910 to 1920. Today, we are no closer to dating weirs or traps made exclusively of stone, but a substantial body of chronological data from fishing sites containing preserved organic artifacts has been obtained. These data derive from radiocarbon dating of wood stakes and structural elements of fishing weirs and traps. Remarkably, they support Pomeroy's speculation that Northwest Coat weir/

trap fishing is very ancient and that this mode of fishing persisted into the twentieth century.

Our knowledge of weir/trap fishing has evolved somewhat sporadically. In an unpublished paper, Chris Rabich Campbell (1982) described a number of fishing weirs in southeast Alaska. In 1985, following his long-term research interest in fishing, Stephen Langdon began what would become sustained efforts at systematically surveying stone and wood-stake fishing traps/weirs on the Prince of Wales Archipelago in Alaska (Langdon et al. 1986; Wooley 1987). Also in 1985, as part of Moss' PhD dissertation research, we radiocarbon dated wood stakes from the Favorite Bay fishing weir identified by Gabriel George of Angoon, Alaska (Moss 1989). We are not completely certain why wood stakes from the numerous fishing structures had not been dated before this time; possibly because such sites were presumed to be relatively recent since they were ethnographically well known. The Favorite Bay weir stakes yielded uncorrected dates of 3015 ± 65 BP, 2685 ± 40 BP, and 2190 ± 45 BP. We found these dates surprisingly old, especially considering the excellent condition of the stakes. In 1987, Ream and Saleeby (1987) documented an even larger wood-stake weir at Exchange Cove, on Prince of Wales Island, which contained a stake with a date of 3220 ± 60 BP. Since the late 1980s, many southeast Alaskan archaeologists have contributed to the database of radiocarbon-dated weirs and traps, and now we know of 71 radiocarbon dates for 42 fishing sites in southeast Alaska (Table 1).

Relatively recently, Fladmark (1986:105) had considered the mass harvesting of salmon to be a late-prehistoric/early historic development on the coast of British Columbia. When we surveyed the Canadian archaeological literature in 1989, we were unable to find any radiocarbon-dated stakes from fishing weirs. From Canadian archaeologists Jim Haggarty and Richard Inglis we knew such sites were numerous in British Columbia, and they were mentioned in a few published reports (Bernick 1983; Hobler 1976). Since publication of our article in *Canadian Journal of Archaeology* (Moss et al. 1990), Morley Eldridge and Steve Acheson (1992) reported dates from four wood stakes from the Glenrose Cannery site, which range between 3950 BP and 4590 BP. The Glenrose trap is the oldest known fishing weir or trap on the west coast of North America. Even more recently, Carlson (1995) has convincingly re-interpreted the function of the wood stakes at Axeti (Hobler 1976) as constituents of a fishing weir. Carlson has suggested that this structure may have been in use for much of the last 2,000 years, based on dates of other sites in the Kwatna vicinity.

The Significance of Mid-Holocene Fishing Sites on the Northwest Coast

In addition to Favorite Bay and Exchange Cove, four other southeast Alaskan sites have produced radiocarbon-dated stakes more than 3,000 years old: Thorne River, Straight Creek, and Snoose Creek on Prince of Wales Island, and Cosmos Cove on Baranof Island. Like other researchers, we generally have interpreted the wood-stake features as salmon-fishing devices, based on their proximity to salmon streams. In a previous paper (Moss et al. 1990), we argued that the wood-stake fishing weirs of southeast Alaska represent a key technological advance with wide ranging consequences for the development of Northwest Coast cultures. We suggested that fishing weirs required considerable planning and effort to construct and resulted in the capture of large numbers of salmon. These salmon would have required efficient processing to provide the storable staple foods on which Northwest Coast aboriginal people relied for winter subsistence. We have viewed weir/trap fishing, its associated activities (processing, storage), and its organizational requirements (planning, labour management) as important milestones in Northwest Coast prehistory. The antiquity of weir/trap fishing is also consistent with Fladmark's (1975) model that mid-Holocene sealevel stabilization allowed for the establishment of abundant salmon populations, which in turn made possible the evolution of the ethnographic Northwest Coast cultures. Putnam (1995) recently provided data that may support claims for reduced salmon population in small streams in southeast Alaska during the early Holocene. By the mid-Holocene, weir/trap fishing seems to have been well established.

Something Different on the Southern Northwest Coast

Several sites in the state of Washington contain wood stakes that are likely associated with weir fishing: Dugualla Bay (Bryan 1963), Fishtown (Blukis Onat 1976), Biederbost (Nordquist 1976), and Wapato Creek (Munsell 1976). In addition, the Hoko River, Ozette, and Conway sites contain lattice-work fragments also thought to be associated with weir fishing (Croes 1992: 102-103). Only two stake weir/trap sites in Washington have been directly dated: 45CL31 at Vancouver Lake (Wessen 1983) and 45PC103, a site recently identified by geologist Brian Atwater (personal communication 1995) in Willapa Bay. Although it is located more than 150 km upstream from the mouth of the Columbia River, the Vancouver Lake weir is thought to have operated much like a tidal fish trap (Wessen 1983:B-70).

Before 1993, only two wood-stake weirs had been reported for the state of Oregon (Draper 1988, Linick 1984:76). Since then, with Scott Byram and Mark Tveskov, we have identified 32 wood-stake weirs/traps on the Oregon coast (Byram 1995). So far, we have 32 radiocarbon dates from 18 of these Oregon sites. Of the 34 radiocarbon dates available from 20 sites in Oregon and Washington, the oldest is 2410 ± 80 BP from the Montgomery Creek site on Yaquina Bay. Five other sites have yielded dates older than 600 BP, but the rest of the dates (63 percent) are younger than 380 BP. In light of

Table 1

Radiocarbon dates from Northwest Coast wood-stake fish weirs and traps

Site no.	Site name	Lab no.	Uncorrected ^{14}C date (RYBP)	Calibrated age range (CAL BP at 1σ)		
ALASKA						
49CRG123	Naukati Creek		2240 ± 60	2340	(2250)	2140*
49CRG243	Little Shakan Weir		1030 ± 60	970	(940)	800*
49CRG280	Staney Creek Weir		2470 ± 80	2720	(2540)	2350*
49CRG334	Little Salt Lake Weir	Beta 75716	310 ± 60	460	(310)	290
49CRG335	Little Salt Lake Weir	Beta 75715	1140 ± 40	1170	(1030)	970*
49CRG335	Little Salt Lake Weir	Beta 72332	1200 ± 50	1170	(1080)	1010*
49CRG335	Little Salt Lake Weir	Beta 72334	1340 ± 50	1300	(1260)	1180*
49CRG335	Little Salt Lake Weir	Beta 72333	1380 ± 50	1310	(1290)	1260
49CRG336	Little Salt Lake Weir	Beta 20072	580 ± 60	650	(590)	530*
49CRG376	Big Creek Fish Weir	Beta 54635	1640 ± 50	1590	(1530)	1420
49CRG433	Thorne River	Beta 75618	3680 ± 60	4090	(3940)	3890*
49CRG433	Thorne River	Beta 75470	3580 ± 60	3960	(3850)	3730*
49CRG433	Thorne River	Beta 75619	2100 ± 60	2150	(2050)	1950*
49CRG434	Trocadero Bay	Beta 74864	1670 ± 60	1690	(1540)	1520
49CRG434	Trocadero Bay	Beta 75617	1440 ± 60	1390	(1310)	1290
49CRG437	Little Salt Lake Weir	Beta 72335	980 ± 50	950	(920)	800
49CRG437	Little Salt Lake Weir	Beta 75717	1060 ± 40	1050	(960)	930
49CRG439	Little Salt Lake Weir	Beta 75713	2280 ± 40	2340	(2310)	2160*
49CRG439	Little Salt Lake Weir	Beta 75712	1720 ± 50	1690	(1610)	1540*
49CRG440	Little Salt Lake Weir	Beta 75714	2000 ± 40	1990	(1940)	1890*
49JUN453	Montana Creek Trap	WSU 4141	700 ± 60[1]	670	(660)	560
49JUN453	Montana Creek Trap	WSU 4140	550 ± 70[1]	620	(540)	510

49KET290	Port Stewart Fish Weir	Beta 28354	1830 ± 70	1830	(1730)	1630
49PET027	Sandy Beach Fish Traps	Beta 60929	2090 ± 60	2150	(2020)	1950*
49PET027	Sandy Beach Fish Traps	Beta 60930	1910 ± 70	1920	(1850)	1730*
49PET027	Sandy Beach Fish Traps	Beta 60931	1860 ± 90	1910	(1780)	1630*
49PET187	Red Bay Weir	Beta 56451	2870 ± 50	3130	(2980)	2890*
49PET187	Red Bay Weir	Beta 75624	2050 ± 50	2110	(1960)	1910*
49PET187	Red Bay Weir	Beta 56458	1880 ± 50	1880	(1820)	1720
49PET203	HRA Fish Weir	Beta 56456	1630 ± 50	1560	(1530)	1420
49PET205	Straight Creek Weir	Beta 56454	3770 ± 80	4350	(4110)	3930*
49PET205	Straight Creek Weir	Beta 56455	2130 ± 60	2300	(2100)	2000*
49PET206	Snoose Creek	Beta 75622	3470 ± 70	3830	(3710)	3590*
49PET206	Snoose Creek	Beta 75621	3240 ± 60	3550	(3440)	3360*
49PET206	Snoose Creek	Beta 75625	2870 ± 60	3140	(2990)	2870*
49PET206	Snoose Creek	Beta 75623	2340 ± 50	2350	(2340)	2330
49PET208		Beta 56453	40 ± 50	60	(0)	0
49PET219	Mable Creek Weir	Beta 55698	710 ± 50	670	(660)	570
49PET319	Exchange Cove Weir	Beta 20709	3220 ± 60	3470	(3430)	3370*
49PET319	Exchange Cove Weir	Beta 56459	2810 ± 60	3000	(2900)	2780*
49PET329	Hole-in-the-Wall Weir	Beta 56460	2500 ± 60	2740	(2540)	2360*
49PET393	McDonald Arm Trap	Beta 73415	1780 ± 50	1770	(1690)	1610*
49PET393	McDonald Arm Trap	Beta 73414	1720 ± 60	1690	(1610)	1540*
49PET393	McDonald Arm Trap	Beta 73416	1690 ± 50	1690	(1590)	1530*
49PET394	Island Point Trap	Beta 73417	1690 ± 60	1690	(1590)	1530*
49PET395	Woody Island Trap	Beta 73419	2180 ± 50	2300	(2150)	2070
49PET395	Woody Island Trap	Beta 73418	1310 ± 60	1290	(1260)	1170*
49PET396	Mitchell Slough Trap	Beta 73420	2000 ± 60	2000	(1940)	1880*
49SIT033	Favorite Bay Weir	SI 6993	3015 ± 65	3330	(3210)	3080

Site no.	Site name	Lab no.	Uncorrected ^{14}C date (RYBP)	Calibrated age range (CAL BP at 1σ)		
49SIT033	Favorite Bay Weir	Pitt 07	2685 ± 40	2790	(2770)	2750
49SIT033	Favorite Bay Weir	SI 6994	2190 ± 45	2310	(2150)	2120
49SIT086	Cosmos Cove Weir	Beta 32110	3460 ± 60	3830	(3690)	3630
49SIT311	Kanalku Bay Weir	Pitt 133	1700 ± 30	1680	(1570)	1540
49SIT311	Kanalku Bay Weir	Pitt 131	955 ± 35	930	(910)	790
49SIT311	Kanalku Bay Weir	Pitt 132	125 ± 35	270	(130)	0
49SIT329	Kanalku Coal Claim Weir	Beta 46338	1720 ± 50	1690	(1625)	1540*
49SIT329	Kanalku Coal Claim Weir	Beta 46337	1690 ± 50	1670	(1580)	1530
49SIT329	Kanalku Coal Claim Weir	Beta 46336	550 ± 50	620	(540)	520
49SIT330	Chaik BayWeir	Beta 46340	2310 ± 60	2350	(2340)	2180
49SIT330	Chaik Bay Weir	Beta 46339	2070 ± 50	2110	(2000)	1950
49SIT330	Chaik Bay Weir	Beta 46341	1610 ± 60	1540	(1520)	1410
49SIT341	Portage Arm Weir	Beta 56337	1790 ± 80	1820	(1650)	1570*
49SIT398	S'aw Geey'ee/Nakwasina	Beta 6532	modern	250	(0)	0
49SUM055	Sandborn Canal Weir	Beta 76053	110 ± 40	260	(130)	0*
49XPA119	Big Creek Weir	Beta 37128	200 ± 60	300	(120)	0*
49XPA130	Aleck's Creek Weir	Beta 37129	540 ± 50	620	(540)	520
49XPA132	Secluded Cove Weir 2	Beta 37130	1730 ± 60	1710	(1660)	1540*
49XPA164	McCallum's Fish Weir	Beta 37131	2450 ± 60	2710	(2470)	2360
49XPA205		Beta 37132	2110 ± 60	2140	(2060)	1990
49XPA217		Beta 37133	1140 ± 60	1080	(1060)	970
49YAK019	Diyaguna'Et	Beta33024	160 ± 50	280	(130)	0*

BRITISH COLUMBIA

DgRr 6	Glenrose Wet	Beta 38808	4590 ± 50	5440 (5300)	5090
DgRr 6	Glenrose Wet	Beta 38811	4370 ± 60	5030 (4930)	4850*
DgRr 6	Glenrose Wet	Beta 38810	4260 ± 70	4870 (4840)	4660
DgRr 6	Glenrose Wet	Beta 38809	3950 ± 60	4500 (4420)	4290
FaSu 1	Axeti	Gak 3208	450 ± 90	540 (510)	330*
FaSu 1	Axeti	Gak 3209	240 ± 80	420 (290)	0*

WASHINGTON

45CL31	Vancouver Lake	Beta 5785	310 ± 60	460 (310)	290
45PC103	South Bend Fishing Weir	Beta 74541	380 ± 50	510 (460)	320

OREGON

35CS122	North Slough #1 (Coos)	Beta 67581	180 ± 50	290 (150)	0*
35CS123	Palouse Slough	Beta 67582	240 ± 70	310 (290)	0*
35CS124	Haynes Inlet #1	Beta 74738	30 ± 50	modern?	
35CS125	Haynes Inlet #2-3	Beta 74739	290 ± 50	430 (300)	290*
35CS125	Haynes Inlet #2-3	Beta 74740	230 ± 70	310 (290)	0*
35CS126	Haynes Inlet #4	Beta 74741	290 ± 60	430 (300)	290*
35CS128	Willanch #2	Beta 67583	210 ± 50	300 (150)	0*
35CS128	Willanch #2	Beta 74742	140 ± 50	280 (140)	0*
35CS130	Osprey Weir	Beta 74746	940 ± 50	930 (830)	760*
35CS130	Osprey Weir	Beta 72790	670 ± 50	670 (650)	560*
35CS130	Osprey Weir	Beta 72791	660 ± 50	660 (650)	560*
35CS132	North Slough #2 (Coos)	Beta 74868	20 ± 60	modern?	
35CS134	North Slough #4 (Coos)	Beta 74869	180 ± 60	290 (150)	0*
35CS143	South Slough(Coos)	Beta 77990	100 ± 60	270 (60)	0*

▲

▼ *Table 1*

Site no.	Site name	Lab no.	Uncorrected ^{14}C date (RYBP)	Calibrated age range (CAL BP at 1σ)		
35CS144	South Slough (Coos)	Beta 77991	70 ± 60	250	(0)	0*
35LA1101	Siuslaw South Inlet	Beta 83330	280 ± 50	420	(300)	290
35LA1101	Siuslaw South Inlet	Beta 74866	130 ± 60	280	(140)	0*
35LA1104	Half Moon Weir	Beta 63843	160 ± 60	290	(130)	0*
35LA1104	Half Moon Weir	Beta 63844	90 ± 60	270	(30)	0*
35LA1104	Half Moon Weir	Beta 63842	modern		modern?	
35LA1105	South Slough #4 (Siuslaw)	Beta 74745	910 ± 50	920	(790)	740*
35LNC76	Ahnkuti	Beta 83325	2120 ± 70	2150	(2090)	1990*
35LNC76	Ahnkuti	Beta 83321	1400 ± 60	1330	(1300)	1280
35LNC76	Ahnkuti	Beta 83326	1330 ± 80	1300	(1270)	1170
35LNC76	Ahnkuti	Beta 77988	1160 ± 40	1180	(1060)	990*
35LNC76	Ahnkuti	Beta 83322	560 ± 70	640	(540)	520
35LNC76	Ahnkuti	Beta 83323	350 ± 70	500	(360)	300*
35LNC76	Ahnkuti	Beta 83324	320 ± 40	440	(410)	300*
35LNC77	RK Weir	Beta 83327	1920 ± 80	1940	(1870)	1730
35LNC78	Montgomery Creek Weir	Beta 83329	2410 ± 80	2710	(2360)	2340
35LNC78	Montgomery Creek Weir	Beta 83328	2220 ± 80	2340	(2250)	2120*
35TI4	Nehalem Bay	LJ 5267	380 ± 60²	510	(460)	310*

Notes: Dates compiled from Moss et al. 1990; Moss 1998; Moss and Erlandson 1995; Maschner 1992; Davis and Lobdell 1992; Eldridge and Acheson 1992; Greiser et al. 1993, 1994; Bernick 1991; McCallum 1993; Putnam and Greiser 1993; Betts and Chaney 1995; Langdon, personal communication 1995; Linick 1984; Wessen 1983; Hobler 1976; Iwamoto, personal communication 1993; Bower 1994; Lively, personal communication 1994; Atwater, personal communication 1995; Putnam, personal communication 1995; Fifield, personal communication 1995. Calibrated ages derived from Stuiver and Reimer (1993). All ages were rounded to the nearest 10 years.

[1] These dates were run on elements of a portable basketry trap that is not known to be associated with a wood-stake fishing weir (Betts, this volume).

[2] This date was run on a twined mat constructed of Douglas fir root associated with a wood-stake weir (Linick 1984).

* Samples with multiple intercepts on the calibration curve.

the antiquity of weir fishing in Alaska and at Glenrose Cannery in British Columbia, we were initially surprised at the relatively recent dates for sites in Oregon. Figure 2 shows the temporal distributions of ^{14}C dates from southeast Alaska and Oregon, the two geographic areas with sizeable samples of dates. These two distributions are significantly different, with dates from southeast Alaska extending back nearly 4000 BP and almost 50 percent of the dates clustered between 2500 BP and 1500 BP. By comparison, the Oregon coast dates are relatively recent. Although it is possible that weir and trap fishing was a late technological development in the southern Northwest Coast, we believe that the explanation for the significant difference in age of fishing sites in the south vs. the north rests with environmental differences and the preservation and accessibility of the archaeological record in these respective areas.

Coastal Subsidence along the Southern Northwest Coast

A flurry of geological studies in Washington and Oregon in recent years has documented evidence for prehistoric earthquakes and tectonic subsidence. These studies have been summarized by Atwater and colleagues (1995), the major source we draw on for this discussion. From southern British Columbia to northern California, evidence for subsidence, tsunamis, and shaking demonstrates that "great earthquakes" (magnitude 8 or larger) have occurred at the Cascadia subduction zone throughout the Holocene. Buried marsh and forest soils indicating sudden earthquake-generated subsidence have

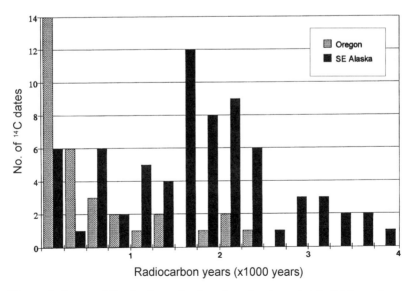

Figure 2. Temporal distributions of radiocarbon-dated wood-stake fishing weirs and traps located in southeast Alaska and Oregon.

been found in more than a dozen estuaries from Clayoquot Sound, Vancouver Island, to Eel River, California. After this sudden lowering of the land, tides deposited mud in areas that were formerly at or above high tide. In some cases, sand layers lie on the buried soils, and these in turn are covered by intertidal mud, providing evidence that tsunamis were produced by some of these earthquakes. In Oregon tidal marshes, buried surfaces dating to 1000 BP have been found to range from 1.5 m to 2.5 m below present surfaces (Nelson 1992). Another signature of seismic activity is evidence of liquefaction, when sand erupts through and onto subsided soil. Evidence for liquefaction in prehistoric times has been identified near Vancouver, British Columbia; east of Grays Harbor in southwest Washington; near the mouth of the Columbia River and upstream near Portland, Oregon; and at Cape Blanco in southern Oregon. Some geologists have estimated that great earthquakes recur in the southern Northwest Coast every 400 to 600 years, but there are several methodological problems with these estimates (Atwater et al. 1995). Nonetheless, two prehistoric earthquakes appear to be well documented: one occurred between AD 1680 and AD 1720 and is evidenced along a 55 km stretch of coast between Willapa Bay and Copalis River in Washington (Atwater et al. 1991); the other evidently occurred near Seattle about 1,000 years ago (Atwater and Moore 1992).

Because prehistoric wood-stake fishing weirs/traps are invariably located in the intertidal zone, they are particularly vulnerable to the consequences of subsidence. In light of the expanding record for subsidence events along the southern Northwest Coast, it seems likely that ancient weirs and traps might be submerged at depths currently below low-tide levels and/or buried under sediments that have accumulated on lowered landforms. Additional complications affecting the southern Northwest Coast archaeological record relate to late nineteenth- and twentieth-century industrial practices. Weirs and traps have probably been destroyed by dredging and "re-claiming" mudflats for pasturing livestock. Sedimentation due to logging, dike building, dredging, and oyster farming may also have buried ancient weirs. Future identification efforts might monitor dredging operations and use underwater survey to try to locate older weirs along the southern Northwest Coast.

Coastal Processes along the Northern Northwest Coast

In contrast to the southern Northwest Coast, the northern Northwest Coast has undergone regional uplift related to isostatic rebound. In our investigation of Favorite Bay on Admiralty Island, we mapped 677 individual stakes exposed along 100 m in the mudflats. We suggested that the weir builders at this site extended the weir in response to shoreline changes caused by isostatic uplift and/or progradational sedimentation (Moss et al. 1990). The weir appears to have been used for about 1,000 years. The oldest date originated from the south end (the upstream or inner-estuary end), the intermediate date came from the central site area, and the youngest date came from the north end of the weir. In 1993, Dave Putnam and Weber Greiser documented a comparable situation at Red Bay, Prince of Wales Island. They dated two stakes: the one from the outer estuary was 1,000 years younger than the one from the central site area. They also suggested that the weir builders extended their weir seaward in response to uplift, pointing out that "weirs were functional in direct relationship to contemporary sea level and tidal range, and as such provided potential radiometric dating of relative sea level change through time" (Putnam and Greiser 1993:9). Putnam and Greiser (1993:13) also discuss how weirs may have influenced sedimentary regimes in estuaries:

> They functioned as sieves in which flotsam borne in and out with the tides would become lodged. They would also form a barrier to storm waves, perhaps resulting in the creation of associated beaches or berms ... they would create erosion resistant barriers in a naturally unrestricted environment of tributary and distributary tidal drainage.

Putnam and Greiser (1993:15) concluded that because the Red Bay weir occupies what is today an intertidal location, there has been only minor sea-level change over the past 3,000 years. This observation might be broadened to include the greater southeast Alaska region and account for why archaeologists have been successful in identifying wood-stake weirs dated to within the past 3,500 years. Putnam and Greiser also suggest that heavy logging on Prince of Wales Island has increased fluvial discharge and sedimentation that may threaten the preservation of these intertidal archaeological features. While some areas of southeast Alaska are protected from logging (e.g., most of Admiralty Island), clear-cutting has accelerated in recent years in many other regions and may result in washing out or burying these archaeological features.

Data Gaps, Unanswered Questions, and Unresolved Issues
The most significant and obvious gap in the database of Northwest Coast wood-stake fishing weirs is the dearth of dated sites in British Columbia. In addition to the studies mentioned previously (Bernick 1983; Hobler 1976), numerous wood-stake weirs and traps have been briefly described. Weirs on the west coast of Vancouver Island have been identified in several reports (Haggarty and Inglis 1985; McMillan and St. Claire 1982, 1991; Marshall 1993; Sumpter 1994). Additional weirs and traps have been reported for the lower mainland region of British Columbia, including the Mary Hill Road site, Mission Weir, and Musqueam Trap, and possibly at Pitt Meadows and Sumas Mountain (Bernick 1991; personal communication 1995; Andrew

Mason, personal communication 1994). Wood-stake weirs are reportedly widespread on the Queen Charlotte Islands (James Haggarty, personal communication 1988). Roy Carlson (1995) recently reported that there are 455 weirs/traps made of stone or wood currently listed in the British Columbia provincial archaeological site files. Nevertheless, the only published radio-carbon-dated wood stakes unequivocally from fishing structures are the ones from the Glenrose Cannery site. As data on the chronology and distribution of fishing weirs and traps in British Columbia accumulate, it will be interesting to see if subsidence has affected the preservation of such sites on the west coast of Vancouver Island as it apparently has farther south along the Cascadia subduction zone. Perhaps the record from the Queen Charlotte Islands will be longer, based on the sea-level history and the greater rate of uplift in that region compared to southern British Columbia. At this time we can only speculate.

In contrast with British Columbia, where numerous weirs and traps have been identified, little information is available for the states of Washington and California. We know of only seven sites with wood-stake weirs in Washington (Atwater, personal communication 1995; Blukis Onat 1976; Bryan 1963; Munsell 1976; Alan Nelson, personal communication to Byram 1994; Nordquist 1976; Wessen 1983), and there is no reported archaeological record of weir or trap fishing in northern California. Ethnographic information (Drucker 1937; Eells 1985; Haeberlin and Gunther 1980), however, suggests that both regions should have considerable evidence of fishing weirs and traps. Further reconnaissance and much more radiocarbon dating will be needed to reach a better understanding of the archaeological record of southern Northwest Coast fishing.

One important issue we have not explored is the range of technological variability represented in weirs and traps (see Byram, this volume). Relatively few of the southeast Alaska weirs we know of appear to have functioned as dams crossing a stream from one bank to the other, even though this type is the most frequently illustrated in ethnographies (e.g., Emmons 1991). More commonly, they are linear arrangements of stakes that run at a variety of orientations to intertidal channels in estuaries that lead to streams. Many southeast Alaska weirs seem designed to entrap salmon as the salmon mill about in estuaries before ascending their natal streams. In this way, the weirs appear functionally similar to the semi-circular stone traps reported from southern British Columbia northward.

Many of the southeast Alaska weirs were probably used in conjunction with portable basketry traps, perhaps like the one found at Montana Creek (Betts, this volume). During our initial studies of the Oregon sites, we observed that some wood-stake structures completely cross relatively narrow intertidal channels, whereas others occur along the shores of large rivers. The latter type is best illustrated by the Osprey Weir described by Byram (this volume) and was clearly used with portable basketry features. Based on ethnographic descriptions and historical records, some weirs and traps served as platforms for spearing, harpooning, or dip-netting. A great deal of additional work is needed to document the technological and functional variability in these features, and this is one of the goals of Byram's current research.

An associated issue is that not all the sites we have lumped together necessarily were used to capture salmon. Ethnographic data suggest a wide range of fish were caught in weirs and traps, including varieties of eulachon, trouts, shiners, perch, flounders, lamprey eels, and others, as well as salmon. Some traps might have been used to capture sturgeon (McHalsie 1995) or sea mammals and water birds as suggested by Monks (1987) for the stone trap at Deep Bay, Vancouver Island.

We also feel uncomfortable separating weir/trap sites based on their primary construction material – wood or stone. Although our research has focused on wood-stake fishing structures because they are easily dated, predominantly stone structures should be carefully examined in the hopes of identifying datable elements. The ethnographic record (Hewes 1947) clearly demonstrates that wood and stone elements were combined in fishing structures.

Revised Assessment of the Significance of Northwest Coast Weir/Trap Fishing

James Petersen and colleagues (1994:216-217) have placed their study of the Sebasticook fishing weir in the eastern United States within a broad global context, as have Putnam et al. (1994) in a recent paper about weirs on Prince of Wales Island. These authors have reviewed a wide range of ethnographic and archaeological sources from North America, Europe, South Africa, Siberia, Japan, and Australia. Putnam et al. (1994:25) have suggested that the widespread occurrence of such sites across many world regions indicates a possible late Pleistocene age for the practice of weir fishing. Although we are unable to support this claim using dates from the Pacific coast of North America, the archaeological record of weir and trap fishing from the Northwest Coast does seem to reflect sea-level histories and Holocene geological events to a great degree. We believe Putnam's hypothesis for an even older record of weir and trap fishing should be considered.

The global record of weir and trap fishing also indicates that not all these sites would have required massive construction efforts. Certainly, the Favorite Bay, Exchange Cove, and Little Salt Lake weirs in southeast Alaska, and the Sebasticook weir in Maine, required significant labour to construct and may represent the activities of corporate groups. However, there is a variety of types of weirs and traps across the Northwest Coast; some of these may have been the products of small task groups. Some of the weirs/traps at Oregon coast sites may be the work of a few persons, in some cases, individuals whom Tveskov (1995) has been able to identify in the ethnohistorical record.

In closing, the chronological record of Northwest Coast fishing has significantly expanded over the past decade. To better address the many questions raised, it will be necessary to identify and date sites in the relatively poorly known areas of British Columbia, Washington, and northern California. Attention to technological, functional, and temporal variation should be especially productive areas for future research.

Acknowledgments

The Oregon coast research has been funded in part through a Historic Preservation Grant-in-Aid administered by the Oregon State Historic Preservation Office. We consider ourselves very fortunate to work with University of Oregon graduate students Scott Byram and Mark Tveskov, whose skills and energy have contributed a great deal to the record of fishing weirs and traps on the Oregon coast. We also acknowledge the field assistance of the Coquille Indian Tribe and of additional University of Oregon students. Tongass National Forest archaeologists who have generously shared data with us include Pat Bower, Terence Fifield, Karen Iwamoto, Ralph Lively, Mark McCallum, and Allison Young. Terry Fifield and Steve Langdon were particularly helpful. We also greatly appreciate Bob Betts and Dave Putnam for sharing papers and correspondence with us. Brian Atwater, US Geological Survey at the University of Washington, has graciously shared data and reprints of his recent research. Special thanks are due to Gary Wessen, who provided sources of information we probably would have missed otherwise, and to Roy Carlson for a new perspective on Axeti.

References Cited

Ackerman, R.E., and R.D. Shaw
    1981 Beach-Front Boulder Alignments in Southeastern Alaska. In *Megaliths to Medicine Wheels: Boulder Structures in Archaeology,* edited by M. Wilson, K.L. Road, and K.J. Hardy, pp. 269-277. University of Calgary Archaeological Association, Calgary, AB.
Atwater, B.F., and A.L. Moore
    1992 A Tsunami about 1000 Years Ago in Puget Sound, Washington. *Science* 258:1614-1617.
Atwater, B.F., M. Stuiver, and D.K. Yamaguchi
    1991 Radiocarbon Test of Earthquake Magnitude at the Cascadia Subduction Zone. *Nature* 353:156-158.
Atwater, B. F., A.R. Nelson, J.J. Clague, G.A. Carver, D.K. Yamaguchi, P.T. Bobrowsky, J. Bourgeois, M.E. Darienzo, W.C. Grant, E. Hemphill-Haley, J.M. Kelsey, G.C. Jacoby, S.P. Nishenko, S.P. Palmer, C.D. Peterson, and M.A. Reinhart
    1995 Summary of Coastal Geologic Evidence for Past Great Earthquakes at the Cascadia Subduction Zone. *Earthquake Spectra* 2:1-18.
Bernick, K.
    1983 *A Site Catchment Analysis of the Little Qualicum River Site, DiSc 1: A Wet Site on the East Coast of Vancouver Island, B.C.* National Museum of Man Mercury Series, Archaeological Survey of Canada Paper No. 118. National Museums of Canada, Ottawa.
    1991 *Wet Site Archaeology in the Lower Mainland Region of British Columbia.* Report on file, British Columbia Archaeology Branch, Victoria.
Betts, R.C., and G.P. Chaney
    1995 The Montana Creek Fish Trap: A 700 Year Old Basket-Style Fish Trap Excavated Near

Juneau, Alaska. Paper presented at *Hidden Dimensions: The Cultural Significance of Wetland Archaeology*, Vancouver, BC, April 27-30, 1995.

Blukis Onat, A.R.
   1976 A Fishtown Site, 45SK99. In *The Excavation of Water-Saturated Archaeological Sites (Wet Sites) on the Northwest Coast of North America*, edited by D.R. Croes, pp. 122-145. National Museum of Man Mercury Series, Archaeological Survey of Canada Paper No. 50. National Museums of Canada, Ottawa.

Boas, F.
   1909 The Kwakiutl of Vancouver Island. *American Museum of Natural History Memoirs* 8.

Bower, P.
   1994 Heritage Resource Investigations for the Northwest Baranof Project. Ms. on file, Tongass National Forest, Chatham Area, Sitka, AK.

Bryan, A.L.
   1963 *An Archaeological Survey of Northern Puget Sound*. Occasional Papers of the Idaho State University Museum No. 11. Pocatello, ID.

Byram, R.S.
   1995 1994-1995 Surveys of Intertidal Fishing Weirs. In *An Evaluation, Survey, and Dating Program for Archaeological Sites on State Lands of the Northern Oregon Coast*, by Madonna L. Moss and Jon M. Erlandson. Report submitted to the Oregon State Historic Preservation Office, Salem.

Campbell, C.R.
   1982 Anadromous Salmon Weirs and Associated Cultural Features in Southern Southeast Alaska. Paper presented at the annual meeting of the Alaska Anthropological Association, Fairbanks, AK.

Carlson, R.
   1995 Survey at Low Tide: Some Intertidal Sites of the British Columbia Coast. Paper presented at *Hidden Dimensions: The Cultural Significance of Wetland Archaeology*, Vancouver, BC, April 27-30, 1995.

Croes, D.
   1992 An Evolving Revolution in Wet Site Research on the Northwest Coast of North America. In *The Wetland Revolution in Prehistory*, edited by Bryony Coles, pp. 99-111. WARP Occasional Paper 6. Dept. of History and Archaeology, University of Exeter, UK.

Davis, S.D., and J.E. Lobdell
   1992 *Cultural Resources Baseline Study: Polk Inlet Environmental Impact Statement*. Report prepared for Ebasco Environmental and submitted to Tongass National Forest, Ketchikan Area, Ketchikan, AK.

de Laguna, F.
   1960 *The Story of a Tlingit Community: A Problem in the Relationship Between Archeological, Ethnological, and Historical Methods*. Bulletin 172. Bureau of American Ethnology, Smithsonian Institution, Washington, DC.
   1972 *Under Mount Saint Elias: the History and Culture of the Yakutat Tlingit*. Smithsonian Contributions to Anthropology, vol. 7. Smithsonian Institution, Washington, DC.

Draper, J.A.
   1988 *A Proposed Model of Late Prehistoric Settlement Systems on the Southern Northwest Coast, Coos and Curry Counties, Oregon*. PhD dissertation, Washington State University. University Microfilms, Ann Arbor, MI.

Drucker, P.
   1937 The Tolowa and their Southwest Oregon Kin. *University of California Publications in American Archaeology and Ethnology* 36(4):221-300.
   1951 *The Northern and Central Nootkan Tribes*. Bulletin 144. Bureau of American Ethnology, Smithsonian Institution, Washington, DC.

Eells, M.
   1985 *The Indians of Puget Sound: The Notebooks of Myron Eells*. University of Washington Press, Seattle.

Eldridge, M., and S. Acheson
   1992 The Antiquity of Fish Weirs on the Southern Coast: A Response to Moss, Erlandson, and Stuckenrath. *Canadian Journal of Archaeology* 16:112-116.
Emmons, G.T.
   1991 *The Tlingit Indians.* Edited with additions by F. de Laguna. University of Washington Press, Seattle.
Fladmark, K.R.
   1975 *A Paleoecological Model for Northwest Coast Prehistory.* National Museum of Man Mercury Series, Archaeological Survey of Canada Paper No. 43. National Museums of Canada, Ottawa.
   1986 *British Columbia Prehistory.* National Museum of Man, National Museums of Canada, Ottawa.
Greiser, T.W, D.E. Putnam, and M.G. Lee
   1993 *Lab Bay EIS Cultural Resource Survey.* Report by Historical Research Associates, Missoula, MO, for Harza Northwest, Bellevue, WA, submitted to Tongass National Forest, Ketchikan Area, Ketchikan, AK.
Greiser, T.W., D.E. Putnam, S. Moorhead, and G.A. Walter
   1994 *Cultural Resources Specialist Report, Control Lake Environmental Impact Statement, Prince of Wales Island, Alaska.* Report by Historical Research Associates, Missoula, MO, submitted under Forest Service Contract 53-0109-3-00369, Tongass National Forest, Ketchikan, AK.
Haeberlin, J., and E. Gunther
   1980 *The Indians of Puget Sound.* University of Washington Press, Seattle. Originally published 1930.
Haggarty, J.C., and R.I. Inglis
   1985 *Historical Resources Site Survey and Assessment, Pacific Rim National Park.* National Historic Parks and Sites Branch, Environment Canada, Ottawa.
Hewes, G.W.
   1947 *Aboriginal Use of Fishery Resources in Northwestern North America.* PhD dissertation, Department of Anthropology, University of California, Berkeley.
Hobler, P.M.
   1976 Wet Site Archaeology at Kwatna. In *The Excavation of Water-Saturated Archaeological Sites (Wet Sites) on the Northwest Coast of North America,* edited by D.R. Croes, pp. 146-157. National Museum of Man Mercury Series, Archaeological Survey of Canada Paper No. 50. National Museums of Canada, Ottawa.
Krause, A.
   1956 *The Tlingit Indians: Results of a Trip to the Northwest Coast of America and the Bering Straits.* Translated by E. Gunther. University of Washington Press, Seattle. Originally published *Die Tlinkit-Indianer,* 1885, in Jena.
Langdon, S.J.
   1977 *Technology, Ecology, and Economy: Fishing Systems in Southeast Alaska.* PhD dissertation, Stanford University. University Microfilms, Ann Arbor, MI.
Langdon, S.J, D.R. Reger, and C. Wooley
   1986 Using Aerial Photographs to Locate Intertidal Stone Fishing Structures in the Prince of Wales Archipelago, Southeast Alaska. Alaska State Department of Natural Resources, Public-data File 86-9, Anchorage.
Linick, T.W.
   1984 La Jolla Natural Radiocarbon Measurements X. *Radiocarbon* 26(19):75-110.
McCallum, W.M.
   1993 Sandy Beach Fish Traps. Paper presented at the 20th annual Alaska Anthropological Association meeting, Anchorage, AK.
McHalsie, Sonny
   1995 Panel Discussion during: A Public Forum on First Nations' Heritage and the Fraser River. Presented at *Hidden Dimensions: The Cultural Significance of Wetland Archaeology,* Vancouver, BC, April 27-30, 1995.

McMillan, A.D., and D.E. St. Claire
  1982 *Alberni Prehistory: Archaeological and Ethnographic Investigations on Western Vancouver Island*. Theytus Books, Penticton, BC.
  1991 *The Toquaht Archaeological Project: Report on the 1991 Field Season*. Permit 1991-31. Report on file, British Columbia Archaeology Branch, Victoria.
Marshall, Y.
  1993 *A Political History of the Nuu-Chah-Nulth People: A Case Study of the Mowachaht and Muchalaht Tribes*. PhD dissertation, Department of Archaeology, Simon Fraser University, Burnaby, BC.
Maschner, H.D.G.
  1992 *The Origins of Hunter-Gatherer Sedentism and Political Complexity: A Case Study from the Northern Northwest Coast*. PhD dissertation, Department of Anthropology, University of California, Santa Barbara.
Monks, G.G.
  1987 Prey as Bait: The Deep Bay Example. *Canadian Journal of Archaeology* 11:119-142.
Moss, M.L.
  1989 *Archaeology and Cultural Ecology of the Prehistoric Angoon Tlingit*. PhD dissertation, University of California, Santa Barbara. University Microfilms, Ann Arbor, MI.
  1998 Northern Northwest Coast Regional Overview. In *The Origins, Development, and Spread of Prehistoric North Pacific - Bering Sea Maritime Cultures*, edited by A. McCartney and W. Workman, *Arctic Anthropology* 35(1), in press. Ms. 1994.
Moss, M.L., and J.M. Erlandson
  1995 *An Evaluation, Survey, and Dating Program for Archaeological Sites on State Lands of the Northern Oregon Coast*. Report submitted to the Oregon State Historic Preservation Office, Salem.
Moss, M.L., J.M. Erlandson, and R. Stuckenrath
  1990 Wood Stake Weirs and Salmon Fishing on the Northwest Coast: Evidence from Southeast Alaska. *Canadian Journal of Archaeology* 14:143-158.
Munsell, D.A.
  1976 The Wapato Creek Fish Weir Site 45PI47, Tacoma, Washington. In *The Excavation of Water-Saturated Archaeological Sites (Wet Sites) on the Northwest Coast of North America*, edited by D.R. Croes, pp. 45-57. National Museum of Man Mercury Series, Archaeological Survey of Canada Paper No. 50. National Museums of Canada, Ottawa.
Nelson, A.R.
  1992 Discordant [14]C Ages from Buried Tidal-Marsh Soils in the Cascadia Subduction Zone, Southern Oregon Coast. *Quaternary Research* 38:74-90.
Nordquist, D.
  1976 45SN100 – The Biederbost Site, Kidd's Duval Site. In *The Excavation of Water-Saturated Archaeological Sites (Wet Sites) on the Northwest Coast of North America*, edited by D.R. Croes, pp. 186-200. National Museum of Man Mercury Series, Archaeological Survey of Canada Paper No. 50. National Museums of Canada, Ottawa.
Petersen, J.B, B.S. Robinson, D.F. Belknap, J. Stark, and L.K. Kaplan
  1994 An Archaic and Woodland Period Fish Weir Complex in Central Maine. *Archaeology of Eastern North America* 22:197-221.
Pomeroy, J.A.
  1976 Stone Fish Traps of the Bella Bella Region. In *Current Research Reports*, edited by R.L. Carlson, pp. 165-173. Department of Archaeology, Simon Fraser University, Burnaby, BC.
Putnam, D.E.
  1995 Holocene Salmonid Habitat Increase in Small Streams, Prince of Wales Island, Alaska. Ms. in possession of the author.
Putnam, D.E., and T.W. Greiser
  1993 The Inter-relationship of Prehistoric Wooden Stake Fish Traps and Estuarine Sedimentological Processes: An Example from Northern Prince of Wales Island. Paper

presented at the annual meeting of the Alaska Anthropological Association, Fairbanks, AK.

Putnam, D.E., T.W. Greiser, and G. Walter
  1994 Tectonic Stream Piracy and Prehistoric Stone Fish Weir Abandonment on Prince of Wales Island, Southeast Alaska. Paper presented at the 21st annual meeting of the Alaska Anthropological Association, Juneau, AK.

Ream, B.A., and B.M. Saleeby
  1987 *The Archaeology of Northern Prince of Wales Island: A Survey of Nineteen Timber Harvest Units in the Tongass National Forest, Southeast Alaska.* University of Alaska Museum, Fairbanks. Submitted under contract #53-0109-6-00214 to USDA Forest Service, Tongass National Forest, Ketchikan Area.

Stewart, H.
  1977 *Indian Fishing: Early Methods on the Northwest Coast.* University of Washington Press, Seattle.

Stuiver, M., and P.J. Reimer
  1993 Extended ^{14}C Data Base and Revised CALIB 3.0.3 ^{14}C Age Calibration Program. *Radiocarbon* 35:215-230.

Sumpter, I.D.
  1994 Ventures in Cultural Heritage Management. *The Midden* 26(5):5-6.

Tveskov, Mark A.
  1995 From Prehistory to History: Continuity in Native American Fishing Practices on the Oregon Coast. Paper presented at *Hidden Dimensions: The Cultural Significance of Wetland Archaeology,* Vancouver, BC, April 27-30, 1995.

Wessen, Gary
  1983 *Archaeological Investigations at Vancouver Lake, Washington.* Prepared by Western Heritage, Olympia, WA, for Cooper & Associates, Portland, OR.

Wooley, C.
  1987 Racing the Tide: Southeast Alaska Shoreline Survey. Paper presented at the annual meeting of the Alaska Anthropological Association, Anchorage.

Fishing Weirs in Oregon Coast Estuaries
Scott Byram

Historically on the Northwest Coast of North America, stationary fishing structures were often built and used on an annual basis to harvest massive amounts of salmon during spawning runs. Salmon harvested in this manner could be processed and stored for several months, and thus provided the staple food for many Native communities. Research into this technology has increased over the past two decades (Byram 1996; Byram and Erlandson 1996; Langdon et al. 1995; Monks 1987; Moss and Erlandson, this volume; Moss et al. 1990; Pomeroy 1976; Stevenson, this volume), and it is becoming clear that on the Northwest Coast other types of fishing structures were also widely used, and that a wide range of fishes and other marine animals were harvested with these devices. Because fishing structures played an important role in many Northwest Coast economies historically, and because of their antiquity and high degree of preservation archaeologically (Moss and Erlandson, this volume), research into the variation in this technology may lead to a better understanding of the development of Northwest Coast economies.

This chapter considers variation in stationary fishing structures in estuaries on the Oregon coast, in the southern portion of the Northwest Coast culture area. In their chapter on Northwest Coast fishing structures, Moss and Erlandson distinguish weirs from traps, with a weir being a kind of fence or barrier, and a trap being an enclosure (c.f., Ballard 1957:38; Smith 1969:258). Both types of fishing structures may be preserved as linear features of wooden stakes or piled rock, possibly in association with brush, wattles, or woven wood lattice panels. Either structure can be composed of the same types of materials, and therefore it may be difficult to distinguish between barriers and enclosures archaeologically. In colloquial use and in the anthropological literature from the Oregon coast (Moss and Erlandson 1995), fishing structures are typically referred to as weirs. Therefore, I use the term "weir" to refer to any fishing structure, recognizing that these may include enclosures as well as barriers. Future analysis of archaeological features on the Oregon coast may allow greater resolution of structural variation.

I use archaeological, ethnographic, and environmental information to examine variability in fishing structures on the Oregon coast. Findings suggest that the greatest variation in these structures involves their relationships to aspects of the local environment.

Oregon Estuaries

Environment
The Oregon coast, south of the Columbia River, features numerous rivers that flow into the sea from the east. The estuaries of these streams range

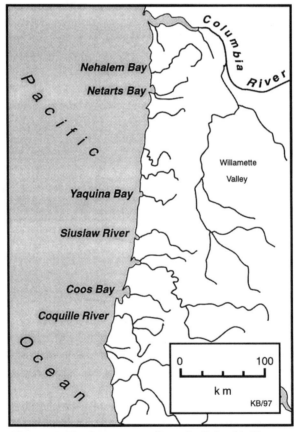

Figure 1. The Oregon coast (from the Columbia River to the California border) showing locations of estuaries in which archaeological weir sites have been identified.

from less than 500 ha to 13,000 ha. Tidal range in these estuaries averages 1.7 m. Some possess substantial intertidal zones, representing up to 70 percent of estuary surface area (Proctor et al. 1980:2-56), whereas others occur in relatively narrow river valleys. Weir sites occur in several of the mid-sized and larger estuaries (Figure 1).

In estuary environments, river-borne detritus mixes with marine upwelling nutrients brought in by tidal currents. The combination results in an exceptionally high biomass. Estuaries are among the "most productive areas on earth, supporting more plant and animal growth per unit of area than even the best agricultural lands" (McConnaughey and McConnaughey 1986:76; see also Proctor et al. 1980:3-77; Thom 1987:32). Although the estuary biomass is highest in summer, fish and other fauna are sustained year-round by the estuary's reservoir of nutrients. For example, eel grass (*Zostera* sp.) represents a large portion of the plant biomass in estuaries such as Yaquina Bay, but becomes an important source of food for estuary fauna only after it dies, in the fall and winter (Proctor et al. 1980:3-82).

Resources in Oregon coast estuaries that are potentially significant for human subsistence include several species of fish (Table 1). Some are present in large numbers seasonally, and others maintain moderate populations throughout the year (Monaco et al. 1990-1991).

Traditional Native Subsistence
Ethnographic information indicates the estuary was central to Oregon coast Native subsistence and settlement during the mid-nineteenth century, the time of initial Euro-American settlement in the region. From the Coquille River north to the Nehalem, the largest and most numerous Native settlements were located on estuaries. South of the Coquille River, where most estuaries are less than 500 ha, estuarine settlements were smaller. In areas of dense population, Native communities were distributed along estuary shores, sometimes from the extreme lower estuary upstream to the limits of tidewater (Jacobs 1931-1934:nb.99:17; Buchanon 1931; Suphan 1974:231, 235; Talbot 1851:112; Tveskov 1995).

Documentary accounts indicate that Oregon coast Native people were relatively sedentary. Often residing near estuaries through much of the year, groups would leave at various times to gather seasonally available resources, upriver or on the outer coast (Buchanon 1931; Drew 1931; Harrington 1942:reel 23:552, 561, reel 26:95-98; Vaughn ca. 1890s:9). The ubiquitous use of canoes allowed resources to be procured from throughout the estuary and returned to towns on a daily basis (Jacobs 1931-1934:nb.91:21, folder 96-22).

Archaeological Survey and Site Characterization
From 1993 to 1995, University of Oregon archaeologists conducted surveys

Table 1

Fish common in two or more Oregon coast estuaries at mainstem channel edges, subsidiary channels, and on intertidal flats

Common name	Scientific name	Comments
Chinook salmon	*Oncorhynchus tshawytsca*	spring and fall races
Coho salmon	*Oncorhynchus kisutch*	
Cutthroat trout	*Oncorhynchus clarki*	
English sole	*Pleuronectes vetulus*	juvenile
Green and white sturgeon	*Acipenser* spp.	
Longfin smelt	*Spirinchus thaleichthys*	not on intertidal flats
Northern anchovy	*Engraulis mordax*	not on intertidal flats
Pacific herring	*Clupea pallasi*	not on intertidal flats
Pacific staghorn sculpin	*Leptocottus armatus*	
Pacific tomcod	*Microgadus proximus*	not on intertidal flats
Shiner perch	*Cymatogaster aggregata*	
Starry flounder	*Platichthys stellatus*	
Steelhead	*Oncorhynchus mykiss*	
Surf smelt	*Hypomesus pretiosus*	
Threespine stickleback	*Gasterosteus aculeatus*	
Topsmelt	*Atherinops affinis*	

Source: Monaco et al. 1990-1991.

in portions of seven estuaries along the central and northern Oregon coast. These surveys, which focused on weir sites, took place during "minus tides," when water levels drop between 0.5 m and 1.0 m below mean low water. Sites were observed from canoes and kayaks and during pedestrian survey on mud flats, channel margins, and along salt marsh channels.

Thirty weir sites were recorded in (from south to north) (Figure 1) the Coquille, Coos, Siuslaw, Yaquina, Netarts, and Nehalem estuaries (Byram 1995, Moss and Erlandson 1995). These were identified by the presence of alignments of vertical wooden stakes protruding from intertidal channel banks or mudflats (Figures 2 and 3). Two additional wood-stake weir sites (originally recorded by Reg Pullen [1985] and John Draper [1980]) were re-visited. No stone weirs have been recorded on the Oregon coast.

The 30 recorded Oregon coast weir sites are located in three of the four estuary settings distinguished in Oregon estuary biological literature (Monaco et al. 1990-1991). These are subsidiary channels (or "tidal slough channels"), the edges of mainstem channels, and expansive tideflats along estuary margins. Weirs have not (yet) been found extending across estuary mainstem channels.

Most of the features at the Oregon coast sites comprise discrete alignments of stakes, though in portions of some sites the identification of alignments has been frustrated by the presence of what appear to be overlapping structures. The buried portions of these stakes are generally well preserved,

▲ **Figure 2.** Left arm of cross-channel tidal weir, Siuslaw River. Looking downstream at extremely low tide. *Photo by S. Byram.*

Figure 3. Tideflat weir, Coos Bay. Looking across tideflat at low tide. *Photo by S. Byram.*

as indicated by those that have been collected for radiocarbon dating. Because the upper portions of these stakes are reduced in size due to weathering, the original height and other characteristics of the top ends are uncertain. Lattice fragments, observed at two weir sites with extensive erosional exposures (Figure 4), are interpreted to be the remains of either weir panels or basket traps. At some sites, other types of artifacts have been observed on the mudflats near weir features.

In addition to documentation and analysis of surface collected artifacts, detailed maps have been made at several sites. Thirty-one weir stakes from Oregon coast sites have been collected and radiocarbon dated (see Moss and Erlandson, this volume), documenting almost 2,500 years of weir fishing. Several of the Oregon coast weir sites are relatively recent, dating within the past 350 years. Historical accounts and the presence of milled wood in some weirs show that weir fishing continued in the region into the late nineteenth or early twentieth century (Harrington 1942:reel 23:437-480; Stafford 1975).

Weir Features in Oregon Coast Estuaries

Oregon Coast Weir Types

An important step in examining variation in Oregon coast weirs has been organizing the data. I have developed a typology based on the archaeologi-

Figure 4. Excavation of lattice panel B8-A, Osprey site (35CS130) in July 1995. *Photo by K. Bernick.*

cal weirs and ethnographic accounts of weirs on the Northwest Coast and in northwest California. Considerable variation exists in weirs used in these regions (see Hewes 1947; Kroeber and Barrett 1960; Rostlund 1952; Stewart 1977). To be useful for archaeological research, this typology is based on characteristics observable under conditions of variable preservation. The foundation of the weir – whether of wood, stone, or other material – is the portion of the weir most often surviving in the archaeological record. Therefore, variability in the position of an alignment of weir stakes in relation to the local environment is an attribute that will likely be present at nearly all weir sites.

I classify Oregon coast weirs based on (1) the presence or absence of marine influence in the waters surrounding the weir, and (2) the configuration of the weir in relation to local hydrology (water flow patterns) and topography (landform characteristics). Variability in these areas can be examined in both ethnographic accounts of weirs and archaeological weir features.

Estuarine vs. Riverine Biomes
The degree of marine influence in the water surrounding a weir site can be measured in terms of salinity. Variation in marine influence relates to weir function in that salinity is a key factor determining the makeup of harvestable fish populations in the site area. In rivers that are tidally influenced, three tiers of salinity are often recognized: saltwater, brackish water, and freshwater (Simenstad 1983, Monaco et al. 1990-1991). Both saltwater and brackish water are estuarine environments, whereas freshwater is riverine. Thus, weirs occurring in saltwater or brackish water settings are estuarine, and those occurring in freshwater settings are riverine. The known archaeological weirs on the Oregon coast are all estuarine (though ethnographic and historical accounts describe both riverine and estuarine weirs in this region).

Tidal vs. Non-Tidal Hydrology
Within both riverine and estuarine settings, weirs may be designed to function with or without tidal fluctuation. Tidal weirs are typically designed to allow fish passage on an incoming tide, blocking or guiding fish on the outgoing tide. Non-tidal weirs do not require tidal action to function. Though they may be built in tidewater, these appear to have been more common in riverine settings above tidewater. Non-tidal weirs block or guide fish under conditions of unidirectional currents and limited water-level variability. These include the large "fish dams" that were often rebuilt annually. Tidal weirs are less often described, but this type is common archaeologically in Northwest Coast estuaries.

Topographic Setting
Non-tidal weirs on the Oregon coast were normally built in channels. Tidal

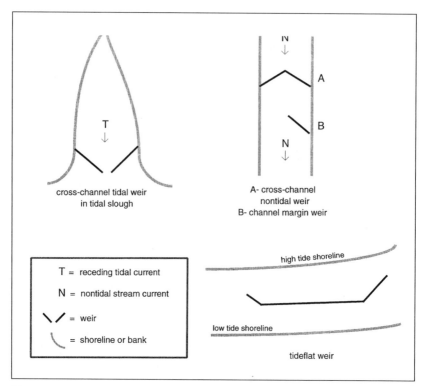

Figure 5. Plan views of selected weir types.

weirs were built and used in various estuary settings, including mainstem channels (tidal rivers), subsidiary channels (tidal sloughs), and tideflats. Among both tidal and non-tidal weirs occurring in channels, further subdivisions can be made based on the position of the weir in the channel. Thus, there are channel-edge weirs, built at the margin of a mainstem channel, mid-channel weirs, built in a mainstem or subsidiary channel but not extending to both banks of the channel, and cross-channel weirs, built across an entire channel, either mainstem or subsidiary (Figure 5). Collectively, cross-channel and channel-margin weirs that occur in the estuary can be referred to as tidal-channel weirs.

Elsewhere, weirs have been classified according to their shape or outline in plan view. Examples include "V-shaped weirs" (Byram and Tveskov 1994) and "chevron weirs" (Langdon et al. 1995). I suggest that weir shape is a useful attribute, but only in reference to its setting. A weir is not necessarily always built in a particular shape for the same reason. For example, Kroeber and Barrett (1960:13) suggest the Kepel weir was V-shaped to give it strength in the heavy current of the Klamath River, whereas Hewes (1947: Figures 1, 5, 13) illustrates weirs that were V-shaped to guide fish toward a trap or net at the apex of the V. In effect, there are considerable differences in fish habitat and fish populations between estuarine and riverine, or tidal and non-tidal, settings, as well as within each of these settings. Whether a weir is linear or curvilinear, of single or multiple lines, its position in relation to its surroundings is the factor that most significantly conditions its use.

Archaeological Weir Sites

Feature Types Present

In Oregon coast estuaries, remains of weirs are most common in subsidiary tidal channels, less so on tideflats, and relatively rare along the edges of mainstem channels (Table 2). Among the 24 weir sites in subsidiary tidal channels, many contain the remains of incomplete tidal-channel weirs of indeterminate sub-type, though in some cases they can be identified as cross-channel weirs (Figure 2). Many of the tidal-channel weirs occur at the mouths of sloughs that drain almost completely during a moderately low tide.

The six sites with tideflat weirs recorded on the Oregon coast occur on extensive intertidal flats along the margins of bays (Figure 3). These weirs are generally longer than the tidal-channel weirs (single features range up to 100 m vs. less than 40 m for most tidal-channel weirs). The stake alignments vary in configuration, including single straight lines, single curved lines (arc open toward the shore), and converging lines forming a V or L shape in plan. One site (35CS130) appears to contain the remains of several channel-edge weirs, consisting of closely spaced, small, branching stakes aligned perpendicular to the mainstem channel of the Coquille estuary. Although built in a mainstem channel, none of these weirs is thought to be a portion of a cross-channel non-tidal weir, or fish dam. The stakes in the channel-edge weirs at 35CS130 are no larger than those in most tidal weirs on the Oregon coast (less than 6 cm in diameter). Larger stakes would likely be present if the stakes formed a fish dam.

Only one Oregon coast weir, in the Nehalem estuary, displays characteristics that suggest it may be a fish dam. It is constructed exclusively of large (8 cm to 15 cm diameter), tightly spaced stakes aligned perpendicular to the stream channel, and it is located in a narrow section of the large tidal channel. For a fish dam to function in tidewater, it would have to be a substantial structure, as tidal range on the Oregon coast may be as much as 3 m diurnally (United States Department of Commerce 1994).

Feature Elements

Aside from the Nehalem River weir, the diameter of most stakes in Oregon coast sites ranges from 1.5 cm to 6 cm, though stouter stakes are present in some sites. Most of the stakes that have been collected for radiocarbon

Table 2

Characteristics of archaeological weir sites in Oregon Coast estuaries

Site	Topographic setting[1]	Feature type[2]	Stake type	Age[3]
COQUILLE ESTUARY				
35CS130	S, M	C, XC, CE	stem, split	660 ± 50, 670 ± 50, 940 ± 50
35CS146	M	C	stem	
35CS147	S, I	C or TF	stem	
COOS ESTUARY				
35CS111	S	C		
35CS122	S	C	stem	180 ± 50
35CS123	S	C	stem, split	240 ± 70
35CS124	S	C	stem, split	30 ± 50
35CS125	I	TF	stem, split	230 ± 70, 290 ± 60
35CS126	I	TF	stem, split	290 ± 60
35CS127	S, I	C, TF	stem, split	
35CS128	I	TF	stem	140 ± 50, 210 ± 50
35CS132	S	C	stem, split	20 ± 60
35CS133	S	XC	stem, split	recent[4]
35CS134	S	XC	stem, split	180 ± 60
35CS143	S	C	stem	100 ± 60
35CS144	S	C	stem	70 ± 60
SIUSLAW ESTUARY				
35LA1101	S	C	stem	130 ± 60, 280 ± 50
35LA1102	S	C	stem, split	

Site	Setting[1]	Weir feature[2]	Components	Date[3]
35LA1103	S	XC	stem, split	recent
35LA1104	S	XC	stem, split	0 ± 50, 90 ± 60, 160 ± 60
35LA1105	S	C	stem	910 ± 50
35LA1106	S, I	C	stem, split	
35LA1107	S, I	C or TF	stem	
35LA1108	S	XC	split	recent
YAQUINA ESTUARY				
35LNC76	S	XC, C	stem, split	320 ± 40, 350 ± 70, 560 ± 70, 1160 ± 40, 1330 ± 80, 1400 ± 60, 2120 ± 70
35LNC77	S	C	stem	1920 ± 80
35LNC78	S	C	stem	2220 ± 80, 2410 ± 80
NETARTS ESTUARY				
35TI68	I	TF	stem, split	
35TI69	S	XC	stem	
NEHALEM ESTUARY				
35TI71	M	XC(NT)[5]	split	

[1] Topographic settings: S = subsidiary channel, M = mainstem channel, I = intertidal flat.

[2] Types of weir features: XC = cross-channel weir, C = unspecified channel weir, CE = channel edge weir, TF = tideflat weir.

[3] Uncorrected ^{14}C dates (see Moss and Erlandson, this volume).

[4] "Recent" age inferred from milled wood components, which indicate that some weir construction took place after the 1850s.

[5] This is the only fishing structure identified in the survey that appears to be a non-tidal weir.

dating are at least 40 cm long, though, due to weathering, the original vertical dimension of the stakes is unknown. Weirs appear to vary more in stake spacing than in stake diameter. Observed stake spacing at Oregon coast weir sites ranges from 2 cm to 3 cm, to as much as 1 m, and considerable variation may exist within a single weir line. Taphonomic processes may account for much of the variation.

Two types of stakes have been identified in Oregon estuary weirs. Most common are stem stakes, consisting of sections of whole stems (usually a branch, less often a trunk), round in cross-section. Many stem stakes exhibit branching, and several retain well-preserved outer wood or bark on buried portions. Somewhat less common, split-wood stakes are reduced from planks, logs, or large branches, or, in recent sites, from milled boards.

Several occurrences of archaeological lattice have been identified at three sites. These may be the remains of lattice weir panels and basket traps used in conjunction with weirs (Byram and Erlandson 1996:51-53; Reg Pullen, personal communication 1994). Most of the information about the lattice is based on observations of exposed eroding pieces, though samples of lattice were excavated from the Osprey site (Byram and Erlandson 1996). Because the lattice is highly regular in construction, attributes such as warp thickness and method of weft twining can be generalized from small exposures of lattice.

Weir Use on the Oregon Coast

The most informative data I have encountered regarding the function of Oregon coast weirs come from numerous ethnographic and historical accounts of weir use, fish habitat data related to weir distribution, and lattice mesh size relative to fish size. Though less direct, fish taxa represented in assemblages from occupation sites near weir sites are also useful as context for interpreting Oregon coast weir use.

Ethnographic and Historical Evidence Related to Archaeological Findings

An extensive survey of mostly unpublished ethnographic and historical documents has revealed numerous accounts of traditional estuary fishing. Most accounts of Native fishing techniques used in Oregon estuaries refer to a single type of structure or fishing strategy. A more general summary of the importance of estuary fishing is found in an unpublished manuscript on Coos ethnology by Melville Jacobs (1931-1934: folder 96-22). Based on interviews with elders of Coos-Coquille ancestry, Jacobs concluded that in the early nineteenth century, the primary source of food for the Native residents of Coos Bay and the lower Coquille River was fish caught in the estuary. Residents of towns along estuary shores were able to harvest all the fish they could process and store during seemingly limitless fish runs, which occurred several times during the year in these estuaries. According to Jacobs, these runs were of two "kinds" of herring; chinook, coho, and one other salmon; two kinds of sardine; two kinds of smelt (including surf smelt); and one other unidentified fish. Tidal weirs were among the tools used to catch these prodigious hauls of fish. A variety of fishes were harvested in other Oregon estuaries as well (see e.g., Drucker 1934, 1965; Harrington 1942; Jacobs 1931-1934). Fishes that were typically caught in the estuary include most of those listed in Table 1.

Ethnographic accounts of estuarine weir use on the Oregon coast are generally brief, but most include information that can be related to archaeological weir-site data. Three types of estuary weirs appear to be represented in the ethnographic literature from the Oregon coast. These are fish dams (estuarine or riverine) and two types of estuarine weirs, cross-channel tidal weirs and tideflat weirs.

Riverine and Estuarine Fish Dams (Cross-Channel Non-Tidal Weirs)
Ethnographic accounts describe riverine weir fishing upstream from the estuary, where some of the occupants of towns along the estuary went at certain seasons. Some people built weirs across rivers above the reach of the tide, in rapids where the water is shallow (Harrington 1942:reel 23:552; Jacobs 1931-1934:nb.91:21). In other cases, people built large weirs across tidal river channels in the upper estuaries (Harrington 1942:reel 24:102, 484; Jacobs 1931-1934:nb.91:21). These upper estuary weirs, though situated in tidewater, were actually non-tidal weirs, as their method of operation did not depend on tidal fluctuations. Several well-known accounts indicate non-tidal weirs in Oregon and throughout the Northwest Coast were typically built in stream channels (Ballard 1957; Barnett 1955:80; Kroeber and Barrett 1960; Smith 1969; Stewart 1977). Non-tidal weirs located in rivers upstream from the reach of the tide targeted both Pacific lamprey and salmon, whereas non-tidal weirs in estuaries appear to have been used for salmon harvesting primarily (Harrington 1942:reel 23:484; Jacobs 1931-1934:nb.91:21).

Estuarine Cross-Channel Tidal Weirs
According to ethnographic and historical accounts (Drucker 1934; Harrington 1942:reel 23:437, 480; Stafford 1975), estuarine tidal weirs were most often built across the mouths of tidal sloughs (subsidiary channels). These were designed to allow fish passage during high tide and prevent fish passage on the outgoing tide. Most accounts describe cross-channel tidal weirs as stake or brush fences with no cross pieces, forming a V or straight line in plan. These weirs sometimes led fish into portable basket traps that were retrieved and then reset after the fish were removed (Drucker 1934; Harrington 1942:reel 24:484; Jacobs 1931-1934:nb.91:42, nb.92:111). In

other cases, fish were scooped from behind the weir with nets or baskets (Charles 1931; Jacobs 1931-1934:nb.99-115; Stafford 1975; Talbot 1851:112). In both cases, these relied on the fish being detained behind the weir or in the basket trap as the tide receded. Salmon, flounder, and herring are often mentioned in these accounts as being targeted with estuarine tidal weirs, though generalized harvests of a wide range of species seem to have been common. These weirs appear to have been built most often on estuary margins close to towns, where they would have been readily accessible. They appear to have been used during large fish runs and on a day-to-day basis at other times. Several of the accounts mention basket traps used with these weirs, especially for small fish such as herring, smelt, and flounder.

Most estuarine cross-channel tidal weirs appear to have been made with closely spaced wooden stakes. Some of these structures may have incorporated lattice weir panels (Figure 6). In an account from Humboldt Bay, on the northern California coast, Hewes (1940:22) describes a cross-channel tidal weir of lattice, used by the Wiyot. The portable panels of this lattice weir were placed across the mouth of a tidal slough during high tide, and fish were left in 5 cm to 10 cm of water when the tide receded. Hewes notes

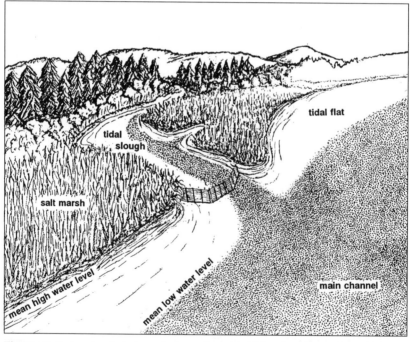

Figure 6. Reconstructed view of a cross-channel tidal weir as it may have looked in operation, at low tide. Based on archaeological and environmental data from the Osprey site (35CS130).

that the weir was used to catch shiner perch, flounders, bullheads (sculpin), and herring, as well as crabs. Although similar accounts have not been found in the Oregon coast ethnographic material, some of the excavated archaeological lattice from the Osprey site (35CS130) on the Coquille River appears to represent the remains of weir panels (Byram and Erlandson 1996:51-53).

Channel-Edge Weirs
I have found no ethnographic accounts of channel-edge weirs used on the Oregon coast, though non-tidal versions of these were used by the Tolowa on Smith River in northwest California (Kroeber and Barrett 1960:23, 53). The non-tidal versions of these weirs were used to divert fish toward nets or spearing stations as the fish moved upstream. Though built in tidewater, channel-edge weirs in the Coquille estuary may have been used in a similar fashion.

Estuarine Tideflat Weirs
There are several accounts of Native people spear fishing on the tideflats of Oregon estuaries during the mid-1800s, and one that mentions a weir built on the tideflats of Coos Bay to corral flounder for spearing (Harrington 1942:reel 23:480, reel 24:223). Some tideflat weirs may have functioned in a similar fashion to cross-channel tidal weirs, allowing fish to pass above the weir during high tide and impounding them as the tide receded. This type of weir is described in use at Shoalwater Bay, just north of the Columbia River on the Washington coast: "made by arranging on the tideflats two long, converging lines of upright poles, which led the fish into a cul de sac, where they remained as the tide receded" (Curtis 1970:50). Lattice may have been used in some tideflat weirs on the Oregon coast, as it was elsewhere. For example, Elmendorf (1992:76) mentions lattice panels used in tidal weirs made by the Twana to catch herring on the tideflats of Hood Canal, in Washington state. As yet, I have encountered no accounts of this from the Oregon coast, and no lattice fragments have been found at the archaeological tideflat weir sites in the region.

Associated Technology
Lattice panels were used in many riverine fish dams described ethnographically on the southern Northwest Coast and in northwest California (Barnett 1955:80; Kroeber and Barrett 1960:14, 22; Smith 1969:260), yet I have found no accounts of lattice panels used in estuarine weirs on the Oregon coast. Several Oregon coast accounts mention that basket traps, constructed of lattice panels wrapped around hoops, were used in conjunction with wood-stake weirs in tidewater settings (Harrington 1942:reel 20:323; Jacobs 1931-1934:nb.92:111).

The Oregon coast literature includes numerous descriptions of tools related to weir and trap fishing, including dip nets, seines, gill nets, gaff hooks, spears, and canoes. Canoes may have been the single most important tool for fishing in Oregon estuaries. They were used for transportation to weir sites and other types of fishing stations, as platforms to stand on while fishing, and for transporting fish back to towns. With the aid of tidal currents, tens of kilometres of the estuary could be traversed by canoe in a single day (Scholfield 1853; Talbot 1851:112; Williams 1878), which would have made it possible for an individual (or a team) to use several weirs simultaneously.

To summarize, aside from the large non-tidal fish dams built across river channels in the upper reaches of tidewater, the ethnographic and historical accounts uncovered at this time do not indicate that particular estuary weirs were built to harvest any one fish species exclusively. Nor do they suggest estuarine weir use was most common during any one season. These accounts suggest a variety of taxa was harvested with estuarine tidal weirs through much of the year.

Weir Site Distribution and Fish Habitat

Most of the fishes listed in Table 1 inhabit all three topographic settings in which weirs have been identified in Oregon estuaries. Most are common or abundant as both adults and juveniles, though herring, longfin smelt, northern anchovy, and Pacific tomcod rarely inhabit tideflat shallows (Monaco et al. 1991:313-317). Tideflat weirs occur in settings inhabited by many estuarine fishes, and both cross-channel and channel-edge weirs are found in habitats frequented by all the species in Table 1. Allowing for changes in fish populations and habitat during the past 150 years, it is likely that most tidal weirs in Oregon coast estuaries were used in settings where a wide variety of fishes would have been present. In contrast to tidal weirs, fish dams appear to have been used in both estuarine and riverine settings. Although these two settings represent different habitats, ethnographic accounts suggest that most fish dams were used to harvest anadromous fish as they moved from saltwater to freshwater habitats.

Lattice Gauge and Fish Size

To date, 16 fragments of split-wood lattice (Figure 7) have been identified in three Oregon coast weir sites. These may have been used in either basket traps or lattice weir panels, or in both devices. "Lattice gauge" refers to the size of openings in the lattice, and represents the average distance between the rigid warps. Typically, this is the smaller of the two dimensions in a rectangular lattice mesh. Nearly all the lattice fragments are of sufficiently fine gauge to prevent the passage of small fish such as herring, smelt, and

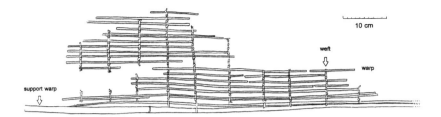

Figure 7. Fragment of lattice panel specimen B8-D (9-mm gauge), excavated from the Osprey site (35CS130).

shiner perch. Fifteen of the 16 fragments have lattice gauge measurements of less than 15 mm, with 9 mm being the average. One has a 30 mm lattice gauge and would probably allow passage of adult herring, smelt, or shiner perch, but not adult salmonids.

In historically documented weirs that targeted large fish such as salmon, lattice panels were generally coarse, averaging 50 mm or more (Barnett 1955:80; Kautz 1900:186; Stewart 1977:102). This gauge measurement is six times the average size of the Oregon coast archaeological specimens. To better understand the differences between coarse and fine lattice, I made two semi-rigid lattice panels of split cedar warps and spruce root wefts, experimenting with the manufacture and twining of warps and wefts of different dimensions. I found that 10 mm-gauge lattice takes nearly twice as long to produce as 20 mm-gauge lattice. Based on this limited experimentation, and assuming raw materials were not in short supply, I suggest that because considerably more effort was required to produce it, fine-gauge lattice was likely used when small fish were targeted, or when generalized harvests of both small and large fish were intended. When large fish such as salmon were exclusively targeted, coarse-gauge lattice (perhaps greater than 50 mm) would most likely have been used, being more efficient to produce. However, manufacturing efficiency and fish size may not be the primary factors conditioning the dimensions of lattice. Other possible factors include resistance to stream current, durability, and aesthetic preferences. But whatever the impetus for producing fine-gauge lattice, its use would have allowed the harvest of numerous small fish that inhabited estuary settings.

Fish Remains at Occupation Sites

Because numerous fishing techniques were used by residents of the Oregon coast, and because the archaeological faunal assemblages are not directly associated with the weirs, fish remains from occupation sites do not necessarily represent fish caught with weirs. However, these assemblages do represent fish that were harvested, and therefore they provide useful contextual evidence for interpreting weir use. Studies that have incorporated fine-grained recovery techniques indicate that a wide variety of fishes was harvested by Native groups at several Oregon coast estuaries, from the mid-Holocene through recent times (Greenspan 1996; Losey 1996). Some of the fishes that are commonly reported from occupation sites near estuaries include salmonids, flounder, herring, perch, sculpin, and others listed in Table 1.

Summary and Conclusions
Archaeological survey and site characterization have demonstrated that fishing structures are preserved in a variety of estuarine settings on the Oregon coast and that most estuarine fishing weirs differ in construction and placement in comparison with the better-known riverine non-tidal fishing weirs. Whereas riverine weirs were often large structures built across rivers to limit anadromous fish passage during spawning runs, estuarine weirs were built often in subsidiary channels and were designed to work in conjunction with tidal action. Although considerable variability exists among estuarine weirs on the Oregon coast, most occur in settings inhabited by a wide variety of fishes during all seasons. Biologists have shown that the biomass of Northwest Coast estuaries is extremely rich in a variety of fishes potentially useful to Native communities. Many of these fishes could have been harvested with weirs, and ethnographic and historical accounts confirm that many different fishes were harvested with estuarine weirs on the Oregon coast. This conclusion is also supported by characteristics of archaeological lattice, which suggest that small as well as large fish could have been harvested, and by the variety of fishes reported from archaeological contexts in occupation sites located near estuary shores.

This study shows that the variability in the weir fishing strategies used by Native peoples of the southern Northwest Coast can be studied through archaeological and archival research. Continued investigation of variability in fishing sites on the Oregon coast and elsewhere will ultimately lead to a better understanding of the importance of estuarine fishing technologies in the development of Northwest Coast economies.

Acknowledgments
I would like to thank Jon Erlandson and Madonna Moss for their encouragement and guidance; Kitty Bernick, Liz Sobel, and Virginia Butler for editing assistance; Gordon Hewes for providing copies of his field notes; Mark Tveskov for his work documenting several weir sites; as well as Robert Kentta and Ben Breon of the Confederated Tribes of Siletz; Reg Pullen, former BLM archaeologist; and Coquille Indian Tribe members Don Ivy, Jerry Running Foxe, Sharon Parrish, George Wasson, Denni Mitchell, Shirod and Jason Younker, and Troy Anderson. Others who participated in fieldwork at fishing sites include Tom Connolly, Ann Bennett-Rogers, Alex Atkins, Rob Losey, Brad Bowden, Dennis Griffin, and many other University of Oregon students and Coquille and Siletz tribal

members. This research was funded by grants from the Oregon State Historic Preservation Office and support from the Oregon State Museum of Anthropology, the University of Oregon Department of Anthropology, and the Coquille Indian Tribe.

References Cited

Ballard, Arthur C.
  1957 The Salmon Weir on Green River in Western Washington. *Davidson Journal of Anthropology* 3:37-53.
Barnett, Homer G.
  1955 *The Coast Salish of British Columbia.* University of Oregon Press, Eugene.
Buchanon, Jim
  1931 Testimony taken on behalf of the defendants, including Mr. Buchanon. Coos (or Kowes) Bay, Lower Umpqua (or Kalawatset), and Siuslaw Indian Tribes, Plaintiff, vs. The United States of America, Defendant. Nov. 10-13, US Court of Claims, North Bend, OR.
Byram, Scott
  1995 Surveys of Intertidal Fishing Weirs. In *An Evaluation, Survey, and Dating Program for Archaeological Sites on State Lands of the Northern Oregon Coast,* by Madonna Moss and Jon Erlandson. Report submitted to the Oregon State Historic Preservation Office, Salem.
  1996 Wet Site Archaeology and Ethnohistory on the Mid-Pacific Coast: The Subsistence Technology of Intertidal Fishing Weirs and Related Assemblages. Paper presented at the 61st Annual Meeting of the Society for American Archaeology, April 10-14, 1996, New Orleans.
Byram, Scott, and Jon Erlandson
  1996 *Fishing Technologies at a Coquille River Wet Site: The 1994-95 Osprey Site Archaeological Project.* Report on file, Oregon State Museum of Anthropology, Eugene.
Byram, Scott, and Mark Tveskov
  1994 Wood Stake Fish Weirs on the Oregon Coast. Poster presented at the 59th Annual Society for American Archaeology Meetings, April 7, 1994, Anaheim, CA.
Charles, Andrew
  1931 Testimony taken on behalf of the defendants, including Mr. Charles. Coos (or Kowes) Bay, Lower Umpqua (or Kalawatset), and Siuslaw Indian Tribes, Plaintiff, vs. The United States of America, Defendant. Nov. 10-13, US Court of Claims, North Bend, OR.
Curtis, Edward S.
  1970 [1907-1911] *The North American Indian: Vol. 9, Salishan Tribes of the Coast.* Edited by Frederick Hodge. Reprinted. Johnson Reprint, New York. Originally published 1907-1911, Plimpton Press, Norwood, MA.
Draper, John A.
  1980 *An Analysis of Lithic Tools and Debitage from 35CS1: A Prehistoric Site on the Southern Oregon Coast.* Master's thesis, Oregon State University, Corvallis.
Drew, Frank
  1931 Testimony taken on behalf of the defendants, including Mr. Drew. Coos (or Kowes) Bay, Lower Umpqua (or Kalawatset), and Siuslaw Indian Tribes, Plaintiff, vs. The United States of America, Defendant. Nov. 10-13, US Court of Claims, North Bend, OR.
Drucker, Philip
  1934 Coos Indians Field Notebook Vol.1. Manuscript 4516, file 78 of the Southwest Oregon Archival Research Project, University of Oregon Library, Eugene.
  1965 *Contributions to Alsea Ethnography.* Reprinted. Kraus, New York. Originally published 1939, *University of California Publications in American Archaeology and Ethnology* 35(7):81-101, Berkeley.
Elmendorf, William
  1992 *The Structure of Twana Culture.* Washington State University Press, Pullman.
Greenspan, Ruth
  1996 Non-Anadromous Fishing on the Southern Northwest Coast: A Perspective from the Vertebrate Faunal Assemblages. Paper presented at the 61st annual meeting of the Society for American Archaeology, New Orleans, April 12, 1996.

Harrington, John Peabody
   1942 Field notes recorded in conversations with individuals of Coos ancestry. John P. Harrington Microfilms: Alaska/Northwest Coast:reel 24, ethnographic and historic notes. National Anthropological Archives, National Museum of Natural History, Washington, DC.
Hewes, Gordon W.
   1940 Field notes from interviews with Indian people of several Northwest California tribes on the topic of traditional fishing techniques. Photocopies provided to the author by Gordon Hewes.
   1947 *Aboriginal Use of Fisheries Resources in Northwestern North America.* PhD dissertation, Department of Anthropology, University of California, Berkeley.
Jacobs, Melville
   1931-1934 Hanis and Miluk Coosan texts and linguistic and ethnographic data. Melville Jacobs Collection, University of Washington Libraries, Seattle.
Kautz, A.V.
   1900 Diary of General A.V. Kautz. *Washington Historian* 1(4):181-186.
Kroeber, A.L., and S.A. Barrett
   1960 *Fishing Among the Indians of Northwestern California.* Anthropological Records 21(1). University of California Press, Berkeley.
Langdon, Steve J., Douglas R. Reger, and Neil Campbell
   1995 Pavements, Pounds, Pairs, Piles, and Puzzles: Research on the Little Salt Lake Weir Complex. Paper presented at the conference, Hidden Dimensions: The Cultural Significance of Wetland Archaeology, Vancouver, BC, April 27-30, 1995.
Losey, Robert
   1996 *Fishing on the Lower Coquille River: A Zoological Perspective.* Master's paper, on file at the Department of Anthropology, University of Oregon, Eugene.
McConnaughey, Bayard, and Evelyn McConnaughey
   1986 *Pacific Coast.* Knopf, New York.
Monaco, M.E., R.L Emmett, D.M. Nelson, and S.A. Hinton
   1990-1991 *Distribution and Abundance of Fishes and Invertebrates in West Coast Estuaries.* 2 vols. ELMR Report No.4. NOAA/NOS Strategic Environmental Assessments Division, Silver Spring, MD.
Monks, Gregory G.
   1987 Prey as Bait: The Deep Bay Example. *Canadian Journal of Archaeology* 11:119-142.
Moss, Madonna, and Jon Erlandson
   1995 *An Evaluation, Survey, and Dating Program for Archaeological Sites on State Lands of the Northern Oregon Coast.* Report Submitted to the Oregon State Historic Preservation Office, Salem.
Moss, Madonna L., Jon M. Erlandson, and Robert Stuckenrath
   1990 Wood Stake Weirs and Salmon Fishing on the Northwest Coast: Evidence from Southeast Alaska. *Canadian Journal of Archaeology* 14:143-158
Pomeroy, J.A.
   1976 Stone Fish Traps of the Bella Bella Region. In *Current Research Reports,* edited by Roy L. Carlson, pp. 165-173. Department of Archaeology, Simon Fraser University, Burnaby, BC.
Proctor, Charles M., John Garcia, David Galvin, Gary Lewis, Lincoln Loehr, and Alison Massa
   1980 *An Ecological Characterization of the Pacific Northwest Coastal Region. Vol.2: Characterization Analysis, Regional Synopsis.* Prepared for the Office of Biological Services, US Fish and Wildlife Service, United States Dept. of the Interior, Portland, OR.
Pullen, Reg
   1985 Water-Saturated Sites on the Oregon Coast. *Current Archaeological Happenings in Oregon* 10(4):12-14.
Rostlund, Erhard
   1952 *Freshwater Fish and Fishing in Native North America.* University of California Publications in Geography Vol. 9. University of California Press, Berkeley.

Scholfield, Nathan
   1853 Autobiographical notes and letters of Nathan Scholfield, 1851-1853. Microfilm, Oregon State Library, Salem.
Simenstad, Charles A.
   1983 *The Ecology of Estuarine Channels of the Pacific Northwest Coast: A Community Profile.* United States Fish and Wildlife Service, Portland, OR.
Smith, Marian
   1969 *The Puyallup-Nisqually.* Reprinted. AMS Press, New York. Originally published 1940, Columbia University Contributions to Anthropology 32, New York.
Stafford, Kim
   1975 Interview with Trygve Nordahl. Ms. typescript (transcript of audiotape). Oral History Series, Pioneer Museum, Florence, OR.
Stewart, Hilary
   1977 *Indian Fishing: Early Methods on the Northwest Coast.* University of Washington Press, Seattle.
Suphan, Robert J.
   1974 An Ethnological report on the Identity and Localization of Certain Native Peoples of Northwestern Oregon. In *Oregon Indians I,* edited by H.C. Taylor, Jr. and R.J. Suphan, pp. 103-165. Garland, New York.
Talbot, Theodore
   1851 *Report of Geological Explorations on the Oregon Coast.* Western Americana Microfilm Series.
Thom, Ronald M.
   1987 The Biological Importance of Estuaries. *Northwest Environmental Journal* 3(1):21-42.
Tveskov, Mark A.
   1995 Archaeological Survey of the South Slough of Coos Bay. In *An Evaluation, Survey and Dating Program for Archaeological Sites on State Lands of the Northern Oregon Coast,* by Madonna Moss and Jon Erlandson. Report submitted to the Oregon State Historic Preservation Office, Salem, OR.
United States Department of Commerce
   1994 *Tide Tables, High and Low Water Predictions, West Coast of North America, Including the Hawaiian Islands.* Published annually by the author agency, Washington, DC.
Vaughn, Warren N.
   ca. 1890s Early History of Tillamook. Oregon Historical Society Manuscript 213, pp. 10-45. Oregon History Center, Portland, OR.
Williams, Loren L.
   1878 First Settlements in Southwest Oregon: T'Vault's Expedition. Bancroft Library manuscripts collection, University of California, Berkeley.

Wet-Site Contributions to Developmental Models of Fraser River Fishing Technology

Ann Stevenson

The Northwest Coast fishery has long been at the heart of discussions about the development of an economy that, although based on wild foods, afforded a level of sedentism, wealth, ascribed status, specialization, and population size usually seen only in agricultural communities. This economy was based on an effective fishing strategy employing an enormous variety of technologies and gear types to take advantage of varying water conditions and available species. This chapter demonstrates that many of these technologies have a long and complex history of development in the Fraser River estuary. In light of evidence from three wet sites, dating between 4,600 and 2,000 years ago, current models of how the fishery developed are re-examined.

Given current management problems in the Northwest Coast fishery, a relatively large and sedentary aboriginal population relying on wild fish for subsistence over many generations is of considerable relevance. Although the Fraser is currently the most important salmon producing river in North America (Fraser River Estuary Management Program 1994:5), this status is seriously threatened by declines of all varieties of salmon and of many other fish species, including sturgeon, eulachon, and steelhead (Glavin 1996: 15-18; see Appendix 1 for nomenclature). Glavin (1996:56-57) asserts that the incidental catch of "non-target" species – or bycatch – is one of the most serious environmental problems facing the fishery. To reduce bycatch, selective gear that targets specific species is needed.

Glavin (1996:95) recognizes that aboriginal fishery strategies and management systems worked over very long periods and therefore warrant careful study to assist in developing a more ecological and community-based management strategy. Although a wide variety of technologies and gear types were employed in the Fraser River fishery prior to European contact, many of the most widespread and effective types, such as traps and weirs, were banned late in the last century (Glavin 1996:57). Whereas the historical standardization of net gauges and methods of deployment obscure which net technologies were traditionally most effective, evidence from wet sites in the region can shed light on development of these fishing devices and raises questions for further research.

Developmental Models of the Fraser River Fishery

Moss and Erlandson (1995:33) point out that an underlying assumption in discussions of Northwest Coast cultural patterns, such as the fishing economy, is that cultures and the technological complexes associated with them evolve from simple to complex. Unfortunately, the nature of local fishing strategies and innovations created or adopted to solve problems are potentially obscured by emphasizing this larger evolutionary picture.

The two primary models that characterize how the Fraser River fishery developed emphasize the importance of salmon net technology evolvement and the advent of processing salmon for storage. Langdon (1977:177-178) and Kew (1992) have discussed how fishing techniques may have developed so that large numbers of salmon could be caught where they are most nutritious – in the approaches to the river or in the river estuary – rather than waiting to catch them upriver, where they have lost some nutritional value ascending the river to spawn. Kew's (1992:197-201) developmental model of net technology shows a progression from relatively simple dip nets used upriver where the banks are narrow to trawl nets used in the muddy waters of the estuary and to reef nets used to capture sockeye salmon in the saltwater approaches to the Fraser. Kew (1992:198) envisions that fishing techniques developed through time so that fish could be caught where they were least accessible but more nutritious. Langdon (1977:178) points out, in discussing an earlier version of Kew's model, that greater technological complexity requires a more complex labour strategy.

In a recently published volume, Matson and Coupland (1995:148) state that salmon processing for storage in large quantities is the critical factor that secured the foundation of the Developed Northwest Coast Pattern. A relatively secure time frame for this storage complex has recently been pushed back to before 3,000 years ago (Matson and Coupland 1995:173). Various lines of evidence may be cited for different areas of the Northwest Coast. Examples include evidence of salmon weirs in southeast Alaska (Moss et al. 1990), the advent of flatfish storage at the Hoko River site on Washington's Olympic Peninsula (Croes 1992b:347-351, 438; Croes and Blinman 1980), and faunal evidence of stored-salmon use at the Crescent Beach site in the Fraser delta (Matson 1992:411; Matson and Coupland 1995:173).

The emphasis of these models exclusively on salmon procurement and processing may obscure how the overall fishery developed. Wet-site evidence shows that although nets have a long history in the Fraser estuary, other devices may have played important roles as well. Certainly salmon is a critical resource; however, understanding how a range of fish was used in the area through time will provide a more complete picture of how the Fraser River fishery operated and developed.

The Nature of the Fraser Estuary Fishery

The development and nature of the Fraser River delta and estuary are complicating factors in evaluating the archaeological evidence of fishing strategies and associated technological developments. During the past five millennia, the delta has built about 25 km westward (Ham 1982:20), so that the conditions one finds at a given location today may be very different from those encountered in past millennia. In addition, seasonal changes in water flow, tides, and shore conditions influence fishing strategies on a very localized basis.

At particular locations and at specific times of the year, aggregated resources appear in the Fraser estuary. Runs of anadromous fish pass through the estuary in predictable seasonal patterns, and resident species amass to spawn. Although the Fraser is most famous for the summer and fall salmon runs, the seasonal arrival or amassing of other fish and waterfowl provide opportunities to harvest large quantities of food within short periods of time (Croes and Hackenberger 1988:45-54; Monks 1987:119; Suttles 1987: 46-47).

Selective harvesting is complicated by several factors, especially in the lower reaches of the river. For example, large fish runs attract significant prey species: the spring eulachon run attracts sea mammals, sturgeon, dogfish, and other fish and birds (Hart 1973:150). In addition, juvenile sockeye and pink salmon spend considerable time near the mouth of the river before moving out to sea and are present when mature salmon return to spawn (Hart 1973:109, 120). Starry flounder and eulachon are both present in the estuary in the spring.

Starry flounder are commonly found in the spring in the tidal flats and sloughs of the Fraser River estuary (Hart 1973:632). Although they are most numerous now in the Boundary Bay tidal flats, they are also found in the Fraser drainage in fairly large numbers as far upriver as the Alouette River sloughs, about 40 km upstream from the Fraser's mouth (Peacock 1982:34). Aboriginal use of starry flounder is not well documented. However, starry flounder bones commonly appear in archaeological deposits in the area throughout the past 4,000 years and on average are second only to salmon in frequency of identified fish remains (Matson 1992).

Although the development of effective butchering methods for salmon to allow this fish to be processed for long-term storage has been seen as a pivotal event in Northwest Coast economic development (see Matson and Coupland 1995:148; for discussion see Moss and Erlandson 1995:20), there may have been greater impetus to develop an efficient filleting technique for starry flounder, regardless of whether storage was a factor. The skin of the starry flounder has a very high iodine content, and if the fish is cooked with the skin on, it has a very unpleasant taste (Batdorf 1990:43). Because this flatfish also has very tough skin, it is reasonable to assume that efficient butchering techniques would have been necessary. Once skinned, the fillets could be cooked or possibly dried. Croes (1992b:438) has suggested that flatfish may have been the initial impetus for storage at the Hoko River site about 3,300 years ago, roughly the same time period Matson (1992:411) asserts that salmon storage initially occurred in the Fraser delta.

Central Coast Salish Fishery

The Fraser River estuary corresponds fairly closely to the traditional territory of the Downriver Halkomelem or Hunqum'i'num-speaking people who live mainly along the lower Fraser and its tributaries below the town of Mission. They include the Kwantlen, the Katzie, the Coquitlam, the Musqueam, and the Tsawwassen First Nations (Suttles 1990b:455), and anthropologists include them within the Central Coast Salish area. During the summer, Island Halkomelem people came to the river for the salmon run.

The fishery predominated the traditional subsistence economy of the Central Coast Salish, and a wide variety of devices and techniques were used to catch a range of species. The fishery relied on entrapment and barrier devices such as tidal traps, weirs, trawl and dip nets, and ensnarement and penetrating devices such as gill nets, hooks, gaffs, spears, and harpoons. These devices range from the simple to the complex and are often used in combination (see Suttles 1990a, 1990b:457 for brief outlines). Although salmon were the most important fish caught, others, including sturgeon, eulachon, steelhead, and flounder, were caught in the river, and herring, halibut, lingcod, Pacific cod, and others were taken in the adjacent saltwater approaches to the river.

The Central Coast Salish salmon weir required the cooperative efforts of a number of people to build and operate, in addition to technical and ritual supervision. Weirs were used by kin groups or entire villages. Tidal traps were built and owned by kin groups (Suttles 1990b:457).

Net Technology

Nets that are pulled through the water or that are easily reset at various locations have practical advantages over fixed tidal structures, especially in a dynamic area such as the Fraser estuary. Nets are portable and can be moved along the shore or out into the water to intercept the fish, providing greater access to fish than can intertidal traps. Many types of nets are reported historically for the Central Coast Salish area, including the Fraser River estuary. Mesh sizes for these nets range from 30 mm to 300 mm (Stevenson 1989:A-16). The Coast Salish used nets to catch a variety of fish and waterfowl, as well as sea mammals and deer. Fish nets were of two types: (1) entrapment types such as seines, bag, or trawl nets and, (2) ensnarement nets of either set or drift varieties. Identifying the function of archaeological net fragments is complicated by the overlap of mesh sizes for different types of nets and by the problem of inconsistency in the method of recording mesh sizes in written accounts. Moreover, a single net could be used for more than one purpose, and different types of nets could be used to catch a single species of fish in differing water conditions (e.g., muddy vs. clear water).

A set gill net has major advantages over a tidal trap in that it can easily be repositioned along the shore or across the entrance to a stream or slough, and it can be used in a wider range of tidal stages. A drift gill net can be used by one or two people in a single canoe. According to Suttles (1974:137), 30 to 40 fish can be caught this way in an evening of good fishing. Gill nets represent a considerable investment in labour, and only wealthy people can afford to maintain one. Gill nets can be a selective technology designed to capture a specific species.

Anthropologists consider salmon trawl nets to be the most highly developed form of indigenous net technology for the lower reaches of the Fraser. Such nets are specifically designed for turbid waters with moderate currents and are used to intercept large runs of salmon, primarily sockeye and chinook, in the summer and fall (Berringer 1982:45-53; Kew 1992:198, 201). Suttles (1990a:149) points out that group subsistence activities such as the use of weirs, complex nets, and some forms of tidal impounds are highly productive fishing techniques. They require cooperative efforts and, compared to individual fishing techniques, such as hook and line trolling, are subject to more restrictions in terms of ownership of sites and of equipment. They also require greater spiritual assistance. I suggest that highly effective fishing strategies such as nets and traps have a long history of use and development in the Fraser estuary, as demonstrated by wet-site evidence.

Non-Wet-Site Fishing Evidence

Analysis of stable carbon isotope ratios in human bone collagen has shown that for the last 5,000 years, people in the Fraser estuary region have obtained up to 90 percent of their protein from marine sources (Chisholm et al. 1983:397). How ancient people obtained these resources has been fairly speculative because, without considering wet-site components, artifactual data are not very informative. What has been recovered from shell middens and other dryland sites includes a variety of bone and antler points, composite harpoon parts, stone net and line weights, and tools made of stone or shell suitable for butchering fish. Chipped stone flake tools and bifacial knives probably fulfilled butchering functions from the earliest times and were replaced, after about 3500 BP, by ground slate knives (Fladmark 1986:58). In addition, microblade-like flakes may have served as cutting blades for fish knives during Locarno Beach times, about 3,300 to 2,400 years ago (Croes 1992a:103-104; Mitchell 1990:341).

Procurement tools include fixed barbed points suitable for spears (Stewart 1977:67). These types of points have a long history in the Fraser estuary region, dating to the Old Cordilleran component (9000 BP to 4500 BP) at the Glenrose Cannery site (Matson and Coupland 1995:70). Unilateral and bilateral barbed points, both fixed and harpoon styles, are found in small numbers through time. Small uni-points and bi-points suitable for arming a variety of fishing devices, including rakes, leisters, trolling gear, and harpoons, are found in modest numbers from St. Mungo times (4500 BP to 3300 BP), increasing in recent components (Ham 1982:237; Matson and Coupland 1995:102-106). Many of these devices could be used by one or two people or in conjunction with weirs or traps.

Ham (Ham et al. 1984:iii, 74, 164) has suggested that seine and dip nets may have been used in the Fraser estuary as early as the St. Mungo phase, based on the presence of bone artifacts he interprets as a net gauge and dip-net rings. However, direct evidence for nets is not found in the Fraser River estuary until the Locarno Beach phase (3300 BP to 2400 BP) in the Musqueam Northeast wet-site component.

Wet-Site Fishing Evidence

The three wet-site components discussed here are on or near the present Fraser delta and estuary (Figure 1). The oldest component is at the Glenrose Cannery site (DgRr 6) and dates between 4,600 and 4,000 years ago. Glenrose is situated in the Corporation of Delta, on the south side of the Fraser River, 25 km from the present mouth of the river. The second component is from the 3,000-year-old Musqueam Northeast site (DhRt 4), which is on Musqueam Indian Reserve Number 2 in Vancouver and is about 1 km from the mouth of the Fraser. The third component is from the nearly 2,000-year-old Water Hazard site (DgRs 30) on the Beach Grove golf course in Tsawwassen, near Boundary Bay.

Glenrose Cannery Site

The Glenrose Cannery wet-site component was excavated by Millennia Research in 1990. Test excavations revealed basketry, cordage, carved wood, cedar-bark clothing, and numerous wooden stakes (Eldridge 1991). This wet-site component is adjacent to one of the largest, oldest, and fully reported shell midden sites in the area (see Matson 1976). The wet-site component is contemporaneous with St. Mungo phase deposits (4500 BP to 3300 BP) reported for this site. A geological study (Harper 1990) shows that the 4,500-year-old wet-site component was intertidal when deposited, that sea levels

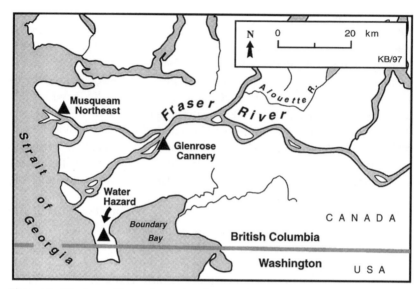

Figure 1. The Fraser River estuary showing wet-site components mentioned in the text.

were similar to present, and that the site was a lower energy location than now – in other words, that water flow was less – and that the site may have been adjacent to a slough. The wet-site faunal remains mirror those found in the contemporaneous shell midden deposits in that both samples contain large numbers of salmon bones followed in number by sturgeon and starry flounder (Pacific ID's 1990). Additional species, including eulachon and stickleback, are identified in the much larger shell midden samples (Casteel 1976:85-86).

In the course of excavating the wet-site component, numerous ancient and recent stakes were found and mapped. Although the patterning of the ancient stakes has been obscured by more recent construction, by loss of stakes, or possibly by ancient re-alignments, there appear to be two or more orientations of the ancient stakes (Eldridge 1991:25). The stakes tend to be aligned either perpendicular to the river or at a 45° angle. Parallel stake alignments are possible but unclear. A systematic dating and seasonality study may help to determine contemporaneous alignments (Scott Byram, personal communication 1995). Eldridge and Acheson (1992:113-115) equate the Glenrose Cannery site stake alignments with the remains of fish weirs, and they assert that the presence of a 4,500-year-old weir implies large-scale salmon fishing and processing for storage nearly 1,000 years before such technology is generally accepted for any area on the Northwest Coast (see Moss et al. 1990).

Alternative explanations for these stake alignments do not necessarily imply that full-scale salmon processing was in place at Glenrose at this time. The faunal evidence recovered at the site is in agreement with the conventional view that whereas a full range of fish resources were used, they were not intensively exploited (Matson and Coupland 1995:114-115). The archaeological literature concerning fish weirs and traps reveals a certain lack of precision in reporting the nature of the types found. This imprecision is relevant because the organizational strategies required to build, maintain, and operate large weir structures differ from those required to build and operate small tidal traps. In some cases, researchers appear to equate stake alignments (Eldridge 1991:79; Eldridge and Acheson 1992:113; Munsell 1976a:49), stakes (Bernick 1991:133), or other trap parts such as latticework elements (Croes 1992a:103) with the presence of weirs, and by implication, with large-scale procurement and processing (Matson 1992:386). The assumption that wood-stake alignments necessarily indicate the presence of weirs obscures the potential diversity of trap types. Moreover, the implication that the presence of stake alignments indicates intensive salmon procurement and processing requires re-assessment. The presence of stake alignments in themselves does not necessarily equate with the major procurement structures we envision when we discuss weirs. Historical descriptions of traps and weirs range from small brush fences used to enhance natural features such as tidal sloughs to enormous constructions that extend hundreds of metres and block entire rivers (Barnett 1955:80; Matthews 1955:177). Therefore, these devices may be expediently constructed tidal traps maintained by a few people or large structures constructed and maintained by whole communities.

The features at Glenrose appear to coincide with what would be expected to remain from the two types of traps, converging fence and latticework-fence tidal traps. Both trap types are useable in a tidal area, particularly in one adjacent to a slough. These could have been used at different times of the year to catch several species of fish. Considerable knowledge of fish behaviour and environmental factors would have been required to make effective use of such traps. One type requires little labour to construct and could be put into place for as short a period as a single high tide, although it is more likely to have been used for repeated tides when the presence of fish was expected. The other type is more elaborate in construction and reconfigurable, to take advantage of varying conditions.

Converging Fence Tidal Traps
The simplest of the many varieties of tidal traps has converging fences made of brush (Figure 2). The trap consists of a series of wooden stakes that are pounded into the intertidal margins of the river with brush or boughs

Figure 2. Idealized converging brush fence tidal trap as it might appear at high spring tide. *Illustration by J. Johnson.*

attached horizontally to the stakes. When the brush is in place, fish that have moved with the tide toward shore or into a slough may be trapped as the tide falls. A person in a boat can block the narrow end of the trap and remove fish with a dip net, a spear, or a basket. The majority of the fish species found in the Glenrose faunal collection dating to around 4,500 years ago (including salmon, eulachon, sturgeon, and flounder) could have been caught in such a tidal trap. A converging fence tidal trap used to catch starry flounder is known to have been used historically at False Creek, in the area now covered by Vancouver's Granville Island (Matthews 1955:12). For this type of trap, a series of stakes are pounded into the mud, and then brush or hurdles of twisted vine maple or hemlock or spruce boughs are used as a barrier to prevent fish from escaping on the falling tide. The trapped flounder can then be easily speared or otherwise removed. This type of trap requires relatively low maintenance, especially if the stakes are reusable. Presumably other types of fish can be caught in this way as well.

Latticework-Fence Tidal Traps
A second type of trap that could account for some of the stake alignments at Glenrose is somewhat more elaborate than the convergent brush fence type and requires significant investments in labour to construct and maintain. This type of tidal trap has fences made of latticework elements attached to stake frames (Figure 3). In the Fraser River estuary, anadromous species moving from saltwater may spend considerable time in the estuary adjusting to the lower salinity levels before moving upriver. Sockeye salmon are known to spend up to a month in the lower reaches of the river before moving upriver to spawn (Kew 1992:191). During this adjustment period,

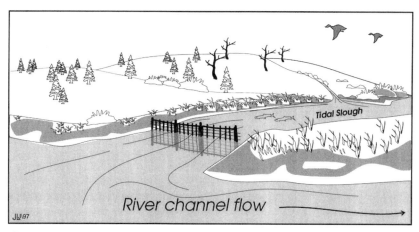

Figure 3. Idealized latticework-fence tidal trap as it might appear with the latticework panels in place at high tide. *Illustration by J. Johnson.*

they move onshore in schools with the tide and, therefore, can be caught in traps. Fences raised at high tide trap the fish when the tide recedes. Similar structures may work for eulachon. Historically, a large version of this type of tidal impound was used near the Fraser's mouth by the Tsawwassen First Nation to catch sturgeon (Barnett 1936:63).

Although no basketry fence structures were encountered in the wet-site test excavation at Glenrose, wrapped-twined basketry technology is present and is analogous to historically known aboriginal latticework trap structures of the region (Barnett 1955:79). Fish trap latticework found in an archaeological context commonly has rigid vertical elements made from whole or split wooden sticks. The horizontal elements are usually applied singly or by multi-strand twining (for examples see Bernick 1983 for Vancouver Island; Croes and Blinman 1980:255 for the Olympic Peninsula; and Munsell 1976a:50, 1976b:102 for Puget Sound). Barnett (1955:79) asserts that latticework fish traps were used exclusively for salmon; however, Byram (this volume) argues that the smaller mesh sizes seen in relatively recent Oregon sites suggest that smaller fish species were sought. Perhaps analysis of the range of mesh sizes in latticework structures and the relative sturdiness of the construction techniques will help determine the range of species that can be caught using the range of known or postulated configurations.

Of course, 4,000 years ago (during the St. Mungo phase), other types of traps may have been constructed in addition to the two described here. However, at this time, the evidence for the Glenrose Cannery site is limited to stakes. Modelling of trap types that takes into consideration environmental conditions (such as stream flow, inter-tidal gradation, turbidity, and seasonality) and variations in construction techniques (such as mesh size, weave structure, frame configuration, and sturdiness) may provide better criteria for describing the nature of this type of fishing technology at this and other sites through time.

The location of the Glenrose Cannery site on the estuary 4,000 years ago may have been ideal for catching a series of fish as they adjusted to lower salinity levels, moved onto shore to spawn, or sought shallow slough waters. However, conditions that may have favoured tidal traps at this location were destined to disappear as the river changed its course and the delta expanded westward.

Musqueam Northeast Site

The Musqueam Northeast wet-site component was encountered unexpectedly during the excavation of a midden site in 1973. Systematic excavations of the waterlogged deposits continued over two summers. It remains the largest and most extensively documented wet site in the Fraser delta area. The deposits date to 3,000 years ago and are identified as a Locarno Beach phase component (Archer and Bernick 1990; Borden 1976; Borden and Archer 1974).

Stiefel's (1985) analysis of faunal remains from this site shows that aggregated resources were exploited, with a marked emphasis on seasonally available fish. Twenty-two species of fish were identified, with salmon accounting for more than 58 percent of identified fish, including large amounts of sockeye salmon. Starry flounder and other flatfish account for 34 percent of the identified species. Diving ducks were secondary only to fish resources (Stiefel 1985:134-147).

The Musqueam Northeast wet-site component contained fishing gear, including netting fragments, wrapped cobbles likely to be net weights, bentwood fishhooks, cordage suitable for fishing line, a wood bi-point, a possible net bobbin, and large openwork baskets suitable for hauling fish. The site was adjacent to a stream and would have faced onto saltwater during Locarno Beach times (Archer and Bernick 1990:16).

Musqueam Northeast Site Netting

The average mesh size (120 mm to 150 mm) for the majority of netting found at the Musqueam Northeast site is consistent with salmon gill nets suitable for catching sockeye salmon (Croes 1980:123), or if used as a seine net, for catching flounder (Suttles 1974:73, 129, 138). Similar mesh size is also reported for entanglement nets for waterfowl (Kennedy and Bouchard 1983:39; Suttles 1955:26). In other words, nets with this mesh size are suitable for catching the main food species reported for this site. The Musqueam Northeast netting is Z-lay, two-ply cedar-bark cordage, and the knots are primarily square knot variations (Figure 4a; Archer and Bernick

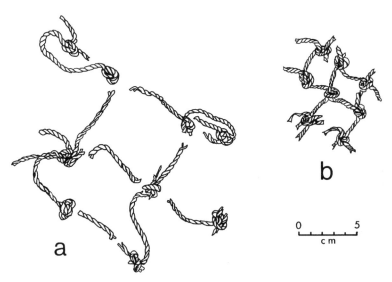

Figure 4. Netting: (a) from the Musqueam Northeast site (DhRt 4:10132). The meshes may appear slightly larger than they are, as the elements are broken; (b) from the Water Hazard site (DgRs 30:1). *Illustration by K. Bernick.*

1990:164-165). Cedar-bark netting is not widely reported for nets in the ethnographic literature; however, it is the only netting material found so far archaeologically in the Fraser delta (Stevenson 1989:A-20).

The introduction of sockeye gill nets 3,000 years ago coincides with the period for which solid evidence exists for the development of salmon storage technology (Matson 1992:411). If salmon storage is assumed for the Locarno Beach phase, then it is also reasonable to assume that effective and selective techniques for procuring fish were in place.

Water Hazard Site
The nearly 2,000-year-old Water Hazard site was discovered in 1988 when a golf-course water hazard was enlarged. More than 100 pieces of basketry, 29 wooden wedges, 7 bentwood fishhooks, and 73 m of cordage were salvaged from mud piles dredged by the golf course's backhoe excavation (Bernick 1989).

Netting
Netting salvaged from this site is S-lay, two-ply cedar bark with square knot variations and a smaller mesh size than the majority of netting found at Musqueam Northeast (Figure 4b). The size ranges from 85 mm to 95 mm. Most likely this netting was used as a salmon trawl, although it could have

functioned as a submerged waterfowl net (Stevenson 1989). Net edge lines were also recovered; however, they are too fragmentary to assist in determining the type of net to which they were attached.

Although the nature of excavations at the Water Hazard site precluded substantial faunal analysis, the nearby Beach Grove site (DgRs 1), which is a Marpole phase (2400 BP to 1400 BP) winter village site, yielded contemporaneous deposits. Beach Grove site deposits contain equal amounts of salmon and starry flounder. Significant numbers of waterfowl remains were also found (Abbott 1962; Matson et al. 1980:68-78). Although Beach Grove is interpreted as primarily a winter and spring occupation site (Matson et al. 1980:96), with some evidence of summer occupancy, the additional data from Water Hazard appears to extend the seasonal occupation into the fall, if the presence of salmon trawl nets is considered valid.

Bentwood Fishhooks

U-shaped bentwood hooks found in Water Hazard and Musqueam Northeast components may have served as fishhooks (Archer and Bernick 1990:24; Bernick 1989:37-39; Figure 5). Similar and apparently barbless hooks are found in a number of archaeological sites in adjacent areas of the Georgia Strait and Puget Sound (Bernick 1983:325; Croes 1992a:102-103; Croes and Blinman 1980:310; Hoff 1980:168-188; Nordquist 1961). Although these hooks were probably used to catch cod in saltwater areas (Croes 1992a:103; Hoff 1980), they may have been used to catch other fish, such as trout (Suttles 1955:23), in estuarine habitats.

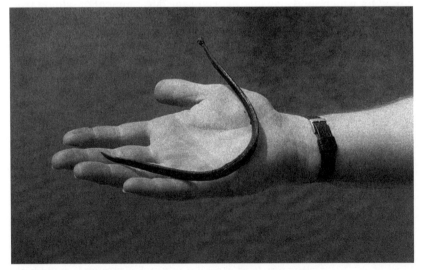

Figure 5. Bentwood fishhook from the Water Hazard site (DgRs 30).
Photo by K. Bernick.

Conclusion

The evidence from wet sites in the Fraser River estuary region supports the suggestion that although the same set of riverine resources were exploited between 4,600 and 2,000 years ago, the primary procurement methods changed significantly during this period. The focus of the technology progressed out from the tidal banks of the estuary into the river itself. Simple traps used 4,600 years ago at Glenrose were, by 3,000 years ago, replaced or supplemented by a gill net technology at Musqueam Northeast. By 2,000 years ago, trawl nets similar to the ones known historically had probably been established to exploit salmon. This scenario does not imply a direct lineage of net technology. When viewed locally, the sequence may have been from tidal traps to nets, rather than a developmental progression of net technology downriver through time.

It is also clear that what may have been a primary technology at a particular time at one location may have continued in use at other locations. Tidal traps appear to have a long history along the lower Fraser. Although a number of sites with stakes or stake alignments have been reported recently (Bernick 1991:55), very little is known about them, and no systematic survey has been undertaken for most of the estuary.

Although the fishery evidence from wet sites may be seen to support developmental models of the salmon storage complex, wet-site evidence has an even greater potential to help explain the diversity and complexity of the fishery. Considerable work could be done to understand the fishery of particular sites at various periods. Careful consideration of the environmental conditions, faunal remains, reconstructions of devices, and experimental use may give a clearer picture of how technologies were used through time. Current concerns with developing selective fishing devices may be informed by a closer look at fishery evidence from wet sites.

Appendix 1

Fraser estuary fish discussed in the text

Local name	Latin name (Hart 1973)
Dogfish	*Squalus acanthias*
Eulachon	*Thaleichthys pacificus*
Flatfishes	Pleuronectiformes
Halibut	*Hippoglossus stenolepis*
Starry flounder	*Platichthys stellatus*
Herring	*Clupea harengus pallasi*
Lingcod	*Ophiodon elongatus*
Pacific cod	*Gadus macrocephalus*
Salmon	*Onchorhyncus* spp.
Chinook salmon	*Onchorhyncus tshawytscha*
Pink salmon	*Onchorhyncus gorbuscha*
Sockeye salmon	*Onchorhyncus nerka*
Steelhead	*Salmo gairdneri*
Stickleback	*Gasterosteus aculeatus*
Sturgeon	*Acipenser transmontanus*

Acknowledgments
The development of this research was supported, in part, by a grant from the UBC Museum of Anthropology's Research and Teaching Committee.

References Cited
Abbott, Donald N.
   1962 *Preliminary Report on the Beach Grove Site, DgRs 1.* Report on file, Laboratory of Archaeology, University of British Columbia, Vancouver.
Archer, David J.W., and Kathryn Bernick
   1990 Perishable Artifacts from the Musqueam Northeast Site. Ms. on file, British Columbia Archaeology Branch, Victoria.
Barnett, Homer G.
   1936 No. 8: Coast Salish – Musqueam, Sechelt, Tswasan, Lummi. Unpublished notes pertaining to field research. University of British Columbia Library, Special Collections and University Archives Division, H.G. Barnett papers, Box 1, Folder/Notebook 8.
   1955 *Coast Salish of British Columbia.* University of Oregon Press, Eugene.
Batdorf, Carol
   1990 *Northwest Native Harvest.* Hancock House, Surrey, BC.
Bernick, Kathryn
   1983 *A Site Catchment Analysis of the Little Qualicum River Site, DiSc 1: A Wet Site on the East Coast of Vancouver Island, B.C.* National Museum of Man Mercury Series, Archaeological Survey of Canada Paper No. 118. National Museums of Canada, Ottawa.
   1989 *Water Hazard (DgRs 30) Artifact Recovery Project Report.* Permit 1988-55. Report on file, British Columbia Archaeology Branch, Victoria.
   1991 *Wet Site Archaeology in the Lower Mainland Region of British Columbia.* Report on file, British Columbia Archaeology Branch, Victoria.
Berringer, Patricia Ann
   1982 *Northwest Coast Traditional Salmon Fisheries Systems of Resource Utilization.* Master's thesis, Department of Anthropology and Sociology, University of British Columbia, Vancouver.
Borden, Charles E.
   1976 A Water Saturated Site on the Southern Mainland Coast of British Columbia. In *The Excavation of Water-Saturated Sites (Wet Sites) on the Northwest Coast of North America,* edited by Dale R. Croes, pp. 233-260. National Museum of Man Mercury Series, Archaeological Survey of Canada Paper No. 50. National Museums of Canada, Ottawa.
Borden, Charles E., and David Archer
   1974 Archaeological Salvage at Musqueam Northeast (DhRt 4), Vancouver, British Columbia. In *Archaeological Salvage Projects 1973,* complied by W.J. Byrne, pp. 6-11. National Museum of Man Mercury Series, Archaeological Survey of Canada Paper No. 26. National Museums of Canada, Ottawa.
Casteel, Richard W.
   1976 Fish Remains from Glenrose. In *The Glenrose Cannery Site,* edited by R.G. Matson, pp. 82-87. National Museum of Man Mercury Series, Archaeological Survey of Canada Paper No. 52. National Museums of Canada, Ottawa.
Chisholm, Brian S., D. Erle Nelson, and Henry P. Schwarcz
   1983 Marine and Terrestrial Protein in Prehistoric Diets on the British Columbia Coast. *Current Anthropology* 24:396-398.
Croes, Dale R.
   1980 *Cordage from the Ozette Village Archaeological Site: A Technological, Functional, and Comparative Study.* Project Reports No. 9. Laboratory of Archaeology and History, Washington State University, Pullman.
   1992a An Evolving Revolution in Wet Site Research on the Northwest Coast of North America. In *The Wetland Revolution in Prehistory,* edited by Bryony Coles, pp. 99-111. WARP Occasional Paper 6. Dept. of History and Archaeology, University of Exeter, UK.

1992b Exploring Prehistoric Subsistence Change on the Northwest Coast. In *Long-Term Subsistence Change in Prehistoric North America,* edited by Dale R. Croes, Rebecca A. Hawkins, and Barry L. Isaac, pp. 337-366. Research in Economic Anthropology, supplement 6. JAI Press, Greenwich, CT.

Croes, Dale. R., and Eric Blinman (editors)
1980 *Hoko River: A 2500 Year Old Fishing Camp on the Northwest Coast of North America.* Reports of Investigation 58. Laboratory of Anthropology, Washington State University, Pullman.

Croes, Dale R., and S. Hackenberger
1988 Hoko River Archaeological Complex. In *Modelling Prehistoric Northwest Coast Economies of the Pacific Northwest Coast,* edited by B.L. Isaac, pp. 19-85. JAI Press, Greenwich, CT.

Eldridge, Morley
1991 The Glenrose Cannery Wet Component: A Significance Assessment. Permit 1990-24. Report on file, British Columbia Archaeology Branch, Victoria.

Eldridge, Morley, and Steven Acheson
1992 The Antiquity of Fish Weirs on the Southern Coast: A Response to Moss, Erlandson, and Stuckenrath. *Canadian Journal of Archaeology* 16:112-116.

Fladmark, Knut R.
1986 *British Columbia Prehistory.* National Museum of Man, National Museums of Canada, Ottawa.

Fraser River Estuary Management Program (FREMP)
1994 *A Living Working River: An Estuary Management Plan for the Fraser River.* FREMP, New Westminster, BC.

Glavin, Terry
1996 *Dead Reckoning: Confronting the Crisis in Pacific Fisheries.* Greystone Books, Vancouver, BC.

Ham, Leonard C.
1982 *Seasonality, Shell Midden Layers, and Coast Salish Subsistence Activities at the Crescent Beach Site, DgRr 1.* PhD dissertation, Department of Anthropology and Sociology, University of British Columbia, Vancouver.

Ham, Leonard C., Arlene J. Yip, and Leila V. Kullar
1984 A Charles Culture Fishing Village. Permit 1982-21. Report on file, British Columbia Archaeology Branch, Victoria.

Harper, John R.
1990 Geological Reconnaissance of the Glenrose Cannery Archaeological Site. Report by Harper Environmental Services, Victoria, BC, for Millennia Research, Sidney BC. Copy on file, Laboratory of Archaeology, University of British Columbia, Vancouver.

Hart, J.L.
1973 *Pacific Fishes of Canada.* Bulletin 180. Fisheries Research Board of Canada, Ottawa.

Hoff, Ricky
1980 Fishhooks. In *Hoko River: A 2500 Year Old Fishing Camp on the Northwest Coast of North America,* edited by Dale R. Croes and Eric Blinman, pp. 160-188. Reports of Investigation 58. Laboratory of Anthropology, Washington State University, Pullman.

Kennedy, Dorothy, and Randy Bouchard
1983 *Sliammon Life, Sliammon Lands.* Talonbooks, Vancouver, BC.

Kew, Michael
1992 Salmon Availability, Technology, and Cultural Adaptation in the Fraser River Watershed. In *A Complex Culture of the British Columbia Plateau: Traditional Stl'atl'mx Resource Use,* edited by Brian Hayden, pp. 177-221. UBC Press, Vancouver, BC.

Langdon, Stephen John
1977 *Technology, Ecology, and Economy: Fishing Systems in Southeast Alaska.* PhD dissertation, Stanford University. University Microfilms, Ann Arbor, MI.

Matson, R.G.
1992 The Evolution of the Northwest Coast Subsistence. In *Long-Term Subsistence Change in Prehistoric North America,* edited by Dale R. Croes, pp. 367-428. Research in Economic Anthropology, supplement 6. JAI Press, Greenwich, CT.

Matson, R.G. (editor)
  1976 *The Glenrose Cannery site.* National Museum of Man Mercury Series, Archaeological Survey of Canada Paper No. 52. National Museums of Canada, Ottawa.
Matson, R.G., and Gary Coupland
  1995 *The Prehistory of the Northwest Coast.* Academic Press, San Diego.
Matson, R.G., Deanna Ludowicz, and William Boyd
  1980 *Excavations at Beach Grove in 1980.* MO 1980-14. Report on file, British Columbia Archaeology Branch, Victoria.
Matthews, James Skitt
  1955 *Conversations with Khahtsahlano 1932-1954.* Compiled by the City Archivist, Vancouver, BC. Copy available at University of British Columbia Library, Special Collections.
Mitchell, Donald
  1990 Prehistory of the Coasts of Southern British Columbia and Northern Washington. In *Northwest Coast,* edited by Wayne Suttles, pp. 340-358. Handbook of North American Indians, vol. 7, William C. Sturtevant, general editor. Smithsonian Institution, Washington, DC.
Monks, Gregory G.
  1987 Prey as Bait: The Deep Bay Example. *Canadian Journal of Archaeology* 11:119-142.
Moss, Madonna L., and Jon M. Erlandson
  1995 Reflections on North American Pacific Coast Prehistory. *Journal of World Prehistory* 9:1-45.
Moss, Madonna L., Jon M. Erlandson, and Robert Stuckenrath
  1990 Wood Stake Weirs and Salmon Fishing on the Northwest Coast: Evidence from Southeast Alaska. *Canadian Journal of Archaeology* 14:143-158.
Munsell, David A.
  1976a The Wapato Creek Fish Weir Site 45PI47 Tacoma, Washington. In *The Excavation of Water-Saturated Archaeological Sites (Wet Sites) on the Northwest Coast of North America,* edited by Dale R. Croes, pp. 45-57. National Museum of Man Mercury Series, Archaeological Survey of Canada Paper No. 50. National Museums of Canada, Ottawa.
  1976b Excavation of the Conway Wetsite 45SK59b Conway, Washington. In *The Excavation of Water-Saturated Archaeological Sites (Wet Sites) on the Northwest Coast of North America,* edited by Dale R. Croes, pp. 86-121. National Museum of Man Mercury Series, Archaeological Survey of Canada Paper No. 50. National Museums of Canada, Ottawa.
Nordquist, Del
  1961 The Fishing Hook as Found in 45SN100. *Washington Archaeologist* 5(3):10-17.
Pacific ID's
  1990 DgRr 6, Glenrose Cannery Salvage: Faunal Remains. Report prepared by Pacific ID's, Victoria, BC, for Millennia Research, Sidney, BC. Ms. on file, Laboratory of Archaeology, University of British Columbia, Vancouver.
Peacock, William R.B.
  1982 *The Telep Site: A Late Autumn Fish Camp of the Locarno Beach Culture Type.* MO 1981-22. Report on file, British Columbia Archaeology Branch, Victoria.
Stevenson, Ann
  1989 Netting and Associated Cordage. In *Water Hazard (DgRs 30) Artifact Recovery Project Report,* by Kathryn Bernick, appendix A. Copy on file, British Columbia Archaeology Branch, Victoria.
Stewart, Hilary
  1977 *Indian Fishing: Early Methods on the Northwest Coast.* J.J. Douglas, Vancouver, BC.
Stiefel, Sheryl Kay
  1985 *The Subsistence Economy of the Locarno Beach Culture (3300-2400 BP).* Master's thesis, Department of Anthropology and Sociology, University of British Columbia, Vancouver.
Suttles, Wayne
  1955 *Katzie Ethnographic Notes.* Anthropology in British Columbia Memoir 2. British Columbia Provincial Museum, Victoria.

1974 The Economic Life of the Coast Salish of Haro and Rosario Straits. *Coast Salish and Western Washington Indians,* I. Garland Publishing, New York.

1987 Coping with Abundance: Subsistence on the Northwest Coast. In *Coast Salish Essays,* edited by Wayne Suttles, pp. 45-63. Talonbooks, Vancouver, BC.

1990a Central Coast Salish Subsistence. *Northwest Anthropological Research Notes* 24:147-152.

1990b Central Coast Salish. In *Northwest Coast,* edited by Wayne Suttles, pp. 453-475. Handbook of North American Indians, vol. 7, William C. Sturtevant, general editor. Smithsonian Institution, Washington, DC.

The Montana Creek Fish Trap I: Archaeological Investigations in Southeast Alaska

Robert C. Betts

The annual salmon runs were of tremendous economic and cultural significance to the Tlingit and allowed the Northern Tlingit, like other Northwest Coast aboriginal people, to achieve high population densities, large winter villages, and a complex material culture and social organization unusual among non-agricultural societies. Salmon were of such importance to the Northwest Coast Indians that "salmon abundance is seen as the key to the emergence of the distinctive Northwest Coast cultural pattern" (Langdon 1989:306). To harvest large salmon runs, the Tlingit employed a variety of techniques that included the use of spears, clubs, unbarbed hooks, gaffs, weirs, and traps (de Laguna 1960; Langdon 1977). Numerous authors (Campbell 1982; de Laguna 1960, 1972, 1990; Drucker 1951, 1965; Emmons 1991; Krause 1956; Langdon 1979, 1986; Moss 1989; Stewart 1982; Wooley 1987) discuss the widespread use of traps and weirs by Northwest Coast Natives as highly effective means of harvesting the seasonal abundance of salmon.

Remains of intertidal stone traps and wood-stake weirs have been documented archaeologically in Southeast Alaska and along much of the Northwest Coast (Campbell 1982; Drucker 1950; Langdon 1986; Moss 1989; Moss and Erlandson, this volume; Moss et al. 1990; Pomeroy 1976; Wooley 1987). Until recently, however, archaeological evidence of the prehistoric use of basket traps has consisted of gaps in stone weirs (in which removable traps were likely placed) and alignments of wooden stakes or posts that represent the remains of fences or leads designed to funnel fish into one or more enclosures. For example, Campbell (1982:18) reports that 16 of 40 fish traps catalogued by her in Southeast Alaska in 1982 were wood-stake alignments representing leads to basket traps. Such inferential evidence, even when supplemented with ethnographic documentation, does not supply details

---

This is a companion to the following chapter by Greg Chaney, "The Montana Creek Fish Trap II: Stratigraphic Interpretation in the Context of Southeastern Alaska Geomorphology."

of size, shape, or materials used in the construction of prehistoric basket-style fish traps.

Unlike the water-saturated lower portions of wooden weir stakes embedded in stream channels and mudflats, effectively protected from decomposition by an anaerobic environment, the wooden traps themselves have generally not survived the ravages of time. The fragile nature of wooden traps, the investment of time and effort to construct a trap, and the need for continued maintenance are some of the factors that resulted in wooden traps being removed from the water when the fishing season was over (Campbell 1982:24; Austin Hammond, personal communication 1992). Traps were commonly stored on land over the winter, either on the stream bank near where they were used or at the fish camp or village where they were taken for repair. A wooden trap left unattended in a creek or river would likely be destroyed by flooding, or would rapidly become clogged with twigs and driftwood. Because of their fragile nature and the fact that they could be removed from the weir after the fishing season, the chances of a wooden fish trap being preserved in an archaeological context are remote, and no intact prehistoric specimen was known from the Northwest Coast until the recent chance discovery of such a trap at Montana Creek, near Juneau, Alaska.

Discovery and Dating

In 1989, a sport fisherman discovered the Montana Creek fish trap (49JUN453) eroding from the left (north) bank of Montana Creek near its confluence with the Mendenhall River (Figure 1). In the spring of 1990, Steve Henrikson, Alaska State Museum curator, and Wallace Olson of the University of Alaska Southeast visited the site to evaluate the significance of the find. Henrikson and Olson confirmed that the artifact was indeed a traditional Native basket-style fish trap and clearly a significant artifact threatened by erosion.

Henrikson and Olson returned to the site in the early summer of 1990 to conduct a one-day emergency salvage excavation. After exposing the upper portion of the trap, it became evident that a full-scale wet-site excavation would be necessary to successfully recover the entire trap. Henrikson and Olson detached and removed the exposed upper section of the main body of the trap and then shovelled gravel over the remaining part as temporary protection from further erosion. The upper section of the trap was transported to the Alaska State Museum in Juneau, where it was submerged in water to await conservation treatment. Samples of wood and lashing from the trap were sent to the Royal British Columbia Museum conservation laboratory in Victoria for species identification. The wooden hoops were identified as Sitka spruce (*Picea sitchensis*) branches, and the longitudinal staves as hemlock (*Tsuga heterophylla*). Sitka spruce root was identified as the lashing material (Mary-Lou Florian, personal communication 1992).

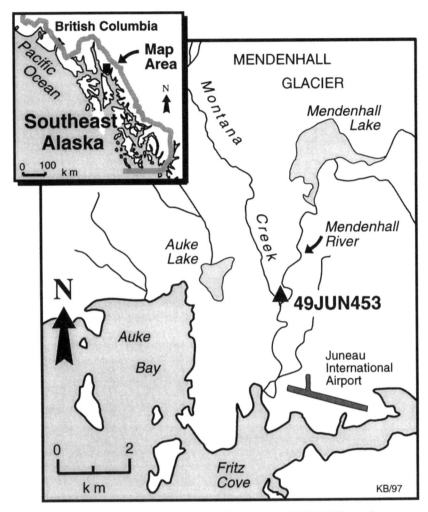

Figure 1. Location of the Montana Creek fish trap site (49JUN453) near Juneau, Alaska.

Two wood samples from the upper portion of the trap submitted by Steve Henrikson for radiocarbon analysis yielded uncorrected determinations of 550 ± 70 BP (WSU 4140) and 700 ± 60 BP (WSU 4141). After calibration, according to Stuiver and Pearson (1986), the average of these dates (640 ± 50 BP) indicates the Montana Creek fish trap was constructed between AD 1270 and AD 1410 (Erlandson 1990).

The 1991 Excavation
Efforts began early in 1991 to find financing for an extensive wet-site excavation, and the Alaska State Museum engaged Jon Loring in the task of

planning the as yet unfunded project. By the spring of 1991, erosion of the north bank of Montana Creek had again exposed a small section of the trap. To prevent further damage, Loring covered the exposed trap elements with a double layer of heavy plastic sheeting over which he placed sandbags and gravel. With financial support from the Sealaska Corporation and with permits secured from the US Army Corps of Engineers and the Alaska Department of Fish and Game to construct a cofferdam in the stream bed, an excavation was scheduled for the early fall of 1991. However, high water in Montana Creek delayed the start of work until the first week of November. The concern to protect the trap proved to be justified. From the time the trap was first discovered in 1989 to the start of the winter 1991 excavation, more than 1 m of the cut-bank containing the trap had been lost to erosion, though the trap itself remained securely in place.

Montana Creek is a shallow clear-water tributary of the Mendenhall River, a silt-laden glacial stream that carries sediment from the Mendenhall Glacier to tidewater in Gastineau Channel (Chaney, this volume). The trap had been located on the left (north) bank of the creek, approximately 100 m upstream from the confluence of Montana Creek and the Mendenhall River

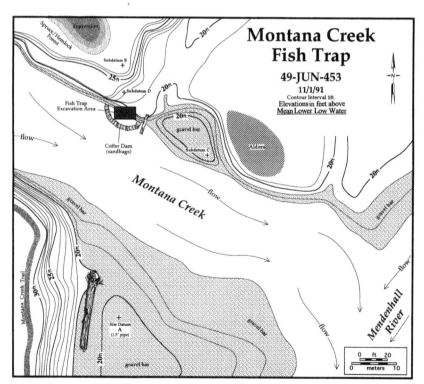

Figure 2. Montana Creek fish trap site (49JUN453).

(Figure 2). In 1991, the excavation site was within an area influenced by tides of 17 ft (5.2 m) or greater, a factor that complicated excavation procedures and, combined with periods of high stream run-off following heavy rains, repeatedly threatened to destroy the fish trap during excavation.

Since the fish trap was below the normal level of Montana Creek, it was necessary to construct a cofferdam around the excavation area using sandbags and plastic sheeting. Water behind the dam was pumped out using a portable gasoline-powered Honda pump with a three-inch (7.62 cm) discharge. Continuous seepage of water through the sandbags and upwelling of water through the gravel streambed required constant use of the pump to maintain a "dry" excavation area. A 2m x 2m square grid was established over the excavation, and the adjacent bank of Montana Creek was cut back to expose a stratigraphic section and to allow a sufficient work area behind the dam. Excavation began with skim shovelling recent bank slumpage and removing the sandbags and plastic previously positioned to protect the trap. Once the excavators had reached the level of the trap, sediments encasing the trap were washed away using a spray nozzle on a one-inch (2.54 cm) diameter garden hose supplied with water from a separate centrifugal pump. Hydraulic excavation was extremely effective as an excavation technique for areas within the trap that could not be reached by conventional methods. Wooden tools (rather than metal trowels) were used to work around the trap so as not to cut the soft waterlogged wooden elements. Sediment and debris removed from the trap was water-screened through a ¼-inch (6 mm) mesh to recover wood and lashing fragments and any associated cultural material. Once the sediment within the trap was removed, structural support was provided by inflated balloons that could be repositioned as needed as excavation progressed.

Preservation of the spruce root lashing was of particular concern due to the fact that upon drying out it became extremely friable. Almost all the lashing had been lost from the upper section of the trap that had been removed in 1990. In 1991, all lashings that could be reached were wrapped with roller gauze bandages to protect the extremely fragile lashing and to strengthen the structure prior to lifting and transport. Keeping the entire trap from drying out for the duration of the five-week excavation was essential to preserve the remaining lashing and the shape of the waterlogged hoops and staves. To achieve this, the exposed parts of the trap were covered with absorbent cotton diapers that were periodically sprayed with water. This effectively shielded the wood from direct sunlight and prevented the trap from drying out after exposure to the air. The main pump was shut down whenever excavation was not in progress, allowing water behind the cofferdam to rise and submerging the trap. This was done also during periods of heavy run-off to prevent flood water from breaching the cofferdam.

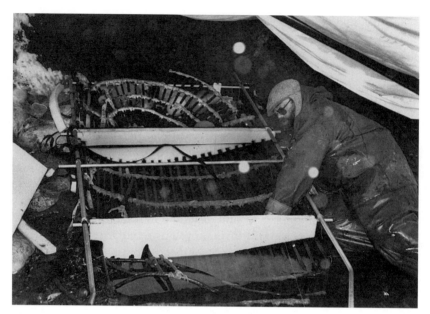

Figure 3. Jon Loring attaching the basketry trap to the lifting frame.

Once the trap was completely free of sediment, but still in situ, a lifting mount was attached. The mount, designed by Paul Gardinier of the Alaska State Museum, consisted of a tubular aluminum frame, ethafoam cut to the curvature of the trap, and nylon webbing (Figure 3). The ethafoam was supported by aluminum cross members on top of the trap. Webbing ran under the trap, holding it snug against the ethafoam. The entire trap, within the lifting mount, was then manually lifted in one piece and placed on a sheet of plywood for transport by jet boat and truck to the Alaska State Museum in Juneau, a total distance of about 19 km. Cold temperatures and a heavy snowfall before and during the transport of the trap to the museum froze the trap and made it unnecessary to keep it wet during transit. Once at the museum, the trap and lifting frame were submerged in water. The trap remained attached to the lifting frame throughout the subsequent polyethylene glycol conservation treatment.

The Montana Creek Fish Trap

The Basket Trap
The basket-style fish trap recovered from Montana Creek is a 2.8-m-long cylindrical wood lattice construction with a funnel insert. The main body is made of 10 spruce branches that have been formed into hoops by lashing their respective bevelled ends together with spruce root (Figure 4), and of hemlock staves that extend the length of the trap and are lashed with spruce

Montana Creek Fish Trap   Excavation Plan View

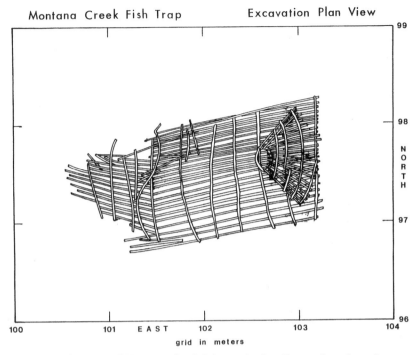

grid in meters

Figure 4. Plan view of Montana Creek fish trap in situ. Top section of trap has been removed. *Drawing courtesy of Jon Loring, Alaska State Museum.*

root to the outside of the hoops. During use, the upstream (distal) end would have been closed, probably with wooden slats inserted through the staves. One slat that may have functioned for such a purpose was found, during excavation, detached from the trap. The distal end of the trap was incomplete, which makes it difficult to determine whether the trap tapered toward the closed end.

A lattice funnel, or cone, constructed of the same material as the main body of the trap, was found inside the main basket at its downstream (proximal) end. Spruce root lashing, still securely in place at the time of the excavation, attached the large end of the cone to the large (proximal) end of the main cylinder of the trap. The cone extends approximately one-quarter of the way into the main body of the trap. Fish moving upstream and entering the trap would have been funnelled through the cone into the main basket and would have had difficulty retracing their way out. Trapped fish would likely have been speared and removed from the trap through a small trap-door opening in the side or top of the main cylinder (direct evidence of which is lacking, but it may have been destroyed when the top section of the trap was removed). This type of trap has been documented ethnographically, but no previous prehistoric examples have been found.

Figure 5. Detail of the funnel portion of the trap showing spruce root lashing attaching hemlock staves to a spruce hoop.

Structural distortion resulting from the weight of the sediments that buried the fish trap, as well as the cutting away of the top section of the trap before the 1991 excavation, makes the original diameter of the body of the trap difficult to reconstruct. When excavated, the distance between the two sides of the trap measured 115 cm, but the original diameter of the trap's body would have been slightly smaller (since the lower portion of the trap, which provided the measurement, was splayed outward). The intact large end of the funnel insert provides the best clue to the original diameter of the body of the trap. The funnel, which is 60 cm long, tapers in diameter from 100 cm to 28 cm. Originally, it would have been round in cross-section, rather than its present oval shape (it has been flattened somewhat by the weight of the overlying sediments), and the diameters of the large and small ends of the funnel would have been somewhat smaller. Thus, the original diameter of the large end of the funnel as well as that of the body of the trap would have been slightly less than 1 m.

The 10 hoops forming the main basket are spaced, on average, 30 cm apart. The staves are fairly uniform in size, with an average cross-section of 2.5 cm x 1.0 cm; spacing between the staves averages 3.5 cm. The lashing used to attach the staves to the hoops features a double- or triple-X pattern that is secured with a cinch loop at each intersection (Figure 5). The staves forming the funnel are of the same width and thickness as those that comprise the main body of the trap. The funnel is constructed with five hoops

Figure 6. The top of the funnel entrance to the trap, when first exposed. Note the spruce-root lashing around the hoops forming the funnel cone.

Figure 7. The Montana Creek trap in situ (1991 excavation) with the funnel entrance clearly visible at the far end. The top section of the trap had been previously removed. Balloons, used for structural support during excavation, are visible around the funnel.

spaced an average of 15 cm apart (Figures 6 and 7). Decreasing the diameter of the funnel was accomplished by using progressively smaller hoops and alternating 36-cm-long staves with 60-cm-long staves (a pattern that avoids clustering all the staves at the small end of the cone).

Associated Cordage

At the funnel end of the trap, four separate segments of a two-strand S-twisted cord were found 5 cm to 6 cm apart in a row, attached to or looped over a single stave (Figure 8). The two outside sections of cord were each tied to the stave with an overhand knot, and the middle two were found looped over the stave without being attached to it. One of the attached pieces of cord was also tied to a second loose 30-cm-long stave with cut marks on both ends, which may have formed part of a trap door used for removal of fish from the cylindrical body of the trap. These four segments of cordage were identified as being made from spruce root (Jon Loring, personal communication 1995). Two fragments of a thicker two-strand twisted cord were found associated with the fish trap, but not in direct contact with it. This detached cord has been identified as being made from cedar bark (Jon Loring, personal communication 1995).

Potentially Harvested Fish Species

The State of Alaska Department of Fish and Game (ADF & G), Sport Fish Division, escapement records contain data on three species of Pacific salmon (*Oncorhynchus* spp.) that currently spawn in Montana Creek (ADF & G 1992).

Figure 8. Detail of the main cylinder of the Montana Creek fish trap, showing spruce root cord tied with an overhand knot around a hemlock stave.

Escapement records for chum (*O. keta*), coho (*O. kisutch*), and pink salmon (*O. gorbuscha*) go back to 1962, 1978, and 1975 respectively. A few sockeye (*O. nerka*) have also been reported in the Mendenhall River as far up as the mouth of Montana Creek. Although not listed in the Sport Fish Division's escapement records, counts of as many as 20,000 Dolly Varden (*Salvelinus malma*) have been reported for Montana Creek by ADF & G. In recent years, eulachon (*Thaleichthys pacificus*) have been observed in the Mendenhall River but are not known to be present in Montana Creek (Mike Bethers, personal communication 1992).

It is fairly clear that the Montana Creek trap was not designed to harvest eulachon. Even if eulachon had, at one time, been present in Montana Creek, the 3.5 cm spacing between the staves on the Montana Creek trap is too wide to contain eulachon, which average 15 cm to 20 cm long and weigh only 55 g on average (Marty Betts, personal communication 1994). The size of the small-diameter opening of the trap funnel is perhaps the best clue to the fish species for which the Montana Creek trap was designed. The original diameter of the small end of the funnel appears to have been approximately 20 cm, which would have been too small to allow mature coho and chum salmon to enter the trap (Mike Bethers, personal communication 1992). Based on the size of the small end of the funnel, the Montana Creek trap would have allowed full-size pink and sockeye salmon, along with small coho and small chum, to enter the trap, as well as full-size Dolly Varden. Since sockeye salmon only ascend streams that discharge from a lake it does not appear that the Montana Creek trap would have targeted this species. If, as Campbell (1982) argues, pink and chum salmon were not the principal species harvested through the use of basket traps, it appears that the most likely species of fish captured by the Montana Creek trap were small coho and Dolly Varden. The size of the small-diameter end of the funnel entrance seems to point to the use of the Montana Creek trap to harvest Dolly Varden rather than coho.

A Further Discovery on Montana Creek

Until recently, the Montana Creek trap had been considered an isolated find not associated with other cultural material. The 1991 excavation did not reveal any evidence that the trap was actually used at the location from which it was recovered. No posts anchoring the trap were identified, and no associated remains of stakes or posts that might have been associated with a wooden weir were discovered. Moreover, no evidence of a fish camp at the mouth of Montana Creek was discovered in 1991 or during a later intensive survey of both banks of Montana Creek upstream from the trap site (Campbell 1994).

However, new information obtained in 1995 requires a re-evaluation of the context of the trap. Further testing of the fish trap site by Jon Loring in

1995, conducted under contract with the Alaska Department of Transportation and Public Facilities, encountered what appears to be a portion of another basket trap immediately to the north of the excavated trap (Jon Loring, personal communication 1995). These additional hoops and staves with spruce root lashing appear to be part of a second, but less well preserved, basket trap at the same stratigraphic level as the trap recovered in 1991. Elements of this probable second trap were left in situ and protected by backfilling the test pit with river gravel. Thus, initial speculation that the trap excavated in 1991 had been used at an upstream location and then been transported by flood water to the location at which it was discovered in 1989 is probably wrong. It is not likely that two traps would have been deposited by river currents in the same location. It is hoped that further excavation at the site will be possible at some point and that additional geomorphology and stratigraphic investigations may reveal the relationship between the two traps and provide information on whether or not they were actually used at the mouth of Montana Creek.

Acknowledgments

The excavation and conservation of the Montana Creek trap was made possible through the generous financial support of the Sealaska Corporation, the regional Native corporation for Southeast Alaska. The Alaska State Museum in Juneau provided essential logistical support and conservation facilities, and the City and Borough of Juneau administered the Sealaska grant and provided additional logistical support for fieldwork. Steve Henrikson and Wallace Olson conducted the initial 1990 salvage excavation, and Jon Loring of the Alaska State Museum coordinated the 1991 excavation. Greg Chaney contributed his expertise as a coastal geomorphologist to the project. Jon Erlandson at the University of Oregon did the statistical calibration and averaging of the 1990 radiocarbon dates on wooden elements from the fish trap. A number of Tlingit Elders, including the late Austin Hammond, Cecilia Kuntz, the late Horace Marks, and the late Bessie Visaya, contributed information on traditional Native use of basket-style fish traps.

References Cited

Alaska Department of Fish and Game
    1992 Peak Salmon Escapement Surveys. Commercial Fisheries – Region I. Survey data on file at Sport Fish Division, Douglas, AK.
Campbell, Chris Rabich
    1982 Anadromous Salmon Weirs and Associated Cultural Features in Southern Southeast Alaska. Paper presented at the 9th annual meeting of the Alaska Anthropological Association, Fairbanks, AK, April 2-3, 1982.
    1994 *An Archaeological Survey of the West Mendenhall River Trail.* Report prepared for the Alaska Department of Transportation and Public Facilities (ADOT & PF), Southeast Region. Project No. 71466. Report on file at ADOT & PF, Juneau, AK.
de Laguna, Frederica
    1960 *The Story of a Tlingit Community: A Problem in the Relationship Between Archeological, Ethnological, and Historical Methods.* Bulletin 172. Bureau of American Ethnology, Smithsonian Institution, Washington, DC.
    1972 *Under Mount Saint Elias: The History and Culture of the Yakutat Tlingit.* Smithsonian Contributions to Anthropology, vol. 7. Smithsonian Institution, Washington, DC.

1990 Tlingit. In *Northwest Coast,* edited by Wayne Suttles, pp. 203-228. Handbook of North American Indians, vol. 7, William C. Sturtevant, general editor. Smithsonian Institution, Washington, DC.

Drucker, Philip
1950 *Culture Element Distributions: XXVI, Northwest Coast.* Anthropological Records Vol. 9, No. 3. University of California Press, Berkeley.
1951 *The Northern and Central Nootkan Tribes.* Bulletin 144. Bureau of American Ethnology, Smithsonian Institution, Washington, DC.
1965 *Cultures of the North Pacific Coast.* Chandler, Scranton, PA.

Emmons, George Thornton
1991 *The Tlingit Indians.* Edited with additions by F. de Laguna. University of Washington Press, Seattle.

Erlandson, Jon M.
1990 Letter to Steve Henrikson, Curator of Anthropology, Alaska State Museum. August 22, 1990.

Krause, Aurel
1956 *The Tlingit Indians: Results of a Trip to the Northwest Coast of America and the Bering Straits.* Translated by E. Gunther. University of Washington Press, Seattle. Originally published *Die Tlinkit-Indianer,* 1885, in Jena.

Langdon, Stephen J.
1977 *Technology, Ecology, and Economy: Fishing Systems in Southeast Alaska.* PhD dissertation, Stanford University. University Microfilms, Ann Arbor, MI.
1979 Comparative Tlingit and Haida Adaptation to the West Coast of the Prince of Whales Archipelago. *Ethnology* 18:101-119.
1986 Traditional Tlingit Fishing Structures in the Prince of Wales Archipelago. In *Fisheries in Alaska's Past: A Symposium,* pp. 67-88. Alaska Historical Commission Studies in History No. 227. Alaska Historical Commission, State of Alaska, Anchorage.
1989 From Communal Property to Common Property to Limited Entry: Historical Ironies in the Management of Southeast Alaska Salmon. In *A Sea of Small Boats,* edited by John Cordell. Cultural Survival Report 26. Cultural Survival, Inc. Cambridge, MA.

Moss, Madonna L.
1989 *Archaeology and Cultural Ecology of the Prehistoric Angoon Tlingit.* PhD Dissertation. University of California, Santa Barbara. University Microfilms, Ann Arbor, MI.

Moss, Madonna L., Jon M. Erlandson, and Robert Stuckenrath
1990 Wood Stake Weirs and Salmon Fishing on the Northwest Coast: Evidence from Southeast Alaska. *Canadian Journal of Archaeology* 14:143-158.

Pomeroy, J.A.
1976 Stone Fish Traps of the Bella Bella Region. In *Current Research Reports,* edited by Roy L. Carlson, pp. 165-173. Department of Archaeology, Simon Fraser University, Burnaby, BC.

Stewart, Hilary
1982 *Indian Fishing: Early Methods on the Northwest Coast.* University of Washington Press, Seattle.

Stuiver, M., and G.W. Pearson
1986 High-Precision Calibration of the Radiocarbon Time Scale, AD 1950-500 BC. *Radiocarbon* 28:805-838.

Wooley, Chris
1987 Racing the Tide: Southeast Alaska Shoreline Survey. Paper presented at the 14th Annual Meeting of the Alaska Anthropological Association, Anchorage, AK, March 13, 1987.

The Montana Creek Fish Trap II: Stratigraphic Interpretation in the Context of Southeastern Alaska Geomorphology

Greg Chaney

Landscapes, like cultures, evolve and change throughout time. Evolving landscapes often modify the distribution of resources and people may be required to adapt to their changing environment. The landscape's natural rate of change in northern Southeast Alaska is among the most dynamic in the world, and it is often misleading to attempt to reconstruct prehistoric sites based on modern environmental conditions. Since archaeological investigations attempt to discover as much as possible about past cultures and about how past people lived, it is important to consider the nature of the geographical setting during the time they were alive.

This chapter attempts to evaluate the sediments surrounding the Montana Creek fish trap in order to gain understanding about how the trap was preserved and exposed (Figure 1). In addition, it attempts to reconstruct the environmental setting before, during, and after the trap was used in order to allow archaeologists to evaluate the probability that a habitation site existed in the vicinity. This information will also be useful for future research if additional archaeological sites are discovered in the region.

Environmental Setting

The Montana Creek fish trap site (49JUN453) is located near the confluence of Montana Creek and the Mendenhall River in the Mendenhall Valley near Juneau, Alaska (see Betts, this volume:Figure 1). Radiocarbon analysis of wood samples from the trap yielded an average calibrated date of AD 1310 (640 ± 50 BP) (Betts, this volume). The landscape surrounding the fish trap site has experienced many changes since the trap's construction nearly 700 years ago.

Southeast Alaska is a seismically active fjord coast that still retains tidewater glaciers. The Mendenhall Valley has been geologically active during

---

This is a companion to the previous chapter by Robert C. Betts, "The Montana Creek Fish Trap I: Archaeological Investigations in Southeast Alaska."

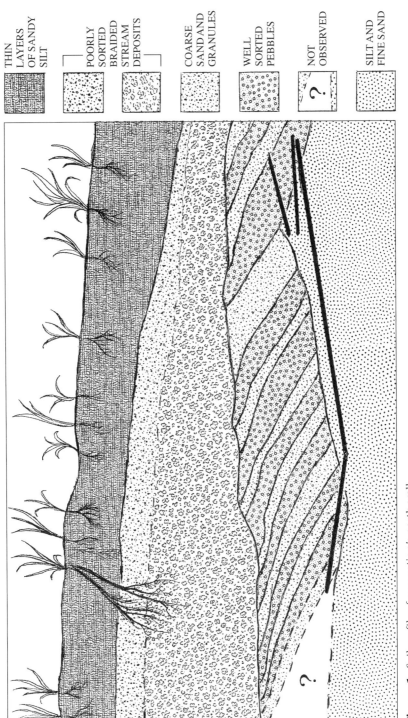

THIN LAYERS OF SANDY SILT

POORLY SORTED BRAIDED STREAM DEPOSITS

COARSE SAND AND GRANULES

WELL SORTED PEBBLES

? NOT OBSERVED

SILT AND FINE SAND

Figure 1. Soil profile of excavation's north wall.

the late Holocene. Juneau experiences an extreme annual tidal range of 25 ft (7.6 m). In 1991, spring tides of at least 17 ft (5.2 m) – measured as tide height above Mean Lower Low Water – reached the fish trap's location (see Betts, this volume, Figure 2). Juneau's tide level reached at least 17 ft (5.2 m) on 172 occasions in 1991, which represents 24 percent of the year's high tides (Kawaky 1991). This tidal exposure has been greater in the recent past due to the rate of uplift in northern Southeast Alaska, which is the most rapid measured for the coastal United States. In downtown Juneau, uplift measured between 1936 and 1980 averaged 0.042 ft/yr (1.3 cm/yr) (Figure 2) (Hicks et al. 1983:24). Uplift rates measured in the Menden-hall Valley between 1937 and 1959 were reported to average 0.062 ft/yr (1.9 cm/yr) (Hicks and Shofnos 1965).

The Mendenhall Glacier's terminal moraine has retreated inland over 5 km in historical times (Miller 1972). Land-level changes have also resulted in lateral movements of intertidal estuaries of more than 1 km. This has caused significant changes in sediment load and gradient for rivers and streams in

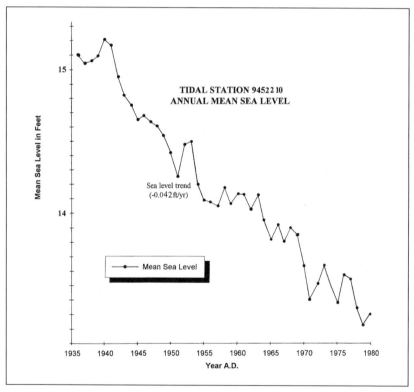

Figure 2. Mean sea level change recorded in downtown Juneau, Alaska, AD 1936 to AD 1980; sea level trend -0.042 ft/yr (-1.3 cm/yr). *Data for graph from Hicks et al. 1983.*

the area (Barnwell and Boning 1968). Therefore, the region appeared significantly different when the trap was in use in AD 1310, compared to AD 1991.

Paleogeography

The Mendenhall Valley

The history of glacial fluctuations for the Mendenhall Glacier has been reconstructed for the last 2,000 years (Motyka and Begét 1996). Evidence gathered from dendrochronology indicates that the Mendenhall Glacier began retreating from its maximum neoglacial position soon after AD 1750 (Lawrence 1950, Lawrence and Lawrence 1949). Of particular interest to this study is a stump rooted in bedrock that has recently been exposed by the currently retreating Herbert Glacier. (The Herbert Glacier is adjacent to the Mendenhall Glacier, and they share a common ice accumulation region on the Juneau Ice Field.) The exposed stump has yielded a radiocarbon date of 610 ± 50 BP (Motyka and Begét 1996:48) and has been interpreted as indicating that the Herbert and Mendenhall Glaciers were in recession for approximately 200 years before that time and that they began advancing approximately 610 ± 50 BP. The Mendenhall Glacier is thought to have reached its maximum advanced position by 300 years ago (Motyka and Begét 1996).

The rapid rate of uplift documented in northern Southeast Alaska was originally attributed to isostatic rebound following the retreat of glaciers (Hicks and Shofnos 1965). Some researchers have correlated prehistoric land-level changes near Glacier Bay with Holocene glacial advances and retreats (Derksen 1976). Recent geophysical measurements and geological evidence suggest that northern Southeast Alaska is influenced by tectonic processes that may be of greater magnitude than isostatic adjustment, and that uplift associated with glacial recession may only be coincidental (Barnes 1990; Brew 1990; Horner 1990). This information implies that past land-level changes may have been driven by processes largely independent of local glacial fluctuations. Therefore, the regional glacial retreat observed since AD 1750 may not have signalled the beginning of uplift currently observed in northern Southeast Alaska, and the total amount of land-level change that has occurred since the fish trap was buried is unknown at this time. It is probable that during the last 600 years land-level change has experienced dynamic fluctuations driven by the elastic compression of tectonic plates. The only tangible evidence indicating the total magnitude of uplift in the Mendenhall Valley is the Mendenhall River's 12 ft- (3.7 m-) high banks lining its entrenched meanders. If the 1.9 cm/yr rate of uplift documented by Hicks and Shofnos between 1937 and 1959 in the Mendenhall Valley has remained relatively constant, then the 12 ft- (3.7 m-) high riverbanks indicate that uplift began about 200 years ago.

A radiocarbon date obtained from an upright sheared tree rooted in peat that was observed eroding from the banks of the Mendenhall River indicates that a forest was established in the Mendenhall Valley before 860 ± 260 BP and that it was over-ridden by rapid deposition of glacial outwash deposits at that time (Miller 1972:56). The dated sample was collected roughly 1 km north of the Montana Creek fish trap site. Statistically, this date overlaps with the construction of the Montana Creek fish trap and may indicate that the trap was constructed when the Mendenhall Valley supported a mature forest. The current elevation of this relict forest horizon indicates that this stratigraphic layer was at or above its current elevation relative to the reach of high tides. Radiocarbon dates for timing of the Mendenhall Glacier's advance, burial of the forest in the Mendenhall Valley, and construction of the Montana Creek fish trap all overlap statistically. This implies that the period when the fish trap was constructed was one of rapidly changing conditions in the Mendenhall Valley.

The Fish Trap Site
The foregoing information requires a re-evaluation of previous interpretations of the paleogeographic setting of the Montana Creek fish trap site (Betts and Chaney 1995; Chaney 1994). It now seems that when the trap was constructed, the horizon containing the fish trap was near its current elevation relative to the reach of high tides. However, the landscape 600 to 800 years ago did not appear the same as today because approximately 12 ft (3.7 m) of glacial outwash sediment has been deposited since that time. It is assumed that some erosion accompanied glacial outwash sedimentation. Erosion and deposition have masked the previous landscape's contours and make accurate regional paleogeographic reconstructions difficult.

It seems likely that in AD 1310 the Montana Creek fish trap site was near the mouth of Montana Creek, bordering tidal flats similar to those at the mouth of the Mendenhall River today. The surrounding landscape would have been low and forested. The Mendenhall Glacier's terminal moraine was near its current recessional position or farther up the valley beginning its re-advance. The location from where the trap was recovered may have been tidally influenced by extreme high water. This reconstruction is offered with caution because it presumes that the trap was buried soon after it was constructed. A delay of 100 years between construction and deposition would put the site in a different context relative to the Mendenhall Glacier in an advanced position. A delay of this magnitude seems unlikely considering the near-pristine condition of the artifact. Furthermore, prehistoric land-level changes have not been researched in detail for the Mendenhall Valley.

After the trap was buried, subsidence seems to have occurred because surficial deposits indicate that during the neoglacial period, the tidal flats of Gastineau Channel were only 0.5 km from the fish trap site (Barnwell and Boning 1968) (Figure 3a). Further evidence of regional depression is provided by Whidbey in 1794 and by Sir George Simpson in 1841, who

(a)

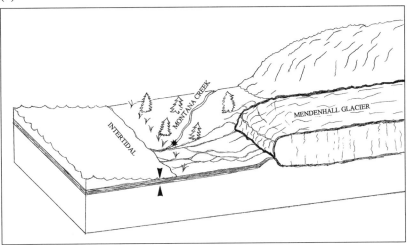

(b)

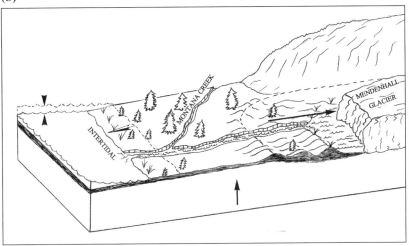

Figure 3. Schematic diagrams:
(a) Braided streams from the Mendenhall Glacier deposited approximately 12 ft (3.7 m) of sediment in the Mendenhall Valley between 860 ± 260 BP and AD 1750. Montana Creek fish trap deposited near location of star on diagram. Regional subsidence also occurred at some time during this interval.
(b) Between AD 1750 and AD 1989 the Mendenhall Glacier retreated approximately 5 km. Land level uplifted 12 ft (3.7 m), causing intertidal estuaries to retreat 1 km in the opposite direction of the glacier. The Mendenhall River establishes a channel and cuts banks 12 ft (3.7 m) high.

both observed ice from the Mendenhall Glacier being discharged into Gastineau Channel (Wentworth and Ray 1936). Although it is possible that the ice observed in the channel was from the Taku Glacier, it is also possible that ice was washed downstream over the relatively short distance between the advanced position of the Mendenhall Glacier and the inland reach of spring tides. The terrace adjacent to the lower reaches of Montana Creek is covered with a forest that appears to have developed after the deposition of glacial outwash sediments ended. The shallow organic soil horizon and the low concentration of forest litter imply that this forest may have become established after AD 1750, when the Mendenhall Glacier began to recede.

Stratigraphic Interpretation

The advance of the Mendenhall Glacier, which occurred 610 ± 50 BP, probably supplied the sediment that eventually accumulated to a depth of approximately 12 ft (3.7 m) (Miller 1972). This depositional sequence, which covered and protected the fish trap, was responsible for the trap's preservation. During the time when this sediment was deposited, the Mendenhall

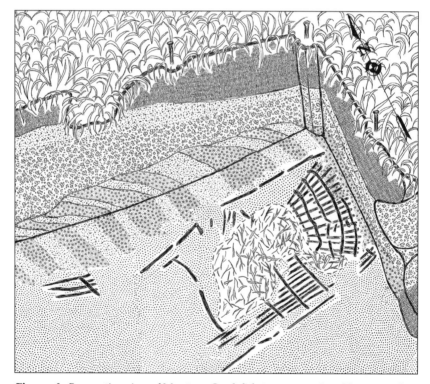

Figure 4. Perspective view of Montana Creek fish trap excavation. View toward northeast. Streambed is in the foreground and flows from left to right. Note distribution of debris captured on the trap's upstream side.

(a)

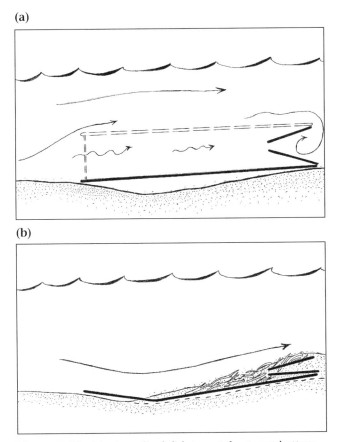

(b)

Figure 5. The Montana Creek fish trap at the stream bottom:
(a) Cross-sectional view of the trap as it first came to rest before
burial. Note how the trap disrupts and reduces stream flow
velocity in its immediate vicinity. Dashed lines show trap
elements that were exposed in the 1980s by stream bank
erosion. Their stratigraphic context was lost.
(b) The fish trap captured driftwood and other debris that
caused the trap's upstream side to become clogged. Dashed
line shows contour of stream bottom before the fish trap
was present.

River was probably a braided stream that wandered across the Mendenhall
Valley (Barnwell and Boning 1968). The Montana Creek drainage basin did
not contain large valley-filling glaciers, therefore Montana Creek's run-off
characteristics were probably similar to its recent flow patterns. Currently,
Montana Creek experiences seasonal flooding and periods of extremely high
run-off (Miller 1972).

(a)

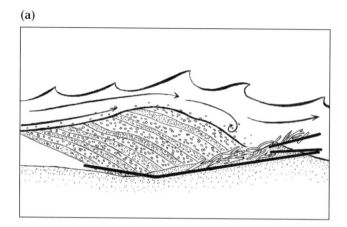

(b)

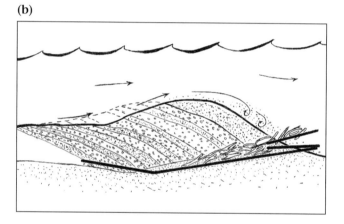

(c)

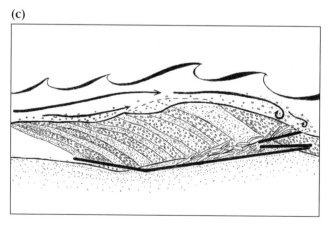

(d)

(e)

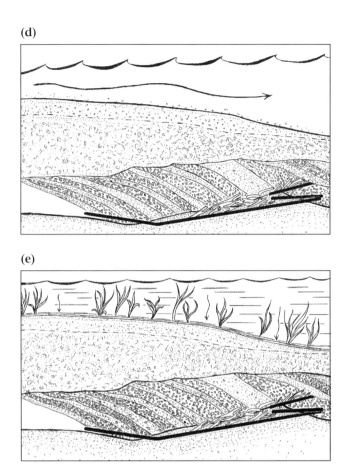

Figure 6. Reconstruction of the burial process:
(a) River bar advancing downstream covering the fish trap. Alternating beds of coarse and fine sediments are deposited. Note gravel moving across top of bar and deposition occurring on "slip face" of bar on the downstream side.
(b) Reduced stream velocity at high tide. Erosion on upstream side of river bar and deposition of fine sediment on downstream side of bar.
(c) Increased stream velocity at low tide. Erosion on upstream side of river bar and deposition of coarse sediment on downstream side of bar. Note abrasion of exposed trap elements by high velocity flow and associated coarse sediments.
(d) Alternating coarse and fine cross-bedding sequence complete. Deposition of poorly sorted sand, granule, and pebbles. Structure poorly defined. Sediments of this type are characteristic of glacial outwash braided stream deposits.
(e) After the Mendenhall River established its channel, sandy silt (glacial flour) is deposited during over-bank flooding. Grass helps slow stream velocity in its vicinity, which enhances silt deposition.

Depositional Sequence

Sedimentary deposits immediately surrounding the fish trap tell a story of initially slow-moving water, followed by rapid burial from a swift current probably associated with a large flood. Cross-bedding and the orientation of detritus trapped within the trap's structure indicate a paleostream flow direction that parallels the present course of Montana Creek (Figure 4). The lower portion of the fish trap was buried in silt (glacial flour) and fine sand. This probably occurred during a period of low stream flow velocity, possibly at high tide (Figure 5a). Deposition of silt and fine sand was probably enhanced by the presence of the trap, which would have slowed water flow in its immediate vicinity. Reduced stream velocity would have resulted in deposition of sediment in suspension. The fish trap proved to be an effective strainer of driftwood and other debris that clogged the trap's upstream end (Figure 5b).

The presence of silt, sand, and associated debris demonstrates why this type of trap was seldom left in a river channel for an extended period. The trap would catch drifting debris, slow current flow, and cause sedimentation. This process alone could bury a large portion of a trap in a relatively short period. It is probable that this style of fish trap required frequent maintenance to counteract a natural tendency to become clogged and buried.

Above the layer of silt, fine sand, and organic material, there was a stratigraphic sequence of well-defined cross-bedding. The cross-bedding featured alternating layers of coarse sand with granules and beds of well-sorted pebbles. This pattern seems to have been created by a river bar that advanced downstream over the trap (Figure 6a). The alternating layers of relatively fine and coarse material may have been caused by tidal influences. In Southeast Alaska, there are two high and two low tides in an average day. During high tides, stream velocity in the lower Mendenhall River and in Montana Creek is reduced. Extreme high tides can even cause a reversal in stream direction. During low tides, the lower reaches of these rivers display normal current velocities. Therefore, the lower reaches of these rivers experience four tidally driven changes in stream velocity per day. Assuming the fish trap was deposited in a tidally influenced location, the stream velocity would have rhythmically increased and decreased four times per day. This systematic fluctuation in stream velocity would have resulted in the alternating deposition of sediments of large and small grain sizes (Figures 6b and 6c).

There were a total of 16 alternating beds covering the trap, which may indicate that the trap was buried within four days. The average grain size of sediment deposited in these cross-beds increased downstream. This implies that average stream flow increased as the trap was buried. One of the most dramatic aspects of the cross-bedding was a bright red colour associated with well-sorted coarse sediments. This coloration is likely the result of iron deposited by groundwater percolating through permeable layers. The relatively high iron content of shallow groundwater is well documented in the Mendenhall Valley (Barnwell and Boning 1968).

Overlying the cross-bedding was a layer of poorly sorted sand, granules, and pebbles, roughly 0.5 m deep. This may have been deposited by a meandering branch of the braided outwash streams from the Mendenhall Glacier (Figure 6d). Above this was a 0.5 m layer of sandy silt (glacial flour), which was probably deposited during over-bank flow (Figure 6e). Within 5 cm of the surface, bottle caps and monofilament fishing line were uncovered. The presence of this modern cultural debris indicates a deposition rate from over-bank flooding of at least 1 cm per decade. Considering that this silt layer was probably deposited after glacial retreat began, a deposition rate of 2 cm per decade is more probable (Figure 1). Riverbank deposition is still active, and two months before the excavation in 1991, I observed deposition of glacial flour during seasonal flooding of the Mendenhall River and Montana Creek.

Erosion and Trap Exposure

As mentioned previously, the Mendenhall Glacier began retreating from its advanced position soon after AD 1750. This retreat was accompanied by regional uplift that has totalled approximately 12 ft (3.7 m). The increase in elevation lowered the base level of rivers and streams, causing them to erode their beds. Young forests became established on the newly stabilized and uplifted surface (Carstensen 1995).

Down-cutting has resulted in 12 ft- (3.7 m-) high banks along the Mendenhall River and lower Montana Creek (Miller 1972) (Figure 3b). The steep, unconsolidated stream banks are subject to collapse during floods. As a result of these factors, erosion of stream banks along the Mendenhall River and Montana Creek is now common and caused the exposure of a portion of the fish trap in 1989 (Figure 7).

Conclusion

The results of this geomorphological investigation have helped archaeologists to determine that a permanent camp could have been in the vicinity of the artifact. It has been shown that the trap was probably buried in a tidally influenced stream channel. The site was near large tidal flats, and the adjacent shoreline was low and forested. The elevation of the site relative to sea level in AD 1310 was probably similar to modern times, but there have been significant local land-level fluctuations and sedimentation during the intervening centuries.

Before this stratigraphic and paleogeographical reconstruction, the nature of the region at the time of the trap's construction was unknown. This study has also informed archaeologists that a lack of artifacts near the

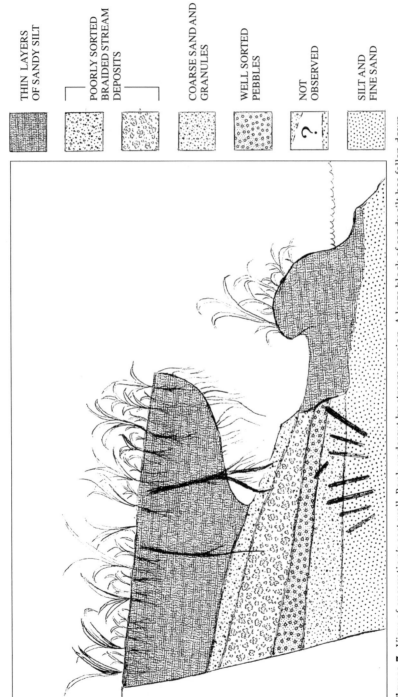

Figure 7. View of excavation's east wall. Bank undercut by stream erosion. A large block of sandy silt has fallen down to the river level.

THIN LAYERS OF SANDY SILT

POORLY SORTED BRAIDED STREAM DEPOSITS

COARSE SAND AND GRANULES

WELL SORTED PEBBLES

NOT OBSERVED

SILT AND FINE SAND

surface in the surrounding forest does not indicate that a permanent habitation site was not there. The contours of the present landscape mask the former setting, and additional artifacts may be buried more than 2 m below the current forest floor. Without geomorphological studies such as this, archaeologists would be left to draw erroneous conclusions by extrapolating modern environmental conditions into the past to explain an artifact's context.

Recommendations for Further Research

Stratigraphy currently exposed along the banks of Montana Creek and the Mendenhall River is complex. There may have been more than one episode of marine transgression and regression between the fish trap's deposition and its exposure. Detailed research and additional radiocarbon dating of sediments would be required to reconstruct land-level changes that have taken place in the Mendenhall Valley. The results of such research could be used to more accurately reconstruct the paleogeographic setting in the region.

Acknowledgments

The Montana Creek fish trap excavation was made possible in part through the Sealaska Corporation's financial support. Much of the credit for the successful recovery of the fish trap goes to Jon Loring and Bob Betts, who were actively involved in all aspects of the excavation. Several individuals were involved with the effort to unravel the secrets locked in the fragile sediments encasing the trap itself. The deepest gratitude goes to my lovely wife Bonnie Chaney, who tolerated an eccentric husband continually distracted from family life by changing sea level, advancing glaciers, and flooding rivers. She also reviewed a draft of this report and offered suggestions that made it more comprehensible. Martha Messick and Bill Elliot generously donated housing, office space, supplies, and encouragement at the critical time when the trap was in danger of being destroyed by flood waters. Significant new information concerning Holocene glacial fluctuations was provided by Dr. Roman Motyka. Richard Carstensen from the Discovery Foundation supplied reprints of relevant articles and provided significant comments that led to a complete restructuring of this report.

References Cited

Barnes, D.F.
  1990 Gravity, Gravity-Change and Other Geophysical Measurements in Glacier Bay National Park and Preserve. In *Proceedings 2nd Glacier Bay Science Symposium, Sept. 19-22, 1988,* edited by A.M. Milner and J.D. Wood, Jr., pp. 12-16. Glacier Bay National Park, Gustavus, AK. Alaska Regional Office, US National Park Service, Anchorage.
Barnwell, W.W., and C.W. Boning
  1968 Water Resources and Surficial Geology of the Mendenhall Valley, Alaska. US Geological Survey, Hydrologic Investigations, Map HA-259.
Betts, R.C., and G.P. Chaney
  1995 The Montana Creek Fish Trap: A 700 Year Old Basket-Style Fish Trap Excavated Near Juneau, Alaska. Paper presented at *Hidden Dimensions: The Cultural Significance of Wetland Archaeology,* Vancouver, BC, April 27-30, 1995.
Brew, D.A.
  1990 Plate-tectonic Setting of Glacier Bay National Park and Preserve and Admiralty Island National Monument, Southeast Alaska. In *Proceedings 2nd Glacier Bay Science*

Symposium, Sept. 19-22, 1988, edited by A.M. Milner and J.D. Wood, Jr., pp. 1-5. Glacier Bay National Park, Gustavus, AK. Alaska Regional Office, US National Park Service, Anchorage.

Carstensen, R.
1995 *Two Centuries on Duck Creek.* Discovery Foundation for Alaska Water Watch, Juneau, AK.

Chaney, G.P.
1994 Montana Creek Fish Trap Stratigraphy Interpretation. Paper presented at the 21st annual Alaska Anthropology Association Meetings, Juneau, AK, March 31-April 2, 1994. Ms. on file, Alaska State Museum, Juneau.

Derksen, S.J.
1976 *Glacial geology of the Brady Glacier region, Alaska.* Institute of Polar Studies Report No. 60. Ohio State University, Columbus.

Hicks, S.D., and W. Shofnos
1965 The Determination of Land Emergence from Sea Level Observations in Southeast Alaska. *Journal of Geophysical Research,* 70(14):3315-3320.

Hicks, S.D., H.A. Debaugh, and L.E. Hickman
1983 *Sea Level Variations for the United States 1855-1980.* National Oceanic and Atmospheric Administration, National Ocean Service, Rockville, MD.

Horner, R.
1990 Seismicity in the Glacier Bay Region of Southeast Alaska and Adjacent Areas of British Columbia. In *Proceedings 2nd Glacier Bay Science Symposium, Sept. 19-22, 1988,* edited by A.M. Milner and J.D. Wood, Jr., pp. 6-11. Glacier Bay National Park, Gustavus, AK. Alaska Regional Office, US National Park Service, Anchorage.

Kawaky, J. (editor)
1991 *Commercial Fisherman's 1991 Guide, Volume 3: Southeast Alaska.* Marine Trade Publications, Port Ludlow, WA.

Lawrence, D.B.
1950 Glacier Fluctuation for Six Centuries in Southeastern Alaska and its Relations to Solar Activity. *The Geographical Review* (American Geographical Society) 40(2):191-223.

Lawrence, D.B., and E.G. Lawrence
1949 Some Glaciers of Southeast Alaska. *Mazama* 31(13):24-30.

Miller, R.D.
1972 *Surficial Geology of the Juneau Urban Area and Vicinity, Alaska, with Emphasis on Earthquake and other Geologic Hazards.* US Geological Survey, Open File Report 72-255.

Motyka, R.J., and J.E. Begét
1996 Taku Glacier, Alaska: Late Holocene History of a Tide-water Glacier. *Arctic and Alpine Research* 28:42-51.

Wentworth, C.K., and L.L. Ray
1936 Studies of Certain Alaskan Glaciers in 1931. *Bulletin of the Geological Society of America* 47:879-934.

Part 4:
Preservation and Conservation in Practice

Introduction

Two dimensions of cultural resource management lie at the base of the contributions to this section. The first is philosophical and involves the goal of preservation for future generations. Accordingly, archaeological materials that are still in the ground and the land that contains them (the sites) fulfil an important purpose by remaining intact and undisturbed; objects that have been removed from their protective environment should be kept safe, as near to their original state as possible, in perpetuity.

The second underlying concern, a focus on water, applies specifically to wetland archaeology. Those who endeavour to preserve the resource in situ contrive to maintain the wet conditions that have preserved the material since antiquity. This task can be extremely challenging as the existence of buried waterlogged material is often known only after the hydrological regime at the site has been disturbed. Conservators, on the other hand, expend their ingenuity at removing water from objects in order that these can continue to exist in a non-waterlogged state.

Scientists and conservators involved in treating waterlogged artifacts, as well as archaeologists who work in land management, are on the lookout for better methods to achieve their respective goals. Research can be experimental, such as the supercritical drying technique described here by Barry Kaye and David J. Cole-Hamilton, or evaluative, such as the re-assessment of commonly used treatments, reported by Dilys A. Johns. Similarly, wet-site field surveys, such as that described by Paul J. Gilman, integrate new technological applications (initially at an experimental level) with traditional methodologies. Mike Corfield's explanation of hydrological factors that are crucial for in situ preservation illustrates the need for scientific research in the context of wetland archaeological resource management.

Throughout the *Hidden Dimensions* volume, various authors comment on the dynamic nature of wetlands and the consequent changes to the water-saturated microenvironments in which perishable materials have been preserved. Threats from natural processes and from accelerating land development continue to prompt the initiation of management plans. The effectiveness of these plans, however, is constrained by the state of methodological knowledge and available funds. Ultimately, the future of wetland archaeology depends on public demand and political will. Achieving the goal of preservation requires demonstrating the significance of resources that merit protection.

Both Robert Van de Noort and Paul J. Gilman illustrate in their respective chapters impressive ventures in long-range planning through programs that incorporate research about the scientific value of the archaeological resources. It is not coincidence that these two contributions, in fact all three that deal with land management issues, describe British projects. Europe, especially England, not only takes the lead in wetland management pertaining to archaeology (e.g., Coles 1995; Cox et al. 1995) but also is enjoying an active period of wetland archaeological research, resulting in numerous conferences, exhibitions, and publications.

Van de Noort discusses a regional approach that recognizes the dynamic character and the diversity of wetlands and emphasizes reconstruction of the ancient, now-eroding, landscapes. The scientific information forthcoming from archaeological sites in the Humber wetlands comprises an important source of data about the very paleoenvironment that the management scheme aims to understand and to protect. (For a detailed example of this type of research, see the chapter by Goodburn in another section of this volume.)

Paul J. Gilman's efforts to develop an effective site management scheme centre on coastal resources, specifically remains of fish traps and weirs in Essex county. The intertidal-zone setting of these sites poses considerable logistical problems, which led to innovative field methodology that promises to be adopted in other places.

The third contribution in this section, by Mike Corfield, argues for the need to understand site hydrology as a critical aspect of site preservation. In noting that wetlands and archaeological sites within them vary and that individual assessment is required if water is to be kept in a site to protect perishable artifacts, Corfield reiterates a point put forth by many other authors in this volume: within a region, be it in New Zealand, the Yucatan, or Sweden, wetlands come in various forms.

The buried nature of wetland sites, where aspects pertaining to water content cannot normally be seen, poses considerable challenges for archaeological assessment. Unlike a dry site that might be protected by relocating a right-of-way or mitigating planned land alteration by designating the area as a park, a wet site can be drained of water due to causes, natural as well as human-induced, unrelated to the development under consideration. For a wet site, drainage signifies destruction, since formerly waterlogged artifacts begin to decay.

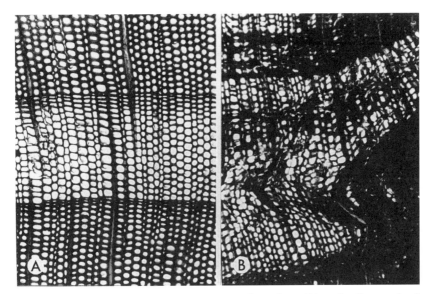

Figure 1. Although wood can survive in waterlogged conditions for thousands of years, it loses internal structural strength. Cross section views at ca. 350X show normal cells (A) and collapsed cells (B) in western red cedar (*Thuja plicata*). Collapsed cell walls challenge the task of conservators who often rely on liquified preservatives to penetrate into the wood by moving through the cell cavities. *Photos by K. Bernick.*

Although it is possible to rescue objects from accidentally or purposefully drained wet sites and to treat them to stem the deterioration process, the costs involved can be prohibitive. Moreover, conservation treatments that appear to produce good results have not been employed long enough to know whether they are truly lasting. In other words, polyethylene glycol (PEG), which has become a popular method of treatment and part of the wetland archaeologist's vocabulary, may not protect objects in perpetuity. Moreover, chemical and physical reactions may produce different results depending on factors as potentially varied as plant part, age, and species; extent of deterioration; alterations during manufacture and use; and depositional environment.

Dilys A. Johns addresses the applicability of PEG treatment to Southern Hemisphere woods that had not been previously tested. She also points out that freeze-drying, touted by many conservators as an excellent method of dehydration following impregnation with PEG, does not always produce good results. This observation echoes opinions expressed informally by wetland archaeologists in other places (including Canada and England) who are becoming increasingly disillusioned with freeze-drying. Understanding the reasons behind differential success of particular treatments seems essential and clearly indicates a direction for conservation research. Equally important is the refinement of new treatments, such as supercritical drying reported here by Barry Kaye and David J. Cole-Hamilton and which requires additional experimentation to identify materials and situations that would benefit from its application.

A huge amount of work is involved in developing management plans, researching effective preservation techniques, and implementing programs of site protection and artifact conservation. Also, the materials and techno-logical devices that enable the procedures to operate require considerable financial investment. Katherine Singley's detailed account of the monetary costs of treating waterlogged artifacts will not surprise archaeologists who have had to budget (and raise funds) for conservation treatment. But, as she notes, it may be news to those who have traditionally accessed facilities at public institutions with little or no cost to their respective projects. Promot-ing increased attention to wet-site archaeology – which is one aim of this volume – will ultimately yield many more objects in need of treatment than existing facilities can accommodate. The difficult task will not be esti-mating costs and retaining the services of a conservator but, rather, decid-ing what to treat and what to forego. The ethical precept of preservation needs to be viewed in practical context and with knowledge of the range of possibilities and their respective advantages and disadvantages.

References Cited

Coles, Bryony
    1995 *Wetland Management: A Survey for English Heritage.* WARP Occasional Paper 9. De-partment of History and Archaeology, University of Exeter, UK.
Cox, Margaret, Vanessa Straker, and Douglas Taylor (editors)
    1995 *Wetlands: Archaeology and Nature Conservation.* HMSO, London.

Essex Fish Traps and Fisheries: An Integrated Approach to Survey, Recording, and Management

Paul J. Gilman

Essex, a county in the southeast of England (Figure 1), has the longest, and one of the most important, coastlines in Britain (English Nature 1993). Including the many estuaries and creeks, it stretches for more than 480 km and consists of five basic habitats: mudflats and sandbanks; saltmarshes; shingle spits; grazing marsh; seawalls and grassland. All these habitats support an abundance of birds and other wildlife. The Essex coast is, therefore, of great international importance for nature conservation. The Essex coast also contains many important archaeological and historical sites. These range in date from the early prehistoric periods through to the very recent past. As well as sites directly associated with the coast, such as shipwrecks, ports, and defences, the intertidal zone in particular contains a rich archaeological resource. This has been preserved as a result of past changes in the coastline and is now being extensively exposed by modern changes in sea level and other coastal processes.

One of the most important aspects of the archaeological resource concerns the ancient ground surfaces that are emerging from the eroding mudflats. These surfaces, which often date to the Neolithic and Bronze Age, have intact soil profiles, whereas at inland sites of similar age, the upper layers have often been removed by ploughing. Thus, sites where these surfaces survive contain information that cannot be recovered elsewhere. However, the continuing erosion of the mudflats within the estuary is a double-edged sword for archaeologists. Sites that have been buried beneath the mud for millennia are appearing, but continuing erosion means they may not survive for long.

In addition to natural processes, human activities also pose threats to archaeological remains. These threats range in scale and effect from large-scale disturbance and development such as dredging, offshore mineral extraction, marinas, and caravan (trailer) parks, to boating, recreation, bait digging, and fishing. Increasing demand for coastal water recreation is a

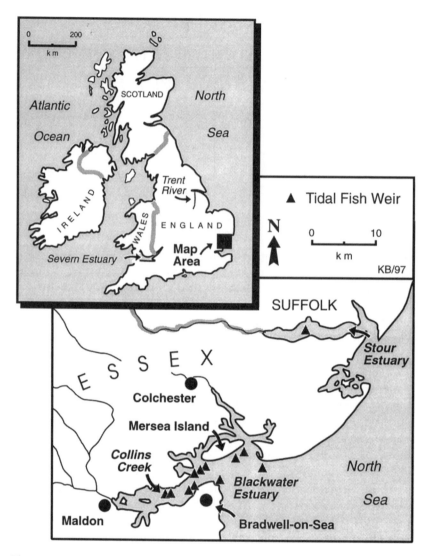

Figure 1. Locations of fish-trap sites and other places mentioned in the text.

particular concern since activities such as jet skiing and water skiing can cause damage to sensitive ecological and archaeological features as a result of wave motion.

National and local government agencies have recently recognized the vulnerability of coastal and estuarine environments and have begun to integrate archaeological requirements into plans for long-term management and conservation.

The First Steps of a Management Plan

Inventory

Essex County Council's Archaeology Section maintains the computerized County Sites and Monuments Record (SMR), which is the most complete and up-to-date source of information about the archaeology of Essex. However, when the SMR was first created, it inherited the biases of the information used to compile it. These sources, such as record cards compiled by the Ordnance Survey and inventories published by the Royal Commission on the Historical Monuments of England (RCHME), were largely terrestrially based in their coverage of the archaeology of the county. Following the initial phase of SMR formation, the Archaeology Section has been continually seeking to enhance and extend the coverage of the SMR, principally through programs of survey and recording. Subject areas where further work is specifically being carried out include post-medieval, industrial, and maritime archaeology.

Intertidal Survey

The importance of the ancient land surfaces in the Essex intertidal zone has been recognized at least since the early years of the twentieth century, notably by the work of Hazzledine Warren, who recorded a number of Neolithic sites on the Essex coast (e.g., Longworth et al. 1971; Warren et al. 1936). Recently, the County Council's Archaeology Section instigated an initial survey project, the Hullbridge Survey, funded by English Heritage. The results were so encouraging that the survey's scope was expanded, eventually covering most of the county's coastline, from the Thames estuary in the south to the Stour estuary in the north (Wilkinson and Murphy 1995). The survey located numerous sites in the intertidal zone, many of which dated to the late prehistoric period. Several of these sites were investigated, including the excavation of a Neolithic settlement at the Stumble, in the Blackwater estuary near Osea Island (Wilkinson and Murphy 1998), where preservation of Neolithic features was far better than at any contemporaneous inland site in the county.

The Collins Creek Project

The Hullbridge Survey was able to examine only those parts of the intertidal zone that could be reached safely on foot. One of the most exciting recent developments in the study of the Essex coast has been the realization that aerial survey can make a valuable contribution to the discovery of sites in the intertidal zone. This realization was prompted by the discovery by a local boatman, Ron Hall, of an extensive series of alignments of timber posts at Collins Creek in the Blackwater estuary (Figure 2). Aerial survey

Figure 2. Aerial view of the mudflats at Collins Creek. *Photo by Steve Wallis.*

revealed the true extent of the structures (some of the alignments are more than 1 km long), which are only visible for short periods at very low tides (Figure 3). Visits were made to the site and two samples were taken for radiocarbon dating. The results were surprising, since one sample dated to the seventh century, and the other to the ninth (AD 640 to AD 675 [UB-3485] and AD 882 to AD 957 [UB-3486], both calibrated to one standard deviation according to Stuiver and Reimer [1986]). The initial work has been followed by further aerial and terrestrial survey by Essex County Council's Field Archaeology Group, funded by English Heritage (Clarke 1993:209).

Survey Methods

The position of the Collins Creek site in the estuary means that it can be reached only by boat. This, together with the fact that the features are accessible only at low tide for at most two hours in any one day, poses serious problems for survey. These problems are exacerbated by the sheer size of the site, with an estimated 13,000 posts, some of which are associated with hurdle structures formed by lengths of interwoven timbers. In designing a methodology for survey, it soon became apparent that it would not be possible to record every post. Therefore, the initial aims of the survey were to produce an overall plan of the alignments and to obtain further dating evidence by means of dendrochronology.

The first attempt at survey involved an aerial photogrammetric survey carried out by the Cambridge University Committee for Aerial Photography.

Figure 3. Aerial view of some of the timber alignments (indicated by arrows) at Collins Creek. *Photo by Steve Wallis.*

This was done using a high-resolution camera during a suitable low tide. Unfortunately, low tides tend to occur early or late in the day, at times of poor light levels. This, coupled with the fact that the flights were actually carried out at too high an altitude, meant that the resolution of features achieved in the photography was low and it was not possible to plot individual posts. However, some of the alignments were sufficiently clear to be plotted from the diapositives by staff of the Department of Land Surveying, University of East London, using a Leica photogrammetric workstation.

The next stage was to use Global Positioning Systems (GPS), with the assistance of the University of East London (Dare 1994), following the "stop-and-go" technique with a mobile receiver (Figure 4). The advantages of this method are that it enables points to be established to an accuracy of a few centimetres while receiving a relatively small amount of data from the satellites. This enabled the work to proceed reasonably quickly, which was crucial since only a few hours were available for survey at any one time. It was impossible to record each of the hundreds of posts that were visible, so recording was confined to strategic points. These were mainly the beginnings and the ends of alignments, points where they changed direction, and points of intersection. Areas with hurdles were recorded, as were the locations where dendrochronological samples were taken. The survey results were subsequently transformed into local grid values, the Ordnance Survey Great Britain 193. The coordinates were then converted to DXF

Figure 4. Stop-and-go survey at Collins Creek using mobile receiver. *Photo by C.P. Clarke.*

format for use in a computer-aided design (CAD) system used by the Field Archaeology Group. The GPS data could then be overlaid with that obtained by aerial photogrammetry. Finally, three sample areas were recorded in more detail, using more conventional surveying methods as well as ground-based photogrammetry (a range of photographs were taken, digitized, and then rectified using a computer).

The combination of the various surveying techniques allowed an overall site map to be produced (Figure 5), together with detailed plans of three areas (e.g., Sample Area 3, Figure 6). Overall, an accuracy of 10 cm was achieved, which was adequate for the purposes of the project.

The Fish Trap Features

Study of the Collins Creek site is still at a very early stage. However, it is possible to make a number of statements about the site. Not all the alignments are alike – some have single lines of posts, some have double rows, and some have lines of posts that hold in place hurdle features (notably in some of the parallel alignments at the southern end of the site). In some areas, for example in Sample Area 3, there are distinct V-shaped features, with the open ends facing upstream into the ebb tide. These can be interpreted as fish traps (Figure 6), but the very long parallel lines of posts are more ambiguous. In this part of the estuary, the ebb tide flows from northwest to southeast and would have carried fish past these lines. Some of the post alignments may, therefore, be the remains of fish weirs sited to catch fish carried out on the ebb tide. Others, notably the ones with hurdles, may represent the remains of trackways built to provide access to the weirs across the intertidal mudflats.

Although many samples were taken with the aim of carrying out a program of dendrochronology, none had enough growth rings for dating purposes. However, the location of Collins Creek, far out in the estuary, means that it would not have been possible to work the site in recent times, since it is uncovered only by the lowest tides of the year. The two radiocarbon dates indicate that part of the site at least is of Saxon age, and the variety of features present indicates that there may have been several phases of activity, possibly extending into the medieval period. If the radiocarbon dates are correct, then there are considerable implications for our understanding of the scale and nature of middle to late Saxon age settlement and economic activity on the coast. To construct and maintain such extensive fishing sites as these would require the expenditure of great resources of time and labour, implying that they played a very significant role in the local economy.

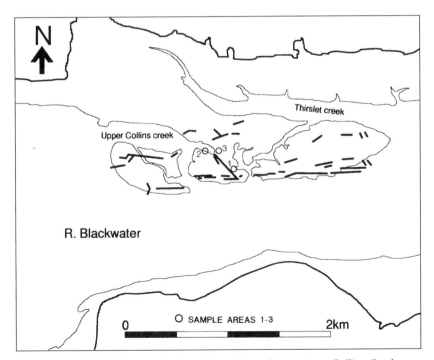

Figure 5. Computer-generated plan of the timber alignments at Collins Creek.

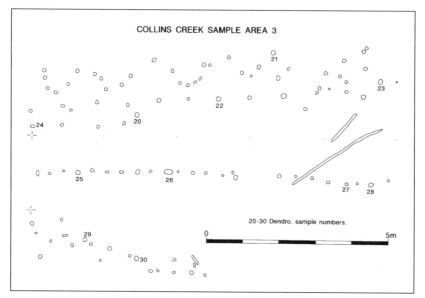

Figure 6. Collins Creek Sample Area 3 showing V-shaped structures.

Data Sources for Integrated Management

Aerial Survey

As a result of the Collins Creek discovery, Essex County Council's Archaeology Section, with the aid of a grant from the RCHME, has carried out a systematic program of aerial survey over other areas of the Essex coast (Crump and Wallis 1992; Strachan 1995a, 1995b; Wallis 1993:193-194, 1994:233). In 1992, this resulted in the discovery of a large fish-trap site at Mersea Flats, southwest of Mersea Island (Figure 1). This is located about 1 km offshore, well beyond the mean low water level, and is shaped like a broad "V" with wings several hundred metres long (Figure 7). Remains of a trap can be seen clearly at the apex of the "V." There are signs of alteration and rebuilding, suggesting that the trap may have been in use over a long period.

The aerial survey also rediscovered a fish trap at Sales Point, near Bradwell-on-Sea. This was previously known from the work of a local archaeologist, Kevin Bruce, who photographed the site from the ground in 1967. The aerial photographs have revealed much more of the site, which, like the Mersea fish trap, seems to have been a multi-phase structure. In 1993, more fish traps in this area were discovered and photographed, including a fine example off Pewet Island, near Bradwell-on-Sea (Wallis 1994). All these sites are in and near the Blackwater estuary, but, in 1995, a V-shaped fish-trap site was found in the Stour estuary, between Essex and Suffolk (David Strachan, personal communication 1995).

Figure 7. Aerial view of fish trap (arrows) at Mersea Flats. *Photo by Steve Wallis.*

No material for direct dating has been recovered as yet from these structures, other than a few shards of medieval pottery from Sales Point. However, the locations of the sites indicate that they are not recent, since they are too far out to be safely worked at modern tide levels. This is especially the case with the Mersea fish trap, which is exposed only at the very lowest tides of the year, during the spring and autumn equinoxes.

Although this project has provided encouraging results, it has also demonstrated the problems of this kind of aerial survey. Flights must coincide with the lowest tides, and these may occur very early or late in the day when the light is poor. Also, even at low tides, parts of some structures may still be underwater and difficult to see. Even when a structure is found, it may be necessary to observe it from different angles to record it fully and to obtain good photographs. As with land-based survey, repeated observations over a long period are needed in order to recover as much detail as possible.

Documentary Evidence

There is extensive documentary evidence from the medieval and post-medieval periods for fish weirs and traps in Essex. Domesday Book, which was completed in 1086, lists many fisheries along the length of the Essex coast (Rumble 1983). For the area around the fish-trap sites, that is, the Blackwater estuary, Domesday Book records fisheries as existing (in 1086) at Bradwell-on-Sea, Osea Island, and Tollesbury, and having formerly (i.e., in and/or before 1066) existed at West Mersea.

Later sources provide more detailed evidence for some parts of the coast. At Foulness Island, fishing was an important part of the economy, supplying income to those who owned shares in fishing rights, as well as providing food for subsistence (Smith 1970). For example, in 1424, the Lord of the Manor of Foulness obtained rents from 57 weirs and 18 kiddles. Most of the fishing was in the hands of a few families from neighbouring mainland parishes, who undoubtedly were professional fisherfolk. In 1424, the most prominent family, the Thurkelds, held or owned shares in 9 weirs and 12 kiddles. Weirs were substantial, permanent structures set between high and low water marks. They were triangular in shape, built of oak posts, 6 to 8 feet (2 m to 2.5 m) high, set several feet (1 m or 2 m) apart, and connected by interwoven hurdles (small pliable lengths of wood and twigs). As the tide fell, large numbers of fish, mainly plaice, dab, sole, and flounder, were trapped in the enclosure, then scooped out at low tide and transported to shore by horse and cart. Kiddles worked on the same principle, but were large square or U-shaped enclosures (Smith 1970).

Documentary sources, such as wills and manorial court rolls, provide valuable evidence of the ownership and distribution of Foulness Island kiddles up to the twentieth century. For instance, the will of John Staples the elder, dated October 28, 1586:

> To Thomas Staples my Son two cottages called Blarescotes, one tenement and 2 acres of land lying in two pieces, late of John Kynge and before Springes, and one Kedell lying between Barnflete Keddle and Crouch Keddell, the pasture for two horses in Estwicke, the fowling upon the marsh called Rugwood Hedd as well within the walls or without, and one summer Keddell lying between the Keddel late of John Hancocke late of John Frend called Southe Kedell and Crouch Kedell and one Keddel called the Halfe Ebbe. To John Staples the elder (?) my son one Kedell called Spedewell, one Kedellplace between Kedellman's Kedell and the Kedell called Le-Tepe on the West. (Essex Record Office D/AER 2 F4.)

The mention of horse pasture in this will is of direct relevance to fishing, as pasture was needed for the horses that drew the carts to bring the fish to shore. Of more interest, perhaps, are the names of the kiddles themselves. Some of these names recur in documents over several centuries, suggesting that the sites were in use for relatively long periods.

A kiddle often produced a cartload of fish from a single tide and could be worked twice daily. Summer kiddles were set closer to the shore since fish swam closer inshore at that season. One problem that might have been encountered was that wave action as a result of the presence of weed could create gullies under the nets, resulting in damage to the structures and sometimes necessitating rebuilding. This, as well as damage from inclement weather, helps to explain why the fish traps observed during the aerial survey exhibit evidence of replacement and reconstruction.

Fish Trap Sites in Other Areas of Britain

It is only relatively recently that coastal and estuarine fish traps have become a subject of study for archaeologists in Great Britain. For example, in the Severn estuary, remains connected with fishing have been recorded in the intertidal zone during fieldwork in advance of bridge construction for the Second Severn Crossing (Godbold and Turner 1994). These remains comprised three types of site:

(1) Post settings, including three sites with V-shaped structures, the openings of which faced upstream. One of these (Site 4) had five "V"s associated with two lines of posts on the upstream side of the structures. The "V"s are readily interpreted as fish traps, and the lines of posts are almost certainly "leaders" situated to guide fish toward the trap. Radiocarbon dates from these three sites place them all in the medieval period (e.g., Site 4: 620 ± 60 BP [Beta-54825], uncalibrated [Godbold and Turner 1994:36]). The V-shaped fish traps are similar in plan to those recorded in Sample Area 3 at Collins Creek on the Blackwater estuary in Essex.

(2) Hurdle structures, which can be interpreted as the remains of "leaders," or alternatively trackways for access to the fish traps.

(3) Large basketry structures that are presumed to have been originally mounted on the V-shaped post settings. They can be compared to modern photographs of a type of trap in the Severn estuary, known as a "putt," for which a long history can be documented – back to the medieval period and possibly beyond. One of the structures, Context 238, which is a large (2.2 m x 1.5 m) interwoven fish trap, produced a late Saxon- or early medieval-age radiocarbon date (960 ± 60 BP [Beta-54832], uncalibrated [Godbold and Turner 1994:36]).

The significance of the Severn estuary fish traps is discussed by Godbold and Turner (1994:48-52), who identify various reasons for their construction:

Individual and small groups of traps may have supplied a local market, but the larger complexes required a significant capital outlay to build and maintain. It is not surprising that many of those ... were built or run by monastic houses. Others may have been built as commercial enterprises, providing a rental income to the owner of the fishing rights, and a supply of fish to urban fishmongers for sale in town or to major households. The three broad periods of the fish traps identified in the study area, the 10th/ early 11th centuries, 13th and 14th centuries, and the early post-medieval period, correspond to the periods of urban prosperity in the main towns around the estuary. (Godbold and Turner 1994:52).

Fish traps have also been reported from several locations in Wales, such as the Gower peninsula in south Wales and the Menai Strait in north Wales (Godbold and Turner 1994:49). Closer to Essex, at Whitstable in Kent, England, a number of V-shaped fish traps are being surveyed and researched by a local society (David Strachan, personal communication 1995). In some parts of Britain, fish traps were built of stone rather than of wood, and many have been recorded recently in Scotland (Deanna Margaret Groom, personal communication 1995). Fish traps have been recorded also in riverine as opposed to estuarine and coastal locations. Comparable structures to those in the Severn estuary have been excavated in the floodplain of the Trent River, at Colwick, Nottinghamshire (Losco-Bradley and Salisbury 1988). Here, a Saxon weir was dated by radiocarbon to AD 872 to AD 949 and a medieval weir to AD 1050 to AD 1245 (both calibrated to one standard deviation, Jordan et al. [1994] and Losco-Bradley and Salisbury [1988], respectively).

The widespread occurrence of these sites is not surprising, since medieval and later documents record the existence of numerous fish weirs around the coast of Britain. Indeed, some medieval kings considered that they were becoming too prevalent, resulting in a menace to navigation and causing a decline in fish stocks, for example, a decline of salmon on the Severn (Godbold and Turner 1994:47).

Management Plans for the Essex Coast

National and Regional Planning Background

At all levels of national and local government in Britain, the coast has received particular attention in recent years, notably as a result of concerns over the effects of global warming (Department of the Environment 1992). This attention has resulted in the issuing of planning policy documents that include recommendations for the protection of archaeological sites. Government planning guidance emphasizes the role of local authorities in the protection and management of the important heritage resource represented by these sites. In carrying out this role, local authorities need to have access to specialist archaeological advice based on up-to-date and accurate records.

In Essex, the County Council, in fulfilling its strategic role for the coast, has long sought to provide relevant coastal plans and policies, notably through a coastal strategy for the county (Essex County Council and Essex Coastal Districts 1994a, 1994b, 1995). The Council's Archaeology Section also liaises with other organizations, such as the National Rivers Authority, Royal Commission on the Historical Monuments of England (RCHME),

English Heritage, and English Nature, to conserve the coast, with its environment, both natural and cultural. At the local level, district authorities are working to prepare coastal zone management plans. For example, Maldon District and Colchester Borough Councils have revised and reissued the Blackwater Estuary Management Plan (Maldon District Council and Colchester Borough Council 1996).

The Blackwater Estuary Management Plan (BEMP)
The recent discoveries in the intertidal zones prompted Maldon District Council, during the preparation of the revised Blackwater Estuary Management Plan (BEMP), to fund Essex County Council's Archaeology Section to produce an assessment report of the archaeology of the estuary (Gilman et al. 1995). The first (1980) version of the plan included only one page of text concerning the archaeological importance of the area covered by the plan. In preparing the revised version of the management plan, a background paper on archaeology was produced, based on the assessment report. The preparation of these documents reflects recent increased awareness of archaeological remains and their significance. This was highlighted in the planning process by the government's Planning Policy Guidance Note 16, *Archaeology and Planning* (Department of the Environment 1990).

The approach adopted in preparing the archaeological text involved the following:

- Enhancement of particular aspects of the Sites and Monuments Record for the study area.
- Extraction of information from the Sites and Monuments Record.
- Visits to selected parts of the estuary, both on foot and by boat.

A map of the management plan area was prepared at 1:25,000 scale, with symbols showing the various categories of sites (Figure 8). The map was accompanied by a report that gave particular emphasis to various aspects of coastal and maritime archaeology, notably intertidal discoveries. The report emphasized that the fish traps and other sites within the intertidal zone are under threat from both natural and human agencies. There is probably little that can be done about the natural erosion that is exposing and damaging the fish traps, although the nature, scale, and effects of the erosion are as yet little understood. However, through the planning system, it is possible to limit and control the risk posed by human activities such as boating and shellfish cultivation.

Implementation
Following completion of the draft text and plan for the Subject Plan (Maldon District Council 1995), Maldon District Council established a

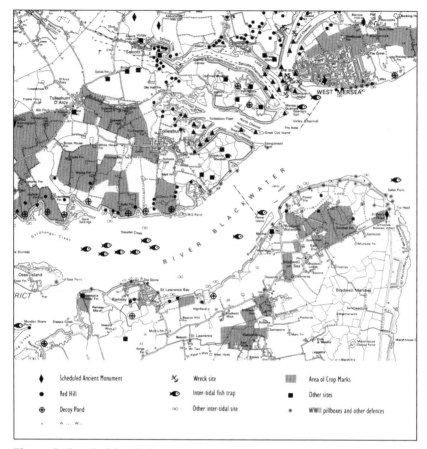

Figure 8. Detail of the Blackwater Estuary Management Plan base map. *Drawing by Stewart MacNeill and Roger Massey-Ryan. Based upon the Ordnance Survey mapping with permission of the Controller of her Majesty's Stationary Office. ©Crown Copyright. Unauthorized reproduction infringes Crown Copyright and may lead to prosecution or civil proceedings. Essex County Council LA076619.*

working committee to consider a number of specific subject areas, one of which was archaeology. Maldon District Council is in a very good position to influence the use of the Blackwater estuary, as a result of a twelfth-century charter that granted ownership of much of the western part of the estuary to the borough of Maldon.

The original BEMP covered only the part of the estuary within Maldon District. However, the area covered by the management plan was, at a relatively late stage, extended to cover the whole estuary, including part of the northern bank which is under the jurisdiction of Colchester Borough. The archaeological papers and the map were revised to take into account this extension.

The published management plan includes summary descriptions of areas of archaeological interest within the estuary, as well as a series of policies and proposals aimed at ensuring future protection of archaeological sites in the estuary and the immediate surrounding. The fish trap sites are covered by four proposals (Maldon District Council and Colchester Borough Council 1996:75):

(1) Survey the intertidal area at five-year intervals, monitoring erosion and recording exposed remains.
(2) Investigate opportunities for charting known archaeological sites and structures within the estuary, in addition to the Collins Creek area, as obstructions on hydrographic and nautical maps.
(3) Establish consultation procedures with Essex County Council Archaeological Advisory Group before any necessary approvals are granted for oyster dredging or block moorings.
(4) Any proposed restrictions to shellfish layings in areas of archaeological importance should proceed in consultation with representatives from the local fishing industry.

Conclusion

Despite documentary evidence that fish traps were once common around much of the British coast, the archaeological study of these sites is still very much in its infancy. In Essex, the County Council is pioneering approaches to the survey of intertidal fish-trap sites. Also, through involvement in the planning process, it is helping to conserve these sites for present and future generations to study and appreciate. The archaeological input provided to the Blackwater Estuary Management Plan shows how the county's Archaeology Section has been able to ensure that full consideration is given to archaeological issues when drawing up policies. By carrying out programs of archaeological survey and recording, and by liaising closely with other organizations, the Essex County Council Archaeology Section has enabled archaeological requirements to be properly integrated with initiatives for coastal protection and management. Moreover, it has been possible to achieve integration at an early stage. Much remains to be done, but the work that has been carried out to date has provided a firm basis for the future protection and management of important archaeological remains of the Essex coast.

Acknowledgments
I am grateful to Dr. Madonna Moss of the Department of Anthropology, University of Oregon, for the invitation to present a paper at the *Fishing for the Past* symposium. I would also like to thank the following: Ann Stevenson and Kitty Bernick of the Museum of Anthropology, University of British Columbia, for their invaluable assistance during

the *Hidden Dimensions* conference; my colleagues of the Essex County Council Archaeology Section, especially the County Archaeologist, David Buckley; the Assistant County Archaeologist, Owen Bedwin; Phil Clarke, Director of the Field Archaeology Group; and David Strachan of the Archaeological Advisory Group, all four of whom read and commented on an earlier draft of this work; and finally the Essex County Council Planning Department for allowing me the time to attend the *Hidden Dimensions* conference.

References Cited

Clarke, C.P.
   1993 Collins Creek, in "Archaeology in Essex 1992," edited by P.J. Gilman. *Essex Archaeology and History* 24:185-210.
Crump, R., and S. Wallis
   1992 Kiddles and the Foulness Fishing Industry, *Essex Journal* 27(2):38-42. Chichester, England.
Dare, P.
   1994 Mapping Ancient Saxon Fish Traps Using GPS. *GPS World* February 1994:28-34.
Department of the Environment [United Kingdom]
   1990 *Archaeology and Planning.* Planning Policy Guidance Note 16. Department of Environment, London.
   1992 *Coastal Planning.* Planning Policy Guidance Note 20. Department of Environment, London.
English Nature
   1993 *Wildlife and Conservation of the Essex Coast.* English Nature, Colchester, UK.
Essex County Council and Essex Coastal Districts
   1994a *The Essex Coast: Issues Report.* Essex County Council, Chelmsford, UK.
   1994b *The Essex Coast: Consultation Draft Essex Coastal Strategy.* Essex County Council, Chelmsford, UK.
   1995 *Essex Coastal Strategy.* Essex County Council, Chelmsford, UK.
Gilman, P.J., D.G. Buckley, and S. Wallis
   1995 Salt Marsh to Managed Retreat in Essex: An Integrated Approach to the Archaeological Management of a Changing Coastline. In *Managing Ancient Monuments: An Integrated Approach,* edited by A.Q. Berry and I.W. Brown, pp. 143-154. Clwyd County Council, Mold, Clwyd, UK.
Godbold, S., and R.C. Turner
   1994 Medieval Fishtraps in the Severn Estuary. *Medieval Archaeology* 38:19-54.
Jordan, D., D. Haddon-Rees, and A. Bayliss
   1994 *Radiocarbon Dates from Samples Funded by English Heritage and Dated before 1981.* English Heritage, London, UK.
Longworth, I.H., G.J. Wainrwright, G.J., and K.E. Wilson
   1971 The Grooved Ware Site at Lion Point, Clacton. *British Museum Quarterly* 35:93-124.
Losco-Bradley, P.M., and C.R. Salisbury
   1988 A Saxon and Norman Fishweir at Colwick, Nottinghamshire. In *Medieval Fish, Fisheries and Fishponds in England,* edited by M. Aston, pp. 329-351. BAR British Series 182. British Archaeological Reports, Oxford.
Maldon District Council
   1995 Blackwater Estuary Management Plan. Final consultation draft, Maldon, UK.
Maldon District Council and Colchester Borough Council
   1996 The Blackwater Estuary Management Plan. Maldon District Council and Colchester Borough Council, Maldon and Colchester, UK.
Rumble, A. (editor)
   1983 [1086] *Domesday Book.* Phillimore, Colchester, UK.
Smith, J.R.
   1970 *Foulness: A History of an Essex Island Parish.* Essex Record Office Publication 55. Essex County Council, Chelmsford, UK.

Strachan, D.
    1995a Problems and Potentials of Coastal Reconnaissance in Essex. *AARG News* (newsletter of the Aerial Archaeology Research Group, UK) 10:28-35.
    1995b Aerial Photography and the Archaeology of the Essex Coast. *Essex Journal* 30(2):41-46. Chichester, England.
Stuiver, M., and P.J. Reimer
    1986 A Computer Program for Radiocarbon Age Calculation. *Radiocarbon* 28 (2B):1022-1030.
Wallis, S.
    1993 Aerial Survey of the Essex Coast, in "Work of the E.C.C. Archaeology Section," edited by A. Bennett. *Essex Archaeology and History* 24:185-194.
    1994 Aerial Survey 1993, in "Work of the E.C.C. Archaeology Section," edited by A. Bennett. *Essex Archaeology and History* 25:226-238.
Warren, S.H., H.S. Piggot, J.G.D. Clark, M.C. Burkitt, H. Godwin, and M.E. Godwin
    1936 Archaeology of the Submerged Landsurface of the Essex Coast. *Proceedings of the Prehistoric Society* 2:178-210.
Wilkinson, T.J., and P. Murphy
    1995 *Archaeology of the Essex Coast,* Vol. 1. East Anglian Archaeology 71. Essex County Council, Chelmsford, UK.
    1998 *Archaeology of the Essex Coast,* Vol. 2. East Anglian Archaeology, in press.

The Humber Wetlands Survey: An Integrated Approach to Wetland Research and Management

Robert Van de Noort

The lowlands in the Humber basin are seen by many as some of the most uninspiring landscapes in England, with no natural landmarks and little or no undulation. These lowlands were formed through sedimentation processes by seas and rivers during the Holocene (i.e., the period since the last glacial period, also, the Flandrian), on the one hand, and by the large-scale drainage projects that began in the seventeenth century, on the other. However, below these alluviated lowlands, a prehistoric landscape exists. It is largely invisible, but parts have emerged through the effects of erosion and desiccation. The known and potential archaeological and paleo-environmental resource in the Humber wetlands is, simply, unique (Van de Noort and Davies 1993).

The Humber Wetlands Survey was commissioned by English Heritage in 1994 as part of a national strategy to address the archaeology of wetlands. The program also includes the Somerset Levels Project (e.g., Coles and Coles 1986), the Fenland Project (e.g., Hall and Coles 1994), and the North West Wetlands Survey (e.g., Cowell and Innes 1994) (Figure 1). The Humber Wetlands Survey has as its prime objective the detailed survey of the wetlands in the Humber basin, in order to create a framework for research and management of important archaeological sites and landscapes in the region.

The Humber Wetlands Survey is conducted by a team of archaeologists and paleoenvironmentalists of the Humber Wetlands Project, which is funded by English Heritage and supported by academic staff of the University of Hull and the Ancient Monuments Laboratory of English Heritage, as well as by local volunteers and others. The survey calls on the expertise of four archaeologists, one paleoenvironmentalist, one geomorphologist, two palynologists, one soil scientist, and one natural historian for fieldwork and analysis of data and samples. This team forms the basis for an integrated multi-disciplinary approach to wetlands and wetland archaeology (Van de Noort and Ellis 1995).

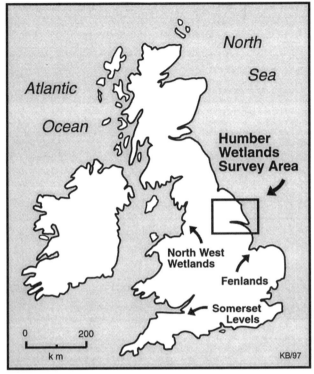

Figure 1. The Humber Wetlands Survey area (boxed) and general locations of other wetland surveys in England.

The Humber Wetlands

The Humber River emerges from the confluence of the Trent and Ouse rivers (Figure 2). The catchment area of the Humber River covers approximately one-fifth of England and is the largest catchment area in the country (Pethick 1990). The lowlands adjacent to the Humber River contain various wetlands that were mainly formed as a consequence of sea-level changes and obstructed run-off of freshwater during the Holocene.

The Humber wetlands, as defined for the purpose of the project, cover approximately 300,000 ha of land below the 10 m Ordnance Datum (i.e., below the 10 m contour above mean sea level) in Yorkshire, Lincolnshire, and Nottinghamshire. Seven physiographic lowland regions can be distinguished. These are delineated by the major rivers and the Cretaceous Yorkshire Wolds to the north of the Humber River, and by the Lincolnshire Wolds and the Jurassic Lincoln Edge to the south (Catt 1990). Probably the most significant feature of the Humber wetlands is the diversity of landscapes and the consequent variety of water-saturated archaeological landscapes. These include raised mire peatlands, which have been extensively worked for the horticultural market. Although raised bogs no longer exist as ecosystems in the area, there are remnants with important archaeological and paleoenvironmental remains (e.g., Buckland 1979). Foreshores occur both along the coast and in the Humber estuary. Lateral movements of the river channel have destroyed many of the prehistoric landscapes in foreshore areas, though pockets remain. At one of these, near North Ferriby, the remains of five prehistoric boats made of timber and several paddles have been recorded, most recently in 1995 (Fenwick 1995, Wright 1990).

In the Humber basin, landscapes buried under alluvium are widespread, and there is great likelihood that they contain preserved archaeological remains. River valleys are the most common type of wetland in the region, the Humber wetlands being for the most part a river delta with numerous channels and paleochannels. Former lakes, locally called "meres," are common in the region of Holderness. These lakes hold important sequences of paleoenvironmental source material for much of the Holocene, and some of them were focal points of prehistoric occupation.

Research Methodology

The Humber wetlands are approached as a continuous archaeological landscape in a dynamic environment. The term "dynamic environment" was chosen in order to underline that natural landscapes are not static backgrounds to archaeological data, but that landscapes, both wet and otherwise, are constantly changing. The words "continuous archaeological landscape" emphasize that the aim of the survey is not only to identify sites but also to record all evidence of human activity in the landscape, including sites.

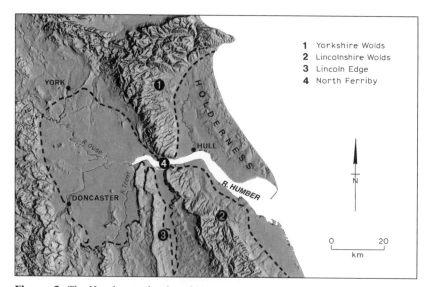

Figure 2. The Humber wetland study area.

Paleoenvironmental Data

The natural development of the Humber wetlands since the Late Glacial period, in response to climatic warming, can be viewed with regard to temporal changes in hydrological, vegetational, and pedological characteristics. The onset of wetland development in the region is mainly the result of sea-level change. There is no doubt that natural processes affected the lives of people and their interaction with the environment throughout prehistoric and historical times. Conversely, the natural environment was affected considerably by human activities, especially drainage, in the historical period. The study of sea-level change and its effect on wetland development, and the drainage and destruction of wetlands, are two of the central themes of the survey program.

The study of sea-level change on the east coast of the United Kingdom has largely been based on radiocarbon dated peat horizons from coastal areas. The dated samples represent, to varying degrees of quality and reliability, indicators of high water levels in the past (cf. Shennan 1994). The regional study of sea-level change that comprises part of the Humber Wetlands Survey commenced with an intensive coring program in one estuarine inlet in southern Holderness (Keyingham Drain, incorporating Roos Carr). Rather than sampling peat for radiocarbon assay from a series of different contexts and later linking the results through a series of calculations, samples for dating were obtained only from the bottom 50 mm of peat that overlies the first marine or estuarine incursion in the area. Such an incursion has resulted, in this region, in deposition of fine clays with impeded drainage and, more importantly, with impeded run-off of both fresh- and saltwater. This physiographic condition resulted in the development of wetland ecosystems and the potential for peat accumulation. In other words, the dates obtained for each sample give a *terminus post quem* for a particular high tide level during the preceding marine incursion. Series of dates and sea-level measurements are gathered by obtaining samples farther and higher up the valleys, from similar contexts.

Furthermore, palynological analysis of samples from the same context that provide the material for radiocarbon dating proves to be a valuable guide to understanding the environmental context of the samples, the development of wetland ecosystems, and the onset of peat accumulation. For example, radiocarbon assay of samples from the *top* of the peat layers, which would provide a *terminus ante quem* for the height of the *second* marine incursion, was ruled out because palynological analysis indicated bracken (*Pteridium* spp.) as one of the dominant plants. A bracken-dominated ground surface would have been vulnerable to erosion, and samples from this context would not yield reliable dates for the cessation of peat accumulation.

It is generally assumed that sea-level changes in the late Holocene followed a strongly oscillating pattern, with a series of transgressions and regressions of varying intensities (e.g., Gaunt and Tooley 1974). Whereas sea-level *rise* may be documented from peat that developed on top of marine sediments, dating sea-level *fall* is difficult because regressions do not result in alluvial accretion. The presence of archaeological sites on the foreshore of the Humber River, however, can be associated with marine regressions, which created opportunities for settlement in low-lying areas that were flooded during the previous and subsequent marine transgressions.

Evolving Landscapes

Once wetlands come into existence, they are characterized by continuing development – for example, from salt marsh via reedswamp, sedge fen, fen car, fen woodland, and transitional poor fen to bog (Godwin 1978; see Waller 1994 for an overview of variations on this model). The study of this transitional character of wetlands is important to understand landscape development, as well as the possibilities for human exploitation of wetland resources. In studying wetland development, the regional survey of Holderness focused on the former meres, or lakes. These lakes were created in the Late Glacial period by ice moving over an area with poor draining soils; all but one were drained or dried up during the Holocene. The stratigraphy of about 30 of the 70 known former lakes in the region was investigated through coring, and significant differences were found between large shallow lakes, continuous water bodies, and small lakes such as kettle holes. The large shallow lakes display typically only an early Holocene stratigraphy. Although these lakes may have been recognized as lakes into the Middle Ages because of seasonal waterlogging, they could not have contained any fish, with the notable exception of eels. The large basin lakes that were connected to rivers usually contain deep depositional sequences that occurred during much of the Holocene, and, as water bodies linked to the Hull or Humber rivers, did contain fish, as well as waterfowl. Kettle holes, such as the bog at Roos, contain continuous sequences of Holocene paleoenvironmental deposits, and because of their small size have sometimes escaped the damaging effects of drainage and ploughing.

Wetlands are not the only landscapes to undergo change; dry lands also are subjected to physiographic modifications through time. One of the lowland regions within the Humber wetlands, Holderness, is largely a morainic landscape. For the most part, its superficial appearance has remained unaltered for much of the past 10,000 years. Since the introduction of drainage and intensive agriculture in the thirteenth century, and, increasingly, with mechanized agricultural practices in the twentieth century, the landform has been changing. A comparative study of colluvium, or ploughwash, has been undertaken in areas of arable land and pasture to assess the effects of recent land use on the landscape. It was found that much of the colluvium is of relatively recent origin; in fact, it can be related to the introduction of mechanized agriculture.

These studies of the dynamic environment address two themes: landscape change and its implications on use through time, and methodological considerations relating to visibility or invisibility of the archaeological landscape.

Archaeological Resources

The Humber Wetlands Survey is programmed to assess a 300,000-ha area over a six-year period. Its activities are geared toward the identification of sites and landscapes and large-scale regional analysis, rather than toward small-scale and intra-site analysis and interpretations. An archaeological survey of wetlands must be three dimensional to allow for the dynamic character of wetlands. The third, or vertical, dimension is mainly observed through extensive coring, supplemented by observing exposures along dikes. Apart from the necessity to understand the development of wetlands through time so that we can appreciate the context of the cultural material found during survey, wetland development is a methodological concern because wetlands are main contributors to the alteration and burial of landscapes and to the relative obscurity of archaeological remains.

In addition to field survey and paleoenvironmental research, the survey investigates the state of preservation of selected archaeological sites with waterlogged components. It had been noted that some archaeological wet sites have good organic preservation, despite the fact that, according to historical records of drainage activities, the hydrological balance must have been disturbed as much as 300 years previously. The study attributes variable states of preservation of water-saturated archaeological sites primarily to hydraulic characteristics of the local soils. Other factors include the age of the archaeological site, its primary character and location, and the time elapsed since drainage and land use.

The results of the systematic survey, both archaeological and environmental, are recorded in a Geographic Information System (GIS), which enables, for example, analysis in the distribution of cultural material in the study area. Artifactual concentrations in specific wetlands assist in determining which parts of the landscape were significant areas of exploitation in the past.

Initial Results from Holderness

The study of sea-level change in southern Holderness has resulted in detailed information for the period between ca. 5100 BP and 2200 BP. It was possible to establish that, prior to 5100 BP, wetland development in the area was limited to several small lakes and to lakes with limited exploitation opportunities. It is hoped that by using digital terrain modelling and the regional sea-level curve it will be possible to determine which wetlands overlie buried archaeological landscapes. Palynological analysis established that the recurrent pattern of large-scale low-energy floods in the southern Holderness region resulted in wetlands evolved, in general terms, along the "progressive series," as suggested by Godwin (1978).

History of the Wetlands

The insight into exploitation and use of wetlands is particularly advanced on a regional scale. Isolated wetlands, such as meres and kettle holes, were not exploited to the same degree as wetlands connected to rivers for hunting, fishing, and gathering in the Mesolithic and Neolithic periods. However, clusters of sites dating to these periods and off-site cultural debris that may be associated with hunting occur in three areas in Holderness. These areas are: (1) the estuarine inlets in southern Holderness, where wetlands developed after the first marine incursion and became connected to the Humber River at the time of the Mesolithic-Neolithic transition, around 5000 BP; (2) the Bail and Low Meres complex in northern Holderness, which had been connected to the Hull River since Late Glacial times; and (3) the environs of Lambwath Mere, which was seasonally connected to the Humber River, as documented by historical records (Sheppard 1956). Many of the large lakes were not focal points for Mesolithic or Neolithic occupation. The evidence from the paleoenvironmental study that identified many of the large isolated lakes as seasonal rather than as permanent water bodies, and thus unlikely to have contained large numbers of fish, provides a clue as to why these larger lakes were of little interest to people who subsisted by hunting, fishing, and gathering.

The results of the archaeological survey add a temporal dimension to this pattern of wetland exploitation. In northern Holderness, a significant number of Mesolithic sites in or adjacent to wetlands were discovered, including the Early Mesolithic site Skipsea-25 (Round Hill), for which a calibrated radiocarbon assay of 8350-7940 BC (GU-5451) was obtained (Van de Noort 1995). In southern Holderness, on the other hand, the earliest cultural debris are dated to the late Mesolithic or the Mesolithic-Neolithic transition phase (ca. 5000 BP), which coincides with the onset of large-scale wetland development after the first major marine incursion.

In the late prehistoric period, when agricultural practices were the major mode of subsistence, some large isolated lakes became focal points for settlements. One such settlement, Barmston Main Drain (Skipsea-63), was partly constructed on peat that began to form in the early Holocene (ca. 10,400 BP), and which eventually buried the settlement (Varley 1968). A totally different form of wetland exploitation was encountered in Seaton, where the in situ remains of a managed woodland were discovered. The

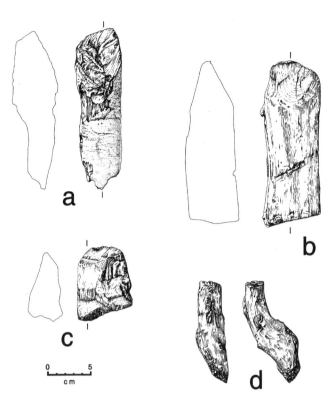

Figure 3. Early Bronze Age coppiced wood from Seaton-3:
(a-c) wedge-ended pieces, (d) heel. *Drawing by Les Turner.*

practice of woodland management has been known for some time (Coles
and Orme 1985; Rackham 1977), but the Seaton site appears to be the first
example of prehistorically coppiced trees in situ in England. The evidence
includes a coppiced heel of alder and a number of wedge-ended pieces of
roundwood that display facets of both stone and bronze axe blades (Figure
3). Considering the coexistence of facets from both stone and bronze tools,
a date in the Early Bronze Age is likely (ca. 2000 BC to 1500 BC).

Archaeological Sites
An example of the special importance of wetlands in antiquity comes from
the site West Furze (Skipsea-38). When it was first excavated in 1880, this
site was believed to be a lake-dwelling, in analogy to lake-dwellings in
Switzerland and the crannogs in Scotland (Smith 1911). Re-assessment of
the site, additional analysis of aerial photographs, and coring and digital
terrain modelling determined that the site is likely to have been a trackway, rather than a lake-dwelling (Van de Noort 1995). According to the

Figure 4. A reconstruction of the Late Neolithic/Early Bronze Age trackway at West Furze (Skipsea-38) in the Holderness region of northeast England. *Drawing by Les Turner.*

excavator, Thomas Boynton, the so-called lower floor consisted of "sharpened upright piles in two rows 5 ft. apart; two of these, higher than the others, and placed opposite one another, may have served as a wicket or narrow entrance at the south-east corner of the platform" (Evans 1885:60).

This description, along with recently obtained evidence from the surrounding area, was used for an illustrated reconstruction of the site (Figure 4). The door or wicket clearly would have acted as a symbolic boundary, whereas the wetland, an elongated mere, was the real boundary. Whether this boundary distinguished the land of the living from the land of the dead, or whether the mere constituted a political territorial boundary, cannot be determined. What is clear, however, is that wetlands in this region helped people in the past to delineate the landscape. With natural divisions already in place, there was no need to construct long earthworks such as those on the Yorkshire Wolds and other high areas surrounding the Humber wetlands.

The Humber Wetlands Survey's assessments of the state of preservation of archaeological sites have, thus far, included the Early Mesolithic site Round Hill (Skipsea-25, dated to ca. 8200 BC), the Late Neolithic or Early Bronze Age trackway at West Furze (Skipsea-38, dated to ca. 1800 BC), the Middle Bronze Age settlement Barmston Main Drain (Skipsea-63, dated to ca. 1150 BC) (Varley 1968), and the managed woodland site at Seaton-3. All these sites are located in the northern half of the Holderness region. The pre-depositional, depositional, and post-depositional processes involved in the formation of these archaeological sites vary greatly, which makes comparison of preservation conditions somewhat difficult. For example, the trackway of West Furze remained exposed after the excavation in 1880 for at least four years, allowing advanced desiccation to take place. On the other hand, Seaton-3 was discovered in 1994, following the construction of a pond, and the site had not been exposed since the Early Bronze Age.

Preliminary results indicate that the most important factor for preserving organic material is soil with low hydraulic conductivity beneath the archaeological deposits. A layer with very low hydraulic conductivity creates, in effect, a perched local water table, while reducing the effect of drawdown from nearby drains. Low hydraulic conductivity is achieved in soils with small particle size. The structure of the soil is also important. The absence of large peds and pores and of root activity is essential for maintaining a low hydraulic conductivity. Successful rewetting of wetland sites in areas with artificial drainage seems feasible only if the local soil conditions are favourable, that is, if they are conducive to the creation of perched water tables.

In the first year of our survey, over 700 archaeological sites, that is, find-concentrations and find-spots related to the wetlands in the region of Holderness, were discovered. The sites range in date from the Early Mesolithic to the Roman period. Most important are the discoveries of water-saturated archaeological sites; prior to the survey, five archaeological sites with waterlogged components were known in the Holderness region (significantly, four of these were discovered before 1890). An additional eight waterlogged sites and sites covered by alluvium were among the 700 sites discovered during the survey, and thought to have been preserved in excellent condition.

Management of Wetland Sites

Creating a framework for managing waterlogged archaeological remains in the Humber wetlands involves identification of archaeological sites and landscapes during the survey, determination of the nature of their water-logged resources and their respective state of preservation, and study of the development of wetlands through time in order to be able to predict the presence of waterlogged or buried archaeological sites and landscapes. The results of the field program will provide recommendations to English Heritage:

(1) for further assessments and fieldwork
(2) for scheduling (designating) sites that are of national importance and can be maintained as wet sites within larger environments (cf. Coles 1995)
(3) for instigation of research, including site excavation and detailed survey in landscapes of national importance that are no longer, or cannot be sustained as, wetlands.

Conclusion

The prime objective of the Humber Wetlands Survey is the creation of a framework for the research and future management of the most important archaeological sites and landscapes in the Humber basin. The research framework is based on an integrated approach to the study of wetlands, including the reconstruction of the processes of wetland development during the Holocene and the relationship of this development to the exploitation of wetlands throughout the prehistoric and historic eras. The work undertaken thus far in Holderness has shown this approach to be successful at a regional level. Further work should be undertaken within the established framework, including detailed analysis of sites and smaller landscapes. Legal protection for wetland sites of national importance will be considered.

Acknowledgments
The Humber Wetlands Survey is undertaken by a team that includes, apart from me, Dr. Mark Dinnin, Helen Fenwick, Ruth Head, Malcolm Lillie, and Henry Chapman, all of whom have contributed greatly to the progress and results discussed in this chapter. Furthermore, information was provided by Dr. David Taylor, Dr. Stephen Ellis, and Richard Middleton, all of the University of Hull, and Dr. David Weir, of English Heritage. I am grateful to them all.

References Cited
Buckland, P.C.
    1979 *Thorne Moor: A Paleoecological Study of a Bronze Age Site*. Department of Geography, University of Birmingham, UK.
Catt, J.A.
    1990 Geology and Relief. In *Humber Perspectives: A Region Through the Ages,* edited by S. Ellis and D.R. Crowther, pp. 13-28. Hull University Press, UK.
Coles, B.
    1995 *Wetland Management: A Survey for English Heritage*. WARP Occasional Paper 9. Dept. of History and Archaeology, University of Exeter, UK.

Coles, B., and J.M. Coles
1986 *Sweet Track to Glastonbury: The Prehistory of the Somerset Levels.* Thames & Hudson, London.

Coles, J.M., and B.J. Orme
1985 Prehistoric Woodworking from the Somerset Levels: 3. Roundwood. *Somerset Levels Papers* 11:25-50.

Cowell, R.W., and J.B. Innes
1994 *The Wetlands of Merseyside. North West Wetlands Survey 1.* Lancaster University Archaeology Unit, UK.

Evans, T.M.
1885 The Ancient Britons and the Lake-Dwelling at Ulrome in Holderness. *Hull Quarterly and East Riding Portfolio* 2:57-61.

Fenwick, V.
1995 A Paddle from the North Ferriby Foreshore (Vale of York). In *First Annual Report Humber Wetlands Survey (1994-95),* pp. 16-8. Humber Wetlands Project, University of Hull, UK.

Gaunt, G.D., and Tooley, M.J.
1974 Evidence for Flandrian Sea-Level Changes in the Humber Estuary and Adjacent Areas. *Bulletin of the Geological Survey of Great-Britain* 48:25-41.

Godwin, H.
1978 *Fenland: Its Ancient Past and Uncertain Future.* Cambridge University Press, UK.

Hall, D., and J.M. Coles
1994 *Fenland Survey: An Essay in Landscape and Persistence.* English Heritage, London.

Pethick, J.S.
1990 The Humber Estuary. In *Humber Perspectives: A Region Through the Ages,* edited by S. Ellis and D.R. Crowther, pp. 54-70. Hull University Press, UK.

Rackham, O.
1977 Neolithic Woodland Management in the Somerset Levels: Garvin's, Walton Heath and Rowland's Tracks. *Somerset Levels Papers* 3:65-71.

Shennan, I.
1994 Coastal Evolution: Controlling Processes and Data Synthesis: Altitudinal Trends. In *The Fenland Project, Number 9: Flandrian Environmental Change in the Fenland.* East Anglian Archaeology, Cambridge, UK.

Sheppard, J.A.
1956 *The Draining of the Marshlands of East Yorkshire.* PhD thesis, Dept. of Geography, University of Hull, UK.

Smith, R.A.
1911 Lake-Dwellings in Holderness, Yorkshire, Discovered by Thos. Boynton, Esq., F.S.A., 1880-1. *Archaeologia* 62:593-610.

Van de Noort, R.
1995 West Furze: The Reconstruction of a Monumental Wetland Landscape. In *Wetland Heritage of Holderness: An Archaeological Survey,* edited by R. Van de Noort and S. Ellis, pp. 323-334. Humber Wetlands Project, University of Hull, UK.

Van de Noort, R., and P. Davies
1993 *Wetland Heritage: An Archaeological Assessment of the Humber Wetlands.* Humber Wetlands Project, University of Hull, UK.

Van de Noort, R., and S. Ellis (editors)
1995 *Wetland Heritage of Holderness: An Archaeological Survey.* Humber Wetlands Project, University of Hull, UK.

Varley, W.J.
1968 Barmston and the Holderness Crannogs. *East Riding Archaeologist* 1:11-26.

Waller, M.
1994 *The Fenland Project, Number 9: Flandrian Environmental Change in the Fenland.* East Anglian Archaeology, Cambridge, UK.

Wright, E.
1990 *The Ferriby Boats: Seacraft of the Bronze Age.* Routledge, London.

The Role of Monitoring in the Assessment and Management of Archaeological Sites

Mike Corfield

Archaeological sites in wetlands are a valuable resource. The normal processes of fungal and bacterial decay that destroy organic materials do not operate in the anoxic waterlogged conditions of wetlands. In temperate climates, wood, leather, textiles, basketry, and other organic-based materials that were used in profusion by our ancestors do not survive in sites that are not permanently waterlogged. The durable materials that survive on non-waterlogged sites do not represent the full range of materials utilized by humans; we therefore have a very biased view of the past, with the major materials used not represented in our museum cases. Postholes might show where the timbers of a hut once were, but it is only in wetlands that we actually see the timber itself.

Organic materials in archaeological sites will be preserved whenever they are permanently in an anaerobic environment. In this context it is not necessary for the site to be in an extant ecological wetland. Many sites, particularly in Europe, survive in areas that have long since been drained and which would not be recognized as wetlands at all. An example of such an area is the Fens of eastern England. Once a complex region of waterways in which fish were hunted and salt was extracted from the brackish water, the Fens have been subject to terrestrialization through silting and progressive drainage beginning in the Roman period and more extensively from the seventeenth century. The Fens today are a rich agricultural landscape with, apart from the extensive system of drains, little evidence of their wetland past. Despite this appearance, archaeological sites still survive below the watertable, and in these sites a rich profusion of waterlogged materials survive.

In addition to their survival in drained landscapes such as the Fens and the major river basins of, for example, the Humber, waterlogged archaeological sites may be found in extant wetlands, as were the Somerset Levels before industrial peat extraction began in the 1960s. They may survive in river estuaries, such as that of the River Severn, and they may be found in the intertidal zone around the coast. Waterlogged sites are not only found in the countryside: they may survive under our great cities, especially those that grew up at river crossings such as London, Carlisle, and York. These city sites are especially rich in the organic detritus of the past as successive generations built on the remains of buildings and on the rubbish left by their predecessors.

English Heritage Management Studies

The recognition that there is such a rich heritage of waterlogged sites has led English Heritage to commission a series of projects to identify the extent of the resource and to devise management strategies for their future survival. These studies have progressed from the seminal work in the Somerset Levels by John and Bryony Coles between 1973 and 1989 (Coles and Coles 1986), through a survey and evaluation of sites in the Fens (Hall and Coles 1994), to similar projects in the Humber wetlands (Van de Noort and Davies 1993) and the scattered wetlands of northwest England. Under the impetus of the proposed Severn Barrage, English Heritage and its Welsh counterpart, Cadw, supported work to survey the archaeology of the Severn Levels. Another English Heritage project is focusing on the intertidal coastal archaeology, and work will soon start on the Thames estuary.

Threats to Wetland Sites

These studies are demonstrating the richness of the wetland archaeological heritage. They are also revealing the considerable threat to the fragile environment that has contributed to the survival not only of organic artifacts from the past but also of the evidence for the natural environment in which people lived and the ways in which their activities changed it. The record of pollen and other microbotanical remains in peat will reveal the changes in vegetation, and studies of the wood that has been preserved will give evidence for woodland management practices such as coppicing or pollarding.

The threats to archaeological wetlands include natural processes beyond our control, such as terrestrialization, climatic change, and changing sea level (Coles 1995; Corfield 1994). Acid rain has been identified as a potential threat (Coles 1995), and though it may not be clear how detrimental increasing acidification will be to organic materials, there will certainly be a risk that corrosion of metals may increase. Changes to the environment can also arise from human activity. These are theoretically controllable, but since the causes of changes may be at considerable distances from the wetland sites, the need for control may not be immediately apparent. Examples of threats in this category include drainage, water abstraction, pollution, and mineral and peat extraction. In urban areas, the threat arises from excavation for foundations or cellars, from ground consolidation techniques, and from the compression of the ground surface. Driving piles through impervious layers may enable waterlogged layers to drain, and when the piles are closely spaced, they may impede the movement of water through the ground.

Given the extent of the threat, why don't archaeologists excavate more sites? In England, the emphasis of national policies is to avoid excavating archaeological sites wherever possible. The reasons for this are twofold. First, the archaeological resource is diminishing constantly under unavoidable threats; where the threat can be controlled, the English archaeological community believes that it has a duty to preserve sites for the future – when improved techniques might be available to enable our successors to understand the evidence better. Second, excavation generates a huge volume of evidence that must be assessed, analyzed, conserved, and recorded, and the costs of this are considerable. There is a further consideration. At the end of the process, the finds must be deposited into a museum where they should be curated in perpetuity. Our museums are overflowing with the archives from past excavations, and there is little enthusiasm for taking on yet more material, no matter how exciting it may be. In other countries, reasons that do not normally apply in England, such as a reluctance to disturb ancestral remains, may be factors in the decision not to excavate wetland sites.

Site Assessment

The main purpose of English Heritage's wetland projects has been to determine the extent of the wetland archaeological resource, to assess the quality of the burial environment and the threats to it, and to seek ways of managing the threats to the integrity of the evidence preserved in the waterlogged deposits. To achieve this, methods are being developed to assess the condition of waterlogged sites. The evaluations being made in the current projects rely far less on excavation, itself a source of risk to the waterlogged environment, and more on minimally interventive techniques, such as augered bore holes. Ideally, non-invasive geophysical methods would be used to determine the extent of a site and to decide where augering might provide the best evidence, but at present there is no technique that will locate buried organic structures, though English Heritage is investigating the potential of ground penetrating radar.

Before consideration can be given to the preservation of a waterlogged site, its hydrological status must be assessed. For some sites, this may simply be a recognition that the status quo can be maintained; for others, a more detailed evaluation involving long-term monitoring may be needed. When it is decided that hydrological evaluation is necessary, the following factors need to be considered:

- nature of the soil
- hydraulic conductivity of the soil

- source of the water supply
- threats to the water supply
- threats to water retention
- level of the water-table
- annual fluctuations of the water-table
- quality of the water
- threats to water quality.

Much of the necessary information may be readily available. Records will often be held by local water supply companies, with agencies concerned with management of the water resource, or with agencies concerned with land drainage. In England, water companies are concerned with the abstraction, storage, and supply of water and the disposal of waste water and effluent; the National Rivers Authority is responsible for management of the water resource; and the local drainage boards are responsible for land drainage and the level of water-tables. Mineral extractors in England are required by law to maintain borehole data, and such information may be useful for archaeological sites in proximity to quarries. Where the site coincides with an ecologically important area, there may be information available from relevant environmental conservation groups. More often, there will be no information available and a monitoring scheme will have to be considered.

Understanding Wetlands

The Hydraulic Conductivity of the Soil

If an archaeological site is to be preserved, there must be a thorough understanding of the soil and the effect it has on the percolation of water down from the ground surface and the ease with which groundwater can move horizontally. A well-drained sandy soil will give little resistance to water flow and therefore will dry out rapidly if the source of the water supply is cut off. A compact clay soil will impede the movement of water. A band of clay may serve to retain water within a restricted basin (within, for example, a terrestrialized ox-bow lake) or it may act as a barrier to an influx of water to the site.

Horizontal flow is, according to Darcy's Law:

$$Q = -k \, (\delta h / \delta l) \text{ or } q = V/ft \text{ (cm}^3\text{s}^{-1})$$

where Q is the rate of horizontal flow, $\delta h / \delta l$ is the hydraulic gradient for head difference (h) over the length of the sample (l), k is the hydraulic conductivity or coefficient of proportionality (cms⁻¹), and *V* is the volume of soil water moving across the cross-sectional area *f* in time *t* (Heathwaite and Göttlich 1993:207).

Hydraulic conductivity depends mainly on the geometry and distribution of the soil-filled pores. Therefore, an open structured soil will have high hydraulic conductivity, and a compact soil will have a low conductivity. Increasing the compression of the soil may decrease its hydraulic conductivity. This may be a significant factor to consider when devising strategies to mitigate the effects of development, for example by embanking or by surcharging the site.

Van de Noort (Van de Noort and Ellis 1995) has made effective use of hydraulic conductivity in the assessment of sites in the wetlands of Holderness, a part of the wider study of the wetlands of the River Humber. Nineteen samples were tested from three different locations; the soil types ranged from an inorganic lacustrine alluvium through clay silts and peats to sands and gravels. The measured saturated hydraulic conductivity ranged from less than 1 cm day⁻¹ to greater than 100 cm day⁻¹. Generally, the clays and silts had hydraulic conductivities less than 10 cm day⁻¹, the peats ranged from 24 cm day⁻¹ to 277 cm day⁻¹, and the sands and gravels from 241 to greater than 100 cm day⁻¹.

The principles of hydraulic conductivity apply equally to the vertical movement of water and to the ability of rainfall to recharge the water-table. In practice, this can be seen in the records of monitoring at two sites. Figure 1 (top) shows the soil moisture measurements at Market Deeping in Lincolnshire, a site on the landward edge of the Fens. The soil is a sandy clay loam and is well drained. The monitoring site is located across a paleochannel that has an organic rich silt in its base. In the top 400 mm of plough-soil, there is considerable variation in the monthly recorded soil moisture; below that level, the environment is much more stable and though there are changes as a consequence of the weather, these are less extreme than at the surface. It is assumed that the water-table acts as a reservoir, allowing soil moisture content to be maintained by upward capillary action.

Figure 1 (bottom) shows the soil moisture readings at Willingham, a site adjacent to the River Great Ouse in Cambridgeshire, also on the fen edge. Here there has been a buildup of heavy clay silt and peat, which seals a layer of sand and silt over gravel. The gradient of soil moisture content is the reverse of that seen at Market Deeping (compare Figure 1, top and bottom). At Willingham, the moisture content decreases with depth, and there is no apparent draw up from the water-table. The clay soil prevents rainwater from reaching the lower levels, and there is an apparent perched water-table 400 mm to 700 mm below the ground surface. In fact, this marks the demarcation between the clay and peat plough-soil and the sand and silt layers that overlie the gravel.

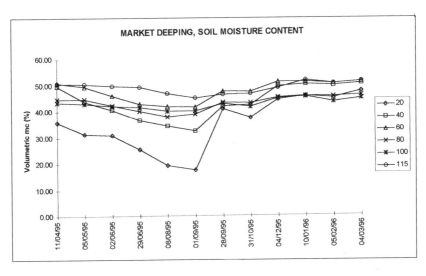

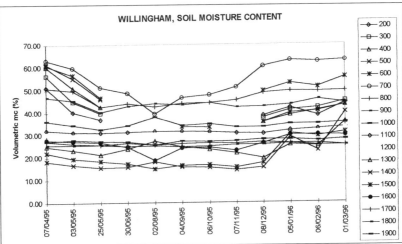

Figure 1. Volumetric moisture contents measured at 20 cm intervals from the ground surface at Market Deeping and 10 cm intervals at Willingham. At Market Deeping, the soil drains well but is fine enough to allow water to be drawn up from the water-table; the moisture content is more or less constant at 40% to 50% from about 60 cm, with the major variations in the topsoil. At Willingham, the topsoil is much denser clay, which holds the moisture; here the soil moisture is much higher, whereas the deeper sands and gravels have a much lower moisture content.

The nature of the soil is a crucial factor for the preservation of a site. In some cases, the management strategy may be designed to prevent the soil from drying out and shrinking and so destroying the site matrix. This was the raison d'être for the site preservation methodology used at the site of the 400-year-old Elizabethan Rose Theatre in London. During excavation, the exposed surfaces of the clay had cracked severely. Had the process continued, there was potential for the integrity of the site to be lost and the possibility that the cracking would penetrate to the underlying peat layers some 1 m to 1.5 m below the ground surface. The water content of the clay is between 56.3% and 82.5%, and tests showed that a reduction of water content from 50% to 40% would result in shrinkage of 13%; drying from 50% water content to 20% would result in the clay shrinking by about one-third. The peat levels have a water content of 226%, and drying would result in severe shrinkage and a possible drop in the levels containing the theatre remains (Huntings Land and Environment 1994). A similar phenomenon has recently been noted in the centre of York, where an evaluation excavation in advance of development showed that the ground surface had dropped by about 300 mm since the existing concrete slab was laid in the 1960s. No apparent reason for this drop could be seen, but it is possible that it is due to interference with the complex hydrology of the city centre as a consequence of piling for new developments (Carrott et al. 1995).

Water Balance

Heathwaite and Göttlich (1993:222) express the water balance in a mire as:

$$P = D + E + (R - C) \text{ mm}$$

where P = precipitation, D = discharge, E = evaporation, R = reserve, C = consumption, and $R - C$ = storage.

Where there is an additional inflow of intrusive water (I), the formula is:

$$P + I = D + E + (R - C)$$

If precipitation and inflow are less than discharge, evaporation, and consumption, there will be a net water deficit.

The influx and efflux from the site affect the level of the water-table. Where the efflux is greater, the water-table will fall; where the influx is greater, it will rise. Figure 2 shows water-table level through one year of monitoring at Market Deeping. There is a fairly regular annual fluctuation. This effect, which is a response to transpirational losses, was first observed by Godwin (1931) in his study of Wicken Fen and is common to most fens and to the Norfolk Broads. Heathwaite (1990) noted a similar effect on the Thorne Moors in South Yorkshire.

The result of changes to the water supply can be dramatic. Bryony Coles (1995) has described the changes in water balance in the Netherlands that

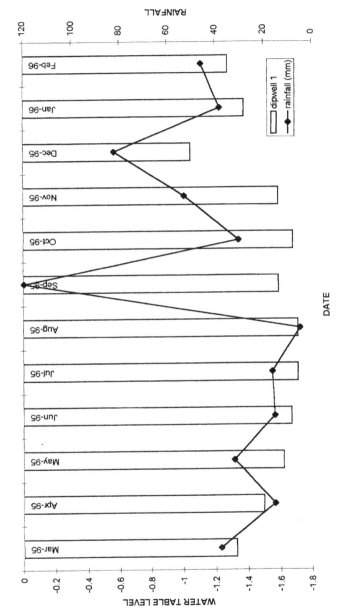

Figure 2. The level of the water-table at Market Deeping over a one-year period. The change through the year is typical of fenland water-tables. Note that the rainfall does not have a significant effect on the water level. This is especially evident during the very wet month of September. (This figure is provided by the UK meteorogolical service and is derived from information on rainfall, evaporation rates, and potential uptake by crops.)

resulted from the damming in 1932 of a large inlet, the Zuiderszee, to create a freshwater lake, the Isselmeer. Subsequently, land was reclaimed in the Isselmeer to create what in the Netherlands are known as polders. At De Weeribben in the Overijssel National Park, records show how Dutch ingenuity in increasing its land affected the water balance. In 1931, before the reclamation of the Zuiderzee began, there was a water balance surplus of 610 mm. Today, there is a deficit of 250 mm. In 1931, there was a contribution of 360 mm per annum to the water balance from upwelling water from the Zuiderzee. Today, groundwater is lost from the site to the polder.

Loss of water may be the result of activities at a considerable distance from the site being monitored. For example, Taylor (French and Taylor 1985) noted that water loss at an Iron Age site at Etton in Northamptonshire was caused by gravel extraction 1.5 km from the site.

The development of effective management strategies depends on an appreciation of the source of the water supply and on an understanding of how it can be managed. Management strategies should be as near to sustainable as possible and ought to have low maintenance requirements. However, in the short term, it may be acceptable to implement elaborate protection methods if it is anticipated that conditions will alter sufficiently in the future to allow simplified longer-term management schemes.

Organic archaeological material will be preserved only when it is permanently below the water-table, or when it is buried in soil above the water-table, which is so saturated that it remains anoxic. At Market Deeping, therefore, we could not expect organic preservation to be good at depths of less than about 1.8 m, since for much of the year, the water-table is at about that level. Moreover, site evaluation in the winter would be inappropriate because that is when the water-table is at its highest. This perhaps demonstrates that Heathwaite's (Heathwaite and Göttlich 1993:237-239) definition of mires as "reservoirs in the landscape" can be applied equally to waterlogged sites.

Water Chemistry
Basic water quality is determined through simple physico-chemical analysis. This is undertaken on site to avoid any post-sampling changes that might occur. Despite this precaution, there are problems obtaining accurate measurements, particularly of sensitive parameters such as redox potential and oxygen content. Both these measurements tend to be higher than is expected on regularly monitored sites and may be caused by the sampling methodology, which involves dropping a sample bottle down a dipwell. As the sample is removed, it inevitably absorbs oxygen, influencing the test results. English Heritage has undertaken a study at Durham University that is intended to lead to improved monitoring methodologies and better understanding of the archaeological waterlogged environment.

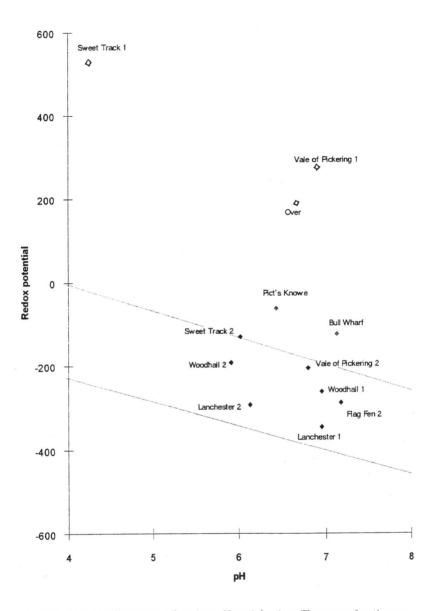

Figure 3. Plot of redox potential against pH at eight sites. The zone of optimum preservation lies between the two parallel lines, which represent the limits of reducing conditions. The measurements at Pict's Knowe (Dumfries) and Bulls Wharf (London) indicate that these sites are intermediate between oxidizing and reducing conditions, so the quality of preservation will not be expected to be as good as those with lower redox potentials. Over (Cambridgeshire), Vale of Pickering 1 (North Yorkshire), and Sweet Track 1 (Cambridgeshire) have high redox potentials; the conditions at the point of monitoring will not be conducive to good preservation. (See Caple and Dungworth 1995.)

The pH of the water and its redox potential are the most useful parameters in characterizing an anoxic environment. The pH value will depend on the location of the site. Upland and ombrogenous peats (those where the water is supplied by rainfall rather than by groundwater) are acidic (ca. pH 4); lowland fens, where there is a substantial contribution to the water supply from groundwater, are neutral (pH 7). The redox potential (E_h) for anaerobic sediments should be low, ideally between +200 mV and -400 mV, which compares with the E_h of +300 mV to +800 mV for well-drained soils (Caple and Dungworth 1995). The relationship between pH and E_h can be usefully presented in diagrammatic form (Figure 3).

The Durham study is using a more sophisticated set of probes and a data logger that records and stores measurements at preset intervals. This is still not proving to be as accurate as we would wish, as the probes are designed to work in a constant stream of water rather than in still and stagnant archaeological deposits. Nonetheless, the study is providing a better understanding of anoxic environments. The results of sampling (Figure 3) show that two of the sites have fully aerobic oxidizing environments, which could signify that they are drying out; four have an anaerobic reducing environment. Testing the Durham equipment at Flag Fen showed that it could take considerable time for the probes to settle down and give a stable value (Figure 4). The high E_h of about 500 mV at the Sweet Track (Figure 3) indicated the need for further investigation, which took place in October 1995.

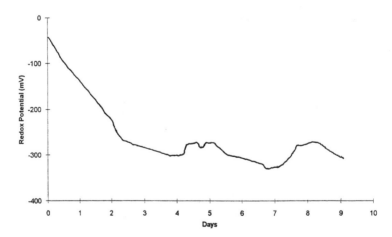

Figure 4. Continuous plot of redox potential measured at Flag Fen over a nine-day period showing the time necessary for anoxic conditions to be re-established after the insertion of the monitoring probe. The disturbance introduces oxygen to the buried environment, which typically takes two to three days to be removed by biochemical activity.

The Sweet Track, a Neolithic trackway between two areas of high ground in the marshy Somerset Levels, is about 1.8 km long. It was discovered in 1970 and subsequently excavated at a number of points along its length (Coles and Coles 1986). A scheme to preserve the trackway within a nature reserve was implemented in 1983, and since then water levels have been managed in an attempt to keep a substantial length of the trackway permanently under the water-table. In 1995, three small sections were cut across the line of the track in the area of the nature reserve, and one outside the managed area. This investigation showed that the condition of wood from which the track was made was visually good, and appeared much as it did when originally exposed. Laboratory and field tests showed that almost all its strength had been lost, but this is not surprising given its great age. A more extensive monitoring program for hydrology and redox using permanently buried redox cells was initiated and the results so far indicate that the site is fully anoxic.

The salts dissolved in groundwater may have an effect on the buried archaeological material and may encourage the activity of some bacterial species that affect both organic and inorganic materials. Modern agricultural soil enrichment causes considerable quantities of nitrates, sulphates, and phosphates to enter the groundwater. When monitoring programs are initiated, the dissolved salts are analyzed to identify what is present, but it would be time consuming and expensive to do this on a regular basis. An indication of changes in dissolved salt concentrations can readily be obtained by measuring the conductivity of the water; the more salts that are present, the higher the conductivity. For example, rainwater has a low conductivity (100µS), groundwater about 1 S, and seawater over 4 S (Caple and Dungworth 1995). The dissolved oxygen content and the temperature of the sample are also measured. An increase in temperature indicates that there may be chemical activity.

Minerals

Reduced iron species (Fe^{2+}) are mobile in low E_h environments, but are readily precipitated by changes in the pH/E_h balance, for example at pH 5 when the E_h is greater than +300 mV or at pH 8 when the E_h is greater than -100 mV. Oxidized iron (Fe^{3+}) is hydrolyzed and may be visible as reddish-brown iron hydrites. Aged ferric hydrites are weathered to form limonite ($Fe_2O_3 \cdot nH_2O$). With carbon dioxide concentrations, ferric hydrites may be either solubilized as iron 2 bicarbonate [$2Fe(HCO_3)_2$] or precipitated as goethite (α FeOOH) according to the reaction:

$$2Fe(HCO_3)_2 + \tfrac{1}{2}O_2 \leftrightharpoons 2FeOOH + 4CO_2 + H_2O$$

Limonite has a strong chemical affinity for phosphate, with which it reacts to form vivianite [$FE_3(PO_4)_2 \cdot 8H_2O$] and this accumulates to form deposits of bog iron ore, from which iron was extracted by people in prehistoric times (Heathwaite and Göttlich 1993:292). Vivianite is also present on iron objects excavated from waterlogged deposits where there has been human activity; it forms a dense protective coating that is often disrupted by cracking following excavation. Sulphur compounds are common in fens, and deposits of hydrogen sulphide (H_2S) and gypsum ($CaSO_4 \cdot 2H_2O$) occur in the Somerset Levels. Sulphur compounds will react with reduced iron to form pyrite (FeS_2). Framboidal pyrite is often found in waterlogged wood, and this, together with other iron compounds, may prove a useful means of assessing the state of a waterlogged environment.

Microbiology

The bacterial species of interest in a waterlogged environment are those concerned with the metabolism of iron, sulphur, and nitrogen. The way in which these interact with organic materials may be of value in site evaluation; English Heritage intends to assess their potential soon. The organisms that destroy organic materials are mainly aerobic, so it is of prime importance that the water be anoxic. However, recent research has identified anaerobic cellulolytic bacteria, and further study will be necessary to determine the role of these organisms in wood degradation (Pointing 1995).

Nutrients

Water quality is also dependent on the level of nutrients it carries. Nutrient levels may be increased by agricultural practices such as fertilization with nitrates, phosphates, sulphates, and ammonia. Initial analysis of the nutrients at Market Deeping indicated that all these were high. Conductivity measurements indicated a sudden increase in dissolved salts in September 1994, presumably as a result of an application of fertilizer. Nitrate pollution is becoming so severe in parts of the UK that nitrate-sensitive areas are being established in which farmers are compensated for cutting back on application of fertilizers to protect groundwater sources (Coles 1995).

A further threat to water quality may arise from the disposal of sewage sludge on the land. Recent European Community legislation has banned the disposal of sewage sludge at sea and also by surface spreading. As a result, all treated sludge is now disposed of by direct injection into the soil. At Flag Fen, part of an important Bronze Age site with a wooden post structure 1.5 km in length has been excavated adjacent to such a sewage sludge disposal site; indeed, the still-buried timber structure extends through the field used. The central platform of the structure has been preserved by constructing an artificial pond over it. The water level in the pond is maintained by encircling it with a polyethylene membrane, which extends from the ground surface down to the clay substratum beneath the peat and alluvium. This is known as bunding. The bund is not totally watertight, so it is still possible for groundwater to enter the pond. The staff at the site had noticed that the pond was becoming more abundant in its plant growth as a consequence of a presumed increase in nutrients from the sewage field, and there was a danger that this might lead to its eutrophication. A similar increase in algal bloom was noted in the Must Dyke that bisects the site and the archaeological structure. A collaborative research project has been set up with the Robens Institute of the University of Surrey to determine whether the increase in algal and plant growth is a consequence of the sewage injection, and also to investigate the effects of sewage injection on archaeological materials. Initially, a series of dipwells will be installed so that the levels of nutrients can be monitored and the microbiological populations assessed.

The central area of the Flag Fen archaeological site has been preserved as an archaeological park with public displays. It is largely funded by the local water company, Anglia Water, which has also supported the preliminary stages of the water quality research at the site; a further grant has been approved by the Natural Sciences Research Council for research that will focus particularly on the effects of the contaminants on a range of archaeological materials. Anglia Water is also sponsoring an extensive planting program along the access road to the site. Plant species ranging from dryland types through to wetland types will be planted in sequence so that the visitor will approach the site through a progressively wetter environment. Water entering the site will be channelled through this vegetation so that by the time it reaches the site, it will have been stripped of its nutrients. In this way, it is hoped that the site environment will be protected.

Non-Archaeological Wetland Investigation and Management

Environmentalists and ecologists have a particular concern for the protection of wetland sites. Wetlands are important for the survival of many rare plant species and provide vital feeding grounds for many species of birds. In addition, it has recently been recognized that wetlands are major reservoirs of greenhouse gasses such as carbon dioxide and methane. There is a considerable body of research into the hydrochemistry of wetlands, and clearly archaeologists have much to learn from workers in this field; Godwin, during his investigation of the wetland environment in the 1930s, recognized the extent of archaeological survival and encouraged the development of wetland archaeological research.

A major project, funded by the European Commission and with partners in England, Ireland, France, and Spain, is under way to develop protocols for the investigation and the assessment of wetlands (Maltby et al. 1994).

This project is concerned with all aspects of wetlands, and the participants are anxious to incorporate parameters for archaeological preservation alongside those for ecological benefit. Close collaboration in this project will be of great value to the development of an understanding of the nature of the environment that preserves archaeological evidence in wetlands, and researchers in the project are now using their techniques to monitor archaeological sites.

Protection for wetland ecological habitats is far more clearly identified through statements such as the Ramsar Convention on Wetlands of International Importance, and by the Directives of the Council of the European Communities (1992). The Trondheim Declaration (1994) further reinforced the importance of mires and peatlands and made recommendations for promoting their conservation. No such generally accepted statement has been prepared setting out the importance of wetland environments as an archaeological resource. Loss of wetlands is a matter of international concern, and one that archaeologists should make common cause with those whose interests lie with ecological conservation.

Conclusion

Wetland environments are enormously varied and range from acidic, rain-fed upland mires through fen-like environments of former river basins to saline intertidal zones and mangrove swamps. The evidence preserved in waterlogged environments gives archaeologists a much broader understanding of the life of earlier communities and the effect they had on their environment than can be obtained from non-waterlogged sites. The preservation of this evidence depends on an understanding of the physical, the chemical, and the biological processes that take place in wetlands and how the wetlands may be affected by changes to the environment. Recent research has indicated the factors to be considered, but further research is needed to determine the influence that these have on archaeological materials. In particular, the assessment of a waterlogged site and its potential for the preservation of the remains in situ will require a thorough understanding of the site hydrology, as well as the ability to maintain a stable environment.

Acknowledgments

I must thank Matthew Davies of Huntings Land and Environment who does much of the monitoring work at our sites and who has helped me to understand the principles involved. Chris Caple and David Dungworth undertook the Durham study into the flaws in our monitoring methodology and further helped in developing the ideas put forward in this chapter. Ed Maltby at the Royal Holloway Institute for Environmental Research has been highly supportive of me as an amateur in a field that he has long experience in, and my colleagues at English Heritage have given me the opportunity to study the hydrology at many sites across England. Particular thanks to Geoff Wainwright, English Heritage chief archaeologist, for his interest and financial support for the research that underpins this chapter.

References Cited

Caple, C., and D. Dungworth
1995 Investigations into Waterlogged Burial Environments. In *Archaeological Science 1995*, edited by E.A. Slater and A. Sinclair. Oxbow, Oxford, in press. Ms. 1995.

Carrott, J., K. Dobney, A. Hall, M. Issitt, D. Jacques, C. Johnstone, H. Kenward, and A. Millies
1995 An Evaluation of the Biological Remains from Excavation at 44-45 Parliament Street, York (Site code 1994.3210). Environmental Archaeology Unit, University of York, Heslington, York, YOL 5DD.

Coles, B.
1995 *Wetlands Management: A Survey for English Heritage*. WARP Occasional Paper 9. Department of History and Archaeology, University of Exeter, UK.

Coles, B., and J. Coles
1986 *Sweet Track to Glastonbury: The Somerset Levels in Prehistory*. Thames and Hudson, London.

Corfield, M.
1994 Monitoring the Condition of Waterlogged Archaeological Sites. In *Proceedings of the 5th ICOM Group on Wet Organic Archaeological Materials Conference, Portland, Maine 1993*, edited by P. Hoffmann, pp. 423-436. ICOM Committee for Conservation Working Group on Wet Organic Archaeological Materials, Bremerhaven, Germany.

Council of the European Communities
1992 Council of the European Communities Directive 92/43/EEC of 21 May 1992 on the Conservation of Natural Habitats and of Wild Fauna and Flora. *Official Journal of the European Communities* No. L 206/7.

French, C., and M. Taylor
1985 Desiccation and Destruction: The Immediate Effect of Dewatering at Etton. *Oxford Journal of Archaeology* 4(2):139-156.

Godwin, H.
1931 Studies of the Ecology of Wicken Fen 1: The Ground Water Levels of the Fen. *Journal of Ecology* 19:449-472.

Hall, D., and J. Coles
1994 *Fenland Survey: An Essay in Landscape and Persistence*. Archaeological Report 1. English Heritage, London.

Heathwaite, A.L.
1990 *The Hydrology of the Thorne Moors National Nature Reserve*. Final report to the Nature Conservancy Council and Fisons. Available from English Nature, London.

Heathwaite, A.L., and K. Göttlich
1993 *Mires: Process, Exploitation and Conservation*. John Wiley, London.

Huntings Land and Environment
1994 *Investigation of Site Conditions and Repair or Replacement of Monitoring Points [at the Rose Theatre]*. Huntings report R898:HER-07 to English Heritage.

Maltby, E., D.V. Hogan, C.P. Immirzi, J.H. Tellam, and M.J van der Piejl
1994 Building a New Approach to the Investigation and Assessment of Wetland Ecosystems Functioning. In *Global Wetlands: Old World and New*, edited by W.J. Mitsch, pp. 637-658. Elsevier, Amsterdam.

Pointing, S.
1995 *Gamma Ray Irradiation and Reburial as a Potential Novel Passive Conservation Treatment for Waterlogged Archaeological Timbers from the Mary Rose*. PhD thesis, University of Portsmouth, UK.

Trondheim Declaration
1994 An International Statement on the Global Conservation of Mires and Peatlands. Sixth International Conference on Mire Conservation, Trondheim, Norway.

Van de Noort, R., and P. Davies
  1993 *Wetland Heritage: An Archaeological Assessment of the Humber Wetlands.* Humber
  Wetlands Project, University of Hull, UK.
Van de Noort, R., and S. Ellis (editors)
  1995 *Wetland Heritage of Holderness: An Archaeological Survey.* Humber Wetlands Project,
  University of Hull, UK.

Observations Resulting from the Treatment of Waterlogged Wood Bowls in Aotearoa (New Zealand)

Dilys A. Johns

Archaeological sites throughout New Zealand frequently yield waterlogged wooden bowls, made from either totara (*Podocarpus totara*) or matai (*Prumnopitys taxifolia*), which are sent to the Archaeological Conservation Laboratory at the University of Auckland for conservation. This comparison of 10 such bowls that have been treated over the past 12 years touches on some of the history of impregnation with polyethylene glycol (PEG) and the way in which refinement of the process has evolved into a treatment that is easily applied and gives consistent results.

One-step impregnation was used at the University of Auckland until 1986. Highly degraded waterlogged wood artifacts were impregnated with incrementally increasing concentrations of aqueous PEG 3350, followed by freeze-drying. During 1986, a two-step procedure was introduced. This involved pre-treatment with aqueous PEG 400, followed by PEG 3350 impregnation. This study evaluates five bowls that have been treated by the one-step process and compares them with five bowls treated by the two-step process. Figures 1 to 5 show several of these bowls.

Aims of This Study

In the mid-1970s, Ambrose published two papers (1975, 1976) on the effects of pre-soaking waterlogged wood artifacts in 5% to 10% aqueous solution of PEG before freeze-drying. This method was adopted by many conservators and has been the subject of many publications (e.g., Cook and Grattan 1985; Grattan 1982b). Subsequent research by Hoffmann (1985, 1986) has shown that a two-step treatment can produce good results for the treatment of waterlogged oak.

The presence of PEG, which shrinks on freezing, is thought to counteract the expansion of freezing water, thereby reducing cellular damage. It also acts as a bulking agent for the cell walls, helping to prevent cell collapse after removal of excess water upon drying. PEG is available in a range of differing molecular weights (MW). Ambrose used PEG 400 (with average

MW 400), but the use of PEG grades of higher MW, such as 1000 and 3350, subsequently became popular for more heavily degraded wood.

Young and Wainwright (1982) and Hoffmann (1985) have suggested that lower MW PEG, such as PEG 400, helps to control cell wall shrinkage, particularly in wood that is not very degraded, and that high MW grades, such as PEG 3350, add some structural strength to the cell lumen of heavily degraded wood. This view has led to the use by some workers of a mixture of PEG grades for the treatment of objects that comprise both lightly and heavily degraded sections, on the basis that the low MW component will help to prevent shrinkage of the less degraded portion, and the higher MW

C166

Figure 1. Treated bowl from Taranaki. Note the fine cracks on base (Taranaki 16).

Figure 2. Treated bowl from Gisborne. The cracking on base, which was a result of drying before arrival in the laboratory, is unchanged (Gisborne C17).

Figure 3. Treated bowl from Te Awamutu. This moderately degraded bowl has responded well to the two-step PEG treatment. The overall appearance is good (Te Awamutu C163).

Figure 4. This large bowl from Taranaki weighed more than 16 kg in its waterlogged state. It has responded well to the two-step PEG treatment. Its overall appearance is good (Taranaki C273).

Figure 5. The two-step PEG treatment produced a pleasing result for this bowl, which had areas of advanced pocket-rot and surface degradation (Te Uku, Raglan C257).

component will add strength to the heavily degraded parts. Such objects, which frequently feature a fairly sound core, were usually treated with a one-step PEG 3350 impregnation at the University of Auckland laboratory from the mid-1970s until the mid-1980s.

As much of the previous work on different impregnation regimes had been carried out on Northern Hemisphere wood species, it seemed desirable to carry out similar treatments on artifacts made from New Zealand native wood species in an attempt to refine techniques used to conserve waterlogged wood artifacts in New Zealand.

The Study Sample

The treated bowls, which were all from archaeological contexts, were selected as being typical of the type often received in the laboratory for treatment. Two frequently found native species of wood are represented, totara and matai.

Totara is a large tree, of which the trunk wood was used by pre-European Maori for the making of canoes, bowls, and numerous small objects. The wood is light coloured with a low, even, shrinkage and is highly impenetrable in its sound state. The heartwood can be very dense. Matai was used to make house planks, bowls, canoes, and fern-root beaters. Though matai has been found in a sound state in wet sites, it is usually partially degraded. Sound matai is a medium density, non-resinous wood. It is highly penetrable when partially degraded. Examples of both extremely degraded and moderately degraded totara and matai are present in the bowls treated with each of the impregnation regimes.

Many rigorous methods of assessing waterlogged wood degradation have been devised by scientists for experimental use. These methods and experiments are essential for the development of treatment methods and have been used on large objects such as ships. However, the taking of samples for chemical or physical analysis from small items of cultural property such as bowls or combs is not permissible, for cultural reasons, in New Zealand. Often, microscopic size samples for wood species identification are all that can be removed. Thus, the choice of suitable treatment may often have to be made with limited information about the state of degradation of some artifacts.

An extensive comparative collection of degraded and undegraded totara and matai was used to assess the extent of degradation in the study sample, as well as direct observation with a needle probe and examination of thin-sections. Moisture contents for samples of the two wood species (totara and matai), both sound and degraded, are shown in Table 1. Higher moisture contents are associated with greater degradation.

Before treatment, each artifact was photographed, measured, weighed, and described. The wood species was then identified, degradation was assessed, and the artifact was cleaned. Impregnation was then carried out, and the artifacts were dried, either by vacuum freeze-drying or controlled air-drying. Surface cleaning and post-treatment documentation of the artifacts completed the treatments.

Treatment Methods

One-Step Impregnation
The artifacts were initially immersed in a 5% (w/v) solution of PEG 3350. The PEG concentration was slowly increased, over 6 to 12 months in 5% increments, to 40%.

Two-Step Impregnation
The artifacts were initially immersed in 5% PEG 400, and the PEG concentration was slowly increased to 15% in 5% increments. They were then washed in warm water and immersed in a bath of 10% PEG 3350, and the PEG concentration was slowly increased to 40%.

The treatment baths all contained 0.2% Bioquat 501 to prevent bacterial and algal growth. (Bioquat 501 is a quaternary ammonium compound manufactured and distributed by Swift New Zealand Ltd., Auckland, New Zealand.)

Freeze-Drying vs. Controlled Air-Drying
Throughout the 1970s and up to 1987, most artifacts that had been impregnated with PEG in this laboratory were subsequently vacuum freeze-dried. During 1988, several artifacts treated in the laboratory were too large to fit in the freeze-drier, so they were air-dried in a plastic tent in which the relative humidity (RH) was slowly lowered, the artifacts being dried to constant weight at 55% RH and 20°C.

The results of controlled air-drying were consistently as good as, if not better than, those of the freeze-drying method (see Table 1 for the results of controlled air-drying vs. freeze-drying). Controlled air-drying has the added benefit of being able to be continuously monitored and, if necessary, halted mid-process to allow further impregnation if artifacts begin to crack or disfigure because of insufficient PEG content. Since then, controlled air-drying has been used extensively at the University of Auckland.

Treatment Comparison
Results of the two methods of impregnation are shown in Table 1. For this study, success or failure of a treatment was assessed according to whether or not the treated artifacts resembled their original wet dimensions. The following properties were observed: absence or presence of cracks; retention of shape and size determined by visual inspection and by measurements; and

Table 1

Treatment results of PEG-impregnated, waterlogged wood bowls from Aotearoa

Year	Artifact	Wood species	% H$_2$O content		Method of drying[2]	Bowl degradation	Bowl volumetric shrinkage	Bowl appearance after treatment
			Sound wood[1]	Comparative degraded sample				
ONE-STEP PEG 3350 UP TO 40%								
1983	Waikato [C1]	matai	50.8	76.8	F	Extremely degraded through to the core	0.6%	Degraded areas still fragile; fine cracks present
1984	Taranaki [N44]	matai	50.8	64.5	F	Surface degraded with slightly sound core	0.3%	Wood stable and very dark; slightly oily looking surface
1985[3]	Taranaki [16]	totara	57.1	63.9	F	Surface degraded with slightly sound core	0.0%	Stable with fine cracks; a little dark
1984	Waimate [C31]	totara	57.1	69.1	C	Extremely degraded; large areas of degraded wood extend into the core	0.7%	Surface fragile with fine cracks; feels greasy, especially on the base
1986	Gisborne [C17]	matai	50.8	57.7	C	Soft degraded areas on the base had been partially dried before reaching the laboratory, and the degraded surface had undergone some cell collapse; slightly sound core	0.3%	Many fine radial cracks on the base; the areas that had undergone some cell collapse display a mixture of tangential and radial cracking; see Figure 2

TWO-STEP 10%-15% PEG 400 THEN PEG 3350 TO 40%

1986-87	Taranaki [N52]	matai	50.8	57.5	F	Surface degradation with slightly sound core	0.2%	Stable; good surface condition and colour
1988	Te Awamutu [C163]	matai	50.8	66.6	C	Several large areas soft and degraded; some degradation extended through to the core	0.2%	Stable; soft degraded areas consolidated; overall surface condition good
1992	Taranaki [C247]	totara	57.1	61.3	C	Rim very degraded and fragile; the base and sides had suffered from degradation	0.2%	Stable; the fragile rim now stable and a little stronger; overall appearance good
1994-5	Taranaki [C273]	totara	57.1	74.5	C	Significant losses on the rim; advanced degradation of the surface and core	0.5%	Stable; degraded areas now consolidated; overall appearance good; see Figure 4
1994	Raglan, Te Uku [C257]	totara	57.1	61.5	C	Some patches of pocket rot present in the heartwood; surface degradation also present	0.1%	Stable; surface degradation consolidated; excellent surface condition; see Figure 5

[1] Taken from a selection of sound wood samples averaged to obtain the above figures.

[2] F = freeze-dried; C = controlled air-dried.

[3] Cracks appeared during drying. Dimensional measurements include cracks producing under-estimation of cell collapse.

preservation of texture, colour, and surface condition as judged by visual examination.

Quantitative Evaluation

Table 1 contains the numerical shrinkage data that were used to evaluate the one-step and two-step treatments. Volumetric shrinkage values were calculated from measurements before and after treatment. Such shrinkage was effectively negligible for all artifacts but was higher for those treated with the one-step regime.

Anti-shrink efficiency (ASE) values (described by Grattan et al. 1980), which compare the shrinkage produced after treatment to that which occurs on simple air-drying of a comparable sample, are often used when evaluating different treatment regimes. However, as previously mentioned, small, precious artifacts do not lend themselves to the removal of samples for controls in the test. Accordingly, ASE values are not available for the artifacts in this study.

In their article, Grattan et al. (1980) noted that ASE remains remarkably constant for different kinds of wood and different types of deterioration. Whereas this *is* true, ASE values need to be used with caution, as they can be misleading. This is because the air-dried samples may be distorted or bowed resulting in unreliable measurements. Since these measurements are used as a basis for the calculations, the results may not give a true picture of success or failure of a treatment. Furthermore, for lightly degraded wood, where dimensional changes may be small, precision in measurement is extremely important.

Qualitative Evaluation

At this point the importance of qualitative evaluation, despite its inherent drawbacks of subjectiveness, should be discussed. If one assesses the results of a treatment of an artifact purely through the interpretation of dimensional measurement, the presence of fissures or cracks may not be revealed. The bowl from Taranaki (Figure 1) illustrates this. The surface of the wood displays numerous fine cracks, yet measurements indicate little or no shrinking.

Visual evaluation of stability of shape is also important, as damaged corners or altered surface condition may occur during or after treatment. Dimensional measurements play a significant role in the evaluation of waterlogged wood conservation treatments, but only when used in conjunction with careful inspection.

The qualitative assessment in the right-hand column of Table 1 shows that although both treatment regimes resulted in artifacts that preserved the original dimensions satisfactorily, the two-step treatment gave better results in terms of absence of cracks and preservation of colour, texture, and surface condition. Figure 5 illustrates this well.

Qualitative assessment also appears to favour controlled air-drying as a method of drying after impregnating with PEG. This conclusion appears to be at variance with most published work on post-impregnation drying of artifacts (Grattan 1982a; Hoffmann 1991) and obviously warrants further research.

Conclusion

This brief survey supports the observations of other researchers who concluded from studies of Northern Hemisphere wood species that waterlogged wood artifacts containing areas of both sound and degraded wood benefit from a two-step treatment. Wood species commonly found in waterlogged archaeological sites in New Zealand appear to respond similarly. The University of Auckland conservation laboratory is currently experimenting with sucrose impregnation as a possible improvement over the established PEG treatments now in use.

References Cited

Ambrose, W.R.

1975 *Stabilizing Degraded Swamp Wood by Freeze-drying*. Report to the International Council of Museums Committee for Conservation, 4th Triennial Meeting, Venice.

1976 Sublimation Drying of Degraded Wet Wood. In *Pacific Northwest Wet Site Wood Conservation Conference* Vol. 1, edited by G.H. Grosso, pp. 7-15. Conference held at Neah Bay, WA, September 19-20, 1976.

Cook, C., and D.W. Grattan

1985 A Practical Comparative Study of Treatments for Waterlogged Wood: Part 3 – Pretreatment Solutions for Freeze-drying. In *Waterlogged Wood: Study and Conservation. Proceedings of the 2nd ICOM Waterlogged Wood Working Group Conference, Grenoble 1984,* pp. 219-239. Centre d'Etude et de Traitement des Bois Gorges d'Eau, Grenoble, France.

Grattan, D.W.

1982a A Practical Comparative Study of Several Treatments for Waterlogged Wood. *Studies in Conservation* 27(3):124-136.

1982b A Practical Comparative Study of Treatments for Waterlogged Wood, Part II: The Effect of Humidity on Treated Wood. In *Proceedings of the ICOM Waterlogged Wood Working Group Conference, Ottawa 1981,* edited by D.W. Grattan, pp. 243-252. International Council of Museums, Committee for Conservation, Waterlogged Wood Working Group, Ottawa.

Grattan, D.W., J.C. McCawley, and C. Cook

1980 The Potential of the Canadian Winter Climate for the Freeze-drying of Degraded Waterlogged Wood, Part II. *Studies in Conservation* 25(3):118-136.

Hoffmann, P.

1985 On the Stabilization of Waterlogged Oakwood with PEG – Molecular Size Versus Degree of Degradation. In *Waterlogged Wood: Study and Conservation. Proceedings of the 2nd ICOM Waterlogged Wood Working Group Conference, Grenoble 1984,* pp. 95-115. Centre d'Etude et de Traitement des Bois Gorges d'Eau, Grenoble, France.

1986 On the Stabilization of Waterlogged Oakwood with PEG. *Studies in Conservation* 31(3):103-113.

1991 An Evaluation Study on the Freeze-drying of Waterlogged Wood. In *Proceedings of the 4th ICOM Group on Wet Organic Archaeological Materials Conference, Bremerhaven 1990,* edited by P. Hoffmann, pp. 331-357. ICOM Committee for Conservation, Bremerhaven, Germany.

Young, G.S., and I.N.M. Wainwright
1982 Polyethylene Glycol Treatments for Waterlogged Wood at the Cell Level. In *Proceedings of the ICOM Waterlogged Wood Working Group Conference, Ottawa 1981,* edited by D.W. Grattan, pp. 107-116. International Council of Museums, Committee for Conservation, Waterlogged Wood Working Group, Ottawa.

Supercritical Drying of Waterlogged Archaeological Wood

Barry Kaye and David J. Cole-Hamilton

Introduction to Drying Techniques

Many of the problems of conserving waterlogged organic materials originate from the drying stresses experienced by the material as water is removed from it. These stresses result in shrinkage and frequently cracking and disintegration. There are three (and only three) physical methods for drying solid matrices with included liquid (Kaye 1995). Two of these, air-drying and freeze-drying, have been employed by conservators for a considerable period. Here we describe the third technique, supercritical drying.

The technique can be placed in context by referring to the sketch of a phase diagram shown in Figure 1 (the physical data recorded on this diagram refer to carbon dioxide). A phase diagram defines the equilibrium physical state (or phase) of a material under given conditions. The data required are defined by two independent physical variables (in this case, temperature and pressure). Thus, at point A in Figure 1, the material is a liquid, at point C a solid, and at points B, D, E, and F a gas. At relatively low temperatures and at high pressures above the critical temperature and pressure (point E), the material is frequently referred to as a supercritical fluid, which can be described as a gas with liquid-like properties. The solid lines represent conditions under which an equilibrium between the adjacent phases will persist indefinitely (these are frequently referred to as "tie lines"). In Figure 1, the various drying techniques are described by dashed lines. The line AB refers to air-drying, removing the liquid phase by reducing the vapour pressure below the liquid's saturation point. Under these conditions, liquid evaporates from the sample, and the liquid vapour surface moves through the sample as liquid is lost. It is the stresses associated with this interface that cause shrinkage and collapse. The lines AC and CD define a freeze-drying process in which the temperature of the sample is reduced until the liquid freezes and is subsequently removed by sublimation at some temperature below its triple point.

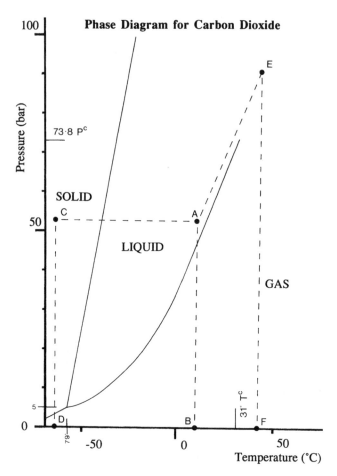

Figure 1. A sketched phase diagram for carbon dioxide.

Neither of these process is well designed for drying weak materials. The sample must be extensively reinforced to resist the stress field associated with the liquid/vapour interface if it is to be air-dried. Cryoprotectants must be added if the sample is to be freeze-dried, to prevent structural damage as the liquid freezes (the water-to-ice phase transition results in an 8% expansion of volume). Much of the time required to conserve samples is thus taken up by introducing foreign material (polyethylene glycol, sugars, alum, etc.) that is required for the sample to survive phase transitions intact.

Supercritical drying is a technique specifically invented (Kistler 1931) to allow low-strength materials to be dried without physical damage. The process is described by the lines *AE* and *EF* in the phase diagram (Figure 1). No tie lines are crossed in this process, which in consequence proceeds smoothly without phase changes occurring in the fluid in the sample. Many conservators have used critical point drying (a method relying on the same physical process) to prepare samples for electron microscopy, but we do not believe that the method has previously been extended to drying artifacts. Large samples cannot be dried economically using critical point drying apparatus, and we have had to simplify supercritical drying equipment, suitable for larger samples, to allow experimental work at a low capital cost (Kaye and Cole-Hamilton 1994).

Supercritical drying has recently been used to conserve complex composite artifacts (Kaye and Cole-Hamilton 1995), but it should be emphasized that the technique is in its infancy, and considerable developmental work remains to be done. Here we address the present state of the technique and its application to materials other than wet wood.

The Application of Supercritical Drying to Waterlogged Wood

The supercritical drying technique has been described previously (Kaye and Cole-Hamilton 1994). Essentially, the sample passes through three stages:

(1) Water in the sample is replaced with methanol.
(2) The methanol is in turn replaced with supercritical carbon dioxide at high pressure.
(3) The sample is decompressed, ready for further study or display.

We have recently introduced one novel approach to reducing the time taken by the methanol water exchange process. Water present in the sample can be reacted with an acetal or ketal to form organic solvents compatible with supercritical carbon dioxide. Equation 1 describes such a reaction using a ketal (2,2 dimethoxypropane [DMP]). DMP must be added in methanol solution as it is immiscible with water.

$$[H^+]$$
$$CH_3C(OCH_3)_2CH_3 + H_2O ==== CH_3COCH_3 + 2CH_3OH \qquad 1$$

The reaction shown in Equation 1 is acid catalyzed. Mineral acids are most efficient, as they co-diffuse into the wood with the DMP and react directly with the residual water. Using this technique, sample preparation time has been reduced to three hours for small test samples. The problem of contamination of the sample with residual acid, however, has prevented us from using this method for artifacts. A less invasive (but slower) treatment is to use a proton-charged cation-exchange resin (highly acidic resin) as the source of catalyst. Here, all the water must diffuse out of the sample to react; time scales of one to two days are required for samples of 100 mm x 30 mm x 30 mm dimensions. The disadvantage of using acetals or ketals is that they are expensive (UK£100 [Can$220] per kg of water removed), and the resultant mixture of solvents is very difficult to recycle. Consequently, we usually remove most of the water from the sample with a single bath of methanol before resorting to the use of DMP. An interesting variation on this technique would be the use of dimethoxy methane [$CH_2(OCH_3)_2$], which is cheaper than DMP and which produces formaldehyde (compared with acetone in Equation 1). The use of dimethoxy methane would result in some handling and storage problems, but it may be useful for organic materials that are suffering from extensive and active biodeterioration processes. (**Note:** care must be exercized when handling formaldehyde. There may be local restrictions; ensure that anyone handling the object is aware of the hazard.)

Once the water in the sample has been replaced with methanol, the methanol can in turn be replaced with supercritical carbon dioxide. The apparatus required is a high-pressure vessel (an autoclave, or, colloquially, a "bomb"), with a tested safe operating pressure of at least 120 bar (12 MPa) static pressure. Even small-scale conservation studies would result in enormous wastage of carbon dioxide with the non-recycling technique used in critical point driers, but the cost of equipment to allow carbon dioxide to be recycled was prohibitive in early experimental studies. For these reasons, we designed a simple "one pot" method. In this method, methanol, extracted from the wood by the carbon dioxide, is trapped by a drying agent present in the same autoclave. The technique is to load the sample, wrapped in a protective bandage of tissue, over a bed of calcium chloride (approximately 1.5 x the mass of the sample), charge the autoclave with carbon dioxide, and warm to an operating temperature of between 40°C and 50°C.

The final stage of the supercritical drying process is to decompress the sample(s). Decompression will damage samples if too great a pressure gradient is created across them (at worst, this might result in "explosive decompression"). Decompression rates of 20 bar per hour had been shown to be suitable for the preparation of aerogels by supercritical drying before our work (Fricke and Emmerling 1992), and this rate causes no problems for archaeological wood. Finally, the wood can be removed from the autoclave, ready for further study or display.

The process is relatively non-invasive, but materials that are soluble in methanol or supercritical carbon dioxide can be leached from the sample. Some loss of methanol-soluble components has been observed from well-preserved or relatively recent timber. Preliminary study by ^{13}C and ^1H nmr indicates that these products are largely "lignin monomers"; no sugars or polysaccharides have been detected. The loss of this material, which is darkly coloured, results in a lightening of the colour of the conserved wood.

Results, and Comparisons with Freeze-Drying

Forty-two samples of wood have been conserved to date by the supercritical drying technique; these are compared with freeze-drying results (Hoffmann 1991) in Figure 2. As can be seen from this figure, most samples show some shrinkage, and a significant number have suffered from transverse cracking. Comparison of the actual transverse shrinkages observed, with those reported for freeze-drying (Godfrey and Kendrick 1991), indicates that supercritical drying is slightly worse than freeze-drying (see Figure 3). There

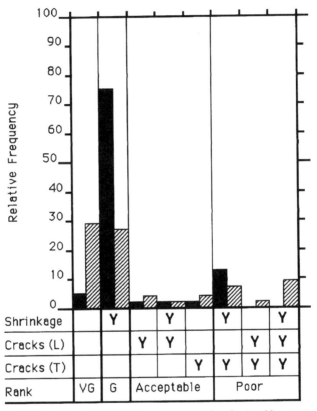

Figure 2. This diagram compares the results obtained by freeze-drying with those obtained by supercritical drying. The format of the assessment and data for freeze-drying results are from Hoffmann (1991). Each sample is assessed in terms of the amount of damage that has occurred during the treatment. Samples that have not suffered shrinkage, longitudinal or transverse cracks (cracks *L* or *T* respectively in the figure) are ranked as being very good (VG), whereas those that show shrinkage but no cracking are good (G), etc. The height of the bar represents the percentage of the total number of samples treated falling into the given category. Freeze-dried results are shown hatched, whereas the results from supercritical drying are shown as solid bars.

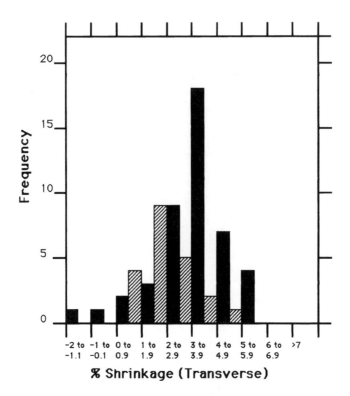

Figure 3. A comparison of the shrinkage observed for wood conserved by supercritical drying with that conserved by freeze-drying (Godfrey and Kendrick 1991). The average transverse shrinkage observed for supercritical drying is 3.2% (42 samples), compared with 2.3% (21 samples) for freeze-drying. Freeze-dried results are shown hatched, whereas the results from supercritical drying are shown as solid bars.

Table 1

Comparison between shrinkage and the moisture content of treated wood

Moisture content	Average transverse shrinkage (%)	Shrinkage (%)		Number of samples
		Min.	Max.	
>400%	3.7	1.6	5.3	9
185%-400%	3.0	1.7	5.4	8
<185%	3.4	2.0	4.6	15

Note: Moisture content is defined as weight of water present in the waterlogged state as a percentage of the dry weight of the sample. It is a rough measurement of the remaining structure of the wood.

is no significant correlation between shrinkage and moisture content of the wood, as shown in Table 1. In some samples, mineral content was too high for this correlation to be meaningful, and only 32 samples are represented in the table.

Anti-shrink efficiency is a measure of how well a technique compares to a control experiment in which the wood is allowed to dry in air. The anti-shrink efficiency is calculated according to Equation 2, where DC^0 = dimensional change as a result of air-drying, and DC = dimensional change as a result of the treatment (in this instance supercritical drying) (Grattan and Clarke 1987).

$$\% \text{ Anti-shrink efficiency} = DC^0 - DC/DC^0 \times 100 \qquad 2$$

We have determined this parameter for a small number of matched pairs of samples, one of the pair being air-dried, the other supercritically dried. The values obtained vary between 75% for well-preserved wood (with a moisture content of less than 185%) and 94% for heavily degraded wood (with a moisture content greater than 400%). The reason for this variability is that the shrinkage results from supercritical drying are independent of the degree of deterioration (see Table 1). In contrast, air-drying may result in shrinkages of between 10% for sound wood and 70% for heavily degraded wood. The variability in anti-shrink efficiency observed here, therefore, reflects the variability in air-drying results.

We have used supercritical drying on a small number of materials other than wood, including wood composite artifacts, shale, hemp rope, and leather. Knife handles, some of which are complex composites containing wood, cloth, iron, and other metals, responded very well to the technique (Kaye and Cole-Hamilton 1995). The single rope specimen treated by the technique was extremely friable after drying, whereas the leather became hard and brittle.

Problems and Possible Solutions
Some of the problems encountered with supercritical drying are due to the methodology we have employed. Others may be intrinsic to the technique. We discuss these problems as they would occur during the supercritical drying process.

Replacement of Water with Methanol
One of the consequences of this stage is that materials that are soluble in methanol will dissolve out of the wood and may be lost. However, as methanol is the most water-like of the organic solvents, it is unlikely that this can be corrected. Fortunately, most archaeological wood samples do not appear to contain large amounts of these extractives.

Figure 4. A plank of oak from the *Dartmouth* (1690), sawn, and each individual section dried separately. After drying, all the parts were reassembled without problems.

It is important to replace as much of the water present in the wood as possible before supercritical drying, as the water influences the shrinkage. This problem can be reduced by increasing the temperature at which the autoclave is run. Samples containing 4% to 5% water can be dried with little shrinkage at 50°C, whereas similar samples would have suffered severe shrinkage at 40°C. The best results are obtained by using a ketal with a strong mineral acid, when average shrinkage drops to between 1% and 2%. This is a very efficient method for removing water and is an indication that trace water content is a cause of the shrinkage. Another possible cause of shrinkage is the loss of solvent swelling upon removal of water from the wood. We do not think it likely that shrinkage could normally be reduced below 2%, due to the high cost of ketal.

The problem of shrinkage is reduced if all the components of an artifact are exchanged with methanol in the same tank, since they will have the same water content and will dry with a uniform shrinkage. We have demonstrated this by drying all the sections of a sawn plank individually after methanol exchange. We observed no distortion, and the sections could be reassembled upon completion of the treatment (see Figure 4).

Replacement of Methanol with Carbon Dioxide

This is the most damaging part of the process, as there are large temperature changes – from ambient to -78°C when the autoclave is loaded with solid carbon dioxide, to 50°C as the autoclave is warmed to its operating temperature, and then back to ambient, as the sample is removed from the autoclave. Since small samples have large surface-area-to-volume ratios, their core temperatures react quickly to external temperature changes, and large temperature gradients between the surface and the core are unusual. Large samples, however, can develop very large thermal gradients between their surfaces and their cores as a result of external temperature fluctuations. These gradients result in the surface and the core expanding (or contracting) by different amounts, putting the wood under stress. We have witnessed the development of surface transverse cracks on large wooden objects as they cool from 50°C to room temperature, once they are removed from the autoclave at the end of the supercritical drying process. We have reduced this problem by allowing the sample to cool slowly in the autoclave. Other temperature changes during carbon dioxide loading and warming to the critical temperature have not been addressed in our experiments. These temperature changes arise from the use of solid carbon dioxide, which sublimes at a temperature of -78°C, and will be addressed when we obtain equipment to allow the autoclave to be charged at room temperature with liquid carbon dioxide.

Decompression

At a decompression rate of 20 bar per hour, no problems have been observed with wood samples.

After Supercritical Drying

Some problems are most apparent after supercritical drying. These include a sample's poor tolerance to changes in its environment and poor mechanical properties, which make the sample difficult to handle. The hemp rope and leather samples mentioned earlier demonstrate the extremes of the most common mechanical problems. The hemp rope is too weak to be easily handled, whereas the leather became hard after treatment.

The treatment of hemp rope fragments could probably be improved by the use of suitable consolidants, which could increase the cohesion between the fibres constituting the material. Leather treatment might be improved by the use of plasticizers, to prevent hardening and embrittlement. In view of these requirements, we have started experimenting with the use of polyethylene glycol (PEG) and other consolidants, either as part of the pre-treatment of the artifact (PEG is compatible with supercritical drying, though the shrinkage is slightly increased) or by introduction of the consolidant into the sample from the supercritical fluid solution (>20% solutions of PEG 400 in supercritical carbon dioxide are possible under our normal operating conditions). This possibility is exciting, as the diffusion process from supercritical fluids is controlled by gas phase kinetics, resulting in a fast infusion process.

Samples of wood treated by supercritical drying have survived without environmental control for periods of up to two years without damage. This monitoring process is still in progress.

Conclusion

Supercritical drying is an experimental method, and considerable work is still required to eliminate problems with thermal control during the drying process. The technique does give rise to slightly more shrinkage than has been reported for freeze-drying, and we do not believe that it will be possible to reduce this shrinkage much further. Fortunately, when all parts of a fragmented artifact are dehydrated in the same methanol bath, the process is reproducible enough to allow the artifact to be reassembled after drying. Despite some problems, supercritical drying has been used successfully to treat small complex composite artifacts, which present a challenge for alternative processes. As consolidants are not used, the appearance of wood conserved by supercritical drying is as close to its natural appearance as is currently possible (whether or not this is desirable). The technique does not obscure fine surface detail, which is easily examined after drying.

Supercritical drying offers some advantages over alternative techniques, including rapid treatment times and a minimum structural and chemical change to the wood. PEG and other consolidants used in freeze-drying and air-drying are implicated in the deterioration of iron and other metalwork. As PEG is not used during supercritical drying, the problems with conserving artifacts containing wood and metals are much less severe.

Other than for the preparation of samples for electron microscopy, supercritical fluids had not previously been used by conservators. To date, we have addressed only drying problems, and it may be argued that these are only part of the conservation problem as a whole. All samples of wood that we have treated by the technique are robust, and it is unlikely that further consolidation is either necessary or desirable, unless they were required for a "hands on" display. The highly degraded hemp rope, described in the text, did not have enough strength to survive handling after drying, and some consolidation would clearly be necessary as part of an acceptable conservation treatment for this type of material. Supercritical fluids may be a useful vehicle for introducing consolidants, and experiments are currently in progress.

Acknowledgments

We would like to thank the NERC's (Natural Environment Research Council) Science Based Archaeology Committee, and English Heritage, for funding. Samples were supplied by Theo Skinner (National Museums of Scotland), Robin Daniels and John Buglass (Cleveland County Council), and Jacky Watson and Mike Corfield (English Heritage).

References Cited

Fricke, J., and A. Emmerling
   1992 The Nano-Structure of Aerogels: Preparation, Investigations, Modifications, and Utilisations. In *Chemical Processing of Advanced Materials,* edited by L.L. Hench and J.K. West, pp. 3-17. John Wiley & Sons, New York.

Godfrey, I.M., and A. Kendrick
   1991 Freeze Drying of Pretreated Waterlogged Wood. In *Proceedings of the 4th ICOM Group on Wet Organic Archaeological Materials Conference, Bremerhaven 1990,* edited by P. Hoffmann, pp. 349-357. ICOM Committee for Conservation, Bremerhaven, Germany.

Grattan, D.W., and R.W. Clarke
   1987 Conservation of Waterlogged Wood. In *Conservation of Marine Archaeological Objects,* edited by C. Pearson, pp. 164-206. Butterworths, London.

Hoffmann, P.
   1991 An Evaluation Study on the Freeze Drying of Waterlogged Wood. In *Proceedings of the 4th ICOM Group on Wet Organic Archaeological Materials Conference, Bremerhaven 1990,* edited by P. Hoffmann, pp. 331-348. ICOM Committee for Conservation, Bremerhaven, Germany.

Kaye, B.
   1995 Conservation of Waterlogged Wood. *Chemical Society Reviews* 24:35-43.

Kaye, B., and D.J. Cole-Hamilton
   1994 Novel Approaches to the Conservation of Wet Wood. In *A Celebration of Wood,* edited by J.A. Spriggs, pp. 35-48. WARP Occasional Paper 8. York Archaeological Wood Centre, UK.
   1995 Conservation of Knife Handles from the Elizabethan Warship *Makeshift. International Journal of Nautical Archaeology* 24(2):147-158.

Kistler, S.S.
   1931 Coherent Expanded Aerogels and Jellies. *Nature* 127:741.

Footing the Bill: Conservation Costs in the Private Sector

Katherine Singley

The Challenge of Conserving Wet Artifacts

In the past 30 years, waterlogged organic artifacts have been preserved in a variety of settings in the United States. Laboratories at larger museums, such as the National Museum of Natural History at the Smithsonian Institution in Washington, DC, and the American Museum of Natural History in New York, have processed waterlogged materials, as have departments of anthropology at various universities. Recently, some cultural resource management firms have treated wet artifacts recovered through mitigation.

However, this kind of specialized conservation usually has been limited to isolated finds and to small assemblages from inundated sites (MacDonald 1977). With the notable exceptions of the extensive collections excavated and conserved in Florida, from sites such as Hontoon Island and West Bay (Purdy 1988, 1991), and in Washington state, from sites at Ozette (Grosso 1976) and Hoko River (Croes and Blinman 1980), the conservation of artifacts from water-saturated terrestrial sites in the United States has not been addressed. American archaeologists may indeed avoid excavating sites with potentially large numbers of waterlogged material remains *because* of the anticipated problems, time, and costs presented by the need to conserve the artifacts.

The United States lacks adequately equipped laboratories, trained conservators, and consistent financial support for conserving waterlogged artifacts. These issues were addressed by the National Institute for Conservation in a 1984 study, *Ethnographic and Archaeological Conservation in the United States*. A greater commitment to conservation appears to exist in other countries, especially in Canada, Japan, the United Kingdom, Germany, Switzerland, and Sweden. The handful of American conservators who do process wet organic and inorganic artifacts depend heavily on the experimental work of researchers in other countries. A network called WOAM (Waterlogged Organic Archaeological Materials) is a working group of the conservation committee of the International Council of Museums (ICOM) and is devoted to research into conservation treatments for wet materials and the exchange of information (Hoffmann 1991, 1993).

Because the conservation of waterlogged artifacts has been limited in the United States and mainly performed "on the side" at public institutions such as universities and museums, the real costs of preserving these artifacts go unrecognized. Often treatments are undertaken as professional courtesy, slipped in between other projects. The treatments are often carried out by technicians or graduate students, whose salaries may come from other, indirectly related, sources. The amount of money that is available for conservation is usually nowhere near what is needed to pay for analytical procedures, rental of equipment and bench space, chemicals, supplies, and utilities, as well as the salaries, insurance, and health benefits of personnel. Institutional conservators know that the costs of preserving large numbers of waterlogged artifacts are high, but published information addressing the costs is lacking.

Archaeologists, cultural resource managers, land-use planners, and tribal Elders and administrators should take note that detailed information about the costs of preserving waterlogged artifacts is available from those conservators experienced in treating artifacts from shipwrecks. Costs can be identified with some degree of certainty, particularly when this type of conservation is performed in the private sector through contractual awards, rather than in a government laboratory.

The *De Braak* project serves to illustrate the high cost of preserving waterlogged artifacts. After three years of conserving a variety of organic and inorganic artifacts from this shipwreck, I can say with assurance that this cost is due not only to the length of time involved in treatment but also to expenditures for:

- photography and documentation
- reagents and solvents (including their disposal)
- specialized equipment.

The *De Braak* Project

The assemblages of artifacts recovered from the H.M.S. *De Braak* (1798) consist of a variety of organic materials similar to those that could be present in much older water-saturated deposits: wood, rush, horn, ivory, bone, hair, leather, and wool. The quantity of artifacts (20,000) from the *De Braak* is comparable to that anticipated at a rich waterlogged terrestrial site such as Ozette (Grosso 1976).

The *De Braak* was a British brigantine armed with 16 cannons. During a return voyage from the West Indies in 1798, the *De Braak* capsized and sank in a violent thunderstorm off the coast of Delaware. Known to be in shallow water and rumoured to be a treasure ship, the *De Braak* was the subject of at least three salvage attempts in the nineteenth and twentieth centuries. During the last of these, from 1983 to 1985, the State of Delaware brought suit against the salvagers in order to establish ownership. The controversy surrounding the recovery project and the court case are discussed by Shomette (1993).

Conservation of the artifacts could not begin until 1993, when clear title to the collection was established. The State of Delaware then released some classes of artifacts for conservation: footwear, clothing, tools, personal artifacts, arms and armaments, and navigational equipment. These artifacts offer a unique look into the world of the English sailor during the Napoleonic era (Fithian 1994; Lavery 1987). Because Delaware has no government conservation laboratory, the treatment of these artifacts is being performed by self-employed conservators working for the state on contract.

The Bidding Process

The awarding of contracts for conserving the artifacts from the *De Braak* is by competitive bid, the same way the government would handle contracts for paving roads or repairing windows. The process is by the book, with everything accounted for. The required work is described in a lengthy prospectus mailed to interested conservators, and calls for bids are published in local newspapers. All interested parties must attend a meeting at a specified date and time to view the assemblages in question. Conservators have this one chance to examine the artifacts, take measurements for determining sizes of containers and equipment, estimate volumes of chemicals that will be needed, and assess the number and nature of incompatible artifacts that will require different treatments. Failure to appear at the mandatory meeting results in disqualification.

Sealed bids are submitted within two weeks, and the contract generally is awarded to the lowest bidder. The artifacts are delivered to the selected conservator within 45 days, because the clock begins ticking as soon as the contract is awarded. The contracted conservator must finish the work within a set time – usually 12 to 18 months. Performance bonds do not have to be posted by the conservator, but he or she is not paid until the treatments are completed and the artifacts are returned with documentary photographs and reports.

Such constraints imposed by this particular contractual system mean that this kind of conservation is quite different from that carried out in public institutions. Since time is literally at a premium, established treatments often have to be modified and/or streamlined. Artifacts composed of similar materials must be processed in batches. Little time is available for experimentation and research into alternative treatments. Although treatments are outlined in a prospectus with some latitude, a substantial change in a proposed treatment must be approved by the state curator.

Lastly, the way in which the conservator is paid is different under this particular contractual arrangement. Because it is difficult to carry over government funding from one fiscal year to the next, the treatments must be finished on time. Multiple extensions of contracts are rarely granted by the State of Delaware. Also, in this case, there is no means of receiving payments in instalments when prolonged treatments, such as a polyethylene glycol soak, are involved. The peculiarities of the *De Braak* contracts, especially with regard to payment, mean that I must be exceedingly thorough in preparing my estimates.

Big Expenditure #1: Documentation

The *Code of Ethics* and the *Guidelines for Practice* of the American Institute for Conservation (AIC) require all conservation treatments to be documented with written records. The record incorporates photographs taken before and after treatment. In the past, archaeological artifacts have been documented as individual, unique works of ancient art. The revised edition of the AIC *Guidelines* (1994) recognizes that the degree of documentation needed for mass treatments of archaeological artifacts recovered in bulk may vary from the more thorough documentation traditionally given to individual artifacts.

For the *De Braak* artifacts, photographic documentation is in accordance with the AIC *Guidelines*. The artifacts are photographed with black-and-white film, and two sets of contact prints are prepared. The state receives one set of contacts, as well as the negatives. Colour slides to record unusual detail are prepared at the discretion of the conservator. These are prepared in duplicate because one set is provided to the state and one retained by the conservator.

A roll of 36-exposure film can record 15 to 20 individual artifacts; by clustering small artifacts, the number can be increased to 60 artifacts per roll. With the cost of the film, processing, and duplicate printing estimated at US$25 per roll, an assemblage of 300 artifacts may cost as much as US$1,000 for black-and-white photographic documentation.

Although archaeologists often regard documentary photography prepared by conservators as redundant, for the *De Braak* project the expense of documentation is more than justified. Because the artifacts were stored for 10 years awaiting treatment, the conservator's "before" photograph can demonstrate the degree of deterioration that has occurred in that time. The photographs also aid in reconstructions. Most important in mass treatments, the photographs aid in identifying artifacts. Despite multiple methods of recording provenience numbers on waterproof tags, the photographs provide another check in the recording system.

A written treatment record is created on a standardized form that has been photocopied onto archival quality bond paper. This form (see

Appendix 1) was developed specifically for waterlogged artifacts. Information such as provenience, field notations, dimensions, and material composition is recorded on the obverse. Photographic documentation before and after treatment is noted by date, roll number, and frame number. A sketch indicates identifying features such as pronounced grain patterns or stains. Treatment objectives are outlined at the bottom of the page. On the reverse, adequate space is provided to describe the practical work in progress. A checklist of key words summarizes treatment for a quick cross-check.

This form is placed in a protective 2-mm polyethylene sleeve and remains with or near the artifact during treatment. Magnetic literature files have been mounted directly on vats, refrigerators, and the freeze-drier in order to hold the documentation. By having the treatment record at hand, there is less chance that the record will be written after the fact, from memory. At the end of the treatment, the original form is shipped with the artifact, and a photocopy is made on acid-free paper for the conservator.

I use archival quality bond paper instead of waterproof or water-repellent papers because of cost. Spun polyethylene paper (Tyvek and Nalgene), drafting films, and acetate are difficult to photocopy onto, or they buckle in damp conditions. Some water resistant papers, such as "Rite in the Rain," contain formaldehyde and their longevity is questionable. Other methods of recording waterlogged materials have been presented by Spriggs (1980) and Keene (1977).

Computers are used to track artifacts as they progress through treatments and to prepare bimonthly status reports for the state. Treatment summaries can be produced for specific assemblages. Computers have limited use in recording the *De Braak* treatments, even though creating a "hard copy" as treatment progresses is preferred by most conservators. The pervasive dampness, grit, gunpowder residues, slime, solvents, and chemicals rule out the use of a laptop unit at the bench. Hand-held electronic notepads, however, may be useful to efficiently and safely record treatments.

The stage of preparing an artifact for treatment may include some rudimentary analysis. Also, the artifact may require rehousing, in a protective support of netting, for example, before treatment begins. After three years of conserving more than 450 artifacts from the *De Braak*, I have found that the cost of documenting and preparing artifacts for treatment is a minimum of US$100 per artifact – even before mixing the chemicals.

Big Expenditure #2: Chemicals
It is not likely a surprise to hear that the costs of the reagents and solvents used in conservation treatments are a large part of the high price associated with stabilizing organic artifacts. What is often overlooked, however, is that the cost of disposing of the chemicals can be equal to or more than their purchase price.

Treatments for stabilizing various kinds of organic artifacts are presented in Pearson (1987). A thorough study of the chemistry, degradation, and conservation of wood can be found in Rowell and Barbour (1990), and a review of the use of polyethylene glycol (PEG) in stabilizing wood has been provided by Grattan (1982).

PEG, at US$56 per US gallon (3.78 litres) for small quantities of grade 400, becomes extremely expensive when large amounts are required for large objects such as hull sections or canoes (Singley 1982). Some money can be saved by ordering directly from the manufacturer (Union Carbide); nevertheless, a 55-gallon (207.9-litre) drum of PEG 400 costs about US$1,000 (1995 price). The high cost of PEG has stimulated a search for alternative, cheaper bulking agents, notably sucrose (Hoffmann 1993, Parrent 1985).

To illustrate relative costs, several chemicals used to replace water and/or bulk the microstructure of waterlogged materials are compared. Solutions of 18.9 litres (5 gallons) were prepared as 20% concentrations in deionized water, except for ethulose (ethylhydroxyethyl cellulose). The calculations are based on using 100 g or 100 ml of solute per litre of solution.

Chemical solution	Cost of solute (US$)
20% glycerol	$100.00
20% PEG 400	56.00
20% sorbitol ($C_6H_{14}O_6$)	48.00
3% ethulose	15.00
20% sucrose ($C_{12}H_{22}O_{11}$)	7.50

If dewatering solvents such as acetone or ethyl alcohol are used in treatment, the costs rise considerably. The successful drying of waterlogged leather through step baths of acetone as described by Ganiaris et al. (1982) doubles in cost when, for every 18.9-litre (5-gallon) soaking bath of 20% glycerol, 37.8 litres (10 gallons) of acetone (US$100) are needed for the subsequent dehydration baths. The cost of 3.78 litres (1 gallon) of acetone (approximately US$10) is less than half that of reagent alcohol (US$27), and so may become the solvent of choice for removing water from large numbers of artifacts.

Solvents used in step dehydration baths often can be rotated and reused with new, purer dewatering agents in the final bath. Also, molecular sieves can be used to dewater acetone and ethanol for reuse (Sease 1987). Bulking agents such as PEG and sugars also may be reused; the more highly concentrated endpoint solutions can be filtered and diluted for use again.

Cost savings also might be realized through refrigeration and/or circulation of PEG solutions, which can help prolong the life of the bulking agent. This is preferable to biocides for controlling contaminating fungi and bacteria (Dawson 1982). Fungicides such as orthophenyl phenol, besides posing a

toxic threat to the conservator who handles the solutions, can also compli-
cate the eventual disposal of the preservative (Mouzouras 1994).

In addition to bulking agents, some other chemicals are commonly used
to pretreat organic materials before replacing the water and subsequently
drying. These reagents help to remove contaminants such as iron salts and
gunpowder residue that can react with both the chemical substrate of the
material and the preservative. Iron salts, for example, can degrade PEG by
catalyzing the scission of its long hydrocarbon chains. The costs of preparing 18.9-litre (5-gallon) batches of these reagents (in 5% solutions) are compared below.

Pre-treatment reagent	Cost of solute (US$)
5% ammonium citrate (dibasic)	$60.00
5% oxalic acid	46.00
5% hydrochloric acid	44.00
5% EDTA (di-sodium salt)	30.00
5% Iron Out	8.00

(*Note:* "Iron Out" is a commercially available product used to remove iron
oxide stains from clothing, enamel, and porcelain. It is a mixture of sodium
metabisulfite and sodium hydrosulfite, and has a pH of 5.6 in a 5% solution. It is manufactured by Iron Out, Inc., 1515 Dividend Road, Ft. Wayne,
IN 46808-1126.)

In contrast to bulking agents such as PEG, sugars, and glycerol, pre-
treatment chemicals are rarely reused. The efficacy of EDTA or ammonium
citrate may be enhanced by the use of ultrasonic cleaners, but once con-
taminated, the solutions must be thrown out.

The cost of disposing reagents has increased significantly with the tight-
ening of government regulations for the disposal of chemical waste. In the
United States, the Environmental Protection Agency (EPA) has established
required standards for the packaging, transporting, and disposing of chemical wastes. The business, the institution, or the individual generating the
waste must have an EPA number, which is used to track used reagents during transport and disposal, usually in landfills or in incinerators.

Most conservation laboratories would fall under the category of "small
quantity generator" (less than 200 kg of hazardous waste per month). A 55-
gallon (207.9-litre) drum is the equivalent of 200 kg. A maximum of five
drums of waste may be kept on site before more stringent regulations apply.
A private contractor has no umbrella agency, such as a university, on which
to piggyback disposal-related expenses and responsibility.

To package, label, transport, and incinerate a 55-gallon (207.9-litre) drum
of a dilute Level I waste (such as 5% EDTA or ammonium citrate, or 10%

PEG 400) costs about US$500 to US$800. Waste disposal may cost more if the waste includes biocides, biological contaminants, heavy metals, or high levels of sulfide.

Big Expenditure #3: Equipment

Stabilizing waterlogged materials requires expensive laboratory equipment. A list of major equipment and supplies is provided in Appendix 2. To equip even a modest laboratory would require an initial investment of US$60,000 (excluding the cost of a freeze-drier).

A freeze-drier is by far the most expensive piece of equipment and easily doubles the cost of setting up a laboratory. A unit with a chamber 120 cm x 60 cm (48 in x 24 in) costs about US$24,000. However, for stabilizing large numbers of waterlogged artifacts efficiently, a freeze-drier is truly a necessity. Freeze-drying has been used in conserving waterlogged materials for about 25 years, with good results (Adams 1994; Ambrose 1972; Morris and Seifert 1978).

There are three principal manufacturers of freeze-driers in the United States: Northstar/IPC (Nisswa, MN 56468), VirTis (Gardiner, NY 12525), and Edwards (Tonawanda, NY 14150). All three companies offer units for pharmaceutical processing and taxidermy preparations. Generally, pharmaceutical driers have smaller chambers but more controls for balancing the temperature and relative humidity in the chamber as drying proceeds. Auxiliary probes to monitor the artifacts are also available. Taxidermy units have bigger chambers (up to 2.7 m, or 9 ft) but fewer controls.

Besides the initial investment, freeze-driers are costly (and often fussy) to operate. Trouble usually results from the exceptionally high amount of moisture that must be pulled from the waterlogged materials. The moisture can condense in the vacuum pump despite the presence of a moisture trap. Replacing the seals on the vacuum pump is often necessary, and US$1,000 to US$2,000 should be budgeted for such repairs each year. Eventually, the pump may have to be replaced (US$4,000). Other annual maintenance costs include US$500 for oil, which should be changed after every run (at US$15 per litre each oil change costs about US$60). Another US$250 per annum should be allowed for filters (US$30 each).

The final cost to run a freeze-drier is for electricity (about US$200 a month). Runs last from one to 12 weeks, depending on the thickness and density of the material being dried. For greater efficiency, similar materials usually are processed together. An average run of drying costs about US$1,000 – based on the costs of electricity, of maintenance, and of monitoring weight changes in the materials in order to determine completion of processing. If the freeze-drier is packed with many small artifacts, this cost is spread over the whole assemblage. However, a dedicated run to dry one artifact may mean the cost of freeze-drying is prohibitive.

The Cost of Conserving Wet Artifacts

After four years of conserving almost 870 artifacts from the *De Braak*, I can confirm that the conservator's time does not contribute as heavily to the cost of conserving artifacts as do chemicals and equipment. By limiting the amount of hands-on time and letting the chemicals and equipment do the work, costs can be kept down.

I have found that small, wooden artifacts involving only one kind of material and few complications cost US$300 to US$500 *each* to stabilize. These include tool handles, shot canister bases, seam rubbers, and pistol stocks. Costs were contained by processing the artifacts in small batches. The price would have been much higher for larger artifacts, composite artifacts, or artifacts requiring complicated reconstruction or reshaping as part of the treatment.

A complete leather shoe from the *De Braak*, for example, cost about US$600 to treat because of the hands-on work entailed. First, the shoe had to be washed, then pre-treated with ammonium citrate and intensively rinsed. Although soaking in PEG for a few months was quite passive, this period of inactivity was followed by painstaking, labour-intensive reconstruction and reshaping of the shoe before freeze-drying. The final finishing was also time consuming.

The smallest, simplest-to-conserve artifacts (e.g., by step dewatering in a solvent), cost at least US$100 each to stabilize. Most of that cost was for documentation that was done in groups. Individualized documentation would have increased the cost.

In summary, the cost of conserving an assemblage of waterlogged artifacts can be estimated as follows. First, determine the number of artifacts and their volume. Then calculate the costs of:

- photographing each artifact twice
- chemicals and solvents needed to process the artifacts in batches
- removing waste chemicals
- materials and supplies (adhesives, consolidants, detergents, supports, packing materials)
- freeze-drying runs
- hands-on work throughout the treatment cycle (including taking photographs, preparing solutions, writing reports, monitoring solutions, monitoring drying, and finishing).

Once this subtotal is calculated, add a 25% surcharge (similar to an institutional overhead). This surcharge covers electricity, water, photocopying, and rental of small equipment and space. The surcharge also serves as a cushion for an unexpected snag in treatment. Divide the total of the costs plus the surcharge by the number of artifacts in the assemblage to estimate the average cost of conserving each artifact in the assemblage.

Putting a price on a treatment needed to conserve a waterlogged artifact is by no means an indication of the worth of the artifact to archaeologists, anthropologists, or the public. But in an economic climate of limited resources, some choices will need to be made. Not every artifact is going to be preserved. I hope that this discussion will reveal another perspective on the promises – and problems – of wet materials.

Appendix 1

Sample treatment record form

86.13.1415

Artifact Name **SCRUB BRUSH**
Artifact Number **86.13.1415**
Provenience **de Braak**

Date Logged **2-26-92**
Date Started **3-11-92**
Date Completed **2-1-93**
Conservator **Singley**

MATERIAL(S): **wood, prob. ~~pine~~ oak**   Dimensions: **19 cm x 6½ cm**

Interment conditions **unknown**
Post excavation history **kept wet since 1986 in tap water, changed often**
Photographic Documentation
    before treatment b&w **Roll 6, #1-3, 4+5**   slide **yes**
    after treatment b&w **Roll 14, #20+22**   slide **yes**

SKETCH: bevelled edges unworn

fibers in some holes but no bristles sticking up

holes on side

EXAMINATION:

Appears to be hard wood -- oak?
Some residues of fibers in holes. Fibers held by wire(?)
No stains, overall even in color.   now gone

magnification_____   magnet _____   chloride test____+ ____-

TREATMENT OBJECTIVES AND PROPOSAL:

1. Wash to remove loose dirt &/or iron encrustation.
2. Chemically treat to remove iron or black sulfide staining. Rinse.
3. Soak in PEG 400 (bulking agent).
4. Freeze-dry to give dimensional stability.

PREPARE FOR:

X Museum exhibit
__ Park study collection
__ Arch study collection
__ Deep Storage

▶

Date

3·11·92   PLACED IN 5% PEG 400 to SOAK.

4-26-92   REMOVED. PUT IN 5% AMMONIUM CITRATE TO DISSOLVE Fe.

5-4-92   After a week, iron appears largely removed.
Artifact removed + placed in tap water to hold.

5-8-92   Placed for 8 hrs. in running tap water (lukewarm)
After 8 hrs., placed in cold tap.

5-9-92   TAP WATER CHANGED.

5-10-92   Placed in deionized water.

5-15-92   Deionized tested: pH @ 6.2 + TDS @ 60 p.p.m. Done.
Put in New deionized to hold.

5·18·92   TDS @ 33 + pH @ 7.2.
REMOVED & PUT IN 15% PEG 400 (NO FUNGICIDE) TO SOAK.

11-22-92
to   Frozen @ -14°F FOR 48 hrs.
11-24-92

11-24·92   Freeze.dried. Ts in chambers averaged -22°F + -65°F.
to   Highest vacuum achieved = 10 millitorr.
12-6-92   Run until wts. of samples were Ⓢ, but brush not
thought to be finished. ∴ put in domestic freezer

12-6-92   Kept in freezer A MONTH. WT. AFTER > 231.69
to
1/6/93

1-6-93 ⎱ Freeze DRIED AGAIN. WTS. MONITORED FOR ENDPOINT
to   ⎰ HIGHEST VACUUM IS 12 millitorr. Ts av. -20°F + -65°F
1-29-43   ⅟₁₁ 205.4   ⅟₁₃ 203.8   ⅟₁₄ 199.6   ⅟₁₅ 148.6   ⅟₁₉ 194.15   ⅟₂₇ 185.7   ⅟₂₉ 185.25 (END)

TREATMENT SUMMARY:
- o brush/gbb_____
- o airbrasive_____
- o scalpel/pick_____
- ✓ chemical cleaning 5% Am CiT
- o chelating agents_____
- o electrolytic reduction_____
- ✓ cold washing_____
- o hot washing_____
- o inhibitor_____

- o solvent drying_____
- ✓ freeze-drying_____
- o filling/mending_____
- ✓ impregnation PEG 400_____
- o consolidation_____
- o coating_____
- o special housing_____
- o biocide_____
- o other_____

1/29/93   Acclimatized in CHAMBER.   NO OTHER TREATMENT

Appendix 2

**Equipment and supplies for a conservation laboratory
processing wet artifacts**

The Working Environment   US$25,000
    floor drain
    cabinets and chemical-resistant worktops
    double sink with drain trap
    shelving
    chairs and stools, adjustable height
    fumehood, solvent approved, with explosion-proof motor and light
    safety cabinet for solvent storage
    fire extinguisher
    eyewash station
    first-aid kit
    220 V electrical line/master cut-off
    overhead gantry and/or floor crane

Major Equipment   US$20,000 to US$30,000
    binocular microscope with swing arm stand
    fibre optic illuminator
    drum dollies, cradles, heaters
    halogen desk lamps
    deionizing column, bracket, cartridges
    Nalgene storage tank (207.9 litre/55 gallon) with spigot
    airbrasive system with on-line filter
    pneumatic pen
    compressor
    vacuum pump
    glass or Nalgene desiccator
    ultrasonic tank (30.24 litre/8 gallon) with heater
    large industrial hotplate, with thermostat
    large Dutch oven, with thermostat
    conductivity meter
    pH meter
    electronic balance
    mechanical stirrer/hotplate
    industrial oven
    electrolysis set-up: Nalgene tank, power source, transformer
    mini-refrigerator
    chest freezer
    photographic set-up

Equipment Available on Loan
    X-ray unit
    freeze-drier (if part of permanent equipment, approximately US$25,000)
    scanning electron microscope

▶

◀ *Appendix 2*

polarizing microscope
large sandblaster
moisture meter

Minor Equipment   US$5,000 to US$8,000
industrial blower/heat gun
small lamps: tensor, illuminated magnifiers
vibrotool or electric engraving pen
Dremel tool, variable speed with heads
hammer, jeweller's screwdrivers, screwdrivers
fine rasps
scalpels, variety of blades
artist's brushes, variety of sizes and qualities
fibreglass brushes, variety of sizes
wire brushes, variety of sizes, brass and steel
dental picks, pin vices
plaster tools and spatulas
scissors
tweezers, tongs, basters, cake spatulas, spoons
X-Acto knives
respirator, with cartridge replacements
ear protectors
goggles
aprons
vacuum tweezers
wet/dry vacuum
stainless steel or enamelled commissary containers
plastic containers: buckets with lids, garbage cans, wash basins, aquarium
    filters for larger containers
callipers
electronic label machine

Disposable Supplies and Chemicals   US$3,000 to US$5,000
glassware: graduated cylinder, beakers, dishes, droppers
particle masks
gloves, variety of sizes and materials
cotton wool
applicators
pH paper
foil
polyethylene and zip-lock bags
Tyvek or Nalgene polypaper
acid-free tissue
silk crepeline
gauze
tapes: surgical, Scotch, masking

▶

◀ *Appendix 2*

acrylic paints and medium
non-ionic detergent
enzymes
adhesives: Acryloid B-72, cellulose nitrate, PVA emulsion, epoxies, cyanoacrylates
consolidants: Acryloid B-72, Butvar, PVAs, Rhoplex, acrylic dispersions
gap-fillers: plaster, acrylic gesso, filled fibreglass, cellulose putty
casting resins and mould-making materials: orthopedic fibreglass tape, polysulfide rubbers, RTV silicones
solvents: acetone, toluene, naphtha, ethanol, isopropanol
waxes: microcrystalline, polyethylene
lacquers: Incralac, Acryloid, Frigilene
water replacements: PEGs, glycerine, ethulose, Bavon, Neutralfat
dewatering fluids and corrosion inhibitors: BTA, CRC
reagents: sodium carbonate; hydrochloric, sulfuric, nitric, oxalic, thioglycolic, citric, tannic, and formic acids; EDTAs; hydrogen peroxide; silver nitrate; thiourea; ammonium hydroxide; sodium sesquicarbonate; sodium hexametaphosphate; ammonium citrate and dithyonate

References Cited

Adams, Gerald
    1994 Freeze-Drying – Art or Science? In *A Celebration of Wood,* edited by James A. Spriggs, pp. 49-54. WARP Occasional Paper 8. York Archaeological Wood Centre, York, UK.

Ambrose, W.R.
    1972 *The Treatment of Swamp Degraded Wood by Freeze-Drying.* Report to ICOM Committee for Conservation, Plenary Meeting, Madrid 1972. International Centre of Conservation, Rome.

American Institute for Conservation (AIC)
    1994 *Code of Ethics* and *Guidelines for Practice,* revised eds. American Institute for Conservation of Historic and Artistic Works, Washington, DC.

Croes, Dale R., and Eric Blinman (editors)
    1980 *Hoko River: A 2500 year old Fishing Camp on the Northwest Coast of North America.* Reports of Investigations No. 58. Laboratory of Anthropology, Washington State University, Pullman.

Dawson, John
    1982 Some Considerations for Choosing a Biocide. In *Proceedings of the ICOM Waterlogged Wood Working Group Conference, Ottawa 1981,* edited by David W. Grattan, pp. 269-277. International Council of Museums, Committee for Conservation, Waterlogged Wood Working Group, Ottawa.

Fithian, Charles
    1994 An Archaeological Analysis of the Armaments from H.M. BRIG *De Braak. Military Collector and Historian, Journal of the Company of Military Historians* 66(4):146-157.

Ganiaris, Helen, S. Keene, and K. Starling
    1982 A Comparison of Some Treatments for Excavated Leather. *The Conservator* 6:12-23.

Grattan, David W.
    1982 A Practical Comparative Study of Treatments for Waterlogged Wood: Part I. *Studies in Conservation* 27:124-36.

Grosso, Gerald H. (editor)
    1976 *Pacific Northwest Wet Site Wood Conservation Conference.* 2 Vols. Conference held at Neah Bay, WA, September 19-22, 1976.

Hoffmann, Per (editor)
    1991 *Proceedings of the 4th ICOM Group on Wet Organic Archaeological Materials Conference, Bremerhaven 1990.* ICOM Committee for Conservation, Bremerhaven, Germany.
    1993 *Proceedings of the 5th ICOM Group on Wet Organic Archaeological Materials Conference, Portland, Maine 1993.* ICOM Committee for Conservation Working Group on Wet Organic Archaeological Materials, Bremerhaven, Germany.

Keene, Suzanne
    1977 An Approach to Sampling and Storage of Waterlogged Timbers from Excavation. *The Conservator* 1:8-11.

Lavery, Brian
    1987 *The Arming and Fitting of English Ships of War, 1600-1815.* Naval Institute Press, Annapolis, MD.

MacDonald, George
    1977 The Problems and Promise of Wet Site Archaeology. *CCI: Journal of the Canadian Conservation Institute* 2:3-10.

Morris, K., and B. Seifert
    1978 Conservation of Leather and Textiles from the *Defense. Journal of the American Institute for Conservation* 18:33-43.

Mouzouras, Renos
    1994 Micro-Organisms – Mechanisms of Control. In *A Celebration of Wood,* edited by James A. Spriggs, pp. 21-34. WARP Occasional Paper 8. York Archaeological Wood Centre, York, UK.

National Institute for Conservation
    1984 *Ethnographic and Archaeological Conservation in the United States.* National Institute for the Conservation of Cultural Property, Washington, DC.

Parrent, James M.
  1985 The Conservation of Waterlogged Wood Using Sucrose. *Studies in Conservation* 30: 63-72.
Pearson, Colin (editor)
  1987 *Conservation of Marine Archaeological Objects.* Butterworths, London.
Purdy, Barbara A.
  1988 *Wet Site Archaeology.* Telford Press, Caldwell, NJ.
  1991 *The Art and Archaeology of Florida's Wetlands.* CRC Press, Boca Raton, FL.
Rowell, Roger M., and R. James Barbour (editors)
  1990 *Archaeological Wood. Properties, Chemistry, and Preservation.* Advances in Chemistry Series 225. American Chemical Society, Washington, DC.
Sease, Catherine
  1987 *A Conservation Manual for the Field Archaeologist.* Archaeology Research Tools, vol. 4. Institute of Archaeology, University of California, Los Angeles.
Shomette, Donald G.
  1993 *The Hunt for H.M.S.* De Braak. *Legend and Legacy.* Carolina Academic Press, Durham, NC.
Singley, Katherine
  1982 The Recovery and Conservation of the Brown's Ferry Vessel. In *Proceedings of the ICOM Waterlogged Wood Working Group Conference, Ottawa 1981,* edited by David W. Grattan, pp. 57-60. International Council of Museums, Committee for Conservation, Waterlogged Wood Working Group, Ottawa.
Spriggs, Jim
  1980 The Recovery and Storage of Materials from Waterlogged Deposits at York. *The Conservator* 4:19-24.

Contributors

Cathryn Barr
Consultant Archaeologist
P.O. Box 242
Whangamata, New Zealand

Kathryn Bernick
c/o Laboratory of Archaeology
Department of Anthropology and
  Sociology
University of British Columbia
6303 NW Marine Dr.
Vancouver, British Columbia
V6T 1Z1
Canada

Robert C. Betts
Vanguard Research
7000 E. Shingle Mill Road
Sandpoint, Idaho 83864
USA

Scott Byram
Department of Anthropology
1218 University of Oregon
Eugene, Oregon 97403-1218
USA

Greg Chaney
60° North, 715 Sixth Street
Juneau, Alaska 99801-1026
USA

David J. Cole-Hamilton
The School of Chemistry
University of St. Andrews
Fife KY16 9ST
UK

J.M. Coles
Fursdon Mill Cottage
Thorverton
Devon EX5 5JS
UK

Mike Corfield
Head, Ancient Monuments
  Laboratory
English Heritage
23 Savile Row
London W1X 1AB
UK

Elena B. Décima
320 D Harvard St.
Cambridge, Massachusetts 02139
USA

Dena F. Dincauze
Department of Anthropology
University of Massachusetts
Amherst, Massachusetts
01003-4805
USA

Jon M. Erlandson
Department of Anthropology
1218 University of Oregon
Eugene, Oregon 97403-1218
USA

Scott L. Fedick
Department of Anthropology
University of California
Riverside, California 92521
USA

Paul J. Gilman
Essex County Council
Planning Department
County Hall
Chelmsford CM1 1LF
UK

D.M. Goodburn
Museum of London,
    Archaeology Service
Museum of London,
    London Wall
London EC2Y 5HN
UK

Dilys A. Johns
Anthropology Department
University of Auckland
Private Bag 92019
Auckland, New Zealand

Barry Kaye
c/o the School of Chemistry
University of St. Andrews
Fife KY16 9ST
UK

Yaroslav V. Kuzmin
Pacific Institute of Geography
Far Eastern Branch of the Russian
    Academy of Sciences
Radio St. 7
Vladivostok 690041
Russia

Lars Larsson
Institute of Archaeology
University of Lund
Sandgatan 1
S-223 50 LUND, Sweden

Madonna L. Moss
Department of Anthropology
1218 University of Oregon
Eugene, Oregon 97403-1218
USA

George P. Nicholas
Department of Archaeology
Simon Fraser University / Secwepemc
    Cultural Education Society
345 Yellowhead Highway
Kamloops, British Columbia
V2H 1H1
Canada

Wojciech Piotrowski
Biskupin Museum
Department of the State
    Archaeological Museum in Warsaw
Dluga 52
00-241
Warszawa, Poland

Katherine Singley
1083 Oakdale Road, NE
Atlanta, Georgia 30307
USA

Ann Stevenson
UBC Museum of Anthropology
6393 NW Marine Drive
Vancouver, British Columbia
V6T 1Z2
Canada

Robert Van de Noort
Manager Humber Wetlands Survey
University of Hull
Hull HU6 7RX
UK

Index

References to illustrations are in **bold type**

A

acid rain, effects of, 65, 303
aerial photography, 11, 95, **116**, 276-277
agriculture. *See* cultivation, of wetlands
anaerobic bacteria, 314
anti-shrink efficiency (ASE), 326, 335
Aotearoa (New Zealand), initial colonization, 47-48
Atlantic period, 58, 60, 64, 79
Axeti site, **xiii**, **xiv**, 182

B

basketry, 139-152, 246; weaving techniques, **xii**, **86**, **143**, 145-147, 229. *See also* lattice, weir parts
biocides, 323, 345-346
Biskupin site, 89-93; ethnicity, 98-99
Blackwater estuary, sites, 275-281
Boylston Street fish weirs, 157; reinterpreted, 169-172
boats, 77, 79, 292. *See also* shipwrecks
bog bodies, 18-22, 70
Boreal period, 66, 67, 68, 70, 79
botanical remains, 51, 59, 69. *See also* wood species, of finds
Bronze Age: economy, 58-59, 61; finds, 8, 74-75, 79, 99, 297, 299; house construction, 11
Bulleid, Arthur, 10
burials, 72, 74. *See also* bog bodies

C

caches, in wetlands, 21, 51, 71-72
Canadian Conservation Institute, 96
cedar bark, 145, 230, 231, 248
cemeteries, 38, 71

ceramics: used to date sites, 92, 115, 119, 281
Charavine Colletière (Lake Paladru site), 3-7
chemicals: disposal, 332, 344-346, 346-347; in sites, monitoring presence of, 313. *See also* sewage, effects on wet sites
clothing, 14, 19, 20, 225
Coast Salish, 223
Coles, John and Bryony, 13, 97, 303
Collins Creek site, 275-279
computers, use of: to keep records, 275, 344; to map sites, 278
conservation, care during excavation, 243
conservation laboratories, 96, 340-341; equipment, 347, 352-353
conservation treatments, metals, 338
conservation treatments, waterlogged wood, xvii, 96, 317-323, 329-332; costs, 331, 343-349; evaluating results, 323-327, 332-338
conservators, contractual agreements, 342-343
coppicing, 135-136, 297
cordage, 248, 335. *See also* nets
cultivation, of wetlands, 50, 108-109, 121-122
cultural resource management, 269-270; strategies, 284-287, 290, 299-300, 303-305; monitoring hydrology, 308-313
Cushing, Frank, 10

D

damage, to wet sites, 93, 191, 263, 273-274, 285, 303-304. *See also* drainage, effects of; wetlands, anthropogenic impact on
De Braak (ship), 341-342

defensive sites. *See* fortified settlements
Delaware (state), contracts for conservation, 342-343
dendrochronology, 132; dates, 12, 98
Denmark, wet-site finds, 19-20, 68, 74
deterioration, of exposed wood, 93, 299
dietary protein, 224
drainage, in antiquity, 50, 109
drainage, effects of, 270, 294
drowned sites, 3-7, 51-52, 65-67, 71

E
earthquakes, effects of, 52, 189-190
English Heritage, projects, 290, 303, 304, 310
erosion, temporary protection from, 240, 242, 250
estuaries, environmental characteristics of, 201, 222; fish species, 169, 202, 214, 234, 248-249
excavation projects, 159-161, 240-244
experimental archaeology, 100, 131, 135, 215

F
faunal remains: domesticated animals, 13, 59; fish, 169, 216, 226, 230, 232; mammals, 58, 61; marine molluscs, 59-60
Finland, wet-site finds, 70
fish traps: basketry, 211-212, 244-248, 250, 283; stone, 180-181, 192, 193, 202, 284. *See also* fishing devices; weirs
fisheries management, 220
fishhooks, bentwood, 232
fishing devices: species targeted, **178**, 192, 193, 214-215, 249; terminology, 164, 178-179, 180, 199, 227
fishing gear, 69, 225, 214, 230. *See also names of specific items*
fishing technologies: complexity, 171-172, 193-194, 221, 224; dry-site evidence, 215-216, 224-225; ethnographic and historical accounts, 210-214, 223-224, 239, 240, 281-282; temporal variability, 233
Flag Fen site, 312, 314-315
Florida (state), wet-site finds, 10, 32
flounder (*Platichthys stellatus*), 212, 213, 222-223
forest management. *See* woodmanship
fortified settlements, 4-7, 49, 51-53, 79, 90-92
Foulness Island, sites, 282
France, wet-site finds, 4, 13
freeze-drying, 271, 323; equipment, 347

G
geomorphology, of regions, 64-65, 111, 252-265, 293-294
Germany, wet-site finds, 12-13, 21
glaciers, 254-256
Glastonbury Lake Village, 10, 13
Glenrose Cannery site, 145, 182, 225-227, 229-230; mentioned, 151-152
Global Positioning Systems (GPS), 277

H
history of wetland archaeology, 8-10
Holderness wetlands, 295-296, 306
houses. *See* structures, remains of
human skeletal remains, 73. *See also* bog bodies
Humber River, 291
hurdles, 276, 278, 282, 283. *See also* lattice, weir parts; wattles

I
interdisciplinary research, 94-95, 290
Iron Age: economy, 58-61; finds, 19-20, 75-77

L
lakeshore villages, Alpine, 8-9, 11
Late Archaic period, 170
Late Glacial period, 57, 65
lattice, weir parts, 183, 204, 210, 212-215, 228-229, 246. *See also* Osprey site
Latvia, wet-site finds, xvi-xvii
London (UK), wet-site finds, 131, 308
Lusatian culture, 98

M
Maori, 47-48, 49, 52, 322
Market Deeping site, 306-307, 308-310, 314
Marpole (phase), 151, 153
Maya, 107, 111-114
medieval finds. *See* Middle Ages
Mendenhall Valley, 255-256
Mesolithic, 66-72, 296, 299
metal artifacts, in wet sites, 74-75, 92, 297, 314. *See also* conservation treatments, metals
microregional studies, 95
Middle Ages (medieval times): economy, 58; finds, 4-7, 99, 281, 283, 284; woodmanship, 132-136
minerals, in wetlands, 313-314
Montana Creek trap site, 242-243, 256-258, 252
Museum of London Archaeology Service (MOLAS), 130-131
musical instruments, 6

Musqueam Northeast site, 225, 230; mentioned, 139-152

N
New Zealand. *See* Aotearoa
Neolithic, 130; economy, 13, 58-61, 99; finds, 71-74, 275, 297-299, 313
Netherlands, water-table, 310
nets, 214, 221, 223-224, 225, 230-231

O
oral traditions, 3-4, 7, 52
Osprey site, **178**, 192, **204**

P
pa, 49, 51-53
paleoenvironmental settings, 57-58, 171, 225-226, 256-258, 294. *See also* sea level changes; woodmanship
Paleolithic, 57, 58, 65-66
peat digging, finds uncovered during, 8, 18-19, 65, 77
PEG. *See* polyethylene glycol
periphyton, 122, 123
pH values, 312
pollarding, 134-135
pollen: as food, 33, 53; paleoenvironmental interpretations, 168, 293
polyethylene glycol (PEG), 244, 271, 317-322, 323; cost, 345
preservation, of organic materials: environmental conditions, xii-xiii, 20, 65, 299, 302, 310
preserving excavated structures, at sites, 96-97
preserving sites: archaeological parks, xvii, 90, 102, 315; hydrology, 98, 313, 314-315
public audiences, interpreting archaeology to, xv, 16-18, 99-101, 315

R
radiocarbon dates, 139, **147**, 296; fishing features in North America, 162-163, 185-188, 241; fishing features in UK, 276, 283, 284; shells, 59, 60. *See also* dendrochronology, dates
reconstructions, buildings, 17, 101-103
reconstructions, pictorial: clothing, **20**; fish weirs, **171**, **212**, **228**, **229**; habitation structures, **5**, **9**, **11**, **78**; trackways, **298**
Robbins Swamp, 34, 36-37, 38-39, 39-40, 42
rock alignments, 115-120, 181. *See also* fish traps, stone

Roman era, 77, 99, 136, 299
Rose Theatre (London), 308

S
sacrifices, in bogs, 21-22, 71-72, 74-75
salmon fishing, importance on Northwest Coast, 183, 221, 239
Saxon era, 279, 283, 284
sea level changes, **254**, 293-294; human responses to, 59-60, 70-71, 169-170, 190-191; submerged sites, 65
sediments, interpreted, 165, 262-263
Severn estuary, sites, 283-284
sewage, effects on wet sites, 315
shellfish. *See* faunal remains, marine molluscs
shipwrecks, 341-342
site formation processes, 258-262, 299
Slavic tribes, 98-99
soils, properties of, 65, 122, 295, 299, 305-308
Somerset Levels. *See* Sweet Track
spatial analysis, activity areas, 69
stake alignments: Boston, 161, 164; Northwest Coast, 192, 202-203, 207, 226, 239; UK, 275-281, 283
stone artifacts, in wet sites, 8, 71-72
stone fish traps. *See* fish traps
stories, wetland themes, 36. *See also* oral traditions
Stour estuary, sites, 280
stratigraphy, **160**, **253**, 262-263, **264**
structures, remains of: ceremonial, 72-73; fortifications, 79; houses, 12, 68; trackways, 279, 283, 297-299, 313; weirs, 161-165, 182-183, 191-192, 207-210, 278-281
Subboreal period, 60, 64
surveys, aerial, 280-281
surveys, field projects, 114-120, 201-204, 275-278, 295, 299. *See also* microregional studies
Sweet Track, preservation of, 312-313
Switzerland, wet-site finds, 8-9, 12

T
textiles, 14
tides, logistical challenges, 243, 276-277, 281
Tlingit, 239
tools, wet-site finds: wooden, 51, 70; other materials, 8, 68, 72, 75, 92
trackways. *See* structures, remains of

U
underwater investigations, 9, 66-68, 95

V

Viking Age, 77-79
votive deposition. *See* sacrifices, in bogs

W

Water Hazard site, 225, 231-232; mentioned, 139-152
water levels, regulating in antiquity, 50
waterfowl, hunting techniques, 37, 40, 50, 223-224, 230
waterproof paper, 344
wattles, 136, 164, 179. *See also* hurdles; lattice, weir parts
weapons, 6, 74
weirs, 204-207, 227-230; antiquity, 165, 193, 226; how used, 159, 282; effects on sedimentation, 191, 262. *See also* fishing devices; structures, remains of: weirs
wet sites: definitions, xii-xiv, 49; excavation techniques, xiii, 94, 131, 243-244; reasons not excavated, xi, 304, 340; types of remains preserved, 6, 8, 10, 13, 69-70, 86 (*see also names of specific items*)
wetland archaeology, significance, xi, 31-32, 43, 302
wetland ecosystems: heterogeneity, 33-34, 41-42, 109, 120, 291-292; protection, 111, 315-316

wetland-human relationships: attractions and limitations of wetlands, 7-8, 33-36, 53; changes in land-use, 39-42, 59-61, 69-70, 296-297
wetland resources, 33-37; fertilizer, 122; food, 5, **15**, 35, 53, 123. *See also* faunal remains; waterfowl, hunting techniques
wetlands: anthropogenic impact on, 7, 41, 65, 190, 294; archaeological potential, xvii, 29, 85; as boundaries, 36, 298-299; biodiversity, 33, 111, 201; foci for settlement, 36, 38-39, 201, 296; restoration, 38; vegetation, 33, 117-120. *See also* soils, properties of
Willingham site, 306-307
wood, construction materials, 11, 131, 132-136; season of felling, 165, 168
wood species, of finds: Alaska, 240, 248; Boston, 164, 165, 168-169; British Columbia, 145; England, 132-136; New Zealand, 317
woodmanship, 130, 136-138, 296-297

Y

Yucatán Peninsula, natural environment, 109-111

Set in Stone by Irma Rodriguez

Copy editor: Judy Phillips

Proofreader: Randy Schmidt

Printed and bound in Canada by Friesens